CHRISTY MOORE

LIR

Hodder & Stoughton

Copyright © 2000, 2003 by Christy Moore

First published in Great Britain in 2003
by Hodder and Stoughton
A division of Hodder Headline

A Hodder Lir paperb

5

A CIP catalogue for t

ISBN 978-0-340-8307:

Typeset in Minion by Palimpsest Book Production Limited,
Polmont, Stirlingshire

Printed and bound in Great Britain by Clays Ltd, St Ives plc

Hodder and Stoughton
A division of Hodder Headline
338 Euston Road
London NW1 3BH

Contents

Acknowledgements
page 7

When, What, Where so far…
page 8

Foreword
page 10

The songs
page 12

Discography
page 544

Index of songs
page 546

Index
page 550

Picture and lyric credits
page 558

I dedicate this book

to the late

Dr Patrick Nugent

Acknowledgements

I wish to extend my gratitude
to the following people:

To Mattie Fox who has overseen the
project since its inception and his
assistant Bernie Mulfaul; Rowena
Webb at Hodder who has edited the
work and offered invaluable advice
and encouragement with patience
and humour. Jo Nutley did copy-
editing while Clare and Yannie at
Cover to Cover did proof and index.

To all the writers and singers
who lent me their work and to
the Traditional Music Archive,
Martin Carthy, Frank Harte,
Tom Munnelly and Ronnie Drew
who helped me retrieve some of it.

Also, to Derek Spiers,
Jill Furmanowsky, John Minihan,
Kieran Kelly, Pete Cassidy,
Michael Traynor, Pat Ryan,
Ronnie Nolan, and most of all
my family Valerie, Andy, Juno
and Pádraic who have lived with the
making of the work.

When, what, where, so far...

1945 Born on 7 May
in Newbridge, Co. Kildare

1949 Entered infant school
with Holy Family Sisters

1953 Moved to primary school
with the Patrician Brothers

1956 Daddy died in the Jockey Hospital,
Curragh Camp, having an ingrown
toenail removed (1915–1956, RIP)

1958 Continued learning with
the Dominican Fathers

1961 Sang with school choir and
performed in opera
in Newbridge College

1962 Heard The Clancy Brothers
and Tommy Makem in
the Olympia Theatre, Dublin

1963 Joined the National Bank,
in Clonmel, Co. Tipperary

1966 Became a professional singer
and moved to London

1967 Heard Ewan McColl at the Singers
Club in London and met
Hamish Imlach in Glasgow

1968 Met Luke Kelly in Manchester.
Did my first radio broadcast
at the BBC in London

1969 Met Dominic Behan in Shepherd's
Bush, London. Recorded my first
album *Paddy on the Road*

1970 My first performance on
a television show, *Capital Folk*,
in Ireland

1971 Returned to Ireland to record
the album *Prosperous* which led
to the formation of Planxty

1973 Married Valerie Isaacson
and went to live in Inchicore, Dublin

1974	Left Planxty to resume solo career	**1987**	Suffered a heart attack and gave up the drugs
1976	Andy Isaac Moore born and we moved to Coolcullen, Co. Carlow	**1989**	Having, at long last, drunk my fill, I gave up the looney soup
1977	First visit to H-Blocks, Long Kesh	**1990**	Granted Hon. Membership of The Kildare Association in NSW, Australia
1978	Juno Nancy Moore born and we moved to Rialto, Dublin		
1979	Produced the *H-Block* album. Launch party in Dublin raided by secret police	**1991**	Played twelve sell-out shows at the Point Theatre, Dublin, to 70,000 people
1980	Collaborated with Donal Lunny to form a band which became Moving Hearts	**1992**	Mammy died, RIP. Nancy Power (1919–1992)
		1997	Toured Ireland, UK, Germany, USA, Australia, New Zealand. Suffered a nervous breakdown
1982	Pádraic Ernest Moore born. Caitlín Moore died at birth, 24.12.82. RIP	**1998**	Cancelled all work
1983	Resumed solo career managed by Mattie Fox from Ballinlee, Co. Longford	**1999**	Released *Traveller* album and gave up live performances
1984	Performed three sell-out shows at the National Concert Hall, Dublin. Released *Ride On* album and 'Lisdoonvarna' single	**2000**	Finalised work on *One Voice*. Commenced work on boxed set. Commenced work on new album. Commenced work on television series. Read about workaholism. Forego ambition to play tight-head prop for Ireland. Learn how to make nut roast, assemble muesli. . .
1985	'They Never Came Home' challenged in the High Court, Dublin		
1986	Played Albert Hall, London and Carnegie Hall, New York. Also Caesar's Palace in Bunclody		

Foreword

To be quite honest, it had never crossed my mind to consider writing any kind of book. Then, in the early Nineties a number of writers made contact with me expressing interest in doing a biography. The prospect did not entice me, and I could raise no enthusiasm. As I had already done interviews with most of these potential biographers, the prospect of having to spend endless months with any one of them sent me scurrying to my guitar for comfort. (Doubtlessly some of them were quite relieved, too.)

Then I got word that one of them was considering an unauthorised biography, and this put the wind up me to the extent that, in 1992, my manager Mattie Fox made contact with some publishing houses and introduced me to Rowena Webb, now of Hodder & Stoughton. For a number of years I wrestled with writing about this life but I could never find a satisfactory starting point. In 1995 the family were away on Cape Clear Island off the Co. Cork coast, and I began collecting and writing down all the songs I'd sung in my lifetime. This became a labour of love for it was very revealing to meet some of these old friends again. I had to retrace my steps, but still I was not able to locate all the songs I had once sung. Some were lost forever, but many of them had not escaped my memory. Some, unsung for 25 years, were still there at the tip of my tongue just waiting for the opening chord.

When I had 500 songs recalled and accounted for, I set to writing about them: where I had first heard them, who sang them, why I wrote them, why I sing them. I found that I could write about my life through writing about the songs themselves.

I took a current set list from 1995 and that became my starting point. Some of the writing was done on the road in Ireland, Germany, Britain, Australia, New Zealand and America, but most was done on The Sheep's Head Peninsula near Bantry in Co. Cork. Here, my only distractions were Concorde

thundering overhead each morning at eleven, and the milk lorry trundling up the mountain in the afternoon.

I've not visited every nook and cranny of my life; I've only gone where the songs have taken me. Nor was I able to include all 500 songs, and some of the pruning was very painful.

'Let the music keep your spirits high.'

Christy Moore
11 May 2000

After the Deluge
by Jackson Browne

Some of them were dreamers; some of them were fools, who were making plans and thinking of the future

With the energy of the innocent, they were gathering the tools they would need to make their journey back to nature

When the sand slipped through the opening, and their hands reached for the golden ring, and their hearts turned to each others' hearts for refuge

In the troubled years that came before the Deluge

Some of them they knew pleasure, some of them knew pain, and for some of them it was only the moment that mattered

On the wild and crazy wings of youth, they went flying around in the rain, till their feathers once so fine were torn and tattered

In the end they traded their tired wings, for the resignation that living brings, they traded love's bright and fragile glow, for the glitter and the rouge

In a moment, they were swept before the Deluge

So let the music keep your spirits high

Let the buildings keep your children dry

Let creation reveal its secrets by and by

When the light that's lost within us reaches the sky

Some of them were angry, at the way the Earth was abused, by those men who learned to forge beauty into power

And in trying to protect us from them, only became confused, by the magnitude of the fury in the final hour

When the sand was gone and the time arrived, in the naked dawn only a few survived, and in trying to understand these things, so simple and so huge

Believed they were meant to live after the Deluge

In the early days of Moving Hearts, there was a repertoire of songs which I brought and a style of music that Donal Lunny and I discussed.

Moving Hearts commenced in 1980 when Donal and I spoke about some songs and music we would like to play. The ideas were quite diverse and the general feeling was to create a band that could embrace these different aspirations. Our first recruit was guitar player Declan Sinnott. He taught me this song which has become a constant in my repertoire. As further members joined what became the Moving Hearts Collective, the original ideas were expanded upon as everyone brought in their own influence. The band was to assume an ideology that was both exciting and fulfilling, but could also be exasperating. As we grew from two to seven to ten, we toured the country and also played Monday, Tuesday and Wednesday every week in the Baggot Inn, Dublin. These gigs were hot, loud and intense and always stuffed to the gills. We recorded our first album in Windmill 2 in St Stephen's Green – it is a good album, but not always as good as the demos that preceded it. I was also managing the band (badly) and I recall it as a crazy time in my life. Songs and music only occupied my mind while I was on stage, for life was too hectic for there to be time to work on the essence.

I met Jackson Browne twice. Once he came to my gig in Culver City, LA. At the time I was working on a song by Floyd Westerman, and that tied in with our meeting. I like the substance of Jackson's work and he strikes me as being the genuine article.

When the Hearts were working in full flight it was quite awesome. We slept head-to-toe on the bus in freezing conditions, cooked our own scran, and Davy Spillane was the laundry officer until we court-martialled him in Galway. We flew high for a while, but in '83 we began to lose our feathers.

This song has become my regular opening number. It allows me to settle into the audience on the night and I've found endless ways of performing it. I keep finding new colours and the accompanying picture in my head continues to change and update. Some nights the dreamers in the opening line can be hunger strikers, more times guardians of the forests standing defiantly in the woods near Blackburn defending trees, women neutralising Harrier jets, or children at war. I keep putting it down when I feel the need to rest it, but after one or two nights I begin to miss it and it always returns refreshed and ready to be sung again.

I remember recording 'On the Blanket' in Colloney, Co. Sligo the night that young Martin Hurson died on hunger strike. Moving Hearts were playing in the Community Hall. Mick Hanly and I shared the vocals. Some days later we were performing at an open-air festival in Castlebar, Co. Mayo. I heard on the radio that Kieran Doherty had succumbed to the Hunger. I remember going into the Artists' Bar feeling numbed by the news, and I was taken aback at the total lack of interest amongst the liggers and giggers. Something stirred inside me that day. I began to realise that the showbiz community was not where I belonged. I think back to a thousand backstage bars; sure, we needed to be anaesthetised to put up with the endless hours of waffling. As a young singer I gazed longingly at the inner sanctum of the Artists' Bar. As an ageing singer I thank God that I've escaped those empty citadels.

The original Hearts were Donal Lunny, Declan Sinnott, Keith Donald, Eoghan O'Neill, Davy Spillane, Brian Calnan, Matt Kellighan, Norman Verso, Cid Isaacson. Clive Hudson was very supportive in recording the early repertoire at a time when no Irish company would touch us. Terry O'Neill and Mr Clarke were other early footsoldiers. We also had the attention of secret police at the gigs, although their presence was never much of a secret as their cars always looked overloaded and down on the suspension. Those were the days when to miss Mass was a subversive act, and to disagree with state brutality was a sure sign of terrorism.

The music keeps my spirits high. When I sing on stage to an audience I go into a place that is very special. I am out of it and locked into a white light space that is seldom penetrated. Nothing is quite like it and I am thankful for the key to it, whatever it is.

Natives
by Paul Doran

For all of our languages, we can't communicate
For all of our native tongues we're all natives here
Sons of their fathers dream the same dream
The sound of forbidden words becomes a scream
Voices in anger, victims of history
Plundered and set aside, grown fat on swallowed pride

With promises of paradise and gifts of beads and knives
Missionaries and pioneers are soldiers in disguise
Saviours and conquerors they make us wait
The fishers of men they wave their truth like bait
With the touch of a stranger's hand innocence turns to shame
The spirit that dwelt within now sleeps out in the rain

For all of our languages we can't communicate
For all of our native tongues we're all natives here
The scars of the past are slow to disappear
The cries of the dead are always in our ears
Only the very safe can talk about wrong and right
Of those who are forced to choose some will choose to fight

29 November 1996

Last night I performed for two hours in The Forum, Kentish Town. It was a very extreme night and my emotions were totally rattled by the sheer rawness of it all. Before the show I was in an uptight and nervous, even frightened place. During the first two songs – 'Nancy Spain' and 'Ordinary Man' – I suffered a panic attack and prayed for survival and it passed over. Thank God. What followed was very special. The standing audience members close by were beautiful, encouraging, gentle people who had taken the trouble to come early and be beside me. They chatted up banter and requests and I thanked them. In the nether regions there were mainly listeners but the odd few Yahoos, Terrorists, Alcoholics, Sham Chuckies, Spoilt Priests, Plain Clothes and other various neurotics who prevented it becoming an easy audience and kept me on my toes. I played for two hours and finished with

'The Time Has Come'. I also performed: 'Nancy Spain'; 'Ordinary Man'; 'Natives'; 'Fairytale'; 'Yellow Triangle'; 'Veronica'; 'Mainland'; 'Minds Locked Shut'; 'Strange Ways'; 'North and South'; 'Smoke and Strong Whiskey'; 'Biko Drum'; 'Back Home'; 'Missing You'; 'Black is the Colour'; 'Quiet Desperation'; 'City of Chicago'; 'Joxer'; 'Delirium Tremens'; 'Rose of Tralee'; 'Bowrawn'; 'Middle of the Island'; 'The Voyage'.

When I left the stage I was very emotional, more so than through the performance. I rang Val for a few words and I thanked God for the gifts of voice and songs and guitar and music and so many friends to listen. Mattie came and we talked for a while, then Tony Rohr, my good friend and brother of 25 years, visited and then I chatted with Neil McColl about his life and work, and then a bunch of merry women down from Lancashire for the gig ('Why didn't you sing "Lisdoonvarna"?') Then, like a zombie, back to the hotel with my driver Mick Devine. I'm looking forward to being with Val, Andy, Juno and Pádraic tomorrow in France. Goodnight.

This song was written by Paul Doran. I don't remember where we first met, but we first worked together on the song 'Make It Work' which was the theme number for Self-Aid, a well-intended day of action to support the unemployed. He wrote this song for me to sing and it has travelled well and touched listeners round the globe with its universal quality.

I think of a sea of young, beautiful faces in Gütersloh, Hamburg, Berlin, singing, humming, swaying to this song and a dark red rose offered up in gratitude for the night we were having. Of the connection made on a cold, cold winter's night in a dirty kip of a nightclub with no creature comforts and a bar staff from Hell doing everything in their power to break the spell and Jim Donohoe from Mullingar trying to quell the roars of drunken Paddies in the Mannheim Fire Station. I think of a priest amok in The Roundhouse, London, a baby born at a Belgian festival, a helicopter above the Whiterock Leisure Centre during 'Irish Ways and Irish Laws'.

I believe that the language of the heart is the only true means of communication. Look at powerful leaders with their diplomats, civil servants, translators, publicists, minders – they talk in photocall sound bites and people get blown apart and starve and die and the charades go on and on.

I sing these words in a thousand halls for a million people and the words wrap themselves around our own lives and we stand in harmony, all our worlds side by side in community and the unifying factor is Language of the Heart.

Ordinary Man
by Peter Hames

I'm an ordinary man, nothing special nothing grand, I've had to work for everything I own
I never asked for a lot, I was happy with what I got enough to keep my family and my home
They say that times are hard and they've handed me my cards they say there's not the work to go around
When the whistle blows, the gates will finally close tonight they're going to shut this factory down
Then they'll tear it down

I never missed a day nor went on strike for better pay for twenty years I served them best I could
With a handshake and a cheque it seems easy to forget loyalty through the bad times and the good
The owner says he's sad to see that things have got so bad but the Captains of Industry won't let him loose. . .
He still smokes a cigar and drives a brand new car still he takes his family on a cruise
He'll never lose

It seems to me such a cruel irony, he's richer now than ever he was before
Now my cheque is spent I can't afford the rent there's one law for the rich one for the poor
Everyday I've tried to salvage some of my pride to find some work so as I might pay my way
But everywhere I go, the answer is always no! no work for anyone here today
No work today

So condemned I stand just an ordinary man like thousands beside me in the queue
I watch my darling wife trying to make the best of life, God knows what the kids are going to do
Now that we are faced with this human waste, a generation cast aside
For as long as I live, I never will forgive, you stripped me of dignity and pride
You stripped me bare

There are a number of writers who have given me only one song. Some of them never wrote much else and seemed to rise up, write one song and go back to the day job. Some writers have given me *carte blanche* to mould their song to my own style, while others are like Rottweilers around the Crown jewels. I've had to let go of songs once or twice because the writers would not allow any alterations, as is their right.

Christ, it was terrible: the Winter Gardens in Cleethorpes of a dirty winter's night in 1984. I was half on and half off the drink. Jim Donohoe and Alan O'Leary were looking after me and the gig was not great. I had a few shots of brandy and port before going out to face a half-folkie, half-Irish audience and I ploughed on as best I could. After the gig I dived into the bevvy until Jim and Alan frogmarched me to the Volvo for the miserable trip to London. A man pressed a cassette into my hand as I left and it contained this song. I got stuck into it straightaway and when I came to record it I could not trace the author.

Peter Hames got in touch with me subsequently and we now meet occasionally. He has been most generous in his praise of my recording of his song. This is not always the case. I have been frustrated by the attitude of some songwriters towards the recording of their work; perhaps they resented not being able to record it themselves. But this is the exception and I am privileged to have received the work of such great writers as Ewan McColl, Jimmy MacCarthy, Wally Page, Pierce Turner, Johnny Mulhearn, Shane McGowan, Johnny Duhan and many, many others. The writing of a song can be such a very precious act, sometimes laying bare the very essence of a life, and the interpreter carries a big responsibility to the writer. A few times I have inadvertently strayed from the path of the writer's journey, but as I've grown older I've understood more.

21 November 1996
Last night in Derry two teenage women shouted repeatedly for this song. Maybe seventeen or eighteen years of age, they would have been in nappies when I first recorded it and here they are, fifteen years on, asking to hear the words of Peter Hames. That's part of this great world I move in – words and music moving across the boundaries.

The 'ordinary man' moniker has been used many times for the handy headline. It came back again recently when Blackie Connors sang 'I'm an ordinary man, I only sing for twenty grand' – I really liked that one. The potential irony of me singing this great song has not escaped me, but I'm comfortable with it and I feel all right about taking the brickbats that occasionally come.

It was a deadly vibe at the opening of The Mean Fiddler in Dublin. The crowd were wedged in and it was a bit like 100,000 in a room that held 850. The audience really went for it that night so I can still see them singing 'Ordinary Man'. I wished that Peter Hames and his wife and daughter could have been there to experience it.

Those scrunched-up, stand-up gigs can be very special. Things happen round the room that would never happen in a seated auditorium. The audience is uninhibited and tends to sing louder and sway better and talk more personally. I think of The Arcadia in Cork, The Mean Fiddler in Dublin, a hellhole in Cologne... I realise the disappointment these venues bring to ageing folkies who need certain comforts, but I confess to loving these mad gigs myself, and I'll confess even more by saying I only love them as the act and never as an audient!

I've seen people get off with each other, total strangers becoming friends, swapping all sorts, having fun, and I compare it to the stiff atmosphere of concert halls and opera houses – very plush and comfy but also very stiff and safe and very dear to hire and sometimes staffed by those who feel their venue should not have to entertain the likes of me or my audience, God love them.

Welcome to the Cabaret
by C. Moore

How's it going there everybody, you're very welcome to this evening's cabaret
Thank you for the trouble that you've taken to come and to hear me play
I know the effort that you make and all the trouble that you take
When you decide to go and see a show
Your husband says 'Who is Christy Moore?
'I've never heard of him before
'And we're goin' to miss Gay Byrne and the Late Late Show'
('Tough shit Pascal, we're going')

There's people here upon my word from every corner of the world
Portarlington, Portlaoise and Tullamore
Two-Mile-House and Poolaphouca
Blacktrench, Cutbush and Boolea
Such a crowd I never seen before
You're welcome, welcome everyone, if you're Special Branch or on-the-run
Fine Gael, Fianna Fáil or Sinn Féin
When the elections are all over we'll all be pushing up clover
And everyone in the graveyard votes the same

My belly thought my throat was cut and all the restaurants were shut
As I was heading west for Kinnegad
I drove on to Mother Hubbard's, where I saw a swarm of truckers
Begod said I and this place don't look too bad
In came a forty-foot lorry, leaking lines of slurry
And the King of the Road jumps down and says to me
'Hey John! I think I know your face are you Paddy Reilly or Brendan Grace
'Are you Mary Black or Freddie White' says he

Wait till I tell you what happened to me today
I was coming down the dual carriageway
Half a mile the far side of Naas, the Irish Army were all over the place
So I pulled in and rolled my window down
The Saighdíurí they surrounded my car
I thought it was the Third World War
And some of them were throwing Sh'ite shapes
'Brigadier General what's the trouble'

Said he 'Don't forget your shovel'
'Have you any auld autographs or tapes'
'Well sir you've a neck on you like a jockey's bollix'
What about the LEB?

I tailormade this as an icebreaker, to settle us all down in whatever circumstance we might find ourselves. Before I moved on to the concert stage I performed in over a thousand kips that had the sale of liquor as the primary object and the stage was often situated in the least likely place. These kips are the places I love dearly for it's there I learned my craft and discovered the love of an audience and how to deal with any situation that might arise.

The song is about nothing in particular, I love the images it creates in my head. It all happened in some shape or form and there are another eight verses somewhere if I ever find them.

In 1972 we drove into Claremorris. Planxty were playing in Andy Creighton's Lounge to celebrate the launch of the Claremorris Ham Festival. This festival consisted of a smoked leg of ham in Andy's window and eight late-night bar extensions. We arrived at 2pm and were amazed to find a long queue. We giggled with joy that at last the band was taking off, until someone noticed that the entire queue was made up of the sick and infirm. Finbar Nolan, the seventh son of a seventh son, was holding a faith-healing clinic in the venue and none of them waited for the gig.

Planxty was a band I formed in 1971 with Donal Lunny, Andy Irvine, and Liam O'Flynn. We recorded six albums and the music we made has become the stuff of legend! We played for fun and fame followed. My happiest times on the road and in the studio were with the original Planxty band. Thirty years on and the music is ageing very well. All four of us are still making lots of music. We may have diverged and diversified, but we're all still on 'the Island'. Once a year or so we get together and talk about playing again, we have dinner and a good time and then we part again for another year and maybe that's the way we should leave it.

It would be a shame to tarnish the legend – we'll have to wait and see.

Fairytale of New York
by Shane McGowan and Jem Finer

It was Christmas Eve babe, in the drunk tank, an old man said 'Son, I won't see another one.'
And then he sang a song, the rare auld mountain dew, I turned my eyes away and I thought about you

Got on a lucky one, came in at eighteen to one, I've got a feeling, this year's for me and you
So happy Christmas, I love you baby, they're gonna be good times when all our dreams come true . . .

They've got cars big as bars they've got rivers of gold
Where the wind blows right through you it's no place for the old
When I first took your hand on a cold Christmas Eve
I told you that Broadway was waiting for you
You were handsome and pretty Queen of New York City
When the band finished playing the crowd howled for more
Sinatra was swinging all the girls they were singing
We kissed on the corner and danced round the floor

And the boys from the NYPD choir were singing Galway Bay
And the bells were ringing out on Christmas Day

I could have been someone, and so could anyone, I took my dreams from you when I first met you
I kept them with me Babe and I put them with my own, I can't make it all alone, I've built my dreams around you

You're a bum you're a punk you're an auld hure on junk lying there on the drip nearly dead in the bed
You scumbag you maggot you cheap lousy faggot happy Christmas me arse I'd rather be dead

And the boys from the NYPD choir were singing Galway Bay
And the bells were ringing out on Christmas Day

He was looking for the broad majestic Shannon

Kneeling by the sick bed of Cúchalainn

Praying for the whores down the Old Main Drag

Thinking about a pair of brown eyes that were waiting

Dreaming of the thousands who were sailing

Of Sally McLennane

And the summers in Siam

Of Aisling his darling black-haired diamond

Asking Kitty my darling to remember

While the madness from the mountains was crawling

I've met Shane on and off these past fifteen years, but I know him mainly by the songs he sings. More than any writer I've heard, his lyrics bring me to a place that I know. I know his country, I've been through his meadow, across his bog, down his street and I love his work dearly. I sang with him once – a version of 'Spancilhill'. I had recorded the song in 1971 and when we rehearsed it in 1995 he pulled me up for having changed it – he is a man of words and raw emotion and understated pain that comes crawling out of the lyrics like the madness crawling out of the mountain. When he sent me 'Aisling' I could not decipher a melody so I made one up and I hope he likes it.

All the London mullarkey I understand. I went over there for the summers of 1961, '62 and '63 and I discovered my culture in the pubs of Hammersmith and Fulham Broadway. There was nothing in Newbridge bar card schools and horses and GAA and tennis clubs, but when I got over to the Big Smoke I encountered Roland, Farrell, Sherlock, McGuire, McGlinchey, Maggie Barry, Mairtín Byrnes, the three Dwyer brothers, Packie Manus Byrne and the flame was lit. Then, when I encountered The Clancy Brothers, I was on my way.

There is an edge to my Irishness when I'm in the ghetto, and McGowan's lyrics take me back there. I wear it like a badge of exile – it was macho and violent and sexist and racist and wild and drunk and stoned and kinky and loud, and underneath it all lay tenderness but no words to describe it, and from that to show tenderness or affection could be misconstrued as weakness so fuck them all just in case.

Shane acts as a magnet and touchstone for many lost and wandering souls who see reflected in him their own confusion and awkwardness. It disturbs me when I see the self-violation that takes place but we all have the right to choose and he knows that there are many doors open to him if he decides to take a rest from the mayhem.

Black Is the Colour (of my True Love's Hair)
from the singing of Hamish Imlach

Black is the colour of my true love's hair
Her lips are like some roses fair
She has the sweetest smile and the gentlest hands
And I love the ground whereon she stands

I love my love and well she knows
I love the ground whereon she goes
And I wish the day it soon would come
When she and I could be as one

I go to the Clyde and I mourn and weep
For satisfied I never can be
Then I write her a letter just a few short lines
And I suffer death, a thousand times

In 1967 I was living in Manchester. I had a room in Rusholme and I was out and about every night looking for gigs. There were a hundred folk clubs within twenty miles of Manchester Piccadilly and in that time I played most of them. My system was to show up early at a club and ask the promoter whether I could do a few songs to warm up the crowd. When I got the nod, I'd go and give it my best shot and this would usually lead to a support gig. Promoters from other clubs were always trawling the circuit for new voices and the 1967 diary gradually began to fill up. I got booked for clubs like the Golden Lion in Middleton, St Clare's in Victoria Avenue, and most importantly the Manchester Sports Guild run by the legendary Jenks. This man was the kingpin of the north of England folk circuit and he took to me early on. I began by singing my two songs at his Monday talent night, and then progressed to support slot on the Sunday night, and after three or four years I had moved on to the main event slot on Saturday night, getting paid £20 for two 30-minute sets.

My contemporaries on the Manchester circuit were Mike Harding, Tony Downes, Marie Little, The Beggarmen, The Grehan Sisters, Harry Boardman, The Oldham Tinkers, The Valley Folk, Rosemary Harding, Tom and Smiley, Des English, and the principal visiting performers were Noel

Murphy, The Watersons, Martin Carthy and The Corries. The clubs varied in size from 40 seats up to the very large, at 250–300. Only the larger clubs had PA systems, which in those days were very simple indeed and none the worse for that.

Once, I was standing in the queue outside the MSG to hear Hamish Imlach. He walked down the street and, seeing me with a guitar case, he stopped to chat and then invited me in as his guest. It was the beginning of a long friendship that lasted until he died in the first minutes of 1996. I more or less joined him on the road for the rest of that tour. I travelled to his gigs and sometimes he would encourage the promoter to give me a chance and I got many gigs and contacts through his generosity of spirit. I sat and watched him carefully and learned about communicating and the skill of ad-libbing and turning every occurrence during a performance into a part of the gig. When Hamish broke a string he ad-libbed while changing it. If a Chieftain tank or a *Coronation Street* barmaid walked in on his performance, he would incorporate it into his set. He was a very gentle man and also had an acute and sensitive antenna. He was never offensive.

He was a terrible man for drink and drugs and I became a drink-for-drink sidekick and began to experiment with whatever was going around. I was very anti-tobacco and found the smell of smoking nauseating. I discovered that hash could be eaten and I was an instant convert. My first hash experience was in Lincoln where, after a big St Patrick's night concert with Hamish, The Grehan Sisters and Nigel Denver, I ingested a lump of Paki black and lay under a table speechless for eight hours waiting for the effect! I began scoring bits of draw around Moss Side, and over in Bradford and Leeds – £8 an ounce. I travelled around England and Scotland stoned for many years. At the time it seemed wonderful – today I've got my doubts. I prefer my reality; if I'm standing in a beautiful place I do not need hash to see the beauty nor any other substance to kill the pain.

This song was a mainstay of Hamish's set and I only started doing it when I returned to Ireland and off his patch. In recent years it has become part of the national repertoire. There is another fine version I heard sung by the late Liam Weldon. The words are quite similar but Liam's melody was a lot more dramatic and may have been based on a slow air of the same name that I heard Willie Clancy play on the pipes.

Whacker Humphries
by C. Moore

One day as I was walking past the bridge in Dolphin's Barn
Down by the old canal I saw some children in a car
In the back they were shooting up smack, I had a bird's eye view
I dialled 999 they said there's nothing we can do
On both sides of the river clearly to be seen
Down along O'Connell Street and up to Stephen's Green
Heroin sold openly there was no need to hide
The Drug Squad were outnumbered, maintained their hands were tied

John Whacker Humphries he's a family man
Him and Sally give their children everything they can
Plagued with the scourge of heroin he'd not accept defeat
He joined other concerned parents to put the dealers off the street
They marched on dealers' houses and ordered them to quit
Time and time again they warned we've had enough of it
Dirty needles in our doorways, junkies hanging all about
Keep on dealing heroin and you're gonna be moved out

From St Theresa's Gardens to the flats in Ballymun
Concerned parents had the dealers on the run
Until the brass in Harcourt Street got their knuckles rapped
Word came down the line these parents must be stopped

They were rounded up and charged with crimes against the state
Brought to Green Street special court to decide their fate
There was no trial by jury, there was no bail
Concerned parents thrown into jail
I was sitting in the gallery with families, friends and wives
We strained to hear who told the truth and who was telling lies
Dealers, junkies and police on the prosecution side
I swear to God that's what I saw before my very eyes

Whacker Humphries took the dealers on and fought them tooth and nail
And a hundred well-armed soldiers took him down to Portlaoise Jail
Tried to protect his children, found guilty of a crime
One man gets a pension, another man gets time

This morning I was walking past the bridge in Dolphin's Barn
I heard a small bird whisper
'Mind you don't come to any harm'

Ever since the costly litigation over my song 'They Never Came Home', I've been forced on a few occasions to rewrite songs at the urging of counsel. This has always been unsatisfactory and a number of songs I loved have been blanded out by my legal eyes acting in my own interest. I remember trying to mix this song in Brussels and getting faxes by the hour telling me I can't say this and I can't say that. Thankfully, this song survived the brief's microscope, and I am grateful for his counsel.

I was following up the issue of the State versus Concerned Parents Against Drugs. I knew some of the activists. One day out walking with my three children I witnessed what is described in verse one. It seemed totally out of control. I saw this crazy guy selling smack to young teenagers and letting them use the back of his old wreck to bang up. He then drove back down through a public park and people had to jump to get out of his way. I went home and rang the police and they said there was nothing they could do. Later that week I attended the Special Court in Green Street where I saw the State using heroin dealers as witnesses against concerned parents. People attending the courts were also being intimidated by police on the way in. It is a factor of our society that has always appalled me. I've seen the police harass and arrest and beat people who were on the streets supporting the Birmingham Six, Nicky Kelly, Concerned Parents Against Drugs, and various other campaigns like Section 31, No to Europe, SHAG off Ronnie Reagan – for long periods of my life I've felt very removed from the authorities of the State called Home. Recently I've come to be more tolerant and to try to see the good in people and only to dwell on the negative when forced to do so.

I've sung this song many times in different prisons. It is always requested in prison concerts no matter what way the audience is made up.

There have been various reverberations to this song. A few people went to great trouble to convince me that the subject was an unworthy one and tried to blacken John Humphries' name. However, I was able to make my own judgement, for John Humphries and his wife are well known to me and I am happy to call them good friends.

Singing Bird
Author unknown

I have seen the lark soar high at morn
To sing way up in the blue
I've heard the blackbird pipe his song
The thrush and the linnet too
But none of them could sing so sweet
My singing bird as you

If I could catch my singing bird
In its own cosy nest
If I could catch my singing bird
I'd warm it on my breast
And on my heart my singing bird
Would sing itself to rest

The ways my mother could sing. As a small boy I listened to her play the
piano and sing old songs and new songs. One day she'd play 'In the
Mood', the next she'd go through a Gilbert & Sullivan medley and have me
singing along. Another time it could be some Moore's Melodies, or a few
John McCormack songs. All these would be sung very softly as if not to
disturb anyone – her singing could never disturb for it was straight from
her heart and what a good-hearted woman she was.

However, on Sunday mornings there would be nothing soft about her
singing. Mammy was a soloist in the Dominican church choir and when Dr
Josef Cuypers gave her the lead in, her voice would thrill the congregation
below as she gloriously trilled out Panis Angelicus or Ave Maria.

Much later on, when we both had our drinking behind us, we grew very
close again. We would drive out together across the Curragh, down by the
Liffey, up the Hill of Allen, over by Father Moore's well, below the Red Hills
and through the Sandy Hills, once or twice heading off to the Boyne Valley
to see the Boyne meander past Ardmulchan, and she would sing gently again
and we'd drive in silence and the world seemed perfect.

Mother was always interested in my work and I always encouraged and
valued her criticisms. I've uncovered a letter which she wrote in 1985 after
reading some pieces I was writing:

Dear Chris

I heard your tape and then Terry gave me the lyrics you are working on. It is hard to comment as I do not know what you have in mind, a biography perhaps or some little vignettes to go with the songs. It seems to be like you are writing down thoughts which are racing through your head as in 'Don't Start'. This has a Beckett influence.

'The Mission' is a feasible little tale but it is too extreme which takes away its credibility.

The language in 'A Shower' is not like yours and the bitterness is not you, either. Sometimes when we say things or sing things they float on the air and are soon forgotten, but the written word remains to be read by your children and their children – that is why it is such a difficult art. All of these thoughts – you are quite capable of expressing them in plain English without the adjectives.

'7/5/66'. In your great, varied and adventurous life I feel that this adventure is not of much importance, your being embarrassed by a sick man. Some day I must tell you of my experiences as a child of eleven and twelve.

'Fr Gorman' is natural and a nice little memory.

'The Hanging' is strong and has a realism that is credible and thought-provoking.

'No Change'. I never knew what my father's wages were. My mother was a very private person in all matters and did not like anyone knowing her business. I never knew how they managed to give me a wedding reception in The Gresham Hotel for 120 people – she was a great believer in keeping 'the side up'. I suppose I inherited that quality as when your Daddy died people said 'It is a terrible tragedy to lose your husband so young, but you are lucky that you've plenty of money.' I always said I had a lot to be thankful for. Like my mother, I felt it was nobody's business but my own.

'Baz & Suzie' is a beautiful story – this is the Christy Moore that people know and love.

'Goggi & Gogga'. We were reared in Ardmulchan. Daddy was born and reared in Hayestown. The language here would not have been my mother's but you have paid them a nice little tribute.

'Uncle Frank'. Also very nice, but it was Father Byrne who was in Milltown then. He inadvertently introduced me to your Daddy.

'Great Uncle Frank' brought happy memories to me, too. As a child, I thought for years that bottles of wine grew in the ground like potatoes.

'Second Time'. Another good teenage memory, although I can't imagine Uncle Frank saying 'Jasus'!

'8-10-56'. Too moving for me to write much about; it is beautiful in its simplicity of words, that is your strength.

'Celibates'. Very good and suitable for your work on social issues, could be used beside 'Oxfam Shop'. Valid stuff.

Christopher alanna – this is very bad writing and the prose leaves a lot to be desired but my arthritis is acting up today.

Love to Val and the kids.

> Have a good gig.
> Mammy

Nancy Power, 1919–1992

Most of us believe that our mothers are special, and I am no exception. Mother nurtured me, my bones and flesh grew from her very life's blood. Writing this I can feel her close by, hear her heartbeat, smell her hair, hear her laugh, watch her cry, listen to her sing or whistle at the kitchen sink, making those air sounds without actually whistling.

My mother taught me to talk, sing, walk, swim (she never swam herself), ride a bike, look for the good in people; she made me aware of so much that lies hidden in the crevices. She hit me once for drinking and then later loved to drink with me; she was my most valued critic for she had insight into my work that was deep and experienced.

Mammy was a singer herself. Nancy Power grew up on the banks of the Boyne. Her father, Jack Power, worked at Ardmulchan which is a large Georgian estate near Navan, Co. Meath, in the parish of Senchelstown or Yellow Furze. Her mother was Elly Sheeran from the cotton mills. Mammy had one brother, Jimmy, who died in hard circumstances in Birmingham. Nancy had an idyllic childhood and from what I can gather was a very happy and much-loved young girl. The older people of the parish still remember her from 70 years ago and tell me of her beautiful voice and her laughter and her zest for living. The estate which Jack worked on was owned by Sir Alexander Maguire, an absentee landlord whose fortunes were made from boxes of matchsticks. She sang in the church and school choirs and also became a renowned soloist as her fine soprano voice developed. She knew about lyrics and melody and voice and projection and communication.

All of my early memories of Mammy are musical. I can still imagine myself as a baby sitting at her feet by the piano as she played and sang. Old Irish songs, hymns in Latin, bits of opera, light and classical, pop songs and lullabies. She loved to play and sing. She instilled music in all of us. Of her six children two are professional singers and the other four can get up anywhere and sing as many songs as people would like to hear. It is carrying on down into the next generation where many of her grandchildren show signs of being immersed in the magic of the music.

Our house in Newbridge was mainly a happy one. I have no bad feelings about my early childhood – I never wanted for anything. But all that changed on 8 October 1956.

I cannot even imagine the terrible trauma Mammy suffered that day. To be widowed at 37 and left to rear her six children alone: Christopher, eleven, Eilish, nine, Anne, seven, Terry, five, Andy, three, Barry, eighteen months. It was a strange, dreamlike time, we were all doled out to different neighbours, everyone was in shock and disbelief. I remember being kind of cool about the madness everywhere, I never saw my daddy's corpse, nor did I see his coffin go down. I seemed to have spent the funeral sitting in a car. I do remember the Mass. Lots of big-wig politicos, including An Taoiseach and various other ministers, but I was not interested. Mammy put Daddy's watch on my wrist at the funeral Mass and I wore it until 1968 when I lost it in the washroom of Victoria Station in Manchester.

Mammy went into a deep depression after the mourners departed. Much later, she told me that she was completely lost without Daddy. She loved him deeply and never ceased to mourn his passing. She was given tranquillisers and became dependent for a time and she told me that, for a period, she was suicidal.

Her father, who loved her deeply, came to her and, painful though it was, he had to shake her out of her depression and lethargy. Jack focused her on her dreadful predicament, and she set about picking up the pieces.

When Daddy died he left no legacy. Nancy started from scratch. She went to the small grocery shop and put on a shop coat and got stuck in. She worked harder than any woman I've ever known. She bought for the shop and did the accounts; she supervised the running of the home and also looked after my father's ageing mother, aunt and uncle out in Barronstown. When her own father died, her mother, Elly, came to live with us. As if this were not enough, Mammy also inherited Daddy's Town Commission and County Council seats. Like him she, too, became deeply immersed in politics and was narrowly defeated in 1968 for a Dáil seat.

She educated all six of us and never saw us short of anything. Not only did she provide for us materially, but all of us are still deeply devoted to her and we never speak without invoking her name.

There came a time when Nancy's loneliness began to cripple her and she sought refuge in alcohol. For maybe ten years she drank too much and there were unhappy times between us when we were both under the spell of booze. At Christmas 1982, Mother and I fell out, and did not speak for a year. It was a terrible period. Time and time again I tried to go and see her, but my pride and anger prevented me.

In late 1983 I woke up in Bertie and Olive Barrett's house in Derry. I always stayed with them when I played Derry. I looked around the room and there was a scroll on the wall that contained some philosophy on how we hurt the ones we love. I asked Olive for the scroll and sent it to Mother, for it described exactly the pain that existed between us. The moment she received it she rang me and we got our love together again. She kept that scroll by her bedside until the day she died, whereupon I sent it back to Olive Barrett in Derry, for it had surely done its job.

Nancy ran out of steam with public life around the early Seventies. She became more involved with helping people on a one-to-one basis. Her door was never locked. At one stage every house around her was burgled, yet hers, which was always wide open, was never thieved. Late one night there was a fracas in her back garden. Three or four drunks had come over her wall and were making a din. She got out of bed and down the stairs, picked up the sweeping brush and went out in her nightie to confront the drunken men. She was 70. 'Jasus, Mrs Moore, we didn't know it was your garden.'

Nancy was well-got with all walks of life. A man said to me recently, 'You know, not everyone liked your mother, but I was always very suspicious of people who did not.'

She had many great spakes: 'It's not everyone that money suits,' or, about people who attended Mass daily and had very pious demeanours, 'They must have an awful lot on their conscience.'

Although her social and political views were deep-rooted, Nancy never preached. She always maintained friendships across the political spectrum and only spoke ill of people who, in some way, she perceived to be a threat to her family.

Nancy died on 18 September 1992 in the County Hospital, Naas, Co. Kildare. Before she passed on I only spoke to her face-to-face or on the phone. Now I can speak to her at any time and I often do.

Don't Forget your Shovel
by Christie Hennessy (with some new lyrics by C. Moore)

Don't forget your shovel if you want to go to work
Or you'll end up where you came from like the rest of us
Don't forget your shoes and sock and shirt and tie and all
Mr Murphy is afraid you'll make a claim if you take a fall
We want to go to Heaven but we're always digging holes
There's one thing you can say we know where we are going
Enoch Powell will give us a job digging our way to Annascaul
When we're finished digging he'll close the hole and all
(There are 5,649 Paddies all trying to dig their way back to Annascaul
and very few of them are going to make it at all
But there is no barbed wire around the mailboat)
If you want to do it don't you do it against the wall
There's a shed up in the corner where they won't see you at all
(Mind your sandwiches)

I met Christie Hennessy in the Sixties and recorded his song twenty years later. It became my first hit single and coined a catchphrase that has followed me around since. I knew my life was changing when a London bus pulled up in Oxford Street in 1985 and the driver leaned out the window and called after me: 'Hey, Christy! Don't forget your shovel!'

I've adapted the song a hundred times. I sang it with Billy Bragg in 1991 at a huge building-workers' strike in Western Australia, with Donal Lunny at the gates of Portlaoise Prison, in Carnegie Hall for Joe Doherty and in Clonakilty for Adi Roche – each rendition with different verses appropriate to the situation.

The song was manna to many of my detractors. They heaped scorn upon its simplicity, its lack of music, its crudeness, its crassness, its lack of substance. Bless them, but they missed the point.

City of Chicago
by Barry Moore

1847 was the year it all began
Deadly pains of hunger
Drove a million from the land
They journeyed not for glory
Their motive wasn't greed
A voyage of survival
Far across the stormy sea

To the city of Chicago
As the evening shadows fall
There are people dreaming
Of the hills of Donegal

Some of them knew fortune
Some of them knew fame
More of them knew hardship
And they died upon the plain
They spread throughout the nation
They rode the railroad cars
Brought their songs and music
To ease their lonely hearts

To the city of Chicago
As the evening shadows fall
There are people dreaming
Of the hills of Donegal

When Daddy died the neighbours told me I was the man of the house, and that I would have to look after my mother and brothers and sisters. I believed them and I started running. I ran fast until 1989, so I was exhausted by the time I stopped.

I became aware of Barry's music around 1968. I arrived home from England to find this kid playing guitar, singing good songs and writing beautiful tunes. He came to England with me in the summer of 1969 and played some clubs at fourteen years of age. Later he played support to Planxty in 1972 and he's been doing his music very successfully ever since. He gigs with the stage name Luka Bloom but Barry Moore still comes home when the gigs are over.

The rest of the family are still on the Island. Eilish with her family in Inchicore, Anne and family in Milltown Malbay, Co. Clare, Terry in the home town and Andy and family now living in Cork. Two of the next generation, so far, are playing music. Conor Byrne has recorded his first album and lives in Dublin; Gavin Moore is writing and singing and lives in Cork.

I've been to Chicago four times with varying degrees of success. My first appearance was to a room full of drunks, so I joined them. Next time, US Immigration prevented me from leaving Toronto, so I missed a sold-out show in the Windy City. That was a painful experience brought on by an out-of-date visa and an unsympathetic officer. Next there was an Irish festival at the GAA Park in Chicago. Plastic paddies, leprechauns, buachalls and colleens and an army of would-be Flatleys. It was hard going. Next time I had more luck, I did three nights at The Abbey in Chicago in December 1997. It was so good, I have not played anywhere since at the time of writing.

Daddy's favourite song was 'The Pride of Petravore'.

The Pride of Petravore
Author unknown

Eileen Oge! Me heart is growing grey
Ever since the day you wandered far away
Eileen Oge! There's good fish in the sea
But there's no-one like the Pride of Petravore

Friday at the fair of Ballintubber
Eileen met McGrath the cattle jobber
I'd like to set me mark upon the robber
For he stole away the Pride of Petravore
He never seemed to see the girl at all
Even when she ogled him underneath her shawl
Looking big and masterful when she was looking small
Most provoking for the Pride of Petravore

Boys, O boys! With fate 'tis hard to grapple
Of my eye 'tis Eileen was the apple
And now to see her walking to the chapel
With the hardest featured man in Petravore
Now boys this is all I have to say
When you do your courting make no display
If you want them to run after you just walk the other way
For they're mostly like the Pride of Petravore

Andy Moore, 1915–1956

I remember certain things about Daddy very clearly. He used to sing and whistle this song. I'll tell you bits of his story.

Andy was born in 1915 to Christopher Moore and Bridie Dowling who were in their third year of an arranged marriage. Christopher Moore was manager of the Hibernian Bank in Newbridge and Bridie was the eldest daughter of the Dowling family in Barronstown, Miltown, near Newbridge. He owned a farm of land that adjoined the Dowling farm and this may have been a factor in the wedding. Bridie was 45 years his junior when they wedded and I heard that, as a young woman, she was renowned for her beauty. Christopher Moore had other interests apart from his banking career, and although he died a wealthy man he left an unhappy woman after him. I remember her well for she outlived Daddy by many years – she was a sad, cold, unfulfilled woman who seldom, if ever, saw the bright side.

When Daddy was a six-year-old boy she put him into boarding school with nuns in Kilashee, near Naas. When he was seven, he ran away from Kilashee and made his way on foot back to his mother, whereupon she got a Hackney car and took him straight back to the nuns again. Why a wealthy young widow should have so little time for her only child remains a mystery. After Kilashee she put him into Willow Park and then Blackrock College, both run by Jesuit priests. I've seen two photos of them together and her body language was cold and forbidding. I used to resent her for this until I grew to realise that she, too, suffered from the lack of affection in her life.

From what I can gather my father left college in 1933 and became a bit of a wild boy. I've no idea what he did between 1933 and 1939, but hearsay and photos would suggest he became a sort of a gentleman farmer. The company he kept was certainly fun-loving and I often heard stories of legendary drinking escapades, of horse-racing and carousing, and I've also met a good number of older women who spoke fondly of Andy Moore and remembered that they 'knew him very well'.

Andy joined the Irish Army in 1939 at the outbreak of the Second World War, and stayed in during 'The Emergency', being demobbed in 1945 as a commissioned officer, ranked lieutenant. During the war he met and married my mother, in 1943. They settled into the bank manager's house in Newbridge. His mother vacated the premises and returned to the Dowling farm in Barronstown.

Some time later he lost the farm bequeathed him by his father. I don't know the details, but suffice to say that the Land Commission took his farm and divided it into six 40-acre farms that were redistributed. He seems to have taken all this in his stride for I grew up knowing all the families who lived on that land and we had good relationships with them all. He bought a small grocer's shop in 1950 and this became the mainstay of our family.

In 1946, when I was six months old, my mother left home taking me along. She did this as a protest against my father's drinking and cavorting. He was unable to track her down for a week but, finally, with the aid of his father-in-law, we were traced to a guest house in Amiens Street, Dublin, where Daddy swore a vow never to drink again – and he never did.

I still love him dearly. I can hear his voice and I can remember his clothes and his hair and his hands and nails and the waft of tobacco and Brylcreem.

Today, I think my Daddy put down the drink and became a workaholic.

As well as his business, he became deeply involved in local, and then national politics. He was Chairman of the Town Commissioners and later of the County Council. He ran for the Dáil and was narrowly defeated at his first attempt. He was in the Fine Gael party and was a 'Michael Collins' man. Despite his party I believe him to have been an active socialist. He fought constantly for the oppressed, and was always at the side of the needy. I recall his involvement in an eviction where a local landlord turned out a family down around Roseberry or Clongorey, and Daddy saw to it that the family got housed. I remember him intervening on the street when a drunken man was beating his wife. I can still see him delivering groceries to families who had nothing. As he became more involved in various committees, we saw less and less of him. When we had our family holiday in Tramore, he would drop us off and collect us a week later. Whatever I did, Daddy would drop me off and collect me – poor man never had time for himself.

One Sunday night he went into the Jockey Hospital. He was to have an ingrown toenail removed first thing on Monday morning. He never came out of the anaesthetic. He was 41.

He was a beautiful man and I still miss him.

Burning Times
by Charles Murphy

ISIS - ASTARTE - DIANA - HEGATE - DEMITRE - KALI - INARNA

In the cool of the evening they used to gather 'neath the stars in the meadow circled near an old oak tree

At the times appointed by the seasons of the earth and the phases of the moon

In the centre often stood a woman equal with the others and respected for her worth

One of the many we call the witches, the healers, the teachers of the wisdom of the earth

People grew in the knowledge she gave them herbs to heal their bodies smells to make their spirits whole

Hear them chanting healing incantations calling for the wise ones celebrating in dance and song

ISIS - ASTARTE - DIANA - HEGATE - DEMITRE - KALI - INARNA

There were those who came to power through domination they were bonded in their worship of Jesus on the cross

They sought control over all people by demanding allegiance to the Church of Rome

And the Pope commenced the Inquisition 'twas a war against women whose powers were feared

In this holocaust in this century of evil nine million European women died

And the tale is told of those who by the hundred holding hands together chose their deaths in the sea

Chanting the praises of the Mother Goddess a refusal of betrayal women were dying to be free

Now the earth is a witch and we still burn her stripping her down with mining and the poison of our wars

Still to us the earth is a healer a teacher and a mother a weaver of a web of light that keeps us all alive

She gives us the vision to see through the chaos she gives us the courage it is our will to survive.

ISIS - ASTARTE - DIANA - HEGATE - DEMITRE - KALI - INARNA

This song came to me via Roy Bailey in England and Martha McClelland in Derry. It is one of those songs that I heard and immediately wanted to sing. I re-recorded it for the 1999 *Traveller* album. The imagery is stunning and I get very inside the movie of the song when I sing it. I've never cracked performing this song on the home turf. On mainland Europe it is well received and the vibe that it creates allows me to develop an atmosphere. But when I sing it at home I always feel a stiffening in the audience and a discomfort. Whether it's the criticism of the Papal See or discomfort with the history of the Catholic Church I don't fully understand, but it is one of the essential songs of my repertoire, and one I wish to record again, preferably live and preferably abroad. I feel this song allows me to express my own feelings about the sustained and modern persecution of women, and my feelings about the femininity of the Deity – my mother nature, my love of the natural way and my belief in The Healing Powers. I have witnessed many of the scenes that Chuck creates in his song. I've never spoken to the man, nor heard him sing, but I hope to meet him some day.

I have never received a song from a woman writer. To the best of my knowledge I've only recorded a woman's writing once in 30 years, the beautiful folk tale by the poet Paula Meehan.

I have encountered great women in my life. In my fifties, I now feel closer to women than to men. There are a few things that I prefer to do with men, but in the main I prefer the company of women. Their strength of character, their humanity, their warmth and kindness, their practicality, suss and pragmatism – they leave us standing in the battle of the sexes. Give me a woman any day of the week for good company and conversation. Men are fine for walking, playing snooker, going to or playing football, management, production, band membership. I want women priests, bishops, presidents, police, politicians. I want to be ruled and governed by at least 50 per cent women. Goodnight Luke.

1 December 1996
Last night I again played in The Forum, Kentish Town. My audience profile has changed dramatically these past ten years. I was very aware last night of a young audience, 18 to 30, and from what I could see from the stage women were in a slight majority. It is women's voices I hear singing the songs, and there is a powerful vibe around the gigs these nights. I've almost lost the drunken boors, but there was one poor woman last night seriously out of her tree and she finally got to me at the two-hour mark as I finished the set with this song.

I feel very annoyed when I let a heckler get to me. For years now I've gone through a mental preparation, part of which is to preclude drunken hecklers rising my anger. Mostly I can handle the odd time it happens, but every now and then I succumb to senseless fury and sometimes this can badly affect a performance. I'll have it conquered before the last gig, maybe.

The Middle of the Island
by Nigel Rolfe and C. Moore

Everybody knew, nobody said
A week ago last Tuesday
She was just fifteen years
When she reached her full term
She went to a grotto
Just a field
In the middle of the island
To deliver herself
She died
Her baby died
A week ago last Tuesday
It was a sad slow stupid death
Everybody knew, nobody said
At a grotto
In a field
In the middle of the island

I continue to sing this song nightly. It is usually preceded by 'The Well Below the Valley', an ancient song which deals with the same topic. As Fr Joe Young speaks of 'the violence of silence' in Limerick, and Fr Pat Clarke whispers to me of 'the terrorism of apathy' from Sao Paolo, this song talks about The Ostrich (the original title) with its head in the sand.

'Like an ostrich, a sad slow stupid ostrich.'

There was a time when this song angered sections of my audience; nevertheless the song has become a memorial to a young woman who died that we might confront an appalling ignorance, that we might stand up and face those who would have us crawling like mindless slugs in a dark bog of sin and guilt. To Hell with Hell, I say to you who rant and rail about sin and punishment and the wrath of God. God knows no wrath for God is Love. To be wrathful is to have no kindness nor forgiveness.

I know this song challenges my audience, but I need to sing it for my own sake. It also does not always sit comfortably within the concept of entertainment, but I will strive to present it as palatably as such lyrics about our recent history can be. It is not only for the suffering young women of Ireland, but for those children who suffer around the world at the hands of fundamentalists and fanatics.

'God help me find those who seek the truth
and protect me from those who have found it.'

The babies of Islam who are violated in the name of God, the babies of Christ punished for the perceived crime of their gender, the girls sold into white slavery that a family might eat and the young girls left to die in cold stone grottos while a country kneels at the altar, like an ostrich.

It has been whispered to me that I don't know the real story – that I should let the girl rest in peace, what's the good in dragging up the past. On and on they whine, but to no avail.

(Nigel Rolfe sent me his original lyric 'The Ostrich' and I recorded it with him. Subsequently over repeated performances it evolved into this piece which I recorded with Sinéad O'Connor for the *Voyage* album.)

The Voyage
by Johny Duhan

I am a sailor you're my first mate
We signed on together we coupled our fate
Hauled up our anchor determined not to fail
For the heart's treasure together we set sail

With no maps to guide us we steered our own course
Rode out the storms when the winds were gale force
Sat out the doldrums in patience and in hope
Working together we learned how to cope

Life is an ocean love is a boat
In troubled waters it keeps us afloat
When we started the voyage there was just me and you
Now gathered round us, we have our own crew

Together we're in this relationship
We built it together to last the whole trip
Our true destination is not marked on any chart
We're navigating for the shores of the Heart

Johnny Duhan has been writing songs all his life, and performing them too. I first recorded a song of his on my *Ride On* album of 1984, and then this song for my 1989 album *Voyage*. I walked the line with this song pondering whether or not I could sing it. When I look back now at my difficulty in deciding, I realise that it was an aspect of my confusion coming to a head. This is me enunciating love to my partner and singing publicly things that most people say only in private. This song is a pure and simple love song and has passed into the national repertoire. Prior to its being banned at Catholic church weddings, it was a great favourite. But the thought police have not managed to get their censor into the reception yet, so it is still to be heard at many a wedding feast.

Valerie and I met in McDaid's of Harry Street on a summer's evening in 1972. We began seeing a lot of each other and we tied the knot in December 1973.

Andrew Isaac was born on 20 January 1976. It was a wonderful moment for us both as we gazed upon this miracle bestowed upon us. I have enjoyed very much the company of my first son. Across the years we have hurled together and swam and kicked the ball, and when we began playing snooker I could give him any number of points up, but these days I seldom get to match him. Jim Aiken pointed out to me the difficulty for a young man growing up in a house with a famous and successful father. I thought of my own early days and I know his words are true. Andy handles the difficult parts well and makes no complaints about the disadvantages and is grateful for the advantages.

Juno Nancy arrived on 12 April 1978. Val and I were living in Coolcullen, Co. Carlow, and we rented a house in Ballinteer for the last week of the pregnancy. I missed the birth between minding Andy and rehearsing for an album. I'll never forget holding my daughter for the first time, and I've been in love with her ever since. She is a strong woman, like her mother, she has a way with her that keeps us on our toes. She sang beautifully on 'Strange Ways', and also did vocals on *Traveller*.

Pádraic Ernest arrived on 24 November 1982. His twin sister, our beloved Caitlín, did not make it to the birth. It was a scary time, but thank God Val and Pádraic came home safe and sound and he is our third pride and joy. He is now a young man and shows us love and affection. I am blessed with a fine family, immediate and extended. Pádraic was a great gift to Val's father Ernie, who subsequently came to live and spend his final years with us. It was a lovely time, and he doted upon his closest grandson although he loved the others equally.

Bogie's Bonny Belle
from the singing of Muriel Greaves, Davey Stewart, Jimmy McBeath
and Owen Hand

(Not a complete version)

As I went out by Huntleigh Town
one evening for to fee,
I met with Bogie O'Cairney
and with him I did agree

To care for his two best horses
or cart, harrow or plough
or anything about farm work
that I very well should know.

Auld Bogie had a daughter
her name was Isobel,
she was the lily of the valley
and the primrose of the dell

And when she went out walking
she took me for her guide,
down by the Burn O'Cairney
for to watch the small fish glide.

And when three months were passed and gone
this girl she lost her bloom,
the red fell from her rosy cheeks
and her eyes began to swoon.

And when nine months were past and gone
she bore to me a son,
and I was straight sent for
to see what could be done.

I said that I would marry her
but that it would nae do,
for you're no a match for my bonny wee girl
and she is no a match for you.

Now she's married to a tinker lad
that comes frae Huntleigh Town,
he sells pots and pans and paraffin lamps
and he scours the country round.

Maybe she's had a better match
auld Bogie cannae tell,
so farewell ye lads o' Huntleigh Town
and to Bogie's Bonnie Belle.

In 1967 I went to a festival in Blairgowrie in Scotland. Traditionally it was a place renowned for berry picking and this festival was a celebration of traditional Scottish music and song. It was a wild time with great, unusual memories. If memory serves me I travelled in convoy with The Marsden Rattlers from Tyneside. We picked up Old Davey Stewart in Glasgow and we had music all along the way. (He was called Old Davey to differentiate him from many younger Davey Stewarts on the music circuit.) I stayed out at a riverside campsite and I met many many people over the weekend. It was my first time to meet Finbar Furey and for many years we remained good friends. I subsequently visited him and Sheila in Peebles where they settled, and spent many's the happy hour in their good company – more of this later. I encountered both Jimmy McBeath and Davey Stewart who were journeymen singers and both had fine versions of this ballad. I managed to stitch together a version from all the different singers I've heard do it and in 1968 it was to be the first song I ever broadcast on radio. It was a live show for Radio Éireann done to an audience somewhere on O'Connell Street. I was absolutely terrified for this was a large step forward in my career – I was home doing a short tour of Irish ballad lounges when Mick Clarke, who put my dates together, somehow managed to get me on to national radio. (Thanks Mick and God rest you.) I would have been playing Slattery's in Capel Street, The Coffee Kitchen in Molesworth Street, The Old Triangle, O'Mara's of The Quays or The Embankment. The nature of gigs in those days was five to six acts on every bill each doing two fifteen-minute sets. You'd finish a gig in Slattery's and then out for a set in The Embankment and then back into town again for a late night spot and another gig. I earned around £12 a night, which was a princely sum for doing what I loved.

Back at the Berryfields of Blair I heard the great Scottish singer Jeannie Robertson and talked to her about songs and family. I sipped whiskey with Hamish Henderson and went walkabout with the Shetland fiddler Aly Bain. Me and Aly became soulmates for a while sharing snooker, curry and whiskey in many's the city, but then he ran off with a woman I loved and we didn't meet up again until a fleadh in Glasgow Green in 1993. I had some sport with

Roy Williamson of The Corries and got booked for their Edinburgh Festival Show in 1968, which was my first introduction to big concerts.

I love the narrative of this song. I included it on Donal Lunny's album *Common Ground* last year. It is a gentle song that still gives me an angry nudge when the labourer gets shafted. I grew up in a time when farm labourers were treated very badly by rich farmers. Small wonder it's all done by machine now. Farmers can abuse machinery without guilt or remorse. The tinkers have dropped off the social scale way below the space they occupied even when this song occurred. It is a song I sing very rarely, so when it comes out of the treasure chest it glitters all the more. I have a small and secret drawer that contains a number of precious songs that only like to be sung on very special occasions, and this is one of them.

Some other 'songs from the secret drawer': 'Lord Baker', 'Little Musgrave', 'Yellow Bittern', 'Dalesman's Litany', 'Banks of the Lee', 'Someone to Love Me'.

Johnny Connors
by C. Moore and Wally Page

My name is Johnny Connors I'm a Travelling man
My people have been Travelling since time it first began
With my horse and covered wagon and my family by my side
Grazing the long acre I travelled far and wide
I met Bridie Maughan my sweet wife on a fair day in Rathkeale
She was the finest Travelling girl that ever wore a shawl

We worked the tin around Galway on up to Ballinasloe
For a Traveller with a horse to sell it was the place to go
We sold the old linoleum swapped carpet for old pine
As the years went by the Travelling life got harder all the time
Where have all the halting places gone all those friendly doors
Where we'd draw spring water from the well and sell our paper flowers

Now it's guards and jailers and JCBs to roll big boulders in
Temporary dwellings are prohibited
Innocent little Travelling children lost out on them streets
My sons and daughters on the wine and lying around my feet
As they try to dull the hurt and pain the rejection that's imposed
Travellers are not wanted here but there is no place left to go

My name is Johnny Connors I am a Travelling man
I've taken everything that's been thrown at me, now I'm going to make me a stand

I had been struggling with these lyrics for ten years. I had put the song away and forgotten about it until Wally Page caught sight of it and refocused my attention with his enthusiasm. I had spent years trying to finish it but Wally could see that it was finished already.

This song is fragments of many true stories stitched together to make the whole. I've known tinkers since early childhood and I've grown to love their culture and spirituality. I know why they cannot trust settled people for we've been fucking them up for centuries and it continues today – maybe even worse than before.

Although I was finally happy with the song, I could not make the decision whether to record it. I was going into the IFC Cinema for the première of *High Boot Benny*. Me and the painter Brian Maguire were heading in to support the director Joe Comerford who was expecting a roasting because of his new film, and we thought to show solidarity. At the entrance to the cinema there was a young Traveller beggar. I gave him some shamboola and knelt beside him to ask how he was. I asked him his name. He said 'Johnny Connors, sir!'

I recorded the song.

One Travelling man told me very seriously that Rathkeale people would never go to Ballinasloe to sell a pony. But I was well pleased, for to get a response was a good feeling. I love the Travelling people. Thank God they are learning to stand up for themselves. There are lots of well-meaning settled people doing the best they can, but it's only when the Travellers get their own self-confidence and education together that they will get proper rights, and it is slowly happening. I'd love to see a Traveller in the Dáil.

Strange Ways
by C. Moore

There is a ring around the world
It ensnares the little ones
Causes governments to fall
It brings all things to an end

Born of woman born through pain
In the shadow of a man
You are in me I am in you
It's not always easy to understand

Strange ways, strange ways

Bless me Father I have sinned
God the Father of all things
You are my everlasting flame
God works in strange ways

Strange ways, strange ways

There is a ring around the world
It ensnares the little ones
Causes governments to fall
It brings all things to an end

Strange ways, strange ways

Mea Maxima Culpa
(earlier draft)

God works in strange ways
All our children are equal in the eyes of God
Mea culpa, mea culpa, mea maxima culpa

Daddy is the daddy, Daddy is the daddy
Bless me Father for I have sinned
Against the God of (love) fear
God the Father
In whose eyes I heard
For fifteen years without a break
'I own you
You are mine
I love you
I beat you

I blind you
I break your fucking nose
My child my love'

Another day, another time, another place
Some of the women give as good as they get
The policeman said
And nobody likes to interfere
The policeman said
(sure she was probably asking for it anyway)

All our children are equal in the eyes of God
God works in strange ways

Valerie and I were driving to Kerry and we listened on the radio to a young Kilkenny woman talk to Marion Finucane about her terrible life in the family home. We stopped and wrote down her words as she shared her story with the country. The original draft of this song was a litany of her words. As time passed and I developed the lyrics, other things happened that became part of the lyrics. In the end I had a song that was too horrific in content to be sung. I still wanted to address the issue of abuse so I decided to try and sing beautifully about this terrible subject.

The awful confusion for children; to be abused in any way is such an unnatural event, to be abused by your father is too sick for me to understand, to be abused by a man of cloth called Father is a fuck-up and then to be asked to seek forgiveness from God the Father is the last great irony and insult to the little ones.

Yes, there is a ring of sickness around the world and I find it hard to accept the existence of paedophiles. They are cunning and evil people and will try to justify repeat offending. I do not know the answer but there will never be one unless we have it out in front of us to discuss openly and in public. For too long now child abuse, paedophilia, incest and all other unnatural acts have been kept hidden and dark. Let the light shine on the sickness.

Juno sings beautifully on this. It is through her grace that it happened at all. I had hoped she would do it but she was finding it very hard to say yes. It was getting close so I went abroad and asked my second and third choices. Two of the island's supreme divas. Neither could attend for various reasons and then Juno said yes. It was a great joy for me as I stood beside her in the studio and she did it all in one go, no fuss, no bother. You've never seen such a proud father.

Viva la Quinte Brigada
by C. Moore

Ten years before I saw the light of morning
A comradeship of heroes was laid
From every corner of the world came sailing
The Fifteenth International Brigade
They came to stand beside the Spanish people
To try and stem the rising fascist tide
Franco's allies were the powerful, wealthy
Frank Ryan's men came from the other side
Even the olives were bleeding
As the battle for Madrid it thundered on
Truth and love against the force of evil
Brotherhood against the fascist clan

Bob Hilliard was a Church of Ireland pastor
From Killarney across the Pyrenees he came
From Derry came a brave young Christian Brother
Side by side they fought and died in Spain
Tommy Woods aged seventeen died in Cordoba
With the Fianna he learned to hold a gun
From Dublin to the Villa del Rio
Where he fought and died beneath the Spanish sun

'Vive la Quinte Brigada'
'No Paseran' the pledge that made them fight
'Adelante!' was the cry around the hillside
Let us all remember them tonight

Many Irish heard the call of Franco
Joined Hitler and Mussolini too
Propaganda from the pulpit and newspapers
Helped O'Duffy to enlist his Blueshirt crew
The word came from Maynooth, support the Nazis
The men of cloth failed us again
For the bishops blessed the Blueshirts in Dun Laoghaire
As they sailed beneath the swastika to Spain

This song is a tribute to Frank Ryan
Kit Conway, Dinny Coady too
Peter Daly, Charlie Reagan and Hugh Bonner
Though many died I can but name a few
Danny Boyle, Blaser Brown and Charlie Donnelly
Hugh Tomelty and Jim Straney from the fells
Jack Nalty, Tommy Patten and Frank Conroy,
Jim Foley, Tony Fox, Dick O'Neill

Val and I and Andy, Juno, Pádraic and my sister Terry went to Spain for three months in 1983. We lived in Nerja and Frijiliana and it was a lovely time. I was reading Mick O'Riordan's book *The Connolly Column* and I began this song as I read on. I was working on a batch of songs at night and being a tourist by day.

Through singing this song I've encountered a bunch of relations of the International Brigade, their children and their grandchildren. It has opened many doors and brought many new friends. In particular, Peter O'Connor and his wife Biddy in Waterford.

Those who fought in Spain sacrificed everything. Many gave their lives to fight fascism. Whenever I run up against resistance to my work from political or associated quarters, I think of the sacrifices these soldiers made.

Peter O'Connor returned to a Waterford that scorned him. He claimed his beautiful bride who had waited for him and the early days of their marriage were lonely ones. Because of his efforts in Spain, many backs were turned against them. But they lived through all this adversity which only seemed to bring them closer together, and today they live with their children and grandchildren in Waterford City. In 1998, Peter and all the surviving members of 'La Quinte Brigada', received their citizenship of Spain from the king himself. Peter invited me to attend, but I was on ballad duty.

A couple of years ago, John Longstaffe made me a presentation to mark the song. John is from Ormsby in Teeside where he lives with his wife Pauline. My earliest knowledge of the Spanish Civil War was from a song called 'Jarama' sung by Johnny Morrissey from Clonmel. I'd love to have the song; it is written to the same tune as 'Take it Down from the Mast', which I used to sing years ago.

14 February 1997

Val and I were invited to a function in The Mansion House where four of the five surviving members were honoured by Dublin City Corporation, 60 years on. But, never too late, these proud gentlemen were welcomed back to Dublin after giving everything in the fight against Franco. Peter O'Connor, Michael O'Riordan, Bob Doyle and Maurice Levitas kindly accepted the flat, lifeless spiel of the Lord Mayor. Michael O'Riordan gave an emotional oration and recalled the deeds of his comrades both present and past. He also welcomed the families of many of the fallen comrades. Val and I and brother Andy were struck by the kind and quiet nature of these four men. The general demeanour of the gathering was that of good people. There was no opportunism here, apart from a number of particularly insensitive media photographers. In his speech Michael O'Riordan quoted loudly from the song 'Quinte Brigada' but never mentioned that the song was lifted entirely from his book *The Connolly Column*.

Since writing this, both Peter and Biddy O'Connor have passed away. God rest them both.

Back Home in Derry
by Bobby Sands, MP

In 1803 we sailed out to sea
Out from the sweet town of Derry
For Australia bound, if we didn't all drown
And the marks of our fetters we carried
In our rusty iron chains we cried for our wains
Our good women we left in sorrow
As the mainsails unfurled our curses we hurled
On England and thoughts of tomorrow

At the mouth of the Foyle bid farewell to the soil
As down below decks we were lying
O'Doherty screamed, woken out of a dream
By a vision of bold Robert dying
The sun burnt cruel as we dished out the gruel
Dan O'Connor was down with a fever
Sixty rebels today bound for Botany Bay
How many will reach their receiver

We cursed them to Hell as our bow fought the swell
Our ship danced like a moth in the firelight
White horses rode high as the devil passed by
Taking souls to Hades by twilight
Five weeks out to sea we were now forty-three
We buried our comrades each morning
In our own slime, lost in a time
Endless night without dawning

Van Dieman's Land is a hell for man
To end up his whole life in slavery
Where the climate is raw and the gun makes the law
Neither wind nor the rain care for bravery
Twenty years have gone by and I've ended my bond
My comrades' ghosts walk behind me
A rebel I came and I'm still the same
On the cold winds of night you will find me

I wish I was back home in Derry

had received a number of poems simply signed 'Marcella'. At the time I was corresponding a fair bit with the POWs in the H-Blocks as a result of the song 'Ninety Miles to Dublin Town'. I was staying in a house in Derry after an H-Block concert and a young lad recently released sang this song. It was subsequent to this that I put 'Marcella' and Bobby Sands together and realised they were the same person.

I love this powerful piece of writing. It has that great quality of a song which can be about two different times in history simultaneously. When I began singing Bobby Sands' songs it caused terrible problems for some people in the Free State. They could not accept that an IRA man could be a poet, and could also write a wonderful song – it proved a difficult fact for some people to accept and, betimes, some of them reacted abusively to the song.

One famous bard asked me, 'How can you sing songs written by a hood?' It shows the power of the media. Eighteen years on they still label freedom fighters as hoods, but it sounds hollow. The thought police did their best on this one, but despite it being banned it has entered the national repertoire and has been recorded by a thousand ballad bands and will long outlive its detractors and severest critics.

Another night in Galway a couple of drunken intellectual lads laid into me for insulting the memory of Woody Guthrie by singing his song beside a Bobby Sands song. I now understand when Northerners are suspicious of Free Staters. Like Travellers, we have abused them once too often and their mindset is inevitable.

Quiet Desperation
by Floyd Westerman

My soul is in the mountains, my heart is in the land
I'm lost here in the city, there's so much I don't understand
There's quiet desperation coming over me
Coming over me

I've got to leave I can't stay another day
There's an emptiness inside of me
I can't bear the loneliness out here
There's another place I've got to be
Another place I've got to be

I long for you Dakota, smell of sweet grass on the plain
I see too much hardship and I feel too much pain
There's quiet desperation coming over me
Coming over me

I've got to leave I can't stay another day
There's an emptiness inside of me
I can't bear the loneliness out here
There's another place I've got to be
Another place I've got to be

Sometime in the early Eighties I attended a concert organised by Joe Cahill. A group of Native Americans came to Belfast, Derry and Dublin on a cultural exchange. They performed in the Geantraí in Monkstown and I met Floyd Westerman who was part of the group who performed.

I presented them with a bowrawn from Portlaoise Prison that had been beautifully painted. Floyd sang 'Quiet Desperation' for me and I sang 'Irish Ways and Irish Laws' for him and we did a swap. I've heard that the song is being sung in America now as 'Indian Ways and Indian Laws'.

I've sung 'Quiet Desperation' in many countries, in places a long way from Dakota, but the song always finds its way into the hearts of people who have known loneliness and isolation. The bigger the city, the deeper the loneliness.

I recorded this song on the 1985 album *Ordinary Man*. Nicky Ryan engineered it in his own studio. Nicky was Planxty's first sound engineer, coming to the band in 1972. He subsequently went on to work with Clannad and then became part of Enya's career with his wife Roma. He was a great engineer and has deservedly achieved great things. Nicky had many great ideas for Planxty but we weren't ready for them. Having a sound engineer in itself was about as much as we could handle.

Recording *Ordinary Man* was a good experience for me. Donal Lunny and Arty McGlynn were my sidekicks, and Liam O'Flynn, Andy Irvine, Tony Molloy and Enya also contributed. All Enya's overdubs were done by Nicky and Enya without Donal and I being around. I'd come into the studio and Nicky would put up the tape and the amazing layered voices came out to me. I was not surprised when she conquered the world a short time later.

The Time Has Come
by C. Moore and Donal Lunny

The time has come to part my love I must go away
I'll leave you now my darling girl no longer can I stay
My heart like yours is breaking together we'll prove strong
The road I take will show the world the suffering that goes on

The gentle clasp that holds my hand must loosen and let go
Please help me through that door though instinct tells you no
Our vow it is eternal and will bring you dreadful pain
But if our demands aren't recognised don't call me back again

How their sorrow touched us all in those final days
When it was time she held the door and touched his sallow face
The flame he lit while leaving is still burning strong
By the light it's plain to see the suffering still goes on

The time has come to part my love I must go away
I'll leave you now my darling girl no longer can I stay

The Hunger Strike came, ten men died, we marched and cried and went home again. I was left with a feeling of helplessness and thought to write a song for the families of the strikers; Peggy O'Hara from Derry was the main source of information with regard to what they had to endure. I also spent time with Mr and Mrs Hughes, who made me very welcome in their home.

I am very glad I wrote these words. Donal Lunny wrote the music. It has the power to evoke a feeling of collective sorrow even when I sing it to audiences who do not know the history of the piece. When I perform it I do not burden the listeners with the background for this would preclude them having their own feelings, their personal experiences evoked by the song.

There are songs that need to be set up and benefit greatly from a good intro. There are songs that I cannot perform without setting a landscape in which they can live. But there are others that are best left completely alone, songs that can touch the hearts and minds without any embellishment. This is one such song.

Joxer Goes to Stuttgart
by C. Moore

It was in the year of '88 in the merry month of June
When the gadflies they were swarming and dogs howling at the moon
With rosary beads and sandwiches for Stuttgart we began
Joxer packed his German phrase book and jump leads for the van
Some of the lads had never been away from home before
'Twas the first time Whacker put his foot outside of Inchicore
Before we left for Europe, we knew we'd need a plan
So we all agreed that Joxer was the man to drive the van

In Germany the autobahn was like the Long Mile Road
There was every make of car and van all carrying the full load
Fod transits and Hi-Aces and an old Bedford from Tralee
With the engine overheating from long hauling duty-free
There was fans from Ballyfermot, Ballybough and Ballymun
On the journey of a lifetime and the crack was 91
Joxer met a German's daughter on the bank of the River Rhine
And he told her she'd be welcome in Ballyfermot any time

As soon as we found Stuttgart we got the wagons in a ring
Sean Óg got out the banjo Peter played the mandolin
Fans there from everywhere attracted by the sound
Of the first fleadh ceol in Europe Joxer passed the flagon around
The session it ended when we finished all the stout
Air mattresses inflated, sleeping bags rolled out
As one by one we fell asleep Joxer had a dream
Dreamt himself and Jack Charlton sat down to pick the team

Joxer dreamt they both agreed on Packie Bonner straight away
Moran, Whelan and McGrath were certainly to play
Tempers they began to rise, patience wearing thin
Jack wanted Cascarino, Joxer wanted Quinn
The dream turned into a nightmare Joxer stuck the head on Jack
Who wanted to bring Johnny Giles and Eamon Dunphy back
The cock crew in the morning he crew both loud and shrill
Joxer woke up in his sleeping bag many miles from Spancilhill

Next morning none of the experts gave us the slightest chance
They said the English team would lead us on a merry dance
With Union Jacks those English fans for victory were set
Until Ray Houghton got the ball and stuck it in the net
What happened next was history brought tears to many eyes
That day will be the highlight of many people's lives
Joxer climbed right over the top and the last time he was seen
Was arm in arm with Jack Charlton singing Revenge for Skibbereen

Now Whacker is back in Inchicore he's living with his mam
Jack Charlton has been proclaimed an honorary Irish man
Do you remember that German's daughter on the bank of the River Rhine
She showed up in Ballyfermot last week

Me and my mucker Cid were coming along the Portlaoise by-pass in '88 when I got the flash. What's needed is a song about young Dublin people that is not about heroin, that doesn't mention guards or TDs or church or abortion or divorce or corruption. A hard task until I remembered the Black Pearl of Inchicore, the safe house and clean sheet he kept and I began to write. By the time we hit Mountrath the song was finished. Ray Houghton has a lot to answer for. I know a woman who was on her holidays in Spain and was watching the match in a Spanish bar. When Houghton buried it the fellow beside her grabbed her in his ecstasy and now they are married! My mother, God rest her sweet soul, was never at a soccer match in her life but she had to send out for a naggin when the ref blew full-time. What's wrong with them GAA arseholes that they won't allow soccer or rugby at Croker? It's hardly any more foreign than Neil Diamond or American bore-ball. I've no problem with Cracklin Rosie in the Hogan stand, nor the Refrigerator making shite of Hill 16. But surely Paul McGrath or Mick Galway have as much right to play there as our Yankee brothers. Nor is it today or yesterday they started their sectarian shite. If Ian Paisley wants to play full forward for the Antrim footballers, why the hell not? (He'd nearly get his place, too.) There would be a right queue to mark him. Those GAA rules. I still have to get my senior championship medal in Tipperary when I played for Clonmel Commericals against Ardfinnan in the county final of 1964 (against Babs Keating). They denied me my medal because I played rugby with Cashel. Talk about resentments (mine, that is).

I always wanted to be a jockey. I used to see Jimmy Eddery strive for home from two furlongs and then when I saw Billy Burke ride Santa Claus in a two-year-old maiden at the Curragh and win by 40 lengths at 33–1 and me and Parkinson had £2 to win, I knew my destination in life. Problem was I haven't been 9 stone 7 since I was about ten, so that was that.

The Reel in the Flickering Light
by Colm Gallagher

As I was walkin home one evening I know this takes believing
I met a group of creatures with the strangest looking features
A poor old dog and a worm and a weed and a fine auld pigeon yes indeed
Then a daddy long legs jumped up sprightly and danced to the reel in the flickering light

Round we go heel to the toe
Then a daddy longlegs jumped up sprightly and danced to the reel in the flickering light

On his thin and whispy spindles he was deft and he was nimble
His eyes were scientific and his dancing was terrific
And the rats and the worms they made a din and the nettles in the corner took it in
God says I tonight's the night we'll dance to the reel in the flickering light

Then the daddy longlegs looked at me directly with a gaze that could dissect me
And he asked me in a whisper hey have you got any sisters?
Good God almighty says I to him what sort of a man do you think I am?
I've only one and she is not your type she wouldn't dance to the reel in the flickering light

Said he 'Does she come from another planet, does she have a bee in her bonnet
Does she do her daily duties, you'd never know we might be suited?'
And the rats and the worms began to laugh and some of them started shuffling off
We're going to have some fun tonight getting ready for the reel in the flickering light

I could see he had no scruples when I looked into his pupils
They were purple or magenta like a statue during Lent
Says I I'll get her right away, good man said he now don't delay
We're going to have some fun tonight getting ready for the reel in the flickering light

Then up stepped a red carnation and they gave her an ovation
She was warm and enchanting as she slowly started dancing
And the poor old pigeon peeled his eye and the nettles and the weeds began to sigh
Daddy longlegs said my oh my then he flipped his legs in the flickering light

She was bright and she was charming and I heard him call her darling
He was graceful as a whisper on his delicate legs of silver
And the rats and the worms were still as mice and the poor old pigeon said that's nice
A shimmering veil on a lovely bride and they danced to the reel in the flickering light

Colm Gallagher went to America a long time ago and he sings and plays in Los Angeles. I went to hear him play one night. I had the number of the street but nobody told me the street was 28 miles long. Fair play to the Yanks – no short cuts. I love this song. I recorded it in 1985 on *Ordinary Man*. I want to do a few more of his songs, particularly 'Spanish Arches' and 'Easter Lilies'. He has many songs – I believe Tommy Makem has recorded a few. He has another cracker about the St Patrick's Night Dance in San Fernando, with all the plastic paddies on the spree. I hope he's doing well and that we meet up again.

This story of Colm's is such a wonderful fantasy. It was difficult to get it into my own shape, but once I settled down with it I've never tired of singing it. Occasionally I can hear people in the audience sigh in wonderment at the pictures; more times I'll hear a squeal of delight at the mad fun. This is not a song for cynics – more for those of us who will never completely grow up. Some young ones have grown up with the song – some old ones love the tale, to dance to the Reel in the Flickering Light.

The Song of Wandering Aongus
by W. B. Yeats with music learned from Richie Havens

I went down to the hazelwood because a fire was in my head
I cut and peeled a hazel wand and hooked a berry to a thread
And when white moths were on the wing and moth-like stars were flickering out
I dropped the berry in a stream and hooked a little silver trout

When I had laid it on the floor I went to blow the fire aflame
When something rustled on the floor and someone called me by my name
It had become a glimmering girl with apple blossoms in her hair
Who called me by my name and ran and faded in the brightening air

Now I am old with wandering through hollow lands and hilly lands
I will find out where she has gone and kiss her lips and hold her hands
And walk among long dappled grass and pluck till time and times are done
The silver apples of the moon the golden apples of the sun

Fr Clandillon, Fr O'Beirne, Fr Flanagan, God rest these men. Each of them tried to educate me in English-language poetry. Fr Kelly and Fr O'Donovan tried too, but their technique never got to me. It was an old tinker that taught me the beauty of words. In a snug in Co. Roscommon amidst glasses of porter I first experienced duende. The hairs stood up on my neck and I felt home and dry. Then Richie Havens brought to me the beauty of Yeats. Was it backstage at Woodstock or sidestage at Carnegie Hall or in a stagecoach near Tombstone in the middle of a stormy head trip? Wherever it was, Richie sang me 'Wandering Aongus' and we were bathed once more in duende.

How I love to sing this song. On the special nights when I've gotten it just right and the atmosphere has wrapped us all together in the white light and we've wandered by the stream around the fire and beneath the moths and stars.

I saw Richie Havens again in Dublin recently and he gave an uplifting performance at the HQ venue. I sat and watched him as he took the trouble to talk to each and every one of the audience who wished to meet him, generously sharing his time with those who came to listen. Nor was he flogging merchandise – simply giving of himself. Goddammit, but I was too shy to join the queue.

Biko Drum
by Wally Page

They went home on an Easter road
On a silent night trying not to show
Who goes where and who goes when
Thinking some day soon they'll get it back again

From the ghetto in Cape Town to dig the gold
Little black baby can't be sold
Under tin roof and a plastic wall
Thinking some day soon we're gonna leave it all

And the renegades sing all the renegade songs
And the ones who know hope they're doin wrong
The blacks and the coloureds play the Biko drum
All the blacks and the coloureds play the Biko drum

Transvaal kids on a Transvaal day
Little by little they show the way
To a city of dreams on solid ground
Thinking some day soon we're gonna come around

Steve he's living in a prison cell
All the friends that know hope he's doing well
Down here they listen to the Biko drum
Down here they listen to the songs he sung

Nelson listen to the people sing
Nelson Mandela the people sing
Twenty-seven years in a white man's jail
Twenty-seven years they couldn't make him say

Don't ask me when or how I met Wally. He played The Meeting Place gig I did around 1974/5 and we got friendly maybe ten years later. He is one of my favourite singers and I feel I've known him a lifetime. We've done a grand bit of collaborating and he has written good music for some words I have written. He has played fine support for me and I've enjoyed a few good sessions with him.

I sing this song regularly for I like to sing about Steven Biko. His spirit lives on so long as we sing about him and talk about him.

I left Planxty in 1974 and had to struggle to revive my career. Although the band had been very popular I had no standing in Ireland as a soloist. There were further complications in that I was under contract as a member of Planxty and, despite previous assurances to the contrary, the holders of the contract were most reticent about releasing me to continue my career. Mean-spirited is a word that springs to mind. They were breadheads with lots of dosh and the arse was out of my trousers and they were not taking my calls.

I was on the lookout for a venue to run my own club. My brother-in-law Sid Isaacson knew a pub in Dorset Street and he brought me to meet Paddy Spillane who ran The Meeting Place with his brothers Shay and Sean. Over several gin and tonics we decided to try it out and I started running gigs there in 1974 on Monday nights. These soon spread to Saturdays as well, and by then I had a backing band with Declan McNelis, Jimmy Faulkner, Kevin Burke and sometimes Robbie Brennan on drums. This was a very trad and folk and hash-cake ensemble and we recorded an album or two in the mid-Seventies for John Woods at Polydor. We made some fine music and had good times too, but it finally fell asunder. Jimmy Faulkner and I continued as a duo and played many gigs in Ireland, UK, Germany and France, and once in Liechtenstein, where we were invited up to meet the king for a cup of tea and he showed us all his guns and Princess Nora von Liechtenstein, the king's most beautiful daughter.

I still play occasionally with Jimmy Faulkner; he is my favourite guitarist. Declan McNelis died tragically after a gig in Limerick. Kevin Burke is big in America.

This was my first experience of managing and playing in a band and I don't recommend it. Referring back to The Meeting Place, I stopped running gigs there in 1976 when my sister Eilish took over the Saturday nights. It was by then a well-established quality music venue and most of the top bands played there. It held 100 people comfortably, but more often had 160 struggling to breathe. I ran a festival there in 1975 which continued on under Eilish's tute-lage and grew to become the Dublin Folk Festival. I recall wild nights in The Meeting Place with bands of the calibre of The Bothy Band, De Danaan and Clannad. Planxty played there once to warm up for a European tour. Many of these gigs were followed by fierce sessions that often went on into the next day. As time went on, the music base of the place broadened out to include residencies and gigs by many other artists, including Red Peter's Floating Dublin Blues Band, Rob Strong, Don Baker, to name but a few. Downstairs was a different shop altogether, where the £10 deal was always readily available, the pint was excellent and you could be offered anything while drinking it.

I recall a TV show on ABC in Sydney, Australia – the national network. It was a magazine show leaning very much towards politics and the arts. They went to great lengths to assure me that I need not feel constrained by any censorship, and encouraged me to sing about anything I wished. In rehearsal I sang 'Smoke and Strong Whiskey', 'No Time for Love' and 'Biko Drum'. They couldn't handle the third song and somewhat shamefacedly requested that I drop it as, at the time, there was a curfew in Australia on reporting matters South African because of some delicate negotiating that was taking place. I saw the humorous side, but the people in ABC were embarrassed that their liberal assurances had been exposed as somewhat flawed.

Allende
Don Lange

The nighthawk flies and the owl cries as we're driving down the road
Listening to the music on the all-night radio show
The announcer comes on says if you've got ideas, I'll file the patent for you
What's an idea that's not in the store, making a buck or two

We drive to the town but the shutters are down and the all-night restaurants closed
It's the land of the free, they've got booze and TV and there's tramps in the telephone booths
The stars and the trees and the early spring breeze says forget what assassins have done
Take our good soil in the palm of your hand and wait for tomorrow's sun

It's a long way from the heartland
To Santiago Bay
Where the good doctor lies with coins in his eyes
And the bullets read U S of A

A truck driver's wife leads a rough life, he spends his time on the road
Carrying the goods all the copper and wood that's what makes America great
But the dollars like swallows they fly to the south where they know they've something to gain
Allende is killed, and the trucks soon are rolling again

The nighthawk flies and the owl cries as we're driving down the road
The full moon reveals all the houses and fields where good people do what they're told
Victor Jara he lies with coins in his eyes there's no one around him to mourn
Who needs a poet who won't take commands who'd rather make love than war

I don't know Don Lange. He's an American singer. I have two theories about how I got this song and only one of them is correct, but I'm not sure which: a) I was listening to AFN coming at me out of Hilversum and I heard this song sung by Peggy Seeger, or b) the journalist/radio producer/TV producer Julian Vignoles sent me the song, which became part of the Moving Hearts repertoire. Either way, I was playing in North Carolina on a cold night in 1986. A weird bit of a kip that was a bit like a folk club-cum-coffee house that also sold bottled Guinness. Triona Ní Dhonail was also sharing the bill and I dived into the Guinness and then on to the stage where, of course, I had to sing every anti-American song in my repertoire: 'Allende', 'El Salvador', 'Ronnie Reagan' – the whole shaggin' lot. I nearly paid the price, too. I recall a large member of the audience, a crew-cutted quarterback type, coming up to the stage and yelling, 'Leave my country you Goddam cock-suckin' motherfuckin' pink mick!' He was right, of course, and I left next morning (never got paid, either).

I believe 'Allende' is a wonderful song. Don used all these simple, everyday scenes to tell the great story of the big picture: big country bullies little country into subjection for the purpose of exploitation. The image of driving down the country road and the music of the announcer making such a cynical statement. I'd like to meet this writer.

American global policies have made that country an easy target for the agitprop balladeer; there is no easier way to get the crowd going in a folk gathering than to blast out the old anti-imperialist ballads. However, it was never quite so easy to sing about oppression on the home doorstep. We love the microscope, but we are not so keen on the mirror.

The Two Conneeleys
by C. Moore and Wally Page

Hear the Atlantic seethe and swell
Hear the lonesome chapel bell
God save their souls and mind them well
The two fishermen Conneeleys

Yesterday at half past four
They pushed their currach from the shore
One took the net one took the oar
The two fishermen Conneeleys

From Connors Fort and from Synges Chair
Towards Inis Mór and Inis Iarr
They scour the sea in silent prayer
As they go searching for their neighbours

Dia bíobh a bheirt jascairí brea
Nác mbeidh stair ar barr na trá
Jo mbeidh síobh sonas sásta ar neain
Tomás agus Seán Ó Coinjíle

Draw the seaweed up the hill
Sow potatoes in the drill
Try to understand God's will
And the loss of the two Conneeleys

In 1972 I visited Inis Mór and Inis Iarr when Planxty performed concerts on both islands. For some reason we did not play Inis Méan and I'd always harboured a desire to visit. In 1991, Valerie and I with Andy, Juno and Pádraic flew out to Inis Méan for a holiday. We stayed in the guest house of Angela Faherty and walked the length and breadth of this wonderful sacred place. One morning we got up and I became aware of a change in the atmosphere. Everyone was looking out to sea. All the currachs were out and the women were in the gardens viewing the ocean. Two men from Inis Iarr had failed to return from fishing the previous evening, and all three islands were on alert. These two men were never found. God rest their souls.

I had been asked by many young Islanders if I would be playing a few songs. I said I'd love to do a concert and left them to decide the venue. They opted for the local hall. When disaster struck the neighbouring island, I again let the Islanders decide what to do and they resolved that the concert should go ahead. We had a lovely night, with great contributions from the audience.

It brought to mind a concert I performed on Sherkin Island in 1986 to raise funds for the planting of trees. Every single person on the island attended that night, and all their dogs followed. The concert was disturbed quite a number of times by dogs settling old scores and creating new ones. My abiding memory of that evening was a tractor pulling up with haycock lift behind carrying a wheelchair in which was sitting the island's oldest inhabitant. Island concerts always have a very special vibe.

St Brendan's Voyage
by C. Moore

A boat sailed out of Brandon in the year of 501
'Twas a damp and dirty morning Brendan's voyage it began
Tired of thinning turnips and cutting curly kale
When he got back from the creamery he hoisted up the sail
He ploughed a lonely furrow to the north, south, east and west
Of all the navigators St Brendan was the best
When he ran out of holy water he was forced to make a stop
He tied up in Long Island, put America on the map
Did you know that Honolulu was found by a Kerryman
Who went on to find Australia then China and Japan
When he was touching seventy he began to miss the crack
And turning to his albatross sez he I'm heading back

Is it right or left for Gibraltar
What tack do I take for Mizen Head
I'd love to settle down near Ventry Harbour
St Brendan to his albatross he said

To make it fast he bent the mast and built up mighty steam
Around Tierra del Fuego and up the warm Gulf stream
When he crossed the last horizon Mount Brandon came in sight
And when he cleared the customs into Dingle for the night
When he got the spuds and bacon he went to douse the drought
He headed west to Krugers to murder pints of stout
Around by Ballyferriter and up the Connor Pass
He freewheeled into Brandon the saint was home at last

The entire population came the place was chock-a-block
Love nor money wouldn't get your nose inside the shop
Fishermen hauled up their nets, farmers left their hay
Kerry people know that saints don't turn up every day
Everything was going grand till Brendan did announce
His reason for returning was to try and set up house
The girls were flabbergasted at St Brendan's neck
To seek a wife so late in life and him a total wreck

Worn out by the rejection that pierced his humble pride
Begod said Brendan if I run I'll surely catch the tide

Turning on his sandals he made straight for the docks
And hauling up his anchor he cast off from the rocks
As he sailed past Innishvickillaune there stood the albatross
I knew you'd never stick it out 'tis great to see you boss
I'm baling out said Brendan I badly need a break
Two weeks of talking to Fungi is more than I can take

Is it right or left for Gibraltar
What tack do I take for Mizen Head
I'd love to settle down near Ventry Harbour
St Brendan to his albatross he said

It was 1985 and I was spending time in Ballyferriter on the Dingle Peninsula. I had concerts in Tralee, Killarney and Dingle. There were a couple of free days so I planned a trip to the Great Blasket Island with Tom McCarthy from Annascaul. We set off for Dunquin Pier but bad weather prevented our departure. We decided to take a bit of an excursion so we drove happily and aimlessly until we arrived into Brandon village at midday. We sought refreshment at Paddy Murphy's pub where we were welcomed by Mary and Kathy Murphy and offered fine hospitality. There was a lone German with a guitar and one Brandon man with a glass of stout. Myself and McCarthy settled in and, after a few glasses, I could not resist the German's guitar and a few songs started up. As momentum gathered I discovered an amazing thing. Half the population in the Brandon region are Moores. The area was teeming with distant relations.

Word got out that there was a session going. Fishermen drew up their nets and farmers left their hay. By mid-afternoon the pub was bursting at the seams and it was like the wedding feast of Cana. There were two nuns in full battle-dress, home from the foreign missions – they were lowering pints and burning Majors and looking for all the latest ballads. There were Gaelic Language Movement enthusiasts gathered around in a cluster of Faínnes, freedom fighters with fertile imaginations, holiday homers, confused continentals, a drug dealer most generous with marching powders, a happy Garda officer feeling no pain, and the entire population. Myself and McCarthy did a twelve-hour shift there. The ladies of the house gave us the dinner before we set out for Dingle, up over the Connor Pass with only the moon to guide us. It was a great day, and 'St Brendan's Voyage' was an outcome.

El Salvador
by Johnny Duhan

A girl cries in the early morning woken by the sound of a gun
She knows somewhere somebody's dying beneath the rising sun
Outside the window of her cabana the shadows are full of her fears
She knows her lover is out there somewhere he's been on the run for a year

Oh! The soul of El Salvador

The bell rings out on the chapel steeple the priest prepares to say Mass
The sad congregation come tired and hungry to pray their troubles will pass
Outside the sun rises over the dirty streets where the crowd gathers round
Flies and mosquitoes are drinking from pools of blood where his body is found

Oh! The soul of El Salvador

Out on the ranch Enrico is preparing to go for his morning ride
They've saddled his horse out in the corral he walks out full of pride
He looks like a cowboy in one of those movies the president made in the past
The peasants in rags they stand back for they know that Enrico gallops real fast

Over the soul of El Salvador

I recorded this song for the *Ride On* album, with Donal Lunny and Declan Sinnott. Again, a very simple song that, for me, paints a broad canvas; so much so that I've grown to know the streets, I can see the church and I recognise the sound of the church bell. I can see the woman, and the crowd around the corpse and the blood on a dust road, and I'm singing the song of Johnny Duhan and I have the picture even though I could not find El Salvador on the map.

There is no shortage of Enricos around the Emerald isle. First up to the altar, top of the list with the Easter dues, buying up every square yard on the market, well in with the local dignitaries, supporting the best-positioned and hungriest politician, always off the mark for the quick buck, squeeze the last ounce of labour out of his workers who must feel grateful and obliged to be in his employ, his big mush in the local paper every week. But at the back of it all there is an emptiness that comes to those of us whose lives are totally dedicated to the acquisition of wealth and power.

The Other Side
by C. Moore

Where John Hinde paints in Caribbean colours
And Tyrone boys dream of loving on the strand
Where the flowers were heaped in gesture on the courthouse steps in Kerry
And the law trampled out the outstretched hand
Roman posters on the wall outside the graveyard
No divorce is all they say
I saw a little Sister of Mercy
Invoke the wrath of God on polling day

When the King of Rome came here to meet his people
He took a soldier by the hand
In the same breath condemned men of violence
To comfort those who occupy the land
High above the clouds a promised heaven
On the street a confused and homeless child
While men in black declare social order
Frightened women sail to the other side

Blue bitch sends squaddies on the water
Geordie don't be afraid to die
In blackened face he dreams of his darling bairns and hinny
On the watchtower overlooking Aughnacloy
In Long Kesh Tyrone boys are dreaming
Of making love upon the strand some day
On the downtown news comes a mid-Atlantic accent
Karen Livingstone has just been blown away

A young body slips quietly through the rushes
As Mountcharles surveys the battlefield
And the silk clad pompadour who played Sun City
Hears little of the corpse among the reeds
The mist comes swirling o'er the mountain
The children have forgotten how to play
The death train sneaks across the island
Deadly poison bound for Killala Bay

All the young ones are leaving the island
Out the door down the steps around the side
Unwanted they file through departure lounges
Like deportees dispersing far and wide
Back home there's cricket in Cloughjordan
And the gentle clack of croquet on the lawn
While our children shackled by illegal status
Hold their heads down behind the Brooklyn wall

Far away from the island
Where Tyrone boys dream of loving on the strand
Far away from the island
Where the law still tramples on the outstretched hands

I was always on the move. On Tuesday I would play in Limerick at The Two Mile Inn, Wednesday I would go to Dirty Nelly's, a roadside tavern between Tramore and Waterford, Thursday night I'd step before the spotlight in the Gleneagles Hotel in Killarney, Friday night could find me in CJ's in Salthill, while Saturday was a great night to be in The Blue Lagoon in Sligo. Come Sunday we'd follow the crowds to Club Cleo in Bandon. This is the type of thing I was doing across the Eighties. I travelled in a basic motorhome with my brother-in-law Sid. We had all essentials on board and we would park up overnight at isolated halting sites, usually lakeside, riverside or on the seashore. We would sleep, wash, cook, eat, wash, walk, swim and then strike camp and on to the next venue. As I criss-crossed the island I was getting information all the way. I saw the flowers for Joanna Hayes on the courthouse steps in Tralee, the posters in Rathmore declaring 'No Divorce in Heaven', the little nun outside the polling booth in Dublin with her placard 'Divorce Means Higher Taxes', frightened women on the boats Travelling alone, all alone, to seek abortions, the Pope diverted from The Gloucester Diamond where good people had built a sacred shrine, all the young squaddies from all those towns I'd played in the Sixties, lost on the streets of Belfast yet ready to do Thatcher's dirty work, queues and queues of youngsters at the American Embassy...

I'd call and visit friends, Annie Kehoe in Clonmel, Joe O'Broin in Charlestown, Peter and Biddy O'Connor in Waterford, Antony and Alberic in

Bolton Abbey, everywhere we travelled there were houses to visit and news to exchange, singing new songs, looking for old ones, stumbling across cricket in Cloughjordan and Freddie Mercury at Slane, always driving to the other side of the island.

Ride On
by Jimmy MacCarthy

True you ride the finest horse I've ever seen
Standing sixteen one or two with eyes wild and green
You ride the horse so well hands light to the touch
I could never go with you no matter how I wanted to

Ride on see you
I could never go with you no matter how I wanted to

When you ride into the night without a trace behind
Run your claw along my gut one last time
I turn to face an empty space where once you used to lie
And look for the spark that lights the night through a teardrop in my eye

'Ride On' has been one of my most popular songs and it has been recorded by many singers. Many people wonder what it's about but Jimmy MacCarthy keeps that to himself. All we need to know is what it means to us individually.

I have lived every word and line of this song, sometimes in more ways than one. My thanks to Jimmy for offering me the first ride.

In 1983 I was recording 'The Time Has Come' in Westland Studios. Mandy Murphy was doing backing vocals and one night she brought in Jimmy MacCarthy. I had met him years previously when Southpaw played The Meeting Place. He played the song 'Ride On' for me. I loved it, and it became the central song for my next album.

I spent a number of months rehearsing a set of songs with Donal Lunny and Declan Sinnott. I had sounds and an approach in my head. I wanted an acoustic album with 'in-house' backing vocals. I also wanted to return to the *Prosperous* kind of recording – in a space that would be conducive to creating something special. We opted for two cottages in Muckross, Killarney, and brought in a mobile studio.

I cannot get truly comfortable in any recording studio. I've worked in the best and less in Ireland and England, but there are always too many ghosts from previous sessions. Somebody else's butts in the ashtrays, someone else's gold disc on the wall, too many artefacts of the business, too many shady-looking shams in the reception area. I once asked Van Morrison about his favourite recording studio, and his answer was that they were all only tape recorders. He now owns his own 'tape recorder' and it's a nice one, too.

This was a special time. Myself, Donal Lunny, Declan Sinnott, Mark Franks, Jim and Peter Donohoe and Peter Eades, we really got entrenched for a while. We were well rehearsed with the material before the recording commenced. The mobile was an awful heap of shite but Mark and Jim and Peter Eades somehow managed to get it running.

From day one the recording went smoothly, and the three of us were cooking nicely together. The *Ride On* album is very much an entity and is ageing very well.

Baz and Suzie

I got to know them when I played the Half Moon in Putney. Baz worked with the sound hire company. Him and Suzie would sit side-stage and drink in the music. They loved the gig and never needed to tell me for it showed. They were a beautiful couple.

A year passed and I was booked to play in Luton. It was a horrible cold winter's night and we had trouble finding the venue. It turned out to be a series of Nissan huts, old, and cold and unwelcoming.

I entered the hall and straightaway spotted Baz setting up equipment on the stage. Even at a distance I could sense his pain and loss. He told me that Suzie was dead, cut down by a motorist who owned the road. The life was gone out of Baz, too.

Another year on and I was in my dressing room at the Royal Festival Hall, London. I got a letter from Baz's mother which read: '*Baz finally went and joined his loved one. When we found him "Ride On" was still spinning on his turntable. It was always their favourite song. All the family are in the audience tonight and we'd love to hear you sing it to their memory. Just for Baz and Suzie.*'

And I always will.

Faithful Departed
by Philip Chevron

This graveyard hides a million secrets
And the trees know more than they can tell
The ghosts of the saints and the scholars will haunt you
In heaven and in hell
Rattled by the glimmermen the boogey man the holy man
Living in the shadows in the shadow of a gunman
Rattled like the coppers in your greasy till
Rattled until time stood still
Look over your shoulder hear the school bell ring
Another day of made to measure history
I don't care if your heroes have wings
Your terrible beauty has been torn

Faithful departed we fickle hearted
As you are now so once were we
Faithful departed we the meek hearted
With graces imparted bring flowers to thee

The girls in the kips proclaim their love for you
When you stumbled in they knew you had a shilling or two
They cursed you on Sundays and holy days
When you stayed away
When you slept there a naked lightbulb hid your shame
The shadows on the wall they took all the blame
The sacred hearts picture compassion in His eyes
Drowned out the river sighs
Let the grass grow green over the brewery tonight
It'll never come between the darkness and the light
There is no pain that can't be eased
By the devil's holy water and a rosary beads

You're a history book I never could write
Poetry in paralysis too deep to recite
Bless yourself and dress yourself you've won the fight
And we're gonna celebrate tonight
We'll even climb the pillar like you always meant to

Watch the sun rising over the strand
Close our eyes and we'll pretend
It could somehow be the same again
We'll bury you upright so the sun doesn't blind you
You won't have to gaze at rain and the stars
Sleep and dream of chapels and bars
And whiskey in the jar

Faithful departed look what you started
An underdog's wounds aren't so easy to mend
Faithful departed there's no broken hearted
No more tristesse in this world without end

In 1972 Planxty did an afternoon gig in O'Connell's School. It was a strange affair but I was very struck by the young guy who ran the gig. He can't have been more than 14 or 15, yet here he was booking Planxty to play at his school. As if that wasn't enough, he was also running a music mag and interviewed us in depth about our work. This boy's name was Philip Ryan.

Roll on ten years, and I receive this song written by Phil Chevron of The Radiators from Space. He told me that he had written the song specifically for me, but didn't know how to get it to me. I took to it straightaway and it became an early part of the Hearts repertoire. Philip Ryan had become Phil Chevron.

It was absolutely terrifying. I sat on the landing of our house in Newbridge and tried to get my young mind around the concept of Everlasting Hell. Brother Alphonsus, God love him, had told us to imagine a fire in the hottest range and multiply it by a thousand, then to imagine the length of a hundred years and multiply that by a thousand – even then Hell would be hotter and longer.

The Bleeding Heart of Jesus was everywhere, the concept of sin and sinning was daily thrust into my face; Everlasting Hell and Limbo, Purgatory a mere end of the world away. But none of these poor Sisters, Brothers or Fathers ever told us about the Love of God – all they drummed into us was fear and loathing and burning and suffering. (I witnessed the Mass a thousand times or more. As an altar boy I got in close to the mystery and there *was* no mystery. There were tired men going through the motions in front of a building full of people fulfilling obligations.)

At all levels of my education I encountered good and kind people. But in my journey through fourteen years of the Irish Catholic education system, I never encountered spirituality nor a loving religion. On parchment and paper they taught me to write and in multiplication in truth I was bright, in Euclid and grammar they opened my eyes, but where was the God of love and compassion that they are supposed to represent on this earth? A number of the Patrician Brothers and Dominican Priests I have met were savages and sadists – most of the rest were good men, but they did not intervene.

One priest slapped me hard across my altarboy face for not giving him enough wine at early Mass. The cruet only held an egg-cup full – he must have mistaken me for some miracle maker. . .

I came out of it unhurt and undamaged. I was never sexually abused and the beatings I got had no after-effect. However, I do know men who *were* badly affected.

In the earliest part of my life I accepted all the religious beliefs that came my way, but at some point in my mid-teens, I cannot precisely identify when, I began to become disillusioned and cynical towards the church of my childhood. I stopped attending, ceased praying and began my descent into spiritual nothingness.

Whilst all the tenets, rules and regulations of Rome were incessantly beaten into us, we were never given any direction towards a true meaning of spirituality. Looking back to my childhood, I can remember many things about the clerics I encountered, but I don't recall any one of them as being truly spiritual. Today, I look around at the power clerics I see and hear and read about, and I still cannot think of one high-ranking Catholic who exudes spiritual love.

In my upbringing, the only sense of God given me was totally tied up in the Catholic Church, when my church crumbled into dust I was left Godless and for many years I walked the dark, cold path of disbelief.

Nancy Spain
by Barney Rush

Of all the stars that ever shone not one does twinkle like your pale blue eyes
Like golden corn at harvest time your hair
Sailing in my boat the wind gently blows and fills my sail
Your sweet scented breath is everywhere

Daylight peeping through the curtains of the passing night-time is your smile
The sun in the sky is like your laugh
Come back to me my Nancy and linger for just a little while
Since you left these shores I've known no peace nor joy

No matter where I wander I'm still haunted by your name
The portrait of your beauty stays the same
Standing by the ocean wondering where you've gone if you'll return again
Where is the ring I gave to Nancy Spain

On a day in spring when snows start to melt and streams to flow
With the birds I'll sing a song
In a while I'll wander down by Bluebell Grove where wild flowers grow
And I'll hope that lovely Nancy will return

As the result of Hamish Imlach's recommendation, I was invited to play the Channel Islands in 1968. It was a meagre two years since I'd been an unhappy bank clerk in Mayo, so I was well chuffed to be flying to Jersey to play three gigs. While performing there I befriended Barney Rush, a Dublin singer domiciled in St Helier, and he taught me a number of songs from his self-penned repertoire. I came away with five of his songs on cassette and I did not listen to them again until 1973 when I offered 'Nancy Spain' to the Planxty collective but, alas, it was refused. I put it away until a subsequent solo album in 1977 when I released it as a single and it straightaway became a favourite with my listeners. In the subsequent 22 years it has entered the national repertoire.

Wise and Holy Woman
by C. Moore and Wally Page

I met a wise and holy woman near the town where I was walking
We both sat down together below the Yellow Furze
She closed her eyes and started singing
A song about the light that shines and the wonders of the world
She sang of the forests in the high, high mountains
The pure clear water and the fresh air that we breathe
Of the bounty we gain from nature's abundance
And how the mighty oak tree grows from a little seed

She had an everlasting notion
The wise and holy woman had a never-ending dream
As she called out to the stars that glistened on the ocean
Shine a light please shine a light on me

She sang a song from the streets of Sao Paolo
For the homeless street children who never learn to smile
She sang of the shrine they built to Chico Mendez
Where the plantation workers laid his body in the soil
She sang of the greed we display before our altars
And the oil-soaked cormorant drowning in the tide
She sang of the halting site, out beyond Clondalkin
Where Ann Maughan froze to death between the dump and railway line

She had an everlasting notion
The wise and holy woman had a never-ending dream
As she called out to the stars that glistened on the ocean
Shine a light please shine a light on me

She sang of the eagle flying high above the island
And the otter that swam through the rivers and streams
Of the lilies that bloomed and the countless wild flowers
And the rainbow that rose from the valley of tears

I began writing this song on the Hill of Allen one day, looking out across the Bog. I finished it some years later in the Sebel Hotel, Sydney after a dramatic electric storm, and sang it for the first time in its completed form to Martin and Lyn Doherty in Maroubra, New South Wales.

It is another song that never did too well on the high stage, but I still perform it regularly to myself and I always enjoy the words and the rhythm. I recognise that I'm coming to terms here with my re-emerging spirituality. I was still a few years short of being able to utter the word God, but I was nevertheless looking outside myself for answers to the imponderable questions that dog us all: Who made the world? Would you have the price of a drink? Can I stay in your gaff tonight?

McIlhatton

by Bobby Sands, MP

In Glenravel's Glen there lives a man whom some would call a God
For he could cure your shakes and a bottle of his poitín would cost you thirty bob
Come winter summer frost all over a-jigging spring in the breeze
In the dead of night a man slips by McIlhatton if you please

McIlhatton ye blurt we need you cry a million shaking men
Where are your sacks of barley, will your likes be seen again
Here's a jig to the man and reel to the drop and a swing to the girl he loves
May your fiddle play and poitín cure your company up above

There's a wisp of smoke to the south of the glen and the poitín is on the air
There's birds in the burrows and rabbits in the sky and there's drunkards everywhere
At Skerries Rock the fox is out and begod he's chasing the hounds
And the only thing in decent shape is buried beneath the ground

In McIlhatton's house the fairies are out and dancing on the hobs
The goat's collapsed and the dog has run away and there's salmon down the bogs
He has a million gallons of wash and the peelers are in the glen
But they'll never catch McIlhatton 'cos Mickey ain't coming home again

The night after I heard Bobby Sands' 'Back Home in Derry' in Chamberlain Street (Olive and Bertie Barrett's), I played in the GAA club in Bellaghy and my billet was with Colm Scullion. He had Bobby's McIlhatton song. The music was by Brendan McFarlane and although Scull was a good man to carry the lyrics God had not blessed him with a great capacity to carry a tune. After repeated efforts to liberate the music from the H-Blocks I got hold of a flattened-out version which I brought to Donal Lunny for a bit of embroidery and titillation. He turned a lively tune around it and this is now an excellent song – one that will pass into the tradition, I think, of a time when some of these songs will be sung and no one will care who wrote them. The best songs outlive the significance of their authors. It becomes incidental after a time, and the songs themselves reverberate down the years. Who wrote 'Lord Baker' or 'The Raggle Taggle Gypsy', or who cares so long as the song helps us through the night?

This song showed me the true poetry of Bobby's writing. When I sing it I think of the men on The Blanket, on the Dirty Protest, singing out through their cell windows at night – having their concerts, telling the stories of films they've seen, countrymen describing farming culture to city men and songs and poems and politics all to try and maintain sanity in the midst of filth and cruel treatment.

Before 1976 I had little or no first-hand knowledge of the Ulster State. My education had taught me lots about the Vikings and the Normans, but shag all about the sectarian abuse that was heaped upon the nationalist community in the north of Ireland. I had been to Belfast once in my childhood, and once or twice in the mid-Sixties. But the truth was I knew London and Manchester better than I knew Belfast and Derry. I began visiting Belfast and Derry during the Blanket Protest and I started to understand what it was like to live in the Bogside or Ardoyne. I stayed in many homes and met many families and soon sang regularly in many places.

I produced an album called *H-Block* in 1979 which was an attempt to focus attention on the situation in the prison, for it seemed that there was silence verging on total apathy with regard to the dreadful conditions in Long Kesh. I performed many concerts for the prisoners during the Smash H-Blocks Campaign, but the apathy continued in the 26 counties as the situation worsened. The Special Branch was very active in harassing and arresting and beating up H-block activists and this scared a lot of people off becoming involved. The morning we released the album the Branch raided the launch in The Brazen Head; they took names and tried to break up the party. They also confiscated the albums that were there, but I suspect they never destroyed them.

Trip to Jerusalem
by Joe Dolan

I'm a stranger here from Ireland's shore
I've been on the road six months or more
Hikin' workin' travellin' in style
I'm a vagabond from Éireann's Isle
Sunburnt thumb stuck up in the air
Manys the lift from here to there
In cars buses vans and trains
In the punishing heat and the snow and the rain

Whack fol de diddle fol de diro de
Whack fol de diddle fol de dayro
Oh Mrs Dolan
Your son he isn't workin

Came from Dublin to Jerusalem Town
Had a drink or two on the journey down
At a railway station called Gare du Nord
I missed my train through garglin' hard
Three days later in Napoli
On a Turkish boat I sailed to sea
Slept in a hot hole down below
Travellin' tourist class you know

It was in the Gulf of Aqaba
I met some Paddies and we had a fleadh
Danced through the streets of Eilat Town
Sang Sean South of Garryowen
I was travellin' I don't know
Ye pack your gear get up and go
Leave the rest for another bout
I could damn well do with a pint of stout (or two)

Planxty were doing four nights in Teac Furbo on a shared bill with The
Dubliners during the Galway Races in 1972. It was a wild kind of a time.
One night I was on stage eight hours after dropping half a tab of very pure

acid and I must have got the strong half, for I was seeing strange stuff and not all of it friendly. I can't remember the precise Dubliners line-up but I vaguely remember a train journey with Ciarán Bourke when no two consecutive drinks were the same. Bottle of stout, gin and tonic, glass of cider, dry sherry, Jameson, bottle of ale, brandy and port – it made no difference for it was only the alcohol we were after. The more we drank, the quieter Ciarán spoke and we drank until I couldn't hear him at all. Another night Luke Kelly wanted to change bands and join Planxty. We were all staying in Teac Furbo and it was generally fairly weird and wonderful. But I'm glad I did it then and not now.

On the Sunday morning I heard a fine Galway singer called Gerry Joyce sing this song in Spiddal. The song was written by retired folky-cum-painter Joe Dolan from Galway, who played guitar in the original Sweeney's Men. I got to know Joe through this song and he played me a lot of his fine songs and we drank a few drops together in the later years of the Seventies.

I never heard the original Sweeney's Men for I was learning my trade in England. When they recorded their first album, it set me thinking. The sound was something I liked very much – it was pushing out the boundaries and it had an attitude.

Looking back across the music that was to influence me, I would put Sweeney's Men into the pot with the Clancys, The Dubliners, Jessie Owens, Joe Heaney, Andy Rynne, The Grehan Sisters, John Reilly, Hamish Imlach, The Watersons, Ewan McColl and Woody Guthrie. My singing was effected and affected in some way by all these sounds, and others too, on and on until I woke up one morning with a voice and style that suited me and I no longer sought influence but rather sang to my heart's content with little worry about what others might think.

This is a road song for me – when I sing it sometimes I'm out there instead of Joe. He actually made this trip to Jerusalem, leaving the band to go and fight in the Six-Day War. But it took him a year to get down there.

I hope I see you soon, Joe.

The Wicklow Boy
by C. Moore and Donal Lunny

As I walked past Portlaoise Prison
I'm innocent, a voice was heard to say
My frame-up is almost completed
And my people all look the other way

Seven years ago his torture started
A forged confession he was forced to sign
Irish men specially trained and chosen
Were on the heavy gang that made him run the line

Give the Wicklow Boy his freedom
Give him back his liberty
Or are we going to leave him in chains
While those who framed him up still hold the key

Others in the Bridewell heard him screaming
Even prison doctors could see
His injuries were not self-inflicted
Those who tipped the scales did not agree

Deprived of human rights by his own people
Sickened by injustice he jumped bail
In the Appalachian Mountains found a welcome
Until his co-accused were both released from jail

He came back home thinking he'd get justice
Special Branch men took him off the plane
For five more years deprived him of his freedom
The guilty jeer the innocent again

The people versus Kelly was the title
Of the farce staged at his appeal
Puppets in well-rehearsed collusion
I often wonder how these men must feel

As I walked past Portlaoise Prison
Through concrete and steel a whisper came
My frame-up is almost completed
I'm innocent, Nicky Kelly is my name

In 1998 Nicky Kelly topped the poll in his electoral area. It seems only a matter of time until he takes a seat in government. We'll have a party that night. Will the secret police still sit outside?

The Free Nicky Kelly Campaign was a lengthy one. There were various events, rallies, raffles and concerts run by a diverse bunch of people. I particularly enjoyed an impromptu performance at the gates of Portlaoise Prison: Donal Lunny and I and a handful of Nicky's supporters faced with a line of hefty guards, a barbed-wire fence, a line of prison officers, 40-foot granite walls with armed soldiers watching the gig, more walls, more wire, machine-gun turrets and somewhere, in there, Nicky Kelly. All those police, prison officers and soldiers were getting paid, some of them overtime and danger money, but there was not a smile among them. They did not even applaud our efforts, never mind pass around a cap.

I recall another gig we ran in Francis Xavier Hall in Dublin, which was filmed by Channel 4. The Free Nicky Kelly Campaign became an industry in itself, unemployment figures jumped upon his release.

He came on the road with me for a spell and got a great welcome wherever we went.

We released 'The Wicklow Boy' as a single and it also features on the 1983 album *The Time Has Come*.

Knock
by C. Moore

At the early age of 38 my mother said Go West
Get up said she and get a job said I I'll do my best
I pulled on my Wellingtons and marched to Kiltimagh
But I took a wrong turn in Charlestown and ended up in Knock

Once this quiet crossroads was a place of gentle prayer
Where Catholics sought indulgence once or twice a year
You could buy a pair of rosary beads or get your candles blessed
If you had a guilty conscience you could get it off your chest

Then came the priest from Partry Father Horan was his name
Ever since he's been appointed Knock has never been the same
Begod said Jim 'tis eighty years since Mary was adout*
'Tis time for another miracle and he blew the candle out

From Fatima to Bethlehem, from Lourdes to Kiltimagh
There's never been a miracle like the airport up in Knock

We had the blessed virgin here Father Horan did declare
And Foster and Allen appeared just over there
Now do you mean to tell me said he in total shock
That we are not entitled to an auld airport here in Knock

TDs were lobbied and harrassed with talk of promised votes
And people who'd been loyal for years spoke of changing coats
Excommunication was threatened upon the flock
Who said it was irreverent building airports up in Knock

Now everyone is happy and the miracle its complete
Father Horan got his runway and it's 18,000 feet
All sorts of planes could land there of that there's little doubt
It would be handy for the yankees to take Gaddafi out

Now poor auld Father Jim is gone to the airport in the sky
And down on Barr na Cuíge he keeps a friendly eye
On Ryan Air and Aer Lingus as they fly to and fro
Oh! we'll never see his likes again on the plains of sweet Mayo

Did NATO donate the dough me boys
Did NATO donate the dough

(* adout as in 'adout in the haggart')

When I was driving myself around the ballad lounges of Ireland I used to have favourite halting places for rolling up a decent spliff before continuing on my travails. One such spot was Barr na Cuíge near Hagfield, Charlestown, Co. Mayo at the time this miracle was being constructed. I used to love lighting up and heading down the runway well toked-up; when I'd had my fill of speed and sweet smoke I'd come down a gear or two and head on to The Traveller's Friend or the Beaten Path or some such joint to strut my stuff. Once, while having tea and sandwiches in Murrays of Charlestown, Gerry suggested I should write a song for Father Horan to help him in his labours. I knew the man from counting his Toureen money in the National Bank in Ballyhaunis in 1965, so I set out to give Jemser a dig out. I wrote this song and everyone was pleased. Father Jim asked me to come in on the inaugural flight and be the first down the stairs, but I was offered a big fee to sing in The Gleneagles the same night so Charlie Haughey got the gig.

Sonny's Dream
by Ron Hynes

Sonny don't go away, I'm here all alone
Your daddy's a sailor never comes home
Nights are so long silence goes on
I'm feeling so tired and not all that strong

Sonny lives on a farm in a wide open space
Take off your shoes, stay out of the race
Lay down your head on the soft river bed
Sonny always remembers the words his mamma said

Sonny works the land though he's barely a man
There's not much to do he just does what he can
He sits by the window of his room on the stairs
Watching the waves gently wash on the pier

Many years have passed on, Sonny's old and alone
His daddy the sailor never came home
Sometimes he wonders what his life might have been
But from the grave Mamma still haunts his dream

H amish Imlach was telling me that he'd like to record a single in Ireland. I
believed that it would get a bit of airplay on RTÉ, that he could get gigs
around the country. I gathered up Declan Sinnott, Donal Lunny, Eoghan
O'Neill and Mary Black, and we recorded Hamish singing 'Sonny's Dream'
and 'Mary Anne'. Gerry Rafferty, an old friend of ours, put up the recording
costs and the job was done. It never got any airplay but Hamish got a good
feeling from it and enjoyed the sessions.

I was rehearsing in Spain a year later for the *Ride On* recording when my
son Andy remembered the Sonny song, and I began singing it. I subsequently recorded it and it was very well received. Other Irish singers have
also had success with it.

I loved most of the Spanish experience. The drink was very cheap. There
was a Spanish brandy called Toro which I found very drinkable at £2 a
bottle. Our local shebeen up in the hills in Malinata had a brew made in the

kitchen by Antonio, the shebeen lord, and it was fair old brain damage indeed. I spent a few nights in there singing the 'The Rocks of Bawn' and 'Dunlavin Green' for the local farmers who rightly thought that I was mad.

Ron Hynes is from Newfoundland. He came to Ireland recently and made a film about his song being so popular here. Everyone knows 'Sonny' and it was a tremendous buzz for him to come here for the first time and to find his song sung all over the island.

Missing You
by Jimmy MacCarthy

In nineteen hundred and eighty six
There's not much for a chippie or swingin a pick
And you can't live on love, on love alone
So you sail across the ocean far away across the foam
To where you're a paddy a biddy or a mick
Good for nothing but stacking a brick
Your best mate's a spade and he carries a hod
Two workhorses heavily shod

Oh I'm missing you
I'd give all for the price of the flight
Oh I'm missing you
Under Piccadilly's neon

Who did you murder or are you a spy
I'm just fond of a drink helps me laugh makes me cry
Now I just drink Red Biddy for a permanent high
I laugh a lot less and I'll cry till I die
All you young people please take this advice
Before crossing the ocean you'd better think twice
'Cos you can't live without love without love alone
And the proof is around London in the nobody zone
Where the summer is fine and the winter is a fridge
Wrapped up in old cardboard under Charing Cross bridge
And I'll never go home now because of the shame
Of a misfit's reflection in a shop window pane

Oh I'm missing you
I'd give all for the price of the flight
Oh I'm missing you
Under Piccadilly's neon

November 1997

Some years ago RTÉ were putting together a tribute to Jimmy MacCarthy and all the various people who had covered his songs were being assembled. Jimmy told me he had something for me and I was well pleased to get this wonderful song. I sang it last week for three nights in Kentish Town to 7,000 people, and I swear to God every one of them sang it with me. It contains some elements which would only apply to a tiny number of people, but as a whole it has something for everyone. It is also two-sided in that it simultaneously embraces the emigrants and the ones left behind in the home place. It has elements of the old emigrant songs, along with the harsh realities of modern building-site life, the racism of police, the comfort of the bottle and the terrible realism of the immigrant at rock bottom gazing into the shop window reflection and knowing how far away home really is.

By now I have no memory of Jimmy's original version, for I wear the song like an old donkey jacket. It has two rhythms going simultaneously and also has a lovely chord sequence and a compelling chorus which rises to the heavens when sung by 3,000 young paddies and biddies abroad. Then I return home and sing it to their mothers and fathers and hear the yearning in their voices as they think of beloved children in Kentish Town, Sydney or Queens, New York.

I still meet Jimmy Mack on and off. He is a quiet man, but very intense when talking about the work. I have no idea of how he writes but he has a unique flow to his words and music. There are a number of his other songs I would like to sing, 'Ancient Rain' and 'The Pyramids of Sneem' being two in particular. I loved Mary Coughlan's 'Ancient Rain'. I see and hear music and painting as being very close together, and Jimmy is my favourite example of the painterliness of music, and maybe Patrick Collins is the example of the musicality of painting. I've grown to love the Irish painters. When I'm away I can look at paintings around the world, but when at home in Ireland I love to see the work of Brian Maguire, Charles Brady, Patrick Collins, George Cambell, Arthur Armstrong, Eric Patton, Maimie Jellet, Mary Swanzy, Harry Kernoff, Nora McGuinness, the list could go on and on. I simply love to look at the work of many Irish painters.

When I recorded this song Elvis Costello dropped in for a cup of tea and a chat and went into a singalong with the track and sang out the lovely stuff that shines. I first heard Costello sing on a documentary made in Nashville as he recorded his country album *Almost Blue* and I was turned on to the way he sang and the sounds he made in his throat. He sometimes sounds so soulful. I worked with him a few brief times later.

Continental Céilí

by Johnny Mulhearn (with additional words added)

Over in McCanns there's a grand type of dance band a-playing
They're spinning out the Continental Céilí
They're coming in their cars from the bars down in Leitir and Killane
Just to hear the famous Gunter Reynolds playing
Out The Star a' Munster with Hans O'Donohoe
Neatly rapping out a tango on the spoons
Such commotion will act like a lotion on the strutting
At the Continental Céilí tonight

Wolfgang is playing on the comb someone shouts at him go home
Klaus is playing a slow air on the bowrawn
Quinn from Corofin his fiddle tucked beneath his chin
Sssh he's gonna play the Bucks of Oranmore now
An old-fashioned lady begins to sing a song
Ah lads a bit of order over there
Clarinbridge for the chowder keep your powder dry
For the Continental Céilí tonight

Corky is closing his eyes pretends he's in disguise
When he sees an old flame coming over
He's singing for the Swedes in their tweeds doing all he can to please
The nights at such a delicate stage
Later on he'll give an audience to one of them and two
He'll sing the dying swan and touch their feelings
Tonight's his night
Tomorrow night'll be just the same

So Ada let me out to the bar where the boys are goin far
And they're spinning out the Continental Céilí
Never mind the liquor the music is in my soul
So long as I can hear the band a-playing
The pipes and the flutes and the fiddles are in tune
Oh I'd love to meet a European girl
Ada now me head is going light and the band is playing tight
At the Continental Céilí tonight

All the publicans are there 'tis like a hiring fair
Trying to figure out how much McCann is making
To keep their pubs outa Stubbs they're lashing out big subs
In a burst of fierce anticipation
Moguls from Muckhill starin at the till
Trying to get the low-down on the line-up
They'll be buying free porter for the members of the band
At the Continental Céilí tonight

Over in McCanns there's a grand type of dance band a-playing
They're spinning out the Continental Céilí
They're coming in their cars from the bars down in Leitir and Killane
Just to hear the famous Gunter Reynolds playing
Out The Star a' Munster with Hans O'Donohoe
Neatly rapping out a tango on the spoons
Such commotion will act like a lotion on the strutting
At the Continental Céilí tonight

Johnny Mulhearn has a wonderful eye and ear and puts them to good use in writing his songs. He allowed me a few liberties with this song, but he always adheres to his original version when performing himself. The song is based loosely on a band who used to assemble and play a residency at The Continental Hotel in Salthill, Galway. I never heard this particular band perform but I do recognise the scenario.

Corky was a good old pal who soldiered for drink. He went home one Christmas on the bus leaving Galway with a good skinful and a decent carry-out. He was still *compos mentis* in Limerick, but when the bus pulled into Cork station Corky was no more. He was a decent man who'd share his last dollar with another suffering drinker.

You're in the corner lashing out chords or rhythming the goat when you spot her and your heart misses a beat. Then you realise the whole shop has spotted her and you try to mask your ardour. You are lost in reels and slow airs and porter and small ones and you never think of her again. Publicans are scanning the session for musicians to hire and fill their own pathetic kips until they, too, have another drink or two and forget the task in hand. Every second person in the room wants to sing or recite or be discovered, there's a woman who whistles 'If I Were a Blackbird', but not before she has a good skite of drink in her, your man there plays 'The Coolin' on the silver paper and comb and then Hacksaw comes in and recites 'McAlpine's Fusiliers' and brings the whole shop to a stop. Everyone wants to do a turn but the band need to keep an eye to business for these amateurs are all very well but they don't pay the rent.

More porter.

Matty

by Johnny Mulhearn (Some additional words have been added)

Matty went out on a frozen night
Making for the pub shoulders hunched up tight
Head down on the railroad track
And his old cow Delia sad lowing him back

He met with a dark and a troubled man
As he passed him by called back at him
Hey Matty can't you see what's become of me
In this country of the blind

This house I've left is dead to me
To my rhyming and my poetry
All I've got is the beat of the stagger
Heading down the Curra Line

But Matty passed on as quick as he could
He couldn't stand such a crooked man sober
All he wanted was the lights of the bar
The nightingale and the wild rover

When he came in they were saying oh! he's back
Did Delia drive you out with your spouting and your swearing
We don't want to hear about The Bunker Hayden
But maybe you'll sing us The Girls of Kinkane

But Matty would not be taken in
By their jibing and regaling
He found himself a fresh blown crew
And fell in with their sporting and their baling

As he was going home in the very same spot
He met with his dark familiar
He seen him coming back down the line
He was bright and strange and fine

As he passed him by Matty threw out his arms
And tried to grab hold of his likeness

In the morning all we found was his frozen corpse
At the butt of the Currah Line

At the wake they were lashing out
The Drops of Brandy and the Auld Fashioned Habit
In the church they were lashing down pounds and fivers
So Matty would be fine in the old bye and bye

Now I don't know what inspired Johnny to write these fine verses, but I do know what it instils in me. It's a song about the loneliness of the long-distance shuffler. I knew Matty before I ever picked up a guitar, he was always up and down the front street or getting his nose tanned at Neesons Corner. I saw him in Bremen Station, opening letter boxes for old ladies. Sure, you'd meet Matty every day of the week, if you only knew how to see him.

Thanks for writing this, Johnny, and letting me sing it.

Back in Kildare in the Fifties, poets were scarce on the ground and we were discouraged from fraternising. Keep away from them fellows, none of them are quite right. Matty was one such and we used to hide behind the hedge and call him names and throw stones at him when he'd be shuffling along muttering his old poetry. He began to get real odd and lonely from the constant haranguing he had to endure. Everyone jeered him and made fun of him and he got so lonely he began to meet himself coming back the other way and he was taken to having chats with the other fellow. One night he made the terrible mistake of trying to embrace his own image. Next morning, on our way to serve early Mass, we found him frozen to death down the bottom of the Curragh line and the whole town knew a collective embarrassment for he had died of loneliness. But our guilt was too late for Matty, God be good to him, was frozen solid.

Delerium Tremens
by C. Moore

I dreamt a dream the other night I couldn't sleep a wink
The rats were trying to count the sheep and I was off the drink
There was footsteps in the parlour and voices on the stairs
I was climbing up the wall and moving round the chairs
I looked out from under the blanket, up at the fireplace
The Pope and John F. Kennedy (and Jack Charlton) were staring me in the face
Suddenly it dawned on me I was getting the DTs
When the child of Prague and Flatley danced across the mantelpiece

I swore upon the Bible I'd never again touch a drop
My heart was palpitating I was sure 'twas going to stop
Thinking I was dying I gave my soul to God to keep
And ten pounds to St Anthony to help me find some sleep
I fell into an awful nightmare, got a dreadful shock
When I dreamt there was no duty-free in the airport up in Knock
Ian Paisley was sayin the Rosary Mother Theresa was on the pill
Frank Patterson on the brandy and he singing Spancilhill

I dreamt that I was in ecstasy up in Heaven in agony down in Hell
Bored in Limbo, ringing that auld bell
There was original sins and venial sins and dirty black mortal sins by the score
So I tied the barbed wire around my underpants and flagellated myself on the floor
I dreamt that I was in the confessional box and the old bishop she said to me
Any impure thoughts my child
God mother
The barbed wire is killing me
Then I dreamt I was doing a concert above in Sandy Row
And the IRA and the UVF took off in a UFO
Gusty Spence was playing the bowrawn Gerry Adams the Lambeg Drum
Gerry sang The Sash and Gusty sang the Old Fenian Gun

(Earlier Verses)
I dreamt Dick Spring and Roger Casement were on board the Marita Ann
As she sailed into Fenit Dick was singin Banna Strand
I dreamt the Bishop of Dublin was in Mountjoy for three nights
Having been arrested for supportin Travellers' rights

Ruairi Quinn was busted smoking marijuana in the Dáil
While Barry Desmond was handing Frenchies out to the scuts in Fianna Fáil
I dreamt of Nell McCafferty and Mary Kenny too
I was in the middle of the two of them (the rest I'll leave up to you)
I dreamt I was in a jacuzzi with that auld hure in number ten
And then I know I'd never ever ever drink again

Here is one of my most popular songs. It was released as a single and subsequently on *The Time Has Come* album. The single disappeared without trace while the album did reasonably well. This song achieved notoriety and popularity through people hearing it at gigs. People had their own favourite image from the song, be it the surfer on his board after fourteen pints or me in a jacuzzi with Nell McCafferty. Over the years there was a myriad of verses that included meeting the Queen in Australia, being on the phone to Sean Doherty, eating rogan josh in Bradford with Enoch Powell, giving Adam Clayton a dig out with Naomi – anything notable on a day's journey could end up in the song.

With all my references to Guinness over the years, not to mention the consumption of a million large bottles, I have always half expected some recognition for my efforts on the company's behalf. Maybe a packet of Y-fronts, or a month at a health farm, but I'm still waiting. Might I offer a possible slogan: 'Guinness makes your shite black'. I did mention this to their Chief Executive in Asia/Australia but he may not have heard me.

No Time for Love
by Jack Warshaw

They call it the law, we call it apartheid, internment, conscription, partition and silence
It's a law that they make to keep you and me where they think we belong
They hide behind steel, bullet-proof glass, machine-guns and spies
And they tell us who suffer the teargas and torture that we're in the wrong

No time for love if they come in the morning
No time to show tears or for fear in the morning
No time for goodbye no time to ask why
And the sound of the sirens the cry of the morning

They suffered the torture, they rotted in cells, went crazy, wrote letters and died
The limits of pain they endured but the loneliness got them instead
And the courts gave them justice as justice is given by well-mannered thugs
Sometimes they fought for the will to survive more times they just wished they were dead

They took away Sacco, Vanzetti, Bobby Seale, the Black Panthers as well
They came for Patsy O'Hara, Bobby Sands and some of their friends
In Boston Chicago Saigon Santiago The Bogside and Belfast
And places that never make headlines the list never ends

The trade union leaders, the writers, the fighters, the rebels and all
And the women who fought with the scabs at the factory gates
The sons and the daughters of the disappeared who paid with their lives
People whose class or creed or belief was their only mistake

They tell us that here we are free to live our lives as we please
To march, to write, to sing, so long as we do it alone
Say it or do it with comrades united and strong
And they'll take you for a long rest with walls and barbed wire for your home

Come all you people who give to your sisters and brothers the will to fight on
They say you can get used to a war but that doesn't mean that the war isn't on
The fish need the sea to survive just like your people need you
And the death squad can only get through to them if first they can get through to you

Frank Connolly introduced me to this song at Carnsore Point in 1978. I can't remember who was singing it but I finally made contact with Jack Warshaw, the author, via The Men of No Property. I first performed it in Switzerland with Planxty, and it fairly rocked. Then I took it out again and the Hearts went to war on it. It was to become an anthem. I don't sing it very often now but I did sing it in the Rialto in Derry in 1996 when Donal Lunny dropped in to the show and we played some songs together.

'No Time for Love' is very much a song in the international tradition; one that comes to life wherever people are denied their basic human rights, denied the right to march, write or sing. Not too many people have covered this one, but I'm not finished singing it yet. I remember hearing it played once on Radio Éireann – I cannot remember the exact time, but it was perhaps a strike of some sort and this song was played and it sounded so strong coming out of the wireless that I felt very good about the work we had done.

The Hearts was a co-operative that swayed from agitprop to rock and roll to MOR to rebel music to fine, fine instrumental music to some terrible crap occasionally. In my day the discussion on material was sometimes controversial and once I was accused of being 'a devious twarth'. I can't say I was too happy about this accusation, for I felt a bit different about it. Some people were more political and I had strong views, as did some others, while some had less robustly offered opinions and others had none at all. I did have a lot to say betimes, but it was my initial approach to Donal that caused the Hearts to happen (as was the case with Planxty). I make no apologies for being an activist, for someone has to make the moves or we would still be playing 'The Jug of Punch'.

Irish Ways and Irish Laws
by John Gibbs

Once upon a time there was Irish ways and Irish laws
Villages of Irish blood waking to the morning
Then the Vikings came around turned us up and turned us down
Started building boats and towns they tried to change our living
Cromwell and his soldiers came started centuries of shame
But they could not make us turn we are a river flowing
Again, again the soldiers came burnt our homes stole our grain
Shot the farmers in their fields working for a living
Eight hundred years we have been down the secret of the water's sound
Has kept the spirit of a man above the pain descending
Today the struggle carries on I wonder will I live so long
To see the gates being opened up to a people and their freedom

The Hearts were hopping in The Baggot every Monday, Tuesday and Wednesday. Cid was on the door and dole cards were half price. We used to rehearse in the top storey, play pool on the second storey and storm the beaches on the ground floor. The *Belgrano* went down and we played on and prayed for survivors. Dr Taxi brought the messages and we zizzed on. Charlie McGettigan was smiling from ear to ear and Jim was licking his fingers. Danny and the Valtones played support and me and Davy looked after the dressing room. Brian Calnan packed his kit and went home to Cork, and Matt Kellighan left the mixing desk and climbed in behind the traps. Norman left his monitor duties and got behind the main console. Mr Clarke was Minister for Transport and Terry O'Neill did posters, PR, T-shirts and God knows what. Various other consultants passed through and we throbbed on. One night, Johnny Gibbs said I have a song for you and began to sing it in my ear after closing time in the Baggot. I tore open a Major packet and wrote the words and got him to sing the melody into Donal's ear. Up we went and got practising and we played it the following night on stage, me still reading the fag packet.

'Irish Ways and Irish Laws' hit the streets and became a very big song around the halls. Fierce criticism came our way. One band member was severely criticised by his brother for being involved with a racist song, while an old friend of mine accused me of singing a fascist anthem. I never saw the song this way and I still don't. People hear the 'Villages of Irish blood' and hear no further – 'Oh, the Hearts are into ethnic cleansing,' was the cry of the safe-bet brigade. Sorry lads. I'm not in today. I'm not playing your games.

There were too many people blind to the UDA, RUC, Paras, Hit Squads, turning the other cheek to the Dublin and Monaghan bombs, reading and believing all the Brit apologists. But I was determined to sing John Gibbs' song and the Hearts did it proud.

One Last Cold Kiss
by Felix Pappalardi

I regret not having these lyrics in my book.

This beautiful song is about the faithfulness
and devotion of the Island Swan for his life partner.
For three years the writer observed the lovers upon
the calm waters of the quiet and peaceful lake.

The scene is shattered by the arrival of the hunter
who slays the female swan. As the cold November winds
blow across the water the male stays lovingly beside
his dying spouse comforting her in the mist before
sharing One Last Cold Kiss.

F elix Pappalardi is from the American band Mountain. I heard his song on
a Sixties' album of theirs and I began to learn it immediately. I felt it was
perfect for the Planxty repertoire, but that was not to be. Subsequently my
infatuation with it was to result in three separate recordings: 1975 on *Whatever Tickles Your Fancy*, 1978 on *Live in Dublin* and 1999 on *Traveller*. But I
would still recommend the original Mountain recording, for that's the one
that turned me on. It is always preferable to get back to the source.

I've travelled around the world with these two island swans and many's
the time the story of their love has helped to sustain me. I've closed my eyes
on a thousand stages and been transported back to the nest of their love-
making. The emotion of this timeless love story has stilled a thousand
crowds and brought us together to that special place where, for a few precious minutes, we all might find a little peace.

The January Man
by Dave Goulder

The January man he goes around in woollen coat and boots of leather
The February man still shakes the snow from off his clothes and blows his hands
The man of March he sees the spring and wonders what the year will bring
And hopes for better weather

Through April rain the man goes down to watch the birds come in to share the summer
The man of May stands very still to watch the children dance away the day
In June the man inside the man is young and wants to lend a hand
And smiles at each newcomer

In July the man in cotton shirt he sits and thinks on being idle
The August man in thousands take the road to watch the sun, sit by the sea
September man is standing near to saddle up another year
And autumn is his bridle

The man of new October takes the rain and early frost is on his shoulder
The poor November man sees fire and mist and wind and rain and winter air
December man looks through the snow to let eleven brothers know
They're all a little older

The January man he comes around again in coat and boots of leather
To take another turn and walk along the icy road he knows so well
The January man is here the start of each and every year
Along the road forever

I met Dave Goulder in the Sixties when he played around the circuit. I believe he is now in the north of Scotland still writing and singing. I recorded this in 1975 for the album *Whatever Tickles Your Fancy*.

We set out for Scariff, Co. Clare to play the Merriman Tavern for Aidan and Síle O'Beirne. We were in a hired VW van. Myself, Jimmy Faulkner on guitar, Declan McNelis on bass, Kevin Burke on fiddle and Colm Flynn was our soundman and driver. The fee was £200. The breakdown would be: van hire £12, PA £20, petrol £20, leaving £148 split six ways. As the leader and manager of the band, I took two shares to cover my management work and expenses. I now realise that this was off the wall, for the hardest part of the job for me was setting everything up. Anyway, that's over and I learned from it. A set list from then: 'Van Dieman's Land'; 'Go Move Shift'; 'Tim Evans'; 'January Man'; 'Dalesman's Litany'; 'Home by Barna'; 'The Crack Was Ninety'; 'One Last Cold Kiss'; 'Trip to Roscoff'; 'Humours of Ballymagash'; 'Slip Jigs'; 'Sligo Maid'; 'The Raggle Taggle Gypsy'; 'Cliffs of Dooneen'; 'Follow Me Up'; 'Sacco and Vanzetti'; 'Pretty Boy Floyd'; 'Tell It to Me'; 'Ponchartrain'. The Merriman was a Saturday night gig and we would have drawn 150–200 people. There was always after-hours to be endured and that could last well into Sunday. There was a snooker table and toasted cheese sandwiches for lining what was left of the stomach.

We left Scariff at 4am and set off back for Dublin on a freezing cold February night in 1975. One by one we fell asleep until only the driver remained awake, and as we made our way across the bogs of south Kildare he too went to sleep and off the road we went. I awoke suddenly lying upside down, all the weight of my body on my head and neck. We were in a mud drain all on top of each other with petrol flowing and the indicator light flashing and I thought it was flame. Such confusion and panic. We managed somehow to get ourselves out of the totally wrecked van and up the embankment on to the road. The shock and fear we felt was partially overcome by the fact that no one was injured or dead, for dead we could have been. We were covered from head to toe in grey mud and were a strange-looking bunch. From the road there was no sign of the van, nor any evidence of a crash, so the very occasional motorist was not inclined to stop.

Eventually, a man did stop and he carried us to Newbridge where my sister Terry took us in and revived us. God was looking over us that night. The van was a write-off, yet apart from stiffness and soreness no one suffered any injury, nor were any instruments damaged.

In my 30 years on the road this was my only brush with death by car crash. There were lots of other prangs and bumps and skids and ditches, but never anything like this.

Recently, I've begun to sing this song again, and I recorded a version that was an out-take from the *Graffiti Tongue* album.

The Galtee Mountain Boy
from Patsy Halloran, with new words by C. Moore

I joined the Flying Column in 1916
In Cork with Seán Moylan in Tipperary with Dan Breen
Arrested by Free Staters and sentenced for to die
Farewell to Tipperary said the Galtee Mountain boy

We tracked the Wicklow mountains we were rebels on the run
Though hunted night and morning we were outlaws but free men
We tracked the Dublin mountains as the sun was shining high
Farewell to Tipperary said the Galtee Mountain boy

We went across the valleys and over the hilltops green
Where we met with Dinny Lacey, Sean Hogan and Dan Breen
Seán Moylan and his gallant men they kept the flag flying high
Farewell to Tipperary said the Galtee Mountain boy

I'll bid farewell to old Clonmel I never more shall see
And to the Galtee mountains that oft times sheltered me
Those who fought for freedom, died without a sigh
May their fight be not forgotten, said the Galtee Mountain boy

I was eighteen years old and working in the National Bank, Clonmel. There were very few ballad singers around in those days and I was in great demand. I detested my bank work; there were six of us in the office and the manager Michael O'Connor was a strict man and was forever sending me home to shave or polish my shoes. I was the junior clerk. Next was Harry Burden, a sort of officer gent who was biding his time until retirement. Then came Michael Butler, the cashier and PR man, who was a golf-mad dazzler forever charming the rich auld ones. Martin Harney was next – he took me under his wing and showed me the ropes, the card schools, after-hours pubs, best lodging houses, who to know and avoid, and after a while we set up a flat together with three other bank fellows: George Collins, Dennis Donohoe and Conor Dwyer.

I had my guitar and got brought around to various gatherings and functions. Tipperary had a great hurling team in this era and I was brought to all the matches by Michael Murray, the local draper, and so long as I sang the drink would fly. My repertoire in those days would include 'Curragh of Kildare'; 'Bard of Armagh'; 'Tim Finnegan'; 'Follow Me Up'; 'Jug of Punch'; 'Liverpool Lou'; 'Rosin the Bow'; 'Whiskey Devil'; 'Wild Colonial Boy'; 'Kevin Barry'; 'Master McGrath'; 'Still I Love Him'.

I was by now playing Gaelic football for Clonmel Commercials and rugby for Cashel. I also played one junior hurling match for Marlfield. I was always looking out for songs, and one night at a late piss-up in the Hillview pitch and putt club I met Patsy Halloran who sang most of this song.

Eventually we had to leave the flat and I moved into Annie Kehoe's guest house. This was the greatest hotel I ever had the pleasure of staying in, and to this day I still return whenever possible. Annie Kehoe was an eccentric and wonderful woman. If you were in you were in, and the opposite applied even more so. The food was the best that rural Ireland could offer and I shared a room with, at different times, a butcher, a council foreman, a technical school teacher, a retired NACA athlete and a painter. The house was famous for its male orientation, card schools and leniency in the matter of closing time. I became the resident bard and barman, much to the chagrin of the bank manager, my boss, who told me I'd have to decide whether I wanted to be a singing loungeboy or a bank man. (I subsequently and thankfully opted for the former. I was on £7 a week and it cost £4 a week to stay at Annie's. At the bank I was expected to cow-tow, bow and scrape to wankers with dosh, and play bridge and golf with airheads, but I had gotten the taste of another way.)

My dear friend Annie has since passed away, but her daughter Nuala and son-in-law John still run the operation.

It was a wild time for me in Clonmel, my alcohol consumption was getting heavy and I had found the company of the hard-drinking set as the one that suited me best. I never got around to serious love affairs, but I did encounter some beautiful women whom I'll never forget and that's all I'll say for they know and you don't need to. I also learned a lot about new things: civil war politics, the class system in Ireland, coursing, greyhounds. I got to know some big wealthy farmers and shopkeepers and, having access to the banking system, I begun to understand how the rich get richer and the poor get poorer.

Many years later I met Sean Hogan whose father is mentioned in 'The Galtee Mountain Boy'. We have become firm friends. He told me that his family greatly appreciated the song being recorded and getting airplay. He views it as a fitting memorial to his father. For me, this means much more than any gold disc on the wall.

I've sung this song around the world; it always creates its own space and atmosphere over and above the particular time it describes. People come to it with their own set of emotional experiences. From Windgap to Mullinahone, Ardfinnan to Kilsheelan, 'The Galtee Mountain Boy' always gets silence around the house.

It rang out around The Glen O'The Downs when I sang it at the campfire side by side with the Eco Warriors. Sitting beneath the ancient trees I sang it with 'Burning Times', 'No Time for Love' and 'Joxer' and we laughed and sang beneath the stars and this magic moment, for me, is frozen in time.

Bright Blue Rose
by Jimmy MacCarthy

I skimmed across Blackwater without once submerging
On to the banks of an urban morning
That hungers the first light much much more
Than the mountains ever do
And she like a ghost beside me
Goes down with the ease of a dolphin
And emerges unlearned unshamed unharmed
For she is the perfect creature
Natural in every feature
And I am the geek with the alchemist's stone

For all of you who must discover
For all who seek to understand
For having left the path of others
You find a very special hand

And it is a holy thing
And it is a precious time
 And it is the only way
Forget me nots among the snow
It's always been and so it goes
To ponder his life and his death eternally

One bright blue rose
Outlives all those
Two thousand years and still it goes
To ponder His life and His death eternally

I recorded this song in 1988 and worked for the first time in a studio with
Paddy Moloney of The Chieftains. He became a different man once the
tape was rolling and turned in a beautiful performance on whistle and harmony pipes to Liam O'Flynn's lead chanter. I love this song. Once in a blue
moon I get a quiet request from down the hall and respond by singing this
song. I never have it on my set list. I think I know what Jimmy Mack is

writing about, but again I have my own pictures that always make me feel good.

I have had many strange and wonderful experiences on stage and one night, performing this song in the Forum Theatre in Waterford, I had a new experience never (yet) repeated. I was in a good head space – well relaxed and prepared before I began. I had done my pre-gig exercises and had achieved a good level of meditation and relaxation. I was deep into 'Bright Blue Rose' when I experienced a very white sensation – it was like a bright light permeating my head and body . It was not disturbing or distressing in any way, nor did it interfere with my singing and playing. No one noticed anything, except Jim Donohoe who saw that I had gone into a different space and remarked upon it afterwards. I have since discovered that what I experienced that night is sometimes known as a spiritual experience – today I accept that explanation. It ties in with my own belief that there are many levels of experience within us if we somehow manage to reach them. I sought out-of-body experiences with all kinds of substances – alcohol, hashish, marijuana, cocaine, mescaline, LSD, speed, sulphate, uppers downers and sideways, opium and, a few times inadvertently, heroin. All it did was give me a false buzz and a few times nearly killed me. When I look back on the chances I took in Paris, Hamburg, Amsterdam, Frankfurt, New York, San Francisco, going into dodgy quarters to score packs of this and lumps of that, what a waste of time and opportunity. Thank God I came through all that with enough life left to experience the bright side of the street. I've no doubt that Jimmy's wondrous song has helped me through and I thank him for all his great music.

A Pair of Brown Eyes
by Shane McGowan

One summer's evening drunk as hell I sat there nearly lifeless
An old man in the corner sang where the water lilies grow
On the jukebox Johnny sang about a thing called love
Saying how are ye kid, what's your name, and what do you know

In blood and death 'neath a screaming sky I lay down on the ground
The arms and legs of other men lay scattered all around
Some cursed and prayed and prayed and cursed and then they prayed some more
But the only thing that I could see was a pair of brown eyes looking at me
When we got back labelled parts One Two Three
There was no pair of brown eyes a-waiting for me

And a roving I will go
For a pair of brown eyes

I looked at him he looked at me all I could do was hate him
While Ray and Philomena sang of my elusive dream
I saw the streams and the rolling hills where his brown eyes were waiting
And I thought about a pair of brown eyes that waited once for me
That waited once for me

So drunk as hell I left that place sometimes walking sometimes crawling
A hungry sound came on the breeze so I gave the walls a good talking
I heard the sounds of long ago down by the old canal
And the birds were whistling in the trees and the wind was gently laughing

And a roving I will go
For a pair of brown eyes

Shane was gracious and generous in his response to my recording of his beautiful song on the 1987 album *Unfinished Revolution*. I consider this to be one of the great songs that I've encountered.

I discovered my grand-uncle Joe Sheeran's name on the Wall of Remembrance in Ypres. He went off to fight for small nations (God love him) along with Francis Ledwidge, among others. Blown to bits in foreign fields not even Joe's cap came back. That night in a large marquee at a festival in Dranouter I sang this song to 10,000 young Europeans, and I spoke about Joe Sheeran and asked them to remember him and they did. I went on to sing 'All for the Roses', 'The First Time Ever I Saw Your Face' and all the songs that night were about the hundreds of thousands of dead whose spirits are still to be experienced in the killing fields of France and Germany.

And in the next World War Joe Sheeran's nephew (my uncle) Jimmy Power joined the British forces and ended up in India. He came back to England and was lost to us all. He was injured in the Birmingham bombs, an innocent bystander, and later he died down an alleyway alone, all alone.

Lawless
by Mick Curry

He was Lawless by name and Lawless by nature
He was trouble right from the start
Hard as nails running wild through the streets
He was breaking his poor mother's heart
Nature played a trick on Lawless
And the human of nature is cruel
He grew up as we all had expected
Into a dangerous fool

He was a hard man and a man for all seasons
Always out for a fight
He couldn't hold drink but still he'd get plastered
In Clarkes every Saturday night
He'd strip to his vest and challenge the best
Till the guards were called to come fast
And they'd lock him away for the rest of the day
Leave him out Sunday morning for Mass

One night he went down to the Ringsend Regatta
Where he met with the bould Dolly Platts
She wasn't exactly what you'd call beauty
But she was the belle of our flats
A whirlwind romance and Dolly took a flier
With Lawless she would settle down
It was pure coincidence three months after
There was a Yankee destroyer in town

The couple were blessed with one of God's miracles
Before six months had elapsed
Dolly gave birth to a nine-pound black baby
And Lawless was fit to collapse
She swore she'd never been touched by another
And Lawless took her at her word
And the neighbours exclaimed he's the spit of his father
And the cuckoo is a wonderful bird

Now Lawless stays in and looks after the baby
While Dolly goes out for the night
The old gossips all say she is free in her ways
And their evil rumours ran rife
When Lawless heard this he waited for Dolly
On the bridge where the river runs low
No-one will ever know what happened next
But Dolly drowned in the Dodder below

There's some say he's crazy and more says he's evil
And everyone says that he's mad
No-one will defend him he was no angel
But I'll tell you he wasn't all bad
They've locked him away for the rest of his natural
Never again will he see
Down the back of Ringsend there's a lonely child playing
Where the Liffey flows into the sea

Barney Rush got back in touch in 1991 after twenty years. We reunited old songs and I organised a soirée in The Ferryman with plenty of singers and players. Barney brought along Mick Curry and I heard him sing a number of brilliant, original songs. At a different time I would have recorded five or six of his songs, but in 1992 only one fitted the bill – 'Lawless'. I had to be sure that the song was fictitious and I was assured by Mick that the characters were not recognisable. This is a great narrative song that audiences love to hear. I like the way it turns from humour to pathos and leaves the laughing listener feeling uncomfortable!

Then I met up with a fair few who tell me they remember the man in the song well and all belonging to him, but he never existed – the story is an amalgam of many people and tales. But when I go out and sing it, it happens for me every night. And, as I do when I sing 'Matty', I always apologise to Lawless for the life he suffered through the consequences of the ignorance and hard-heartedness of vicious tongues.

Giuseppe
by C. Moore

Every time I go to London
I think of Giuseppe Conlon
Who left his home in Belfast
And went to help his son
As he said goodbye to Sarah
And took the boat to Heysham
Little did Giuseppe know
He'd never see that place again

Giuseppe was an ailing man
And every breath he drew
Into his tired lungs
He used
To maintain his innocence
Behind those walls
Behind those bars
For every day remaining in his life
Maintaining his innocence
Giuseppe Conlon
Giuseppe

I was on the plane heading into London and I was thinking of him. I think it was after seeing *Dear Sarah*, a film about the Guildford Four, the Maguires and Giuseppe Conlon. I wrote this originally for the film *In the Name of the Father*.

6 November 1996

Here I am tonight in Belfast in my dressing room at UTV. I'm tuned up and ready to perform 'North and South' and 'Strange Ways'. The show also features OTT, Roger Chapman and a troupe from Riverdance helping Sam Smith preview his book. The studio is agog and agosh and I'm in here and I'm thinking about Giuseppe so I start singing the song here in East Belfast and I'm finding new feelings and I think about all the streets I drove through tonight and all the graffiti and murals and the fog and the chippers and cold and the frost and the billion-pound chopper loitering above in the dark eavesdropping on the misery and I wonder about all the gear that's maybe being moved day after day and the firebombing of little children's schools and the charred prefabs and Paisley ugly and intransigent on the news saying it would be wrong for Unionists to protest about the firebombing of little ones' schools and I wonder at people who will listen to this, and I remember Giuseppe Conlon.

Yes, I was writing the above and also preparing to sing 'North and South' and 'Strange Ways' on *Kelly Live* when the show went up and I heard Sam Smith going on to publicise his Riverdance book and he is criticising Flatley no end. Calls him arrogant and stupid and takes Flatley's earnings unnecessarily apart and suddenly I find myself becoming angry. Why is Sam doing this? He's been brought in to write a coffee-table book and here he is running down the creator of the whole phenomenon. Across the years I've worked with Riverdance supremos John McColgan, Moya Doherty, Bill Whelan and Maurice Cassidy, and I've never seen any of them dance. Forgetting my reason for being there I felt it incumbent upon myself to defend Flatley, which I did. That done, I went and gave a truly awful performance of my song, for all my preparation had fallen asunder.

Aisling
by Shane McGowan and C. Moore

See the bright new moon is rising
Above the land of black and green
Hear the rebel voices calling
I'll not die though you bury me
The aunt upstairs in the bed she's calling
Why has he forsaken me
Faded pictures in the hallway
Which of them brown ghosts is he

Bless the wind that shakes the barley
Curse the spade and curse the plough
I counted years and weeks and days
I wish to God that I was with you now
Fare thee well my black-haired darling
Fare thee well Aisling
At night fond dreams of you still haunt me
Far across the grey north sea

And the wind it blows north and south
To the east and west
I'll be like the wind my love I will know no rest
Until I return to thee

One two three four telegraph poles
Burning on the cold black road
The night is turning into morning
Give us a drop of your sweet poitín
The rain was lashing the sun was rising
The wind was whipping through the trees
The madness from the mountains crawling
When I saw you first my sweet Aisling

Fare there well my black-haired darling
Fare there well Aisling
At night fond dreams of you still haunt me
Far across the grey north sea

Down the dark centuries of dampness, cold, hunger, getting your arse kicked, your land taken, besieged at every turn by invaders and marauders, longing for the fruits of our own soil, downtrodden and fucked about until a new moon began to rise and reflect some light shining in other constellations and slowly, slowly we began to see a new way and a small number of people began to emerge from behind the hedgerows and through their enlightenment and courage began to lead us on a new path of self-determination and confidence for the betterment of the inhabitants of one black and green island.

Shane sent me this lyric. We tried a few times to get the melody from London to Dublin but the landline could never handle it. Then he sent me a tape. Just himself on vocals and guitar recorded at a lock-in in Filthy McNasty's using a free Texaco tape on a disposable tape recorder. I could not truly retrieve his melody so I hammered it out best I could on *Smoke and Strong Whiskey* in 1991. Shane subsequently recorded it using his own melody.

The Well Below the Valley
from the singing of John Reilly with new words and new music by C. Moore

A gentleman was passing by he asked for a drink as he was dry

At the well below the valley O, green grows the lily O, right among the bushes O

My cup is full up to the brim if I were to stoop I might fall in

If your true love was passing by you'd fill him a drink if he was dry

She swore by grass she swore by corn that her true love had never been born

He said to her you're swearing wrong for six fine childer you've had born

If you be a man of noble fame you'll tell to me the father of them

There's two of them by your uncle Dan at the well below the valley O

There's two of them by your brother John at the well below the valley O

There's two of them by your father dear at the well below the valley O

If you be a man of noble fame you'll tell to me what did happen to them

There's two of them buried beneath the tree at the well below the valley O

Another two buried beneath the stone at the well below the valley O

Two of them in the angels field at the well below the valley O

If you be a man of noble fame you'll tell to me what will happen myself

You'll be seven years a-ringing a bell at the well below the valley O

You'll be seven more a-burning in Hell at the well below the valley O

I'll be seven years a-ringing a bell but the Lord above may save my soul from burning in Hell

At the well below the valley O, green grows the lily O, right among the bushes O

In 1972 I spoke to Tom Munnelly, the song man, collector and folklorist, about John Reilly. I had met John in Grehan's Bar in Boyle, Co. Roscommon circa 1963. He was a wonderful singer and exposed me for the first time to a kind of song I did not know existed. John knew nothing about folklore and tradition or revival or any of that, but he knew how to sing and he had great songs. His tunes varied from one performance to the next. Once, while singing a long ballad, I heard him pause for a sup of porter and upon recommencing he entered a new melody and divil the bit anyone cared. Through hearing John and The Grehan Sisters and visiting Tom Munnelly, I have a number of songs from his repertoire: 'Well Below', 'Raggle Taggle', 'Tipping it Up', 'Lord Baker', 'What Put the Blood' and 'The Navvy Boots'. With 'The Well Below the Valley' I discovered for the first time that certain songs can be almost hypnotic. I learned about the experience of escaping into the world that some songs evoke.

There are various folklorists' yarns about this ballad. That it is one of the basic source songs, that the discovery of John singing this was the folklorist's equivalent of the discovery of the Rubik. I don't doubt any of this at all, but the spirit of the song is what makes it important. I listen to the high priests of Irish arts with their notion of grandeur and I think of John Reilly's interpretations of these timeless masterpieces. I think of Séamus Ennis cycling around Ireland with pen and ink and capturing airs and lyrics and I see his beautiful fingers on the chanter and I remember that there was no room at the inn for certain artists, no Cnuas for the piper.

When I began singing this song with Planxty, I was attracted to it without understanding why. Over the following twenty years I was to grow into it and understand why it mesmerised me. God knows who wrote it; it survived for centuries in the Irish tinker culture, and must have come originally from the East. Biblical in its origin, it has travelled across the millennia in the hearts and voices of a thousand singers, nourished by the attention given it by listeners in wagons and caravans, Botháns and bow tents down a thousand roads. The Travelling community had a respect for this song because of its power and durability and many's the night I've understood why.

John Reilly was a Traveller who stayed put around Boyle. He died in 1970, aged just 44. His family (grand-nephews and nieces) are still located around parts of Leitrim. He was a generous and gentle man, totally bemused and very tickled when his singing gained the attention of the folklorists. He could often be found having dinner with Mrs Bridie Grehan in The Square, Boyle. This was a great music house which I first encountered in 1963. The pub would rock when The Grehan Sisters – Francie, Marie and Bernie – let fly with 'Leaning o'er the Half Door' or 'Tippin' It Up to Nancy'. We often travelled up from Kildare to hear these women sing, for they melted our hearts with the wildness of their playing and the raw gusto of their three voices, and we fell in love with them.

We met up with The Grehan Sisters again in London in 1966, when we were all trying to break into the circuit. They gave me support slots and contacts and both the band and their manager Mike Thornley were generous with transport, floor space, mighty dinners and much appreciated friendship.

I have played at many of the world's great venues, stayed at the finest lodging houses, known the fame and the hype and I've been well paid for the most part. But behind all the palaver lies what really makes it worthwhile: the great songs I've encountered and the wonderful singers I have befriended.

Take away all the fame and wealth and glory but leave me the songs and the singers.

The Raggle Taggle Gypsy
from John Reilly

There were three auld gypsies came to our hall door
They came brave and boldly
And there's one sang high and the other sang low
And the lady sang the raggle taggle Gypsy

She gave to them a glass of wine
She gave to them some brandy
And the fine gold ring that the lady wore
She gave it to the raggle taggle Gypsy

Upstairs downstairs the lady went
Put on her boots of leather
It was the cry all around our door
She's away with the raggle taggle Gypsy

Late that night the lord came in
Enquiring for his lady
And the servant girls reply to him was
She's away with the raggle taggle Gypsy

Then saddle for me my milk white steed
My big horse is not speedy
I will ride and seek my bride
She's away with the raggle taggle Gypsy

He rode east and he rode west
He rode north and south also
But when he came to a wide open field
It was there he spied his lady

Why do you leave your house and your land
Why do you leave your money
Why do you leave your only wedded lord
All for the raggle taggle Gypsy

Yerra what do I care for my house or my land
What do I care for money

What do I care for my only wedded lord
I'm away with my raggle taggle Gypsy

There last night you'd a goose feather bed
With blankets drawn so comely
Tonight you'll lie in a wide open field
In the arms of your raggle taggle Gypsy

Yerra what do I care for a goose feather bed
What do I care for your blankets
For tonight I'll lie in a wide open field
In the arms of my raggle taggle Gypsy

Oh for you rode east when I rode west
You rode high when I rode low
I'd rather have a kiss of the yellow Gypsy's lips
Than all of your gold and silver

Bert Lloyd once did a series of seven half-hour programmes on the BBC all dedicated to versions of this song from all over the world. In my life I've encountered five versions, and I love to sing this song for the film that runs in my head is deadly.

As I write this I realise that I recognise the story in the song. I always wanted to run away from the drear of stifledom. I had a romantic view of the horse and wagon heading down the road, or the circus lorry trundling away with Romanian trapeze artists in glitzy costumes. I always seemed to be stuck in a grocer's shop or a college or a bank or a GAA club; I needed to break away. In 1966 'The Raggle Taggle Gypsy' came to my hall door in the guise of a bank strike, and I took off like a hare out of Hell. I kissed the yellow Gypsy's lips and I've never left her since.

When the bank strike ended I decided The National Bank would have to continue without me and I resigned. The manager, Mr O'Leary, bless his heart, beseeched me to reconsider. To sacrifice three years' pension rights (only 42 years to go) was an appalling vista and he had Pat Coakley, my immediate senior colleague, try and talk me out of my rash decision. The choice to me was a simple one: stay in Ballyhaunis, Co. Mayo, for £8 a week, digs with Mrs Nester £5 a week, get turned down when asking fine things to dance in Toureen, or shag off to England where I could get £4 a night for singing songs and backing jigs and reels and there were beautiful women to be loved and friends to be made and goose-feather beds and wide open fields with not a mortal sin in sight.

So I struck out again for London, and this time there was no coming back. This wasn't 'for the holidays' or 'to earn a few bob', this was emigration and I threw myself into it wholeheartedly.

I got a room in Gunnersbury, West London, for £3 a week, and I fell in love with a beautiful woman from nearby Richmond. Our eyes had met in a canning factory in Norfolk and we had planned to meet in London (when the peas were all safely canned).

Hiroshima Nagasaki Russian Roulette
by Jim Page

They dropped the bomb in '45 to end the world war
No-one had ever seen such a terrible sight before
And the world looked on with eyes wide to see where it might lead
The politics of power passed around the seed
It was a time to remember we never can forget
They were playing Hiroshima Nagasaki Russian Roulette

They arose like the saviours of our modern human race
With radiation haloes hung about their face
With the key to the sure cure the treatment of our ills
A hot shot of cobalt and a pocket full of pills
Speaking always of the enemy who lurked across the sea
While they crept in among us like a carrier disease

Deep down in the bunkers of the concrete and the lead
Einstein's disciples working steadily ahead
Building heavy metal power plants to fire the city lights
All you can hear in the underground is the humming through the night
While the walls of tight security circle all around
Where they spill out their poison and they bury it in the ground

Holed up in the harbours hidden secretly away
Warheads and submarines await to make their play
While the military master minds improve on their designs
The soldiers get doped up and stumble through the lines
And the spills into the rivers get carried out by the tide
They call this security – I call it suicide

Our statesmen and leaders on politicians' pay
Quick to heed the hand that feeds careful what they say
They call out experts to assure us to wave their magic wands
This is the power of the future and the future marches on
Then they call in all their favours all their political gains
While the spills fill the rivers and settle in the plains

They've caused the death of millions that's their stock in trade
And they will be affected by this fallout that they've made

They've sealed their own inevitable doom and it must surely come
Not even the moons of Jupiter will be far enough away to run
When this earth that they've assaulted begins to turn around
And the unavoidable gravity sucks them to the ground

I know the minds behind them are riddled full of holes
Not to be trusted with their hands at the controls
Their eyesight is twisted by the glory of their careers
The sweet sound of flattery is music to their ears
To listen to them talk about how it hasn't happened yet
Is like playing Hiroshima Nagasaki Russian Roulette

In 1977 I became involved with Revolutionary Struggle and a small group of very active and political people who, amongst other campaigns, were opposed to the proposed nuclear power station at Carnsore Point, Co. Wexford. Initially the Irish Anti-Nuclear Movement was (as I saw it) driven by the power of RS. I became involved with RS and various anti-nuclear groups without officially joining anything. I campaigned and did benefit gigs in many towns, raising funds for the first anti-nuclear power festival to be held on Martin Ronan's land at Carnsore Point. I was motivated by the determination of RS and I was intrigued by the different approaches of different groups and the dialogue that would emerge at different meetings. It was my first time to become directly involved in a political campaign, and I was to meet many people who became lifelong friends and a few who became somewhat less than that.

Jim Page came from America to sing at Carnsore Point and stayed for years. He is a straight-up singer who does not hide behind any little folkie clichés when giving his message. When he sang this song at Carnsore, I told him I'd like to sing it and he handed it over without a blink.

The festival was a huge success and opened my eyes to the potential of people power and what can be done when we come together to effect change. It was a wonderful collective and to this day I still try to carry the message of Carnsore Point in my everyday life.

Derby Day
by C. Moore

The bishop walked in circles inside the cloistered walls
Pondering in solitude on his leather soles
Outside the palace on his bended knees
Johnny begged for whiskey beneath the lilac trees

Over in the courthouse the judge sat wrestling with a yawn
Wondering would the gardener pluck the daisies off the lawn
Annoyed and irritated by a guilty woman's whim
Mary pleading innocence to an alleged crime

Next day was Derby Day down on the Curragh Plains
Dry old men of cloth and silk watched the sport of kings
Meanwhile back down the town Johnny battered down the door
Beat Mary around the face and kicked her to the floor

Johnny took his own life Mary she passed away
The judge donned his veil of sorrow put the children into care
They became God's little orphans learned to serve and to obey
And to be unobtrusive when the bishop knelt to pray

I was staying in the Cashel Palace Hotel, once the home of the Bishop of Cashel, a great man for throwing in The Ball. I was walking around the lovely gardens behind the cloistered walls pondering upon the sounds of the real world outside the barricade. I wandered up to the Rock of Cashel, once a seat of great power and learning, and I mingled with Belgians and Japanese and learned about the history of Ireland. A local man told me about the cricket in Cloughjordan and as I wended my way back to the palace I thought of Judge —. I thought about the ever-increasing violence upon women, about Spare-a-copper who was always begging for drink, about the children who were put into care and were trained to enter service, be it the service of the rich or the middle class or the clergy men and women.

Derby Day was always a big day in Newbridge – as a boy I'd go up to the Curragh Races and look over at the way the other half lived. Thinking about the Curragh Races I remembered Jimmy MacCarthy telling me that when he was an apprentice his employer would pay him 2/6 to pick the daisies off the lawn on Sunday.

10 January 1997
The Forum, Enniskillen
It's like this. You're on the stage with a guitar and a bunch of songs. There's 2,000 people and they're riding the wave with you and for 90 minutes it's storming along. A quiet moment and a woman asks, 'On the Bridge'. I've got a decision to make. Over the next half-hour I cogitate as I perform. I know this song will affect the gig, but I feel a deep need to sing it for this woman. The way she asked, and the song itself, marks a time for me. I no longer want to sing this song, but tonight I feel I should and I do and it did and I'm glad I did it.

These current shows at the start of 1997 on the last leg of the 'North and South' tour are possibly the best concerts of my life. There is such a great connection at this time and the energy is pure and natural. The hecklers are good-natured, and the age profile of the audience is across the spectrum. Tonight I had children from six and seven, and parents and punks and newly-weds and families and grandparents and all sorts and collectively they were a joyful and spiritual energy and I thank God for the night I've just had.

On the Bridge
by C. Moore

There's thirty people on the bridge they're standing in the rain
They caught my eye as I passed by they tried to explain
Why they were standing there I did not want to hear
When trouble gets too close to home my anger turns to fear

With my eyes turned to the ground I moved along
I covered up my ears and I held my tongue
The rain poured down relentlessly upon the picket line
And the empty words fell from my lips your troubles are not mine

Tho' the rain had made the colours run the message it was plain
Women are being strip-searched in Armagh jail

We kneel in adoration before effigies of stone
Eyes turned to heaven blind to what's going on
Six women hold a naked woman pinned down to the floor
Without trial or jury she is a prisoner of war

Tho' the rain had made the colours run the message it was plain
Women are being strip-searched in Armagh jail

I received a letter from a POW in Armagh Prison, asking that I try and write a song about the campaign of brutalisation being waged against Republican prisoners there. At times it is very difficult to find the way into a song.

I was appearing in the High Court in Dublin in a case resulting from the recording of my song 'They Never Came Home'. I left the court with my manager Mattie Fox, and we fought our way past reporters and TV cameras and into a waiting car. As we drove across O'Connell Bridge there was a picket in support of 'The Armagh Women'. A small group of supporters were walking quietly up and down the centre island of Ireland's busiest thorough-fare. It was raining and the colours of their banners were beginning to run.

I was catching a plane to Cork and then I had to rush to Killarney where I had a show to do. By the time I reached the Gleneagles I had a draft of the song and I performed a rough version that night. I developed a melody over the next four weeks and, before recording, Donal Lunny wrote a different tune. When I sing the song now it can be to either melody, or even both.

I was to have a chance meeting with the woman who asked me to write the song, and shortly afterwards she was shot dead by British agents.

Canberra, Cumbernauld and Craigavon have one thing in common: there ain't no love in the heart of the city. I played in Cumbernauld before the paint was dry and in Craigavon I was welcomed by the large slogan, 'Go Home Ya Fenian Bastard'. But by Jasus we had a great night. They insisted on flying the Union Jack on the Hall even after dark and it only served to sweeten the concert, for the bigots could not permeate the music of the evening. But I particularly recall a rendition of this song in The Labour Club in Canberra. The concert was opened by Judy Small, a fine Australian singer. Among Judy's followers that night was a bunch of drunk militant feminists. The moment I began to play, these women had trouble with my gender and seemed determined to ruin my performance. However, when I sang this song and spoke at length about the suffering of the women in Armagh prison, Judy's followers finally shut up.

By closing time the songs had won them over.

Ballinamore
by Fintan Vallely

Leitrim is a very funny place sir
It's a strange and a troubled land
All the boys are in the IRA sir
All the women are in Cumann na mBan
Every tractor has a Nicky Kelly sticker
Displayed for all to see
Sure it was no wonder that the Gardái made a blunder
Said your man from RTÉ

Today – tonight they went to Ballinamore sir
They were briefed by the Gardái
On a video they showed to them the Provos
Atin' curry and drinkin tea
They were all wearin Russian balaclavas
Each carried an RPG
British scalps around their tummy pockets full of stolen money
Said your man from RTÉ

Leitrim is seething with sedition
It's Sinn Féin through and through
All the task force have joined the local unit
The post office in the GHQ
They've a racetrack underground for training Shergar
No comment! is all they'll say to me
Subversion here is bubblin please take me back to Dublin
Said your man from RTÉ

Every bird upon my word is singing I'm a rebel sir up in Leitrim sir
Every hen indeed is layin hand grenades I do declare sir in Dromahair sir
Every auld crock of a Drumsna cock is longin to be free
Even sheep are advising there'll be another risin said your man from RTÉ

Fintan Vallely is a flute player who also writes and sings songs. He is the trad music critic with *The Irish Times* – one of the last relics of 'auld dacency'.

As is the case the whole world over, news programming in the national stations is driven by various agendas. 'What's the news, what's the news, oh my bold Shelmalier.' I was in Derry City in December 1996 when the security forces exploded a suspected car bomb outside Strand Road RUC barracks. This took place 300 yards from my hotel room. Within 30 minutes life was back to normal, as if nothing had happened. Children were on the move from school, women were shopping and people were worried about how their horses were doing in the betting shop. This event was the leading item on the London news at six, and the Dublin news at six-thirty, and they carried it right through the night. Yet there was not a word about it in Derry.

Political news and war news always carries an agenda and the people who hold the power at any given time decide what slant to give.

When RTÉ went to Leitrim to make a news documentary they encountered many people who had a healthy cynicism towards their presence. Everywhere they went they were met with a 'No comment', so they ended up doing their own thing anyway.

Vallely, as always, was on the ball and he captured the kernel of that programme with this song.

Billy Gray
by Norman Blake

Billy Gray rode into Gantry way back in '83
There he first met with young Sarah McClean
The wild flower of morning the rose of the dawning
She heralded spring time in Billy's life that day

Sarah she could not see the daylight of reality
In her young eyes Billy bore not a flaw
Knowing not her chosen one he was a badman
Wanted in Kansas City by the law

Until one day a tall man came riding from the badlands
That lie to the north of New Mexico
He was overheard to say he was looking for Billy Gray
A dangerous man and a wanted outlaw

Word came creeping to Billy who lay sleeping
There in the Clarendon Bar and Hotel
He ran to the old church that lies in the outskirts
Thinkin he might hide in the old steeple bell

A rifle ball came flying, Billy lay dying
There on the dust of the road where he lay
Sarah ran to him she was cursin the lawman
Poor girl knew no reason why Billy had been killed

Sarah still lives in that old white frame house
Where she first met Billy some forty years ago
But the wild flower of morning has faded with the dawning
Of each day of sorrow the long years have grown

Written on a stone where the dusty winds have long blown
Eighteen words to a passing world did you say
True love knows no season no rhyme nor no reason
Justice is cold as the Grainger County Clay

There must be 50,000 exceptionally good singers in Ireland, and ten times that number able to hold a good song. To my ear, a good singer is one who can reach inside no matter what the song may be. I've heard some with great voices but they weren't good singers, while I know others who have small enough instruments but they can hold a room spellbound with the emotion that reaches out. Every townland has its quota, every pub has its star at closing time and every family has at least one member who can be called upon. I've been blessed in life by coming from a family of singers who will burst out at any opportunity. When Mammy's coffin was being closed, Barry serenaded her before she left the house, and when we gathered in Milltown Cemetery to add the ashes to her beloved Andy, brother Andy ingested some of her ash and burst into song, and we stood arm in arm, tearful but happy, as we sang to the memory of the wonderful mother we had known and loved. My sister Eilish has been known to go into strangers' houses and ask would they like a song, while sister Anne has been promising for years to extend her minute, but excellent, repertoire. Terry has a fine store of revolutionary ballads and will always have a rebel song at hand if the session is becoming a bit too downhomey.

I first heard this song in The Phoenix Pub, Cork in 1976. It was by Noel Shine who stilled the crazy throng with his beautiful rendition of Norman Blake's masterpiece. He had hardly finished singing before I was on to him for the words and music. When I hear a good song I always move quickly and Noel was not lacking for he wrote it out for me there and then. Thanks Noel.

Here is a cowboy song that goes down as well in Crossmolina as in Tucson. It also has one of the great last verses ever. The recording of it was a sign of the nonsense of musical boundaries. Planxty, a renowned Irish traditional band, took this a Wild West song and made total sense of it. The geographical origin of a song, or its players, matters not – it's the soul that counts. If it is a good song, and if it is treated with love and respect and skill and musical spirit, then the end result will be pure stuff.

Let the debate rage among the walking museums of song and the trad watchdogs, between the revivalists and the revisionists; when they are all exhausted with the talk, the singing will begin.

The Crack Was Ninety In the Isle of Man
by Barney Rush

Weren't we the rare auld stock we spent the evening getting locked
Up in the Ace of Hearts where the high stools were engaging
Over the Butt Bridge down by the dock the boat she sailed at five o'clock
Hurry up lads sez Whack or before we're there we'll all be back
Carry him if you can. The crack was ninety in the Isle of Man

Before we left the Alexander Basin the ding dong we did surely raise
In the bar of the ship we had great sport as the boat she pulled out from the port
We landed up in Douglas Head enquired for the vacant bed
The dining room we soon got showed by a grand landlady up the road
Lads ate it if you can. The crack was ninety in the Isle of Man

That night we went to the Texas Bar came back to town in a horse and car
Met Big Jim and we all went in to drink some wine in Yates
The Liverpool Judys it was said used to go drinkin in the Douglas Head
McShane was there in his suit and shirt and the Liverpool girls he was trying to flirt
Sayin here girls I'm your man. The crack was ninety in the Isle of Man

Whacker fancied his good looks on an Isle of Man woman he was struck
But a Liverpool lad was by her side he was throwing the Bulmers into her
But Whacker thought he'd take a chance so he asked your woman out to dance
Around the floor they stepped it out and to whack it was no bother
Everythin was goin to plan. The crack was ninety in the Isle of Man

The Isle of Man woman she fancied Whack your man stood there till his mates came back
Whack they all whacked into Whack poor Whack got whacked out on his back
The police arrived as well we banjoed a couple of them I'll tell
We ended up in the Douglas jail until the Dublin boat did sail
Deported every man. The crack was ninety in the Isle of Man

I love the language of this writing. I love to sing this song to myself. I had a minor hit with it in the Seventies, and it went on to become a standard with every ballad band and for some reason this has made it difficult for me to perform. I think I connect with it in that it describes the way I used to drink. The entire lyric is about getting drink into the body. Between drinks there is a boat trip, a visit to an island, a love affair (of sorts), a riot, a jail cell and a deportation. But everything is chloroformed with lashings of drink and that's the way my life was for many, many days.

It was 1968 and I was booked to play at a folk club in RAF Sealand in Wales. It was tense from the start for the atmosphere was not what I was accustomed to. Among my songs I sang 'The Patriot Game' and 'Kevin Barry', probably not a wise choice but I was drinking plenty and fearless. There was a late session in the NCOs' mess and late, very late, a group of us made our way to the local café near the base. A ruckus erupted, I got one dig in, and then I got seven shades of shite beaten out of me. I woke up next morning back inside the RAF camp in a sorry state. Were it not for the tender loving hands of Sara Clay, I'm sure I'd have curled up and died. Chunks of my beard were gone AWOL, broken teeth, black eyes, and what did I learn – nothing.

My guitar was unharmed, my car started, I pulled out of Wales black and blue and hurting, but I had a gig to play in Manchester and I had a loving girl by my side and the day was looking up.

The First Time Ever I Saw your Face
by Ewan McColl

The first time ever I saw your face
I thought the sun rose in your eyes
And the moon and stars were the gifts you gave
To the dark and the endless skies

The first time ever I kissed your lips
I felt the earth move in my hands
Like the trembling heart of a captive bird
That was there at my command

The first time ever I lay with you
I felt your heart beat close to mine
And I knew our love would fill the earth
And last until the end of time

The first time ever I saw your face

This is one of a very small number of standards I had always wanted to cover. It was pure indulgence for me to record this, for there are some sublime versions.

Recently, an old friend called me from Majorca. He was feeling a bit low and he put on the *Voyage* album. He was moved to hear my version of the song, it helped him through the night – he vindicated my recording of this classic.

I'd been to the Singers Club as an audient in 1967. I'd gone to hear McColl, who was the main figure on the British folk circuit. He had written and recorded numerous albums of the finest of songs, and I entered his club with nervous anticipation. It looked like most folk clubs – upstairs in a dingy pub (the Lloyd George Tavern near King's Cross). The capacity was maybe 150, and there was a small raised stage. The make-up of the audience was very different to any other club I'd visited. This was not a folk club audience, but an assorted gathering of radicals and intellectuals and anarchists and banjo pickers and singers and rebels come to play homage at the shrine of McColl and quite rightly so, too.

In 1968 I got the call to perform at the Lloyd George Tavern, and this was another turning point in my life as a singer. I had begun to get sidetracked by the bawdy-comedy-easy-laugh type of song which always helped me to go down well at the myriad of folk clubs that dotted the nation. But I wanted to do something different.

When I got to the Singers Club upstairs, I was extremely jittery and I'll never forget McColl for recognising my nervousness and giving a few words of comfort and a dram or two of whiskey to settle me down. That night, there were four of us on stage: McColl and Seeger, myself and (I'm nearly certain) Micho Russell. We sang in turn and that night I performed 'Tippin' It Up to Nancy', 'James Connolly', 'The Yellow Bittern', 'The Banks of the Lee' and 'Master McGrath'. The audience were a strange lot, and took their lead in all things from the Buddha of Ballads. If McColl liked it, they went wild, and if McColl was not impressed, neither were the minions. I had a great night and nearly got off with a Trotskyist. I never met McColl again, although we did correspond occasionally – at least his wife Peggy Seeger and I did. At one stage I wrote and asked Ewan to consider writing about the Dirty Protests and impending hunger strikes, but he declined. However, he subsequently sent me the last song he ever wrote and invited me to sing and record it.

In recent times it has been a great experience to work and record with Ewan and Peggy's two sons Neil and Callum. They are a great pair of musicians reared in the Tower of Song. I number Neil as one of my favourite guitar players. He worked with me on the *King Puck* album.

Go, Move, Shift
by Ewan McColl

Born in the middle of the afternoon
In a horse-drawn carriage down the old A5
The big twelve-wheeler shook my bed
You can't stay here the policeman said

You'd better get born in some place else
Move along, get along, move along, get along
Go, move, shift

Born on a common by a building site
Where the ground was rutted by the trail of wheels
The local people said to me
You lower the price of property

Born at the back of a hawthorn hedge
Where the black hoar frost lay on the ground
No Eastern kings came bearing gifts
Instead the orders came to shift

The eastern sky was full of stars
One shone brighter than the rest
Wise men came stern and strict
And brought the orders to evict

Wagon tent or trailer born
Last month last year or in far off days
Born here or a thousand miles away
There's always men nearby who'll say

Additional Verses
Six in the morning out in Inchicore
Sixteen men came through the wagon door
John Maughan was arrested in the cold
A Travelling boy just ten years old

Mary Joyce is living by the side of the road
No halting place no fixed abode

The vigilantes came to her Darndale site
And shot her son in the middle of the night

Who hired the heavy gang in Bantry Town
Who gathered up five thousand pounds
Who paid them thugs to drive a JCB
Thru Liz Burke's wagon and her family

Since my youngest days I've known about Gypsies. In those days we spoke of Gypsies or Tinkers. The Traveller word had not been coined, and the Knacker word had another use. The name Traveller came about when The Johnstons had a huge hit with McColl's 'Travelling People' in 1967. My granny, Ellie Power, always had a welcome for the Gypsies and would buy holy pictures and paper flowers as well as giving out a few pennies or a bit of food if it was there. My other granny was Bridie Dowling, who farmed land with her brother and sister Annie and Frank. The Dowling house was a calling house for Gypsies and they would get a bit of work with buckets or pans and a mug of tea and cut of bread. The Dowlings were welcoming, but with a strictness that was self-protective and they would not tolerate any shilly-shallying. But they never ran the Gypsies, nonetheless. In our house in Newbridge, no one was ever turned away empty-handed, for both Mammy and Daddy had respect and regard for anyone in need.

I never got to know any Travelling people in my childhood days. Once I got into music I began to meet up with musicians from these communities, and I now have many good Travelling friends around the world.

I cannot recall where I first encountered this McColl song – probably from the man himself. I began singing it in 1969 and subsequently recorded it in 1975 for the album *Whatever Tickles Your Fancy*.

I've added various verses across the years to record attacks against the Travelling community. I sang the Bantry verse on national TV on New Year's Eve, 1994 or 5, and it caused quite a controversy and was the subject of animated debate at the following meeting of the Bantry Town Council. I enjoy my work being discussed in such places of power and wisdom!

Lisdoonvarna
by C. Moore

How's it going there everybody from Cork, New York, Dundalk, Gortahork and Glenamaddy
Here we are in the County Clare and it's a long long way from here to there
There's the Burren and the cliffs of Moher the Tulla and the Kilfenora
Micho Russell, Dr Bill, Willy Clancy, Noel Hill, flutes and fiddles everywhere
If it's music you want – go to Clare

Everybody needs a break climb a mountain jump in a lake
Some head off to exotic places others go to the Galway Races
Mattie goes to the south of France, Jim to the dogs, Peter to the dance
A cousin of mine goes pot holing a cousin of hers is heavy into Joe Dolan
As the summer comes around each year, we go there and they come over here
Some jet off to Frijiliana, but I always head for Lisdoonvarna

I normally leave on a Thursday night with my tent and groundsheet rolled up tight
I like to get into Lisdoon in or around Friday afternoon
This gives me time to get my tent up get my gear together
Don't have to worry about the weather
There's a Dutchman playin a mandolin a German lookin for Liam O'Flynn
Adam and Bono, Larry and The Edge getting their photo taken for the Champion
Finbar, Charlie and Jim Hand drinking pints to bate the band
Why wouldn't they for Jasus' sake, aren't they getting it for nothing

The multitudes they flocked in throngs to hear the music and the songs
On motorbikes and Hi-Ace vans with bottles barrels flagons cans
Mighty crack, loads of frolics, pioneers, alcoholics,
Plac and Spuc and the FCA, Free Nicky Kelly and the IRA
Hairy chests, milk-white thighs, mickey dodgers in disguise
McGraths, O'Briens, Pippins and Coxes, massage parlours in horse boxes
RTÉ were making tapes, taking breaks, throwing shapes
Amhráns, bodhráns, amadáns
Hairy freaks Arab sheiks Hindu sikhs Jesus freaks
This is heaven this is hell
Who cares, who can tell
Anyone here for the last few choc ices

A 747 for Jackson Browne they had to build a special runway just to get him down
Before the Chieftains could start to play six creamy pints came out on a tray

Sean Cannon was doing the backstage cookin Shergar was ridden by Lord Lucan
Mary O'Hary and Brush Shields together singing the Four Green Fields
Clannad were playing Harry's Game Chris de Burgh was singing The Spanish Train
Van the Man and Emmy Lou, Moving Hearts and Planxty too

Everybody needs a break climb a mountain jump into a lake
Sean Doherty goes to The Rose of Tralee, Oliver J. to the Holy See
I prefer music in the open air, every summer I go to Clare
Woodstock nor Knock nor The Wedding Feast of Cana couldn't hold a match to Lisdoonvarna

I was beginning to record some of my own songs. This was a very slow
process for me and might not have happened had it not been for the
encouragement of my manager, Mattie Fox. It came to a head with this song.
I had written it specifically to perform at the festival in Lisdoonvarna, but I
had no intention of recording it for I did not attach any worth to it. Mattie
urged me to reconsider and also to take my own writing seriously. He felt,
rightly, that I had always taken more care recording the work of other writers than I would take with my own songs. Since then I've tried to write more
songs and to take the discipline of writing more seriously. I will never be
prolific, but there are plenty of good writers about so I'll never run out of
new and old songs to sing.

Paddy Doherty and Jim Shannon came to meet me in The Meeting Place
in Dublin. They had a plan to run a festival in Lisdoonvarna in a field outside the town. I shared with them all the experience gleaned from the running of Carnsore Point and various other events I'd been around. They went
ahead and their first festival was run in 1979. I headlined with The Chieftains and it was the beginning of a six-year run of great events. Some years
later I was playing the festival again and by this time it had become very different from the first year. The bill had become international in flavour and
the crowds had capitulated from thousands to tens of thousands. I decided
to write a song specifically for the oncoming gig, and I wrote the original
draft over a week and debuted the song at a pub called The Lawns in Bel-
turbet, Co. Cavan. It's a song about my life and my world in those days and
the success of the song would indicate that it was also about the lives of millions of people around the world, for everywhere I get up to play people
want to hear it. Finland, Vancouver, Rome, Paris, Warnambool – people join

in and let rip as they reminisce upon their own days of freedom and madness and adolescence and rock and roll.

Twenty years before I wrote this song I worked in Lisdoonvarna for one day. Myself and another man brought the National Bank sub-office from Ennistymon and set it up in Lisdoon for a day. The man with me was a divil for the sup and soon departed leaving me in charge. It got quite busy as three o'clock approached. A thick man came in and dumped a bag in front of me and said 'Lodge that' and departed. This was highly irregular, for a customer should wait for the lodgement to be checked. When I got around to checking it, I discovered it was £200 over. This at a time when my wages were £44 a month. Before leaving Lisdoon I called at his premises and gave him his £200 back. He never so much as said thanks, and I remembered Mother's words 'It's not everyone that money suits.'

Casey
by Martin Egan

If it's drink you want and plenty of feeding and you'd like the bed as well
Grab the wife throw the kids in the Datsun make for Inch and the Strand Hotel
If talk of turf drives you crazy and you can't face a bale of hay
Make for Foley's work the top shelf talk pucks pints and the GAA

The low road goes from Killorglin all the way to Annascaul
When Eamon Casey came to guide us he never used his brakes at all
A trail of sheepdogs littered Kerry from Killorglin to Macroom
He might have been all soul's salvation but he also was the sheepdog's doom

Casey Casey you're the devil
When you get behind the wheel
'Twas a sad day for Kerry sheepdogs
When your Firestones they did feel

From the holy diocese of Galway Eamon went to London town
Where the traffic cops out on their duty overtook and flagged him down
As he was tearing after luncheon around the city like a loon
Regardless to his rank and station forced him blow up the auld balloon

Geographically he was in limbo faced with justice through and through
No obligations were accepted he was rightly up the flue
No bolt of lightning from the heavens could remove the boys in blue
He wished the force that worked at Cana would turn his wine into water too

When Ronnie Reagan came to Ireland all the wankers made a great furore
But Eamon remembered Bishop Romero said he'd even up the score
Casey Casey said God willing I'll meet Reagan on the road
And Niall O'Brien will hear his confession when I've taught Ronnie the Green Cross Code

Casey Casey you're the right man
To teach them Yankees right from wrong
If it wasn't for yourself and Reagan
There would be no Kerry sheepdog's song

I first encountered Martin Egan in The Meeting Place in the mid-Seventies when we were both partial to the cratur and the capers. I next met Martin in Dingle in the mid-Eighties and we have become good friends. He now lives in Dublin where he continues to write.

In St Conleth's parish church in Newbridge in 1958 the Bishop of Kildare and Leighlin confirmed me into the Catholic Church. There were hundreds of us for he only came once every four years. I suppose the origin of confirmation was of a spiritual nature, but what I encountered as a young boy was certainly not. It was rooted in fear and domination.

I've no doubt that everyone felt the same way as myself. This man was coming to confirm us and we had better be cowering in our pews shipshape and sheepish or Brother Raymond would sort us out for sure. The bishop arrived from Mars and he dressed up like nothing on earth and he shuffled over and back, did his bit of brainwashing and then back to his palace while we went about our coin collecting, for a confirmed child was entitled to his dues and we went forth and collected them. I celebrated my confirmation by going to the Palace Picture House with Joe Coffey and we gorged ourselves on Double Centres and choc ices and Tayto Crisps. The following Saturday I put a shilling on a horse called Vic Rose at the Curragh and it won at 33–1. Maybe this bishop had something after all.

The next bishop I touched was Casey himself. It was at the launch of the film *Cry Freedom* and he was there to speak. After his speech I was called up to sing Wally Page's song 'Biko Drum' before the big picture began.

Smoke and Strong Whiskey
by Wally Page

Kids wear white garters and smell like their mothers whose husbands and fathers alike
Drink black beer in the same public houses smelling of smoke and strong whiskey
Mammies and daddies and skipping ropes and lectures from priests living in hope
That they've not mistaken the brand of their coats paid for by their religious masters
It's Easter again and we can't forget brothers and sisters and all that was said
So practise your pipes and stand proud in the wet for the eyes of the world are upon you
Seventeen years Kelly thinks he's a man as he stands on the street with a gun in his hand
Protecting the Papists who play in the band while the enemy waits with an army

Oh the holy ground
céad míle fáilte there's saints and there's scholars to see
Oh the holy ground
Those far away hills ain't as green as they once used to be

God in his mercy has given us men to lead us to peace but they can't bring an end
To all the young women who are leaving the land and flying away cross the water
Dia le hÉireann suckle the Empire Dia le hÉireann suffer the loss
Of the green and the red and the orange white and blue and the blood
and the pain and the hatred
Father walks home on a colourless night the organisation has blinded his sight
His wife and his kids are sleeping tonight in the arms of Jesus and Mary

Oh the holy ground
céad míle fáilte there's saints and there's scholars to see
Oh the holy ground
Those far away hills ain't as green as they once used to be

Kids wear white garters and smell like their mothers whose husbands and fathers alike
Drink black beer in the same public houses smelling of smoke and strong whiskey

Here is Wally Page's song about the country. I like the way Wally writes them.

This song reads like a film script for me and I have vivid pictures to look at every time I sing it. It has never been a constant in my repertoire for it needs a specific atmosphere in which to live. It covers times in my life that are very far apart and disparate yet all live together. Men drinking porter in a dark smelly pub on a corner near my home, a place of mystery and intrigue and sin and low life and I could not wait to get into it. Girls with plaits playing hopscotch as I sought the courage to light my first cigarette. For me it's all in this song: Revolution–Abortion–Love–Dysfunction. It matters not that Wally wrote it, for as soon as I play the opening chords, for four minutes Wally's words become my song and my life and my pictures and they cannot be explained or painted, only alluded to.

Encore
by C. Moore

I've just heard Willie Nelson he was singing of his hard life on the road
And his song set me thinking it's much the same no matter where we go
Tulsk or Bord na Móna, Arkansas or Arizona, Nashville, Castleblayney or Sneem
People clap you or ignore you, hate you or adore you, some listen while others let off steam

When I first heard Tommy Makem and The Clancys my future it was sealed
I was bitten by the music bug and ever since the wound has never healed
When I got my first guitar my fingers bled until I learned a chord or two
I pulled on my Aran sweater, wrote me Ma a goodbye letter, started throwin shapes up in O'Donoghue's

I've played every lounge in Ireland from Dingle right up to Donegal
I've sung Nancy Spain on stages where no other ballad singers played at all
From The Rising Sun in Brownstown, to The Blue Lagoon by the River in Sligo Town
Ballymurphy and The Bogside, Ballinamore and once in Ballinasloe

If I get an encore I go home feeling like a king
It's a two-way situation I love to play my old guitar and sing

I've played cabaret in Bundoran, marquees for Father Horan and I once stood in for Johnny McEvoy
From Berlin to San Francisco gone on before the disco lashin out The Four Green Fields of Athenry
Mountbellew was like purgatory but Tulsk was just like being in Hell
I received my education in the lounges of the nation after thirty years I'm still going fairly well

I was playing in The Meeting Place when half the Special Branch came through the door
They were looking for McGlinchey stole their trousers back in 1984
They started listenin to some songs and hung around till after the show
If I ever need a taxi plate or a massage at the special rate
Thems the boys could show me where to go

The last thing on my mind was to offend good people of Tulsk or Mount-bellew but there are enough people involved in the re-writing of history and I'm telling my own story here.

At the time of writing I am probably getting on towards the 5,000 gig mark and it still feels good to be given the privilege of an encore. A few times I've taken an encore that was not there and I would hope never to do that again for it is a bad vibe all round. But it's the joy on the faces at the end of a good night, the welcome back out, the way the requests tumble out in abundance and the change of atmosphere. When the gig is over it is extra time and the audience tend to become involved in a more laid-back way. This applies to concerts and clubs. The outdoor stand-up gigs are a different story. They are all a backdrop to the celebration of youth. I remember a huge human pyramid in Thurles as the rain cascaded down – people got so drenched that they began to celebrate their wetness and I sang on and on and we got wet together. In Finsbury Park the sun came out, an evening June sun that was like a spotlight on the audience and stage and I sang 'The Voyage' and the vibe was beautiful. In Glastonbury I did a long bowrawn piece and the audience swelled from 5,000 to 25,000 as people came to hear the ancient drum – out of their tents and out of their heads they came to sing 'Green grows the lily O, right among the bushes O'.

Then you finish and go back to the dressing room and cool down and dry off and say a prayer of thanks and some nights wander back around the venue where the crew are dismantling and getting out and the audience has departed but their spirit still lingers and sometimes it can be a lonely time but a sweet loneliness for the memory gives an inner warmth and Val is keeping the home fires burning and I'll be home soon and there is tomorrow night's show in Caesar's Palace in Bunclody.

Sacco and Vanzetti
by Woody Guthrie

Say there did you hear the news Sacco worked at trimming shoes
Vanzetti was a Travelling man pushed his cart round with his hand

Two good men's a long time gone Sacco and Vanzetti are gone
Two good men's a long time gone left me here to sing this song

Sacco was born across the sea somewhere over in Italy
Vanzetti born of parents fine drank the best Italian wine
Sacco sailed the sea one day ended up in the Boston Bay
Vanzetti sailed the ocean blue ended up in Boston too

Sacco was a family man Sacco's wife three children had
Vanzetti was a dreaming man his book was always in his hand
Sacco made his bread and butter being the factory's best shoe cutter
Vanzetti worked both day and night showing workers how to fight

I'll tell you if you ask me about this payroll robbery
Two clerks were shot at the shoe factory on the streets of Braintree
I'll tell you the prosecutors' names, Katman Adams Williams and Kane
Them and the Judge were the best of friends did more tricks than circus clowns
The Judge he told his friends around that he'd put them radicals down
Anarchist bastards was the name Judge Thayer gave these two fine men

Vanzetti docked in '98 slept along a dirty street
He helped the workers organise, in the electric chair he dies
I ain't got time to tell this tale 'cos the Dicks and the Bulls are on my tail
But I won't forget these men who died to show poor people how to live
All you people in Suassos Lane sing this song sing it plain
Everybody here tonight, sing this song we'll get it right

I know very little about Woody except through his work, and hearsay via a thousand camp followers, and the odd direct snippet from his son Arlo or Jack Elliott. Everything I need to know is in the songs. I was given an entire album of songs he wrote about Sacco and Vanzetti, and hearing Woody's words certainly has enabled me to write many songs using his style and approach. The extent of his work is quite enormous, and considering the number of years he was actually writing he must have worked extremely hard.

I first encountered Woody when I called to Andy Irvine's flat in 1966 to borrow a guitar after mine was stolen from Slattery's in Capel Street. I see this photo on his wall and he tells me it's Woody Guthrie and that was my first introduction. Then I heard Josh McCrea in Kirkcaldy and Tony Small in Finsbury Park and Owen Hand in Edinburgh and Ralph McTell in London, and they all had different Woody songs and I began to get his drift. In '67 I learned my first Woody song, 'The Plane Crash at Los Gatos', and brought it back to Dublin where it took off rapid and hasn't landed since.

Many of us sit around bars and rooms talking about solidarity and romanticising about playing our part in the struggle. Woody's approach was 'Get off your arse and get down to the picket line and sing your song side by side with the proletariat. Never mind singing protest songs in the folk club, you've got to do it at the prison gates, too.'

The Ludlow Massacre
by Woody Guthrie

It was early springtime and the strike was on
They drove us miners out of our homes
Out of the houses that the company owned
Into the tents of the Little Ludlow

We were worried bad about our children
State troopers guarded the railway bridge
Every once in a while a bullet would fly
Kick up gravel around our feet

We were so afraid that you'd kill our children
That we dug a cave that was seven foot deep
Took the children and a pregnant woman
Down inside the cave to sleep

It was late that night the soldiers waited
Till all us miners were asleep
They crept around one little camp town
And soaked our tents in kerosene

They struck a match and the blaze it started
They pulled the triggers on their Gatling guns
I made a run for the children but the firewall stopped me
Thirteen children died from their guns

I never will forget the looks on the faces
Of the men and women that awful day
As they stood around to preach the funeral
And lay the corpses of the dead away

The women from Trinidad took some potatoes
Up to Wallensburg in a little cart
They sold the potatoes and brought some guns back
Put a gun in every hand

We asked the governor to phone up the president
Ask him call off the National Guard

But the National Guard belonged to the governor
I guess he didn't try very hard

Late one night the troopers charged us
They didn't know that we had guns
The red-necked miners shot them troops down
You should have seen those poor boys run

We took some cement and walled the cave up
Where the thirteen little children died
I thanked God for the Mine Workers' Union
And then I hung my head and cried

Here is a song that fired me up and still does. Woody sings about the greed for power that then corrupts. There are no agendas in most of Woody's work – no sub-political motives – just the fight against fascism, racism and the class struggle.

These songs will soon become very relevant again. Woody would not recognise a lot of what we see in the Labour movement today. Power is gone from the workers and trade union officials have become Suits.

During the mid-Seventies my appetite for benefit gigs got totally out of control. I was saying yes to everything and I was in danger of disappearing in a cloud of benefit smoke. Most people who run such gigs are sincere, but some are misguided and a number are downright cynical and self-seeking. The last straw for me was circa 1977 when Val and I were living in Kilkenny. I agreed to do a benefit for some striking building workers in Dublin. The gig was to take place in a hall off Stephen's Green. I drove up from Kilkenny with my guitar and PA and no one showed up – not even the guy who had asked me to do the gig. It was a turning point for me in the area of benefit gigs, and gradually I began to phase them out. Twenty years on I now say No to everything and I do a number of performances on a continuing basis for people, places and things of my own choosing. I also organise these gigs myself and, in the main, they are underground and quite anonymous, unless the subject of the benefit is in need of profile. High-profile benefits have a habit of devouring most of the proceeds. I recall a stuffed Nicky Kelly release campaign benefit in Francis Xavier Hall that ended up in the red, so great were the overheads.

1 January 1997

Two memorable nights in Millstreet. It is a beautiful small town situated between mountains, rivers and hills and is on a crossroads leading to many places. Tonight I had the pleasure of seeing my audience as they made their way to the Green Glens Arena. A mixture of all ages and walks of life all converging through the frosty night to hear the songs. It is such a privilege in this life to have so many good people coming to hear me share God's gift of music and song.

1913 Massacre
by Woody Guthrie

Take a trip with me to 1913
To Cal Michigan and the Copper Country
I'll take you to a place called Italian Hall
Where the miners are having their big Christmas ball

I'll take you through a door and up a high stairs
Singing and dancing is heard everywhere
I'll let you shake hands with the people you see
Watch the kids dancing round the big Christmas tree

You talk about work and you talk about pay
They tell you they make less than a dollar a day
Working their copper claims risking their lives
So it's fun to spend Christmas with their children and wives

A little girl sits down by the Christmas tree lights
To play the piano so you've got to be quiet
To watch all the fuss you don't realise
That the copper bosses thugs are waiting outside

And one of them thugs puts his head round the door
And he yells and he screams and he roars there's a fire
A woman she hollered there's no such a thing
Keep on with your party there's no such a thing

But a few people move, only a few
It's only them thugs and them scabs fooling you
A man grabbed his daughter and carried her down
But the scabs held the door and he couldn't get out

Then more people followed a hundred or more
Almost every one left the floor
But the scabs kept on with their murderous joke
And the children were smothering on the stairs by the door

Such a terrible sight I never did see
They carried them back to the big Christmas tree

The scabs still laughed at their murderous spree
And the children that died numbered seventy-three

The piano plays a slow funeral tune
And the town is lit up by a cold Christmas moon
The women they cry and the men they do mourn
See what your greed for money has done

In January 1972 I was playing in The Chariot in Ranelagh. It was before I was fully immersed in Planxty and I was still doing some solo gigs. I would have been playing two thirty-minute sets and getting £12. When finished, as always, I went to a quiet corner for many drinks. As the last few people were about to leave, the man of the house invited me to stay behind for 'a few'. He cleared the house, and when there was only the pair of us left he took off his Pioneer pin and we set to. It was serious stuff, nothing social or personal about this, it was the all-out oblivion express. I have vague nightmare snippets of the two of us fighting and singing and crying, but the end result came next morning at eleven. The lunchtime staff found us both unconscious on the floor behind the bar. We got out of there and into his car and he drove to Merrion Row, hitting a number of parked cars on the way. We got into O'Donohue's and within a matter of drinks we were way off line again. A good friend of mine, Jake McDonald, came in and, seeing the state I was in, pulled me out of there and into his car and got me to his girlfriend's house. She was a doctor. By now I was losing it and she gave me something and I blacked out.

I woke up late afternoon and I was in the horrors. There was snow on the ground and I tried to cool my head with a snow poultice. The news began to come from Derry. The Civil Rights march had been massacred. Two dead, five dead, seven dead, on and on it went – the news was awful and I was a pathetic shaking drunk and I felt good for nothing. But I still had seventeen years' drinking to do.

In 1968 I used to spend time in Finsbury Park where friends of mine were occupying a squat. One night I heard a Galway man sing '1913 Massacre'. Dylan used the tune for his 'Tribute to Woody', and I employed it partially for 'Another Song is Born'.

Here is an example of Woody at his best: simple basic language and ordinary words used to bring us up the stairs and into the room and to be all but crushed in the terrible fate of events on that dreadful night.

When I hear Woody's songs they give me hope for I don't feel as helpless in the face of the terrible injustices taking place all around me every day. So long as there are people prepared to listen and people prepared to sing, there is a glimmer of light in the darkness. Get down your old guitar and unlock your old accordion, shake the dust off and sing your heart out. Language of the heart will always find a listener and good music brightens up the darkest day.

Unfinished Revolution
by Peter Cadle

From the health centre porch she looks to the north
Where Nicaragua's enemies hide
Polio crippled and maimed before things were changed
Slowly they're turning the tide
In the twilight she stands with a gun in her hand
She's determined deep down inside
To be part of the Unfinished Revolution

Feudal landlords they've known and seen overthrown
Afghanistan comes into view
Learning to read and to write is part of the fight
But for her it's something quite new
Down all the years ashamed of her tears
Hidden behind a black veil
Now she's part of the Unfinished Revolution

Soldiers kicked down the door and called her a whore
While he lingered in Castlereagh
Internment tore them apart brought her to the heart
Of resistance in Belfast today
The living is hard, the struggle is long
She's determined deep down inside
To be part of the Unfinished Revolution

Peter Cadle sent me this song and also allowed me to do some re-writes – nothing too dramatic, but his generosity allowed me to mould the song to my own style. He continues to send me his fine songs, and one in particular, 'Bless This Guitar', I hope to tackle some day soon.

I encountered women in the Seventies who began to expose my chauvinism and, slowly, wash it away. I was a product of the Irish society of the Forties and Fifties, and I grew up in a time when 'men were men and women were women' with all the myths and sexism and chauvinism and brutality that went with the prevailing attitudes.

The view that women be gentle creatures is valid so long as they are normal and no more or no less gentle than men creatures. There are basic differences in our make-up but nature's and God's differences are sufficient without a male-dominated society adding its self-interested tuppence-worth. I grew up in a church-dominated society that proclaimed itself as male superior, that voted in all-male governments, councils and commissions, that was protected by a male army and police force that kept 'its' women under house arrest, that scorned its unmarried mothers as 'fallen women' yet somehow seemed to glorify the unmarried fathers as 'wild young men sowing their oats'.

The nuns that taught me saw themselves as wives of Jesus and some of them took male names: Sister Michael, Sister Gabriel. . . It was a confusing time – battered women were out of sight and out of mind, fallen women got the fare to England and some of them were never seen again. Rape, abuse, discrimination, sexual harassment were not in the vocabulary of my youth so I had to go out into the world to learn about the beauty and strength of women and then come home again to witness what I had missed first time around.

27–28 February 1997

Val and I have come to Paris to visit Juno who is over here studying. I am playing two nights at the Flann O'Brien pub.

The gigs were hot and sweaty and Juno sang 'Irish Ways and Irish Laws'. On the second night I got in touch with John Reilly's spirit and the audience was open to share it. A request for 'High Stool' but I was getting very hoarse.

Paul and Jim and Sorcha and Marie and Speedy were our hospitable hosts. Four Pads and a Yorkshire lass. There are 40 Irish pubs in Paris and I was happy to visit theirs.

I think a change is coming. It is 31 years now travelling down the Blue Tar Road and I think it's time for me to consider an alternative route.

They Never Came Home
by C. Moore

St Valentine's Day comes around once a year
All our thoughts turn to love as the time it draws near
Sweethearts and darlings, husbands and wives
Pledge love and devotion for the rest of their lives

As day turns to evening soon night-time does fall
Young people preparing for the Valentine's ball
As the night turns to laughter some families still mourn
The forty-eight children that never came home

Down to the Stardust they all made their way
The bouncers stood back as they lined up to pay
The records were spinning there was dancing as well
Just how the fire started sure no-one can tell

In a matter of seconds confusion did reign
The room was in darkness fire exits were chained
The firefighters wept for they could not hide
Their sorrow and anger for those still inside

Have we forgotten the suffering and pain
The survivors and victims of the fire in Artane
The mothers and fathers forever to mourn
The forty-eight children who never came home

All round the country the bad news it spread
There's a fire in the Stardust there's forty-eight dead
Hundreds of children lie injured and maimed
. . . .

Our leaders were shocked grim statements were made
They shed tears in the graveyard as the bodies were laid
The injured were forced to wait for six years
It seems like our leaders shed crocodile tears

Thousands paid out in barristers' fees
The insurance claim settled upon Butterly

It was all of eight years before any help came
To the injured families who suffered the pain

The days turn to weeks and the weeks turn to years
Our laws favour the rich or so it appears
A mother still waits for her kids to come home
Injustice breeds anger and that's what's been done

Moving Hearts were doing two nights in an old hall in Thomastown, Co. Kilkenny. On the night of the first concert this terrible tragedy occurred in the Stardust Club, Dublin. Because of the shock that ensued nationwide, we discussed whether or not we should play the second concert. We decided to go ahead, to hold a minute's silence and to forward the proceeds to the disaster fund.

In the aftermath of this tragic time, I wanted to write a memorial to the 48 who died. One night I heard a broken-hearted mother utter the words 'They never came home' as she described the loss of her three beautiful daughters.

I used Woody Guthrie's technique of describing the events to create not only a picture of the event, but also the underlying inequalities and injustice and blatant discrimination that still exists in our society. I recorded the song on the 1985 *Ordinary Man* album. It achieved notoriety when I was hauled before the courts because the original song suggested that the fire exits being chained was the *only* reason for the disaster.

I was scared going into the High Court. It was a high-profile case and I was most concerned, both about the likely outcome and how the case itself would affect the bereaved families and the injured survivors. The court was thronged and there in the front seats were many, many families of the lost and injured who came out to support me. It was a very moving realisation for me. Years later I was asked again by the families to officially open the Garden of Remembrance in Bonnybrook. On the day, there was a great jostling for profile from various public dignitaries. When I got on the rostrum I was so emotional I could barely speak, so I simply sang the song quietly and declared the park open.

The album was banned by Judge Frank Murphy and had to be withdrawn from the shops. I replaced 'They Never Came Home' with 'Another Song is Born'. Costs were awarded against me, and I estimate that the whole sad affair cost Mattie Fox, WEA and myself in the region of £100,000.

However, the court case did refocus public attention on the abuses being heaped upon the suffering families, and certainly helped to bring forward the settlements that ensued. I still get requests to sing this song in halls around the world. One night in Toronto, a woman came up to the stage and gave me a cheque for $100 for the victims' fund back home.

These events have taught me to be careful when recording songs, but they certainly did not affect my desire to use my voice to sing about injustice. Today, I believe that if they ban or censor or bring a song to court it must surely be touching a raw, raw nerve.

Another Song is Born
by C. Moore

I looked over my shoulder but not for too long
It's no place to be lookin when writing a song
Some songs grow ancient survive down the years
Others die young and soon disappear

Open the cloak, lift up the veil
Raise up the hammer to drive home the nail
When flesh gets torn the bone is revealed
Wounds left to fester are seldom healed

Songs written for love, written for gain
Help me to laugh, help soothe my pain
Songs have heart, body and soul
Put one down and another song is born

While we rescue banks and Royal Kilmainham Halls
Hell on earth means nothing at all
My hands are withered, I cannot breathe
In this nightmare of indifference, suffering and greed

The elite on the plinth maintain status quo
In marble and granite all movement is slow
Silk stays unruffled when eyebrows are raised
In satin and mohair your lordship be praised

This was the song that I wrote to take the place of 'They Never Came Home' on *Ordinary Man*. I was in Nicky Ryan's studio in Artane; I had three hours, and it was literally being recorded as it was being rewritten.

Two men stood by me all the way during this confusing time – my manager Mattie Fox and Clive Hudson of WEA never once shirked and I'll always remember their support during the court case.

This song was not born to live except for its recorded performance and subsequently on paper. The original song may have been drawn through the law courts and kicked around, punched and abused by learned men in wigs and cloaks, but they could never do it down for the melody is on the air and the words are out and about in people's hearts and ears. The highest court in the land can never, ever silence a song. The people will decide, and only the people can silence a song for, if no one wants to hear it, the song itself will fall silent.

My life in songs started off as a lovely thing, sitting by my mother on the piano stool, as she played along and sang. I was mesmerised by the music coming out and the lovely sounds that Mammy made. I could play a tune or two at seven years of age, even before I was brought into Sister Michael, who took it all so seriously as she tried to teach me pieces I did not want to play. She would try and twist my fingers into awkward chords that were not to my liking, so I left her and we became much better friends. I went to Mrs Sullivan – a soprano of great stature and poise and fun and laughter and she taught me how to sing and play and speak with elocution and deep breathing and I would perform at her concerts in the Curragh Camp. Once, I sneaked off to a talent contest in The Palace Cinema to sing 'Kevin Barry' and 'The Meeting of the Waters' and I won the prize of a Brownie 127 camera and was booked for variety shows in the locality; between comedians and actors on came me, the boy soprano. Back in school I was featuring in Brother Michael's choir which he ruled with cane and baton. Sing sweet ye little fuckers or I'll bate the Bejasus out of you and thank God my voice broke.

A man called Josef Cuypers from Aarschof in Belgium was a composer who dwelled in Newbridge College and he coached me on piano to years and years of grade As, but my heart was never in it for I'd heard of Elvis Presley, Terry Dene and Gene Vincent so I was only letting on to be listening to his teachings. Henry Flanagan OP, a brilliant sculptor and Dominican priest, taught me Art, English, Music and Discipline. He told me about Renoir and Rodin and he detested Rugby. Henry played Mozart and Beethoven in the Gramophone Club and signed me up for choir and opera. I did Koko in *The Mikado* and Sir Despard in *Ruddigore* and I felt this voice growing in my throat that could knock me and them half sideways so I began to dream about a life in music. I used to get close in at the dances listening to the showbands; at hops I'd lurk beside the skiffle group and at musicals I would be taking it all in. I just wanted some of it and then I went to a fleadh ceol in Bunclody and I heard Liam Clancy singing on the street – just him and his guitar and this life I live began that day. In between, I'd heard Sonny Ghent singing 'Panis Angelicus' and Nancy and Marie Slowey sing their own Ave Marias and Count John and my daddy and all the songs and singers I heard along the way and it all went in there and this is what comes out and I pass it on to whoever wants it for it does not belong to me – it is a gift to a grateful recipient.

Little Musgrave

The source of these lyrics is unknown. I found loose pages (on the floor of Reilly's Auction Rooms in Dublin)
containing most of these lines, which I then married to the music of a Nick Jones version which he played when
opening for Planxty in The National Stadium in 1972. Nick is one of the great singers.

It fell upon a holy day as manys in the year
Musgrave to the church did go to see fine ladies there

And some were dressed in velvet red and some in velvet pale
Then in came Lord Barnard's wife the fairest among them all

And she cast an eye on little Musgrave as bright as the summer sun
Said Musgrave unto himself this lady's heart I've won

I have loved you fair lady full long and manys the day
And I have loved you Little Musgrave and never a word did say

I have a bower in Bucklesfordberry it's my heart's delight
And I'll take you back there with me if you'll lie in my arms tonight

But standing by was a little foot page from the ladies coach he ran
Although I am a ladies page I am Lord Barnard's man

And my Lord Barnard will hear of this whether I sink or swim
And everywhere the bridge was broken he'd enter the water and swim

My Lord Barnard my Lord Barnard you are a man of life
But Musgrave is at Bucklesfordberry asleep with your wedded wife

If this be true my little foot page this thing that you tell me
All the gold in Bucklesfordberry I gladly will give to thee

But if this be a lie my little foot page this thing that you tell me
From the highest tree in Bucklesfordberry, hanged you will be

Go saddle me the black he said go saddle me the grey
Sound you not your horns he said lest our coming you'd betray

But there was a man in Lord Barnard's train who loved Little Musgrave
He blew his horn both loud and shrill 'Away Musgrave away'

I think I hear the morning cock I think I hear the jay
I think I hear Lord Barnard's men I wish I was away

Lie still lie still Little Musgrave hug me from the cold

It's nothing but a shepherd lad a-bringing his flock to fold

Is not your hawk upon its perch your steed eats oats and hay
And you with a lady in your arms why would you go away

So they turned around and they kissed twice and then they fell asleep
When they awoke Lord Barnard's men were standing at their feet

How do you like my bed he said, how do you like my sheets
How do you like my fair lady who lies in your arms asleep

It's well I like your bed he said, and great it gives me pain
I'd gladly give a hundred pound to be on yonder plain

Rise up rise up Little Musgrave rise up and then put on
It will not be said in this country that I slayed a naked man

There are two swords down by my side full dear they cost my purse
You can have the best of them and I will have the worst

Slowly slowly he got up and slowly he put on
Slowly he went down the stairs thinking he'd be slain

And the first stroke Little Musgrave struck it hurt Lord Barnard sore
But the next stroke Lord Barnard struck Little Musgrave ne'er struck more

Then up spoke the lady fair from the bed whereon she lay
Altho' you're dead Little Musgrave still for you I'll pray

How do you like his cheeks he cried, how do you like his chin
How do you like his dead body now there's no life within

It's well I love those cheeks she cried and well I love that chin
It's more I want his dead body than all your kith and kin

He's taken out his long, long sword to strike the mortal blow
Through and through the lady's heart the cold steel it did go

A grave, a grave Lord Barnard cried to put these lovers in
With my lady on the upper hand for she came from better kin

For I've just killed the finest man that ever rode a steed
And I've just killed the finest woman that ever did a woman's deed

It fell upon a holy day as manys in the year
Musgrave to the church did go to see fine ladies there

I've recorded this song twice – in 1974 and 1981. It is one of those special songs which can only be attempted under ideal conditions.

This song is from a time when to hear music was a rare treat. One could go a whole year and never hear a note of music in any quarter, except the trees or bushes or maybe the bark of a distant dog across the bogs and meadows. Today, however, we are bombarded 24 hours a day by aural pollution.

March 1997

Abroad at some Swiss festival there were fierce cavortions. Planxty was a five-piece – the original four and Matt Molloy. Clannad were about too, and there was a bunch of beautiful Brazilian transvestites singing South American Gypsy jazz, or at least that's what it sounded like waltzing in the dawn light after a lorry load of Pernod and cider liqueur. After I straightened my head out with brandy and crème de menthe and crushed ice, we later played on stage. Afterwards in the dressing room, Clannad came in and we played this song and jammed for hours and Matt pulled this glorious slow reel out of his flute and the music rode the brandy all the way to my heart and I felt on top of the world, until I woke up the following morning in the lobby of some Swiss kip hotel and the van was leaving. All the rest were flying, but I had tripped myself out of air travel and was heading back overland in the back of a big ghost of a van with Norman at the wheel, and I began to go into the horrors when a big third eye began staring back into my head. No matter how tight I clenched my eyes this big black staring thing pierced my brain and I got Norman to halt and I bought a two-litre flagon of vino collapso that I sucked all afternoon. When we checked into a motel Norman slept peacefully all night while I sat with the mini bar and kept the third eye at bay. But I learned nothing from this and a multitude of other drunken escapades. Self-inflicted torture repeated again and again. I had a huge desire to stop the madness but I simply could not. I went for one or two and ended up in oblivion, wherever the crazy trail might take me.

But that was then and this is now and here today in Galway I have a clear head and a love for life and a gratitude for something and I trust in God and I no longer have the responsibility of being all things to all people and nothing to myself.

Mullaghmore
by C. Moore

I took a rocky road up Croagh Patrick and a mossy path way up Slieve Gallion Braes
I plunged the deep at Brandon Creek and slept in a glade way up beyond Dún Maeve
All alone along the Wicklow Way peace and solitude I found
When I reached the slopes of Mullaghmore I could have swore that was the holy ground

Minister Minister Minister pause for reflection
As you fly by helicopter in pursuit of re-election
An obsession with affairs of state and high-flying legislature
Leaves little time for a man to share the miracles of nature

Like the Fairy Foxglove and the Rusty Back Fern at Pol Na gCollum
The Silver Cranesbill and the Columbine at Caherconnell
The Juniper at Bellharbour the Wintergreen around Slieve Carron
These miracles of nature surviving in the crevices of the Burren

There's gonna be sewerage schemes, septic tanks, tarmac and concrete mixers
And rumours circling County Clare promising lots of nixers
Car parks to be levelled, in-fills and elevations
And when all the dust has settled a handful of jobs – and relations

Nature took two million years to sculpture Mullaghmore
Carved from the ancient rock by the freezing ice and snow
As the sun shines down on the mountain by the broad Atlantic Ocean
You can hear the small birds singing on the Burren 'round Mullaghmore

Back in 1995 I took to the bed with a weakness that turned into a black depression. I couldn't get up for I had no strength: a black, weak, hopeless feeling filled me and left me languid and useless, good for nothing. I cancelled a tour, failed to get to an awards show and, worst of all, missed a clan gathering that included a guided tour of the Burren and a walk round Mullaghmore. Later that year I played a benefit concert for the Burren Action Group in the hotel in Ballyvaughan. It was a wonderful night. The room was full of good people out to save the beautiful mountain. There was music and poetry and songs and speeches in a celebration of solidarity and in praise of Mullaghmore. At the time of writing, there is no building activity on the sacred place, but there are interested parties always hovering about looking for an opening to recommence their mindless Gombeen development.

The grant culture has some unfortunate people driven demented. They see any potential grant as something that must be harvested, no matter what the environmental consequences. They try to mask their greed with talk of 'creating employment' and 'developing infrastructure', but I know some of these gougers and they only have self-interest at heart. They would poison the seas to swell their own coffers, ruin sacred mountains to sell a few choc ices, cover the last green field and leave the children with no place to play. They wield power in a threatening way, and often have politicians and the clergymen in their arse pockets. Their dream is to cover Ireland in concrete, provided there are grants available and their companies are doing the mixing, shuttering, steel fixing and timbering. Many of them belong to Fianna Fáil.

Lord Baker
from the singing of John Reilly

There was a lord who lived in this land
He being a lord of high degree
He left his foot down a ship's board
And swore strange countries he would go find

He's travelled east and he's travelled west
Half the north and the south also
Until he arrived into Turkey Land
There he was taken and bound in prison
Until his life it grew weary

Turkey bold had one only daughter
As fair a lady as the eye could see
She stole the key to her Dado's harbour
And swore Lord Baker she would set free

Singing you have houses and you have linen
All North Humber belongs to thee
What would you give to the king's good daughter
If out of prison she'd set you free

Singing I have houses and I have linen
And all North Humber belongs to me
I would will them all to the King of Turkey's daughter
If out of prison she'd set me free

She's brought him down to her Dado's harbour
And filled for him was the ship of fame
And every toast that she did drink round him
I wish Lord Baker that you were mine

They made a vow for seven years
And seven more for to keep it strong
Saying if you don't wed with no other woman
I'm sure I'll wed with no other man

And seven years been passed and over
And seven more they were rolling on
She's bundled up all her gold and clothing
And swore Lord Baker she would go find

She's travelled east and she's travelled west
Until she came to the palace of fame
Who is that, who is that called the young foot soldier
Who knocks so gently and can't get in

Is this Lord Baker's palace replied the lady
Or is His Lordship himself within
This is Lord Baker's palace replied the soldier
This very day he took a new bride in

Well ask him send me a cut of his wedding cake
And a glass of his wine it bein e'er so strong
And to remember the king's young daughter
Who did release him in Turkey Land

In goes in goes the young footsoldier
And kneels down gently on his right knee
Rise up rise up my young footsoldier
What news what news have you got for me

Singing I have got news of a grand arrival
As fair a lady as the eye could see
She is at the gate waiting for your charity

She wears a gold ring of every finger
And on the middle one where she wears three
She has more gold hung around her middle
Than would buy North Humber and family

She asks you send her a cut of your wedding cake
And a glass of your wine it bein e'er so strong
And to remember the king's young daughter
Who did release you in Turkey Land

Down comes down comes the new bride's mother
What will I do with my daughter dear
I own that your daughter she's not been covered
Nor has she shown any love for me
Your daughter came here with one pack of gold
I'll avert her home now with thirty-three

He took his sword all by the handle
And cut the wedding cake in pieces three
Singing here is one slice for the new bride's mother
A slice for my new love and one for me

And then Lord Baker ran to his darling
Of twenty-one steps he made but three
He put his arms around Turkey's daughter
And kissed his true love most tenderly.

I spent many days working on 'Lord Baker'. When I previously worked on John Reilly material I would listen to the song until I could make a stab at singing it, and then discard his version. With 'Lord Baker', I stuck at it over a period of four to five years, trying to absorb every nuance and variation in his rendition. It was always a labour of love, and this has grown to become the most important song in my repertoire. I have grown to a level of involvement with this ballad that allows me to know the characters intimately. I performed it once in 1996 in The Forum in Waterford, and once in 1995 in The Varieties in Leeds. Both performances were memorable and were inspired by the two audiences. It takes a special atmosphere to launch into a twelve-minute song to a large audience, most of whom will not have heard the work before. The spirit of John Reilly lives on in this song. When I perform it, he is holding my hand and he leads me through the story line by line.

Yellow Triangle
by C. Moore

(A song based on the words of Pastor Niemoeller, victim of the Holocaust)

Black triangle pink triangle
Red triangle green triangle
Blue triangle lilac triangle
And they wore the yellow triangle

When first they came for the criminals
I did not speak
Then they began to take the Jews
When they fetched the people who were members of trade unions
I did not speak
They took away the Bible students
Rounded up the homosexuals
Then they gathered up the immigrants and the gypsies
I did not speak
I did not speak
Eventually they came for me
But there was no-one left to speak

Black triangle pink triangle
Red triangle green triangle
Blue triangle lilac triangle
And they wore the yellow triangle

In the early Eighties I received a postcard which contained some writings of Pastor Niemoeller, who was a victim of Nazi persecution. I pinned his card to the noticeboard on the wall above my desk and for years I reflected upon the pastor's words, determined that they would become the basis for a song. He was describing the method used by the Nazis to differentiate between the various minorities as they were rounded up prior to execution. The song was years in the making and I recorded it on the *Graffiti Tongue* album.

My disappointment at the lack of response to this song in Ireland was allayed by the feedback from other countries, where it was well received and often requested. In Scotland, a primary-school teacher used the song to illustrate a project his children were doing on racism. He was kind enough to send me the pictures his class had painted. The song could not have received a greater accolade.

Dying Soldier
by Ger Costello

Look at the dying soldier
I heard someone whisper
And then I saw the blood coming through my shirt
I don't want to die here
Don't let me die here
Someone come and pick me from the dirt

I don't want to die here
Please don't let me die here
Oh! No

My hands are getting colder
My thoughts are growing weaker
This must be the way it is
Stop the shooting
Don't you see I'm dying
Someone kneel and say a prayer

My eyes are closing
I hear someone coming
But they turn their back and run away
They've stopped shooting
It's started raining
Oh Jesus this must be the way

Ger Costello sang with a band from Limerick called The Outfit. They played with Moving Hearts and we became friends. I recorded this song on the *Ride On* album and subsequently on a limited edition album called *The Spirit of Freedom*. The second album was to raise funds for Republican prisoners' dependants with a view to purchasing a new vehicle to transport families on their prison visits. I recorded and manufactured the album and all the artists gave their services free.

Some time later I was summoned to the offices of WEA Records who pointed out that under terms of contract they had rights to everything I recorded. So *The Spirit of Freedom* was officially released and was generally available for a number of years.

Boning Hall
by C. Moore

See the rich cowman with fifty boning halls
He weighs up every chop that comes across
his trimming board
He is king of the cattle mart smooth and razor sharp
His scrawny old scrag end tenderised by extra stamping

In the boning hall
In the boning hall
Where the carcass is stripped down to the bone
And all the flesh gets ripped off a country

Bone meal, angel dust, T-bone steak
Hormones, nitrogen, sweet gravy
When the beef is on the block the knife is on the stone
We've just been told the bung is underneath the counter

Of the boning hall
Of the boning hall
Where the carcass is stripped down to the bone
And all the flesh gets ripped off a country

The beef tribunal is over
We're all back in order
Our cleavers are well sharpened
We're all ready for the slaughter

In the boning hall
In the boning hall
Where the carcass is stripped down to the bone
And all the flesh gets ripped off a country

Looking for the Entrance Fee

(earlier draft)

I was looking for the entrance fee
The price of a pint or a fix
Anything to get me head together
Whoever delivered the goods, thank God
Albert was totally vindicated
Dick was left all right
And Larry was well chuffed
He knew nothing about it

How could any man with fifty boning halls
Know the source of every lamb chop
That comes across his trimming board
And sure a few extra border crossings
Never killed a T-bone steak
Only served to sweeten the gravy
And stamping tends to tenderise
The scrawniest of auld scrag end
By the time George Bush is finished with him
Angel dust will be the least of Saddam's worries

Whoever delivered the goods
No man is more entitled
To a dacent bit of a homecoming
For he never went away at all
Don't be turning your back on him
When you're thanking him
Never mind your bleeding diaspora
He stayed on the sinking ship
He didn't bale out and go off digging tunnels
He stayed at home
Burning the candle at both ends
To vindicate
Left right and centre

This piece was derived from two earlier works and was written in the atmosphere of a country defiled by the politics of meat. In truth, I must say that I've been disappointed by the lack of reaction to this song. I will continue to examine the work to see if I can perform it or exhibit it in a different manner. It may need to be re-framed and hung in a different light.

To work in an abattoir or boning hall can be a very brutalising experience. To slaughter and butcher and be knee-deep in blood is not a natural environment for anybody, and pain is suffered subliminally if not always apparently.

We have just come through an era of meat in Ireland where the entire industry has been tarnished and fouled by corruption and greed at every level. Farmers with no scruples going to any lengths to fatten their animals, others concealing the sickness of their herds. Crooked dealers swapping tags and border crossing with impunity, meat factories cutting off the old stamps from carcasses, re-stamping, re-boxing and ripping off butchers, selling poisoned food that kills the unfortunates who eat it, the list goes on and on.

There would appear to be a level of acceptance or even sympathy for the perpetrators of many of these crimes. The most recent example was of a farmer getting a six-week sentence for the use of illegal drugs on his animals, but given a four-month remand in order to get his affairs in order. There's an example of one law for the rich and one law for the poor. It seems we're all equal in God's eyes but not in the eyes of the judiciary.

I am in a dilemma. I aspire to vegetarianism, but I still eat meat occasionally. I will try again to stop eating meat – if I think about it enough I won't eat it. So I need to think about it more.

Folk Tale
by Paula Meehan with music by C. Moore

A young man fell in love with truth
And searching the wide world for her
He found her in a small house
In a clearing in the forest
She was old and she was stooped
And he pledged himself to her
To chop the wood
And to carry the water
To collect the root the stem the leaf
The flowering top and seed
Of every plant she would need
To do her work

Years went by
Until one day
The young man woke up
Longing for a child
He went to the old woman
And asked to be released
From his oath to her
That he might return to the world
Certainly she said
On one condition
You must tell them
That I am young and beautiful

Paula Meehan's poetry is published by Gallery Press

These lines are not laid out as Paula wrote them, but rather as I sang them. I sang this sitting in a hedge once, amidst a Passage East dawn chorus.

Fathers and mothers and husbands and wives and daughters and sons and brothers and sisters. There's a fair old web of inter-relationships to be dealt with in that maze of criss-crossed lines. A man could be torn asunder trying to cope with all the energies that can be unleashed by the love and dependency on the one side and the positive force of sheer love and concern on the other.

The wind is howling up the Moulnaskeha Valley; Dunmanus Bay is well sheltered by the two peninsulas but I can almost hear the Atlantic boiling in the distance.

A stranger told me last night that he was glad to see me 'off the television, out of the black shirt and perspiration'. He told me there was a much better television down below in Bantry Harbour if I wanted to go and look at myself in the water. He said he knew me, that he had booked me many, many times to play at White's Hotel and The Talbot Hotel in Wexford, The Burlington in Dublin and the West Lodge in Bantry. He told me he was always terrified that I'd not be able to deliver the show, so he would give me plenty of drink to bolster me up. I never played at any of these places, but still he read me well in his confusion. He told me I was not a bad person and to stop punishing myself. He also told us all (twelve of us) that we had it all wrong – that he had the answers but, God love him, he was the only one among us who was showing signs of disturbance; he had no peace of mind but he had all the answers.

26 October 1998

I am about to start work on a project with a young producer called Leo Pearson. We've been talking for six months now, on and off, looking at songs and a possible mode of working. He is setting his gear up down the garden and I'm hopeful of fruitful collaboration. (This project subsequently grew into my 1999 *Traveller* album.)

God Woman
by C. Moore

She spent seven days creating the world the Sun the Moon and the stars
The plough and the Milky Way then Jupiter and Mars
Then she opened up her ribcage pulled out a little man
She put him down near Timahoe and the human race began
Go forth said she and multiply, God ma'am and I will by God
What better place to begin the race than below in the Yellow Bog

God woman God woman
God woman God woman

Down by the edge of Clongorey he built a lonely cell
Where he contemplated heaven and drink from St Bridgid's Well
Then he went to the mission fields of Raheens and Ballitore
And he sailed on down the Grand Canal to the town of Lullymore
Where he went breaking up the bordellos smashing the poitín stills
Introducing the love of God herself around the furry hills

God woman God woman
God woman God woman

Many years ago I wrote 'God the mother is your only man', a trite cliché that I devised to coax a wry smile in some bar or lounge. I was weary of the male deity, God the Father and Son and pope and all the maleness. Church, State and power at every level of society was male orientated and dominated. Big, fat, ugly, arrogant men mixing with dry, mean, skinny men all with power and chauvinism in common.

Oh Mother of God, Oh God Woman deliver us from the world of prick power.

The recording of this song in Sulaune Studio, Ballyvourney, Co. Cork was a traumatic experience. A bit like me and The Rose in the same studio. It went to the wall. I was about to give up. I went on my knees and laid my forehead to the Paraná pine and prayed to all the Gods and Goddesses that I might just once get it right, and I gave Jim and Walter the nod and we got her down. I've never sung it properly since. It is one of those songs that does not want to live in performance. It is a flawed song in that at its inception it was of a different nature and has never been able to handle the eventual weight cast upon it. The terrible weight upon this prick world that God Be A Woman.

This prick world will get what it deserves, unless it loses its rigidity.

On the Mainland
by C. Moore

I was over on the mainland doing my act in The Royal Albert Hall
It was the night before we stormed the Hackney Empire
My adrenaline got pumping when the crowd demanded more
I couldn't sleep a wink so I turned on the BBC World Service
Coming at me from New Delhi or some other long lost colonial shore
When a lovely English man came on the wireless
With a gorgeous sweet dulcet Portland Place clipped tone
He announced that the winner of the 1995 Nobel Prize for Literature
Was a British poet
Seamus Heaney from Londonderry sez he as cool as cool could be
So I rang up for tea and toasted muffins
And a pair of hard-boiled eggs to calm my nerves
You never claimed George Best nor Alex Higgins
Nor you never claimed Bellaghy's other boys
But that's the way things are upon the mainland
Where the quare hawks are still sucking
The wee small birds eggs dry

L et us save the World Service. It may not survive the onslaught of world
domination by accountants, and probably needs every colony of the
British Empire to subsidise its huge organisation. It has mindboggling
staffing levels and the building that houses it is as large as government buildings in Dublin and probably even more secure. After being strip-searched
and anally probed I was led handcuffed to a control room that was staffed by
(at least) five women. They all seemed totally occupied and intensely busy as
the man in the studio did a telephone interview with Australia. I was
wheeled in and did my bit. Thank God for the BBC World Service. I've
worked on BBC Radio 1, 2, 4 and 5 and I'm conniving to play the straight
flush and perform on Radio 3.

My most memorable interview was with Sheridan Morley. I sat across the
table from this man who had already done 57 interviews that day. Had I not
known better I'd have sworn that Sheridan had every album I ever made and
hung on to every word I'd sung in my 30-year career. Sheridan, most certainly, pulls it off.

I thank God for the BBC. Seldom a day goes by that I do not listen to or look at its output. We residents of Éire never have to put our hands in our pockets. We get the Beeb for nowt.

Some years ago I was steaming in a Dublin sauna. The woman beside me said, 'I heard you with Ned Sherrin on Radio 4 last Saturday; I never realised you were that good.'

However, it must be said: I love the BBC, but I need RTÉ. Without the endorsements and exposure I've received from Radio and Telefís Éireann I would not be writing this today. Lest I cut off the hand that feeds me, my first choice for viewing and listening is RTÉ and I only switch over to 'the mainland' when the Home Service is off my beam.

Nancy Power,
my singing
bird, aged 17.

Daddy and Mammy on their wedding day in 1943.

Daddy, Mrs McAleavy, my godmother Maeve Laffan, Jack Power, at my christening, 1945.

With Grandmother Ellie Power in Newbridge, 1946.

With Jack Power, my grandfather, and sister Eilish in the Phoenix Park, 1951.

Turlough McGowan (with glasses) with our gang, down by the Liffeyside, 1960.

Mammy and I
dancing in the
Town Hall,
Newbridge,
in 1961.

A gaggle of
bank clerks,
1964.

£3 a night and my chances, 1967.

With Donal Lunny, 1972.

Our only wedding photograph, taken on 19 December 1973.

Valerie, Inchicore, Dublin, 1973.

Valerie and Andy, our first son, in Coolcullen, Co. Carlow, 1976.

With Juno in 1985.

With Pádraic, our second son, 1992.

Moving Hearts: Donal Lunny, myself, Brian Calnan, Declan Sinnott, Keith Donald, Eoghan O'Neill, Davy Spillane.

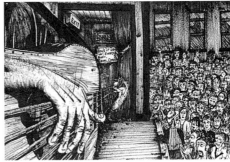

My nephew Turlough Rynne, then aged 14, sent me his impression of Lisdoonvarna.

Barry Moore (aka Luka Bloom) at Ballisodare Festival, Co. Sligo, 1977.

Sherkin Island Festival in 1977 with Johnny Moynihan, Andy Irvine, Frankie Gavin and Paul Brady.

With Kevin Flynn (manager), and Planxty members Andy Irvine, Donal Lunny, and Liam O'Flynn at the Nyon Festival, Switzerland, 1980.

'He was very fond of Black Porter, it was bulgin' out both his eyes.'

I Pity the Poor Immigrant
by Bob Dylan

Sadly I cannot grace this page with Dylan's
powerful words. I recommend his version
of the song which can also be heard on
Words and Music by Planxty from 1981.

Here he paints a savage picture.
Each line has chilling words used
to describe an empty life lived in an alien
and unwelcoming environment.

The poor immigrant who wishes he'd stayed at home.

Ring a ling a ding dong
tooria fol de diddle da
bebop bop a looma
diary fol de diddle dairy o.

What I love most about this song is that it is about many of my own personal experiences. I worked on building sites and oil rigs and factory
floors, on fruit farms, in pubs and on delivery vans, and this song contains
the insights, the inside story. I believe this to be one of the greatest songs I've
ever sung. The melody is that of 'Tramps and Hawkers', 'Homes of Donegal'
and 'Ninety Miles to Dublin' with a bit of Dylan variant. One night I sang
this song in The Hammersmith Odeon, back round 1979, and it was suddenly about my uncle Jimmy Power. He was the man of the song and I recall
the emotion and hurt I felt that night. I sang in front of 4,000 people, but it
felt like only me and Jimmy were there.

The immigrant's place can be a lonely one. Different weather, difficult language, strange culture, rules and regulations, red tape, bad vibes. People look
at me with such hatred. I still wear the badge of home. I have no status or
rights. I came here to better myself and my family and now I seem to be fair
game for nastiness – the butt of jokes, the foil of power-crazy bosses and
foremen and gangers. I've been here for centuries digging and scraping and
washing and drying and arsewiping and hoovering and my conditions are
appalling and I don't even get to save a dime.

The Deportees Club
by Elvis Costello

At the Arrividerci Roma nightclub bar and grill
Standing in the fibreglass ruin watching time stand still
All your troubles you confess to another faceless backless dress
Schnapps, Chianti, Porter, Ouzo, Pernod, Vodka, Sambucca
I love you so
Deportee
There's a fading beauty talking in riddles
Rome burns down and everybody fiddles the deportee

It's a brittle charm but the lady has had enough
She wrote her number down on your paper cuff
It's hard to know when to start and when to stop
All this pillow talk is nothing more than talking shop

When I came here tonight my pockets were overflowing
You stole my return ticket and I didn't even know it
I swear by saints and all of the martyrs and the secret life of Frank Sinatra
That all of these things have come to pass, in America the law is a piece of ass

17 January 1997

You do a thing for 30 years, 5,000 times and then you get ready to do it again. You sit in a dressing room and the confidence is low and the body is tired but there are 4,500 people in their seats and there is an hour to go. Eleanor Shanley goes on stage to play her set and I listen in the distance. Please God the crowd will raise me to do it one more time and I'll tread the boards with a lighter step.

I've seen the men smoking at the street corners in Melbourne, and down the street there are twenty Greek cafés. Their dress and banter has not changed, neither their food, music nor card games, and their children grow up with Australian accents, but with Greek culture and inflections, and they are just like the children in London with Cockney accents and lifestyles who dance the buckles off their shoes to Irish music.

I've never encountered any British or American immigrant ghettoes. They tend to gather in expatriate circles and meet behind high walls and closed doors in clubs and societies where they are somewhat invisible. It takes a lot of money to be invisible.

North and South
by C. Moore, Bono and The Edge

I want to reach out over the Lough and feel your hand across the water
Walk with you along an unapproved road not looking over my shoulder
I want to see, I want to hear, to understand your fear
But we're north and south of the river, north and south of the river

I've been doing it wrong all of my life, this holy town has turned me over
A young man on the run from what he didn't understand as the wind from the lough gets colder and colder
There was a badness that had its way, love was not lost it just got mislaid
North and south of the river, north and south of the river

Can we stop playing these old tattoos, darling I don't have the answer
I want to meet you where you are I don't need you to surrender
There is no feeling so alone, as when the one you're hurting is your own
North and south of the river, north and south of the river

Some high ground is not worth taking
Some connections are not worth making
There's an old church bell no longer ringing
Some old songs are not worth singing

North and south of the river

Hands Across the Lough
(earlier draft) by C. Moore

Before this heart stops beating
I want to know
What turns you on
I want to reach out
And offer you
My hand across the Lough
To embrace you
And hold you tight
To fear you not
Upon some country road

In the dark of night
Maybe we could stand side by side
Beneath the one light

I want to lay down my fear
And surrender my anger
To meet you on an unapproved road
And share with you
How hard it is to get good spuds
Or that I heard the corncrake
Beyond in some distant meadow

But as I stand here at the gable of this ruin
On the edge of Ballyscullion Wood
I wonder who it was that dwelt here
On divided and sub-divided land
Divvied up until no longer worth keeping
What family fled away from here
Driven by a bully's hand

I was flying out of Toronto Airport in 1985 and I met Bono in the check-in area. We got straight into it and I liked him from the start. We cross paths occasionally and I played before U2 in Croke Park in 1987 and enjoyed the experience tremendously. It was my first time to score with a large outdoor crowd and it was an eye-opener. Anyway, in Toronto we agreed to try and sing together and then we met up again at The Dubliners tribute show. I showed Bono a song I was working on, and we sat down and the song became this. Edge wrote the music and we recorded it with various other people in various places. The first verse is all that survived intact from the original lyrics, and a lot of ideas from the first draft are still there for the cutting.

Working with Bono was joy itself as he just bubbles with enthusiasm and ideas and I learnt a lot from the experience. He has the magic and he has the spirit of art within him and I admire him greatly.

At one time, I kept trying to write a song that started 'Is it folk or is it art or is it rock and roll?' Today I leave art out of the equation for it should never be mentioned by the artist (i.e. the singer). Rock and roll is a style, an approach, a bluff, an act, a fuck, a smirk, a tear, a heart, it is not a type of music – nor an adjective. Folk is all of this, too. People who write endlessly about compartmentalised music seldom know very much about it. Most interviews and reviews are of absolutely no interest or consequence. They're merely a tool for commerce or for grandiosement or mutual wanking. If the work needs to be explained or justified, it's probably not working.

I have talked and talked for years about my work, trying to sell albums and concert seats while the interviewers strove to sell magazines. Most of it is all drivel and of absolutely no consequence.

Sing the song.

Tiles and Slabs
by Nigel Rolfe and C. Moore

A country artist making tiles
whilst on a grave slab sleeps a son
Wet clay dug from the earth
wet stone covering the ground
Earth that buried another mother
died dead and gone
And left a torn lonely boy
trying to re-confirm
Trying to re-connect
Trying to know himself
and to contact the country
Whilst the artist celebrates
Connects and confirms
Contacts the country
Knows herself
Tiles and slabs
woman and son
Take away
take a gun
Blow away the blow-in
Kill the mother kill the child in yourself
kill the pain
Kill the father kill the son and the Holy Ghost
kill the pain
Violence from an inner rage
buried in the country

I arrived in Tulla, Co. Clare in 1964 to be relief cashier in The National Bank. Here I encountered music and song and beauty and madness. The work was easy and the hours were short and the money was good. It was a learning time for the life ahead.

Thirty years later I returned there with Nigel Rolfe and we spent a day traversing the hills and back roads of East Clare. We bought bread and cheese in the Co-Op in Scariff and we were moved by the mountains and forests and wild beauty.

Only weeks later, the terrible truth was known of the shocking events of murder and terror that shattered the quiet of East Clare and the whole country. It was that kind of murder that appals us most for there is no apparent motive nor understanding, and suddenly we realise that we are all vulnerable.

Imelda Riney and her child Liam and a local curate, Fr Joe Walsh, were brutally slain in the beautiful hills of East Clare. Brendan O'Donnell, a local lad, was eventually captured, charged and found guilty of their murders. He subsequently died in prison.

I've heard it whispered 'They should be shot,' or 'That fucker should be taken out,' or 'We shouldn't have to put up with this,' or 'Shoot the bastards', and some unfortunate disturbed person hears the whisper and it grows into a screaming tormented order in the mind and he goes out and does it.

This poor song passed almost unnoticed in the night. One London journalist, Colin Randall of *The Daily Telegraph* commented upon 'Tiles and Slabs' and the terrible events in East Clare. I performed it on Donal Lunny's *Sult* programme for Telefís na Gaeilge and apart from that I've not yet found a suitable platform for its live performance. It is a song that will never leave me, for it is too deeply engraved upon the mind's set list.

Rory Is Gone (A tribute to Rory Gallagher)
by Nigel Rolfe and C. Moore

Rory is gone to play the blues in Heaven
Above the clouds with all the angels singing there
His record is scratched like his beaten-up old Fender
But the songs are strong and the notes hang in the air
Gone with Stevie Ray and Jessie Ed. David
Died too young and much too premature
Another rock and roller's gone but not forgotten
As his old guitar still mourns and plays and wails and screams the blues

Sings for Mississippi Fred and Muddy Waters
Sunhouse, Sleepy John and the Nighthawk, too
Blacks Whites Blues and Greens, all the colours mixed together
Since Rory's gone to Heaven, since Rory has gone to Heaven, to play the blues

Rory's gone to play the blues in Heaven
Rory's gone to Heaven to play the blues

I saw Rory play in The Carlton, Dublin in 1973, the National Stadium, The Gaiety and in Glasgow, and met him maybe half a dozen times. He was a wonderful musician and a quiet, gentle man.

He would pull on his guitar and once the music started the shyness would become invisible. He would appear to light up, to walk, talk, strut and nut the music. He could make us laugh and cry and love him and send us home sweating and laughing, but where did he go as we rolled down the South Circular Road?

I was always drawn towards him, yet when I got there I never knew what to say. We would both be embarrassed. Once, backstage at a festival in Glasgow, I saw him from my caravan. He was standing outside his and he looked so lost, so lonely, surrounded by excited fans he tried so hard to be polite and nice – all I could see was pain. I stood to try and talk to him but I began to feel uncomfortable and voyeuristic so I split. We never met again.

I have been so blessed to escape from that prison of loneliness, that being ill-at-ease. Today I feel perhaps I know what Rory sometimes felt, but I was unable to share it with him, just as many were unable to share it with me until I was ready and willing to receive.

I think Nigel Rolfe's lyrics are a fitting tribute to this lovely man.

Riding the High Stool
by C. Moore

I was riding the high stool expanding and expounding
On the price of rice in Sierra Leone and the height of the beef mountain
As to where did Jack Doyle meet Movita how many wives did the Aga Khan
Until dismounting from my high horse I couldn't find the handle of the bar-room door

You see I knew it all then up against the counter I'd weigh you up in ten seconds flat
You see I was a great judge of character instinctively I knew exactly what kind of guy I'd met
Until I turned to go that is
Whereupon I couldn't tell me arse from my well-bent elbow

I was heading down the streets of Laredo singing Red Sails in the Sunset
Sure it was no wonder that we knew it all then
'Twas like drinkin porter off a sore leg said Ber Murphy
Would ye ever ask me bollix said Kathy Barry
And I showed her the colour of me money
When I got back from Katanga
There's no business like show business said Titch Maher in Flood's Bar
After snagging turnips for the Bishop and the Holy Father
But after it got dark, much later
Down by the Pinkeen Bridge I cried buckets in the river
When Mixer sang oh! gentle swallow

For knowing it all is a lonely place to be
Yet still I found it very hard to say
Hey man, this load is all too much for me
Until I was completely terrified whereupon a lightship came upon my way
And caught me up into its beam
Before I went under yet again
For the very last time

I was riding the high stool expanding and expounding
Swimming in the wine lake and climbing the beef mountain

This is a song about many different times in my life. But most of all it's about coming out of the dark into the light to discover the power and great healing capacity of love. To learn about the strength to be gleaned from comradeship and that one need not always be alone, forever alone, in the darkness of addiction. The comradeship of addiction is indeed a shallow one. True friendship cannot be based upon substance, but only upon the power of love and caring.

Many old friends are featured in these verses.

I first met Richie Crosby on Good Friday 1991. He was trying to keep warm, to stay alive. He was looking for the price of a smoke and a bottle of gas to keep his hut warm. He lived in a priest's garden where the good man let him use a timber hut. Richie helped many men to get sober and to join the mainstream of life again, but he could never achieve continuous sobriety himself. He succumbed to his demons in 1996. He died alone in a cold park on an icy February night. The heat from his last bottle did not sustain him until morning. I will never forget Richie Crosby and he was the inspiration for this song.

Ber Murphy was a (retired) cattle drover who also played harmonica and could sing a song or two to gain wet for his whistle. Him and I left the Kildare bus at Rathcoole one evening in the Sixties. God only knows how we made it back to Newbridge, but Ber had his Hohner and Christy had his banjo.

Titch Maher was a gentle man from the other end of the town who always had a friendly word for me and I'll always remember him for that. 'Mixer' is Jimmy Reid from Páirc Mhuire who was my favourite singer in teenage times. Manys the recital we gave down by the river when the pubs were closed and the town was deep in slumber. Mixer and I and our old pal Billy Parkinson would lie on the banks of the Liffey where we'd sing our hearts out until all the cider was gone.

Minds Locked Shut
by C. Moore

It happened on a Sunday afternoon
On a lovely bright crisp winter's afternoon
On a perfect day
On a perfect day for walking

There was gunshots stones and bullets
On a lovely bright crisp winter's afternoon
There was chaos panic and death
Disbelief upon the faces
Fear and bewilderment
Seconds seemed so long
They're firing bullets at us
It was not supposed to be like this
Awesome to behold
And then our minds locked shut
And then our minds locked shut
And then our minds locked shut
And then our minds locked shut
And there remains
Jackie Duddy Willy Nash
Gerry Donaghy Willie McKinney
Gerald McKinney Jim Wray
Johnny Johnston Barney McGuigan
Paddy Doherty Kevin McIlhenny
John Young Micky Kelly
Hugh Gilmore Michael McDaid

Let us remember

It happened on a Sunday afternoon
On a lovely bright crisp winter's afternoon
On a perfect day
On a perfect day for walking

Twenty-five years on and Paddy Mayhew states that it would be wrong to apologise. I went over to England to tour when the Widgery Report came out and I was shocked by the number of English people who believed that the fourteen shot dead on Bloody Sunday were IRA men.

Once our minds lock shut it can take too much to prise them open again. But a little effort might help rather than continuing to heap scorn upon us.

This neighbouring island of ours is inhabited by our closest brothers and sisters, the vast majority of whom bid us nothing but goodwill and friendship, but a small minority of whom treat us as if they deem us to be an inferior people. They do not reserve their upturned noses for the Irish – they also heap scorn upon many sectors of British society. The irony of it all is that there are pockets of them still lording and lodging around Ireland – pomping with aristocratic British ideals, sending their children to England for education and elocution and still holding lands taken by force and awarded to their forefathers for foul deeds in far-off colonies.

By this time the land is theirs. But if only they'd spare us the Lord and Lady shite. We all know how they came by land and privilege – through fraud and coercion and violence and murder.

So, Sir Algernon Mucksavage-Smythe, less of the airs on your old melodeon please.

The Banks of the Lee
Author unknown

When two lovers meet down beside the green ocean
When two lovers meet beneath the green tree
And Mary my fond Mary to her love she is declaring
You have stolen away my young heart from the banks of the Lee

I loved her dearly both true and sincerely
There is no-one in this wide world I loved so much as she
Every bush, every bower, every wild Irish flower
It reminds me of my Mary on the banks of the Lee

So I will pluck my love some roses some wild Irish roses
So I will pluck my love some roses the fairest that ever grew
And I will place them on the mound of my own darling true love
In that cold and silent valley where she lies beneath the dew

Here is a song that has a powerful spirit of its own. When I sing it I am transcended to another place. I know these lovers, I am these lovers. I know exactly where the tree is and I taste the ocean, I am dampened by the dew and I ache with the sorrow, I hold these lovers in my arms and, in turn, I whisper in their ears and share their whiskey. No matter where the water laps upon the shore, the song is placed the same, in the heart and in the mind.

I believe this to be an incomplete version of the song. I first heard Andy Rynne sing it in The Union Tavern, Congleton, Cheshire on a Monday night in August 1967. It was hot and steamy in a cramped and crowded folk club. I was mixing cider and whiskey and I was wild out. Yet when he sang this he chilled the blood in my veins. I fell in love with a dream song.

I managed to record some of the song on *Traveller* in 1999. I want to record it in full, but I cannot find a setting. In the past I have recorded some favourite songs in settings that were far less than suitable, and there are songs that may be impossible to record for their simple beauty and spirit can be tainted by the recording process. The spirit of certain songs will react to the process of recording, like a flower at night or a startled snail they will hide away their beauty.

The Yellow Bittern
by Cathal Buí Mac Giolla Gunna (died 1750)

translated by Thomas McDonagh (died 1916)

(This incomplete version I learned from Andy Rynne of Prosperous, Co. Kildare. There are many translations, the original being in four verses. The bittern is a great bird, now extinct in Ireland. The corncrake is no longer a common bird.)

The yellow bittern that never broke out on a drinking bout he might as well have done
For his bones are thrown on a naked stone where he lived alone like a hermit monk
Oh yellow bittern I pity your case, tho they say that a suck like myself is cursed
I was sober for a while now I'll drink and I'll be wise for fear that I might die in the end of thirst

It is not for the common bird that I would mourn, the corncrake the blackbird or the crane
But for the bittern who is shy (like this poet) and who lives in the quiet of a dark bog drain
Oh had I known you were so near your death with my breath held I'd have run to you
Until I had cracked the ice in your favourite drinking place and stirred your heart to life anew

My darling she tells me do not drink any more or your life it will be over in a little while
But I told her it was the drink gave me health and strength and could lengthen my road for manys the mile
See that bird of the long smooth neck who has got his death from the thirst at last
Come soothe my soul come fill my bowl for I'll get no more drink when my life is past

I was white-knuckle sober. I had come through the first month heavily Valium assisted and after a period of weaning down I'd achieved a 24-hour period without drink. The achievement, however, was so hard gained and so dominant in my thoughts that it was of little use for my mind and body ached for the comfort I thought a drink would bring. I continued, Valium forever in my pocket, on my unmerry way – a martyr to the cause. I would need a good reason if I was to ever drink again and, as always, it's easy to find a good reason if we look hard enough and want badly enough.

Jesus Christ will you look at that poor creature of a bird – oh you rare and beautiful thing to die at your frozen drinking hole, all alone and unnoticed in the beauty of a frozen bog. Christ, had I known I'd have come to you and cracked the icy pool for you to drink and drink and to stay alive. Christ almighty, what good is this so-called life of sobriety when I'm confronted daily by such calamities as this. Give me drink before I die – let me drink freely from comfort's cup and feel the juice slide down my neck to warm my belly and numb my pain.

The Cliffs of Dooneen
Author unknown

You may travel far far from your own native home
Far away o'er the mountains far away o'er the foam
But of all the fine places that I've ever seen
There is none to compare with the Cliffs of Dooneen

Take a view o'er the mountains fine sights you'll see there
You'll see the high Rocky Mountains on the west coast of Clare
The towns of Kilkee and Kilrush can be seen
From the high rocky slopes of the Cliffs of Dooneen

It's a nice place to be on a fine summer's day
Watching all the wild flowers that ne'er do decay
The hare and lofty pheasant are plain to be seen
Making homes for their young around the Cliffs of Dooneen

Fare thee well to Donneen fare thee well for awhile
And to all the fine people I'm leaving behind
To the streams and the meadows where late I have been
And the high rocky slopes of the Cliffs of Dooneen

In Mercury and Mars they love this song. It just goes straight in and does the job. Try and analyse this song and it is pretty plain and simple. A million songs have been written in this category but they don't have the magic ingredient. Early on I heard it sung by Mick McGuane, Ann Mulqueen and Andy Rynne, but I took it and ran with it and made it my own. Every now and then it comes up of a night and never fails to touch.

Mick McGuane was a punk whistle player before Johnny Lydon had hair, and he used to sing a verse about 'dancehalls and cinemas' which I cannot find. Anne Mulqueen used to sing it in a Sean Nós style while Andy Rynne used to do a right job of it in the back of O'Donohue's or in Pat Dowling's of a Wednesday night. But don't go there looking for the magic, it has flown on the wind to calmer quarters. I remember the time when most pub owners would expel a person for life for singing a verse of a song. Now it's almost impossible to find an Irish pub that has not got some karaoke folk group oozing insincerity and forcing unfortunate customers to drink more to kill the pain.

As for Germany, Japan, France, Taiwan and the United Kingdom of Britain, England, Scotland and Wales – every street has an authentic Irish pub with plastic woodworm and a Celtic Tiger growling behind the counter. Now if only a fellow could convince the Blessed Virgin to appear – that would fairly get the statues moving . . .

Give us four pints there Mary, and whatever you're having yourself.

The Dark End of the Street
by Chuck Moman and Dan Penn

At the dark end of the street
That's where we always meet
Hiding in shadows where we don't belong
Living in darkness to hide our wrong
You and me

Time is going to take its toll
We'll have to pay for the love we stole
It's a sin and they say that it's wrong
Oh but our love has grown so strong

And when the daylight comes around
And by chance we're both down town
If we should meet, pass on by, hush little baby and don't you cry
Tonight we'll meet at the dark end of the street
You and me

Let's get out of sight to be together in our love, our guilt, our shame or whatever it is that separates us from those who look at us. Down dark lanes, under bridges, into deserted building sites to huddle together for warmth, to hide away for safety. Let us retreat from the gaze of the righteous.

I made a film once – it is called *Christy* and it has been shown in a few countries around the world. Philip King and Nuala O'Connor directed and produced it and the cinematographer was Declan Quinn. It was a good project for me and I particularly enjoyed performing this song with Keith Donald – we filmed it in The Baggot Inn. I've sung this song occasionally and it invariably stills the room. I live a three-minute life when I sing Dan Penn's words, and it feels like the audience sees the images that I dream.

Johnny Jump Up
From Jimmy Crowley circa 1973

I'll tell you a story that happened to me
one day as I went down to Youghal by the sea
The sun it was high and the day it was warm
says I an auld pint wouldn't do me no harm

I went in and I called for a bottle of stout
says the barman I'm sorry all the beer is sold out
Try whiskey or Paddy ten years in the wood
says I I'll try cider I've heard that it's good

O never O never O never again
If I live to a hundred or a hundred and ten
For I fell to the floor and couldn't get up
after drinking a pint of old Johnny Jump Up

After drinkin a quart I went out to the yard
where I met up with Brophy the big local guard
Come here to me boy don't you know I'm the law
so I jumped up on the counter and kissed him on the jaw

We fell to the floor and we couldn't get up
but it wasn't I kissed him 'twas the Johnny Jump Up
And the next thing I met down in Youghal by the sea
was a poor man on crutches and says he to me

I'm afraid of me life I'll get hit by a car
would you help me across to the Railwayman's Bar
After drinkin a pint of that cider so sweet
he threw down his crutches and danced round on his feet

A man died in the union by the name of McNab
they washed him and shaved him and laid him right out on the slab
And after the undertaker his measurements did take
his wife brought him home to a very fine wake

It was about twelve o'clock and the beer it was high
the corpse he sat up and says he with a sigh
I can't get to Heaven for they won't let me up
till I bring them a drink of old Johnny Jump Up

O never O never O never again
If I live to a hundred or a hundred and ten
For I fell to the floor and couldn't get up
after drinking a pint of old Johnny Jump Up

I've been singing occasionally with Jimmy Crowley since 1976 or so. We've shared manys the song in pubs and clubs along the way. He sang this song to me at the Sherkin Island Festival; I was only after a glass of poitín and a mushroom sandwich. The Bothy Band were on the island with De Danaan and Clannad and the Island House was bursting at the seams. Natie Comerford was in residence and Seamus Creagh had set up camp on the front lawn. Power lines to the island were severed by some wanker yachtie, but we cared little for the alcohol and drugs had us all well lit up and Norman King kept the show running like a human generator.

It lasted for seven days and seven nights and it was only a one-day festival. A local fast-food baron shipped 1,000 fried chickens to the island, but we were all vegetarians and the magic mushrooms had played havoc with the diet. I spent a night looking at luminous marine life, but when I awoke I was in a field untouched by water. That festival was in 1978 and some people are still trying to get off the island.

O never, O never, O never again.

Tony Trout was 5'6" with his hands up. I was seventeen stone at the time – the porter was bulging out both of my eyes as I lay motionless and happy in a deep ditch. That fine hero of England, God rest him, hoisted me out of the drain, up on to his blessed Cockney back and hauled me across the island to my couch.

O never, O never, O never again.

Tippin' It Up to Nancy
From the singing of John Reilly

There being a woman in our town, a woman you all know well
She dearly loved her husband and another man twice as well

With me right finnigan eerio me tip finnig a wall
With me right finnigan eerio tippin' it up to Nancy

She went down to the chemist shop some remedies for to find
Have you anything in your chemist shop to make me aul man blind

Give him eggs and marrowbones and make him suck them all
And before he has the last one sucked he won't see you at all

So she gave him eggs and marrowbones and made him suck them all
And before he had the last one sucked he couldn't see her at all

If in this world I cannot see here I cannot stay
I'd rather go and drown myself c'mon says she and I'll show you the way

She led him to the river and she led him to the brin
Sly enough of Martin it was him that shoved her in

She swam through the river and she swam through the brin
Martin dear Martin don't leave me behind
Yerra shut up outa that ye silly aul fool ye know poor Martin is blind
With me right Finnegan eerio we're tippin' it up to Nancy

I've nine in me family and none of them is me own
I wish that each and every man would come and claim his own

I took off down the road just to escape from whatever it was that was driving me loopy. Some very weird intangible piece of information tucked away into the false memory led me to a dark pub in a grey town. All that's needed is some inane contact to get the show on the road. Soon the company of mad fuckers begins to gather and when the rituals are dispensed the lunatics are bunched together as if from the same cradle. Nothing matters. My world could not survive without the loyal friendship of this mad hure beside me who I'd never laid eyes upon before, whose name or town I cannot now recall – only that I met legions of them. Men who'd die for you so long as drink was in the equation. Women whose beauty was bedazzling so long as there was drink to be taken.

A time of darkness and despair amongst the hurt and suffering.

Sometimes in my wild dreaming I find myself lurking around the entrances of those cul-de-sacs – sleeping rough in Great Yarmouth, Manchester, London, with me right finnigan eerio me tip finnig a wall.

The Sun Is Burning in the Sky
by Ian Campbell

The sun is burning in the sky
Strands of clouds go slowly drifting by
In the park the dreamy bees are droning in the flowers among the trees
And the sun is burning in the sky

Now the sun is in the west
Little babes lay down to take their rest
And the couples in the park are holding hands and waiting for the dark
And the sun is in the west

Now the sun is sinking low
Children playing knowing it's time to go
High above, a spot appears a little blossom blooms and then draws near
And the sun is sinking low

Now the sun has come to earth
Shrouded in a mushroom cloud of death
Death comes in a blinding flash of hellish heat and leaves a smear of ash
And the sun has come to earth

Now the sun has disappeared
All that's left is darkness pain and fear
Twisted sightless wrecks of men go crawling on their knees and cry in pain
And the sun has disappeared

The Jug of Punch folk club in Digbeth, Birmingham was one I wanted to play, for to appear there would look good on my CV. The Singers Club, the Trocadero and Les Cousins in London, The MSG in Manchester, The Glasgow Folk Centre, The Byre in St Andrews, The Topic in Bradford, The Grove in Leeds, Watersons in Hull – all these clubs were recognised as front runners in the development of the UK folk revival.

About 1968 I finally got booked for the Jug in Digbeth. The resident band was The Ian Campbell Group and what a fine band it was. Polished but raw, with two great singers in Ian and Lorna and a fine backing group. I was billeted with Ian's parents Dave and Winnie, where I first sampled haggis and turnip and malt whiskey. I also got introduced to a number of Communist Party members, some of whom remained friends for many years. Two of Ian Campbell's songs entered my repertoire. This one, and 'The Old Man's Song'. I still see him occasionally.

Across my years I've come across many different shades of politics. Early on, I encountered Republicanism from my grandmother Ellie Power, and as a young boy I saw and heard the whole Fine Gael way of doing things. In my teens I began to get a handle on the Fine Gael–Fianna Fáil debate, and then in England I began to meet Trotsksyists, Marxists, British Labour, Communists, Tories and Liberals. And if that was not enough, I then met up with Provos and Stickies, PDs and SDLPs. In all my years of travelling I never met any group to talk like British Communist Party members. They'd talk the hind legs off an ass for days on end, in a language of their own and very difficult to comprehend. They were full of wordy idealism.

This is a powerful song. I recorded it on *The Iron Behind the Velvet* album in 1978 and on the 'Anti-Nuclear' twelve-inch single in 1978.

I can recall some memorable renditions. On the Sunday after the Le Mons bomb in Belfast, I performed it in Buncrana and the song took on a very definite Irish significance and the room was raw at the end of it. On the fiftieth anniversary of Hiroshima I sang it on Merrion Square to a small group of people that included the Japanese ambassador, but not the American ambassador who failed to attend.

Scapegoats
by E. Cowan and C. Moore

There was five men playing poker on the Heysham train
Fate was dealing them a cruel hand
Hugh Callaghan was walking home through the evening rain
Not knowin what lay in store for him

You'll find traces of nitro on cigarettes and matches
On formica table tops and on decks of playing cards
When forensic found traces on the hands of these six men
The police drove up from Birmingham thinking the case was closed

Have you ever seen the mugshots that were taken
After forty-eight hours in custody
Battered and bruised, haunted looks upon the faces
The judge accepted they confessed willingly, please take another look at what you see

If you tell me my family are being terrorised
Keep me awake six days and nights confused and terrified
In the lonely dark of night, I'll swear that black is white
If you'll let me just lie down and close my eyes
I'll sign anything if you'll let me close my eyes

Scales of justice, balance up your act
Am I talking to myself or to the wall
Hugh Callaghan, Paddy Hill, Gerry Hunter, Johnny Walker, Billy Power, Dick McIlKenny, scapegoats all
For sixteen years they were talking to the wall

Men and women were stopped and questioned and harassed by Special Police in Dublin because of their involvement in the movement to free the six men framed for the IRA bombs in Birmingham.

The horror of bombing a city-centre pub is incomprehensible to anyone, like myself, who has not witnessed the atrocity of it all. The English people have suffered greatly from civilian bombing, as indeed have millions of Europeans from the bombing raids on Dresden, Hamburg, Brest, Le Havre, Dublin, Monaghan, Enniskillen, Omagh, the list is endless. Civilians blown to pieces in the name of a 'just' war.

It is too easy for the innocents to get caught up in war. Australian tourists in Germany, children in Warrington, those shot dead because they looked like off-duty soldiers, the others killed because they walked an English street of an afternoon. Children killed with rubber and plastic bullets in Belfast, Aiden Mac An Easpaig going to a match, six men murdered in Loughin Island for looking at Jack's army. It goes on and on.

The West Midlands Police Force had a job to do and they were determined to do it. They wanted arrests and neither ethics, the truth, the innocent nor the guilty would be allowed to get in their way. Many blind eyes were turned in England and Ireland, and once they had secured six Irish men who fitted their requirements and forensic evidence which would comply with their needs, they went for it and got it.

Today the British establishment still disgraces itself by its innuendo and snide comments, be they about the Birmingham Six, the Guildford Four, Giuseppe Conlon or the Maguire family. A whispering campaign surfaces every now and then which forever tries to cover up the way these innocents were treated.

The Limerick Rake
Author unknown

I'm a young fellow that's easy and bold
in Castletownconnors I'm very well known
In Newcastle West I spend manys the pound note
with Kitty and Judy and Mary
My parents rebuked me for being such a rake
and for spending my time in such frolicsome ways
But I never could forget the good nature of Jane Agus Fágaimíd siúd mar atá sé

My parents had taught me to shake and to sow
to plough and to harrow to reap and to mow
My mind being too airy to leave it so low
I went out in high speculation
On parchment and paper they taught me to write
and in Euclid and grammar they opened my eyes
In multiplications in truth I was bright Agus Fágaimíd siúd mar atá sé

If I happen to go to the town of Rathkeale
all the girls there around me do flock on the square
Some give me the bottle and others sweet cake
to treat me unknown to their parents
There's one from Askeaton and one from the Pike
and another from Ardagh my heart has beguiled
Being from the mountains her stockings are white Agus Fágaimíd siúd mar atá sé

If I happen to go the Market of Croom
with a cock in my hat and my pipes in full tune
I'm made welcome at once and brought up to a room
Where Bacchus is sporting with Venus
There's Biddy and Jane from the town of Bruree
Mary from Bruff and we're all on a spree
Such a combing of locks as there was about me Agus Fágaimíd siúd mar atá sé

To quarrel for riches I ne'er was inclined
for the greatest of misers must leave them behind
I'll get a cow that will never run dry
and I'll milk her by twisting her horns

John Damer of Shronel had plenty of gold
and Devonshire's treasure was twenty times more
Now they're on their backs amid nettles and stones Agus Fágaimíd siúd mar atá sé

There's some say I'm foolish and more say I'm wise
but being fond of women I think is no crime
For the son of King David had ten hundred wives
and his wisdom was highly recorded
I'll till a good garden and live at my ease
and each woman and child can partake of the same
If there's war in the cabin themselves they might blame Agus Fágaimíd siúd mar atá sé

And now for the future I mean to be wise
I'll send for those women who acted so kind
And I'll marry them all on the morrow by and by
if the clergy will agree to the bargain
When I'm on my back and my soul is at peace
these women will crowd for to cry at my wake
Their sons and their daughters will offer a prayer to the Lord for the soul of their father

1965. I was gazing out of the window of the National Bank in Askeaton, Co. Limerick. I was trying to ignore the manager as I gazed at the Sheehan girls – long-legged, black-haired, beautiful women forever ambling across the sleepy square. Beyond them stood Mai Collins' dark and beckoning pub where I'd slide in after dark for a large bottle and a game of cards and some nights I'd bring my box and forget for a while that I was a bank clerk.

My first digs in Askeaton were hard living – the woman of the house loved whiskey and was a lonely house-drinking widow. I liked her but it became impossible to stay, so I moved to Mrs Nolan who was a great baker and cook and took great care of myself and one other lodger. He had a record player and through his two Joan Baez records I fell in love with her voice and songs in 1964. As a result of my pub chanting I got asked to sing in the George Hotel, Limerick for a bunch of visiting Americans. I tried out my big numbers – 'Follow Me up to Carlow', 'Curragh of Kildare', 'Mary from Dungloe'. But they were restless for 'Bing Crosby' and 'Leprechauns in Galway Bay', so I left never more to return to the tourist Irish cabaret circuit (not yet, anyway).

Back at the day job, life continued. I learned how to match my manager's ignorance and bullying by ignoring him completely until, eventually, he called an inspector down from head office to deal with his non-compliant teller. But the inspector was quite sympathetic to my plight and I was moved on to Ballyhaunis, Co. Mayo, without a reprimand or penalty. The manager was retired shortly afterwards.

In many ways this song reflects the way my life was in 1964. I came across it in Colm O'Lochlainn's collection. His songs were the basis for many a balladeer's repertoire, although this was seldom acknowledged. It was always sexier to maintain that a song was learned from a sailor in Tierra del Fuego than from a book in bed.

As I Roved Out
Author unknown

Then who are who my pretty fair maid
and who are you my honey
Then who are who my pretty fair maid
and who are you my honey
She answered me quite modestly
I am me mother's darling

With me tooria foldediddle dan diary fole de diddle dairy o

Will you come to my mammy's house
when the moon is shinin clearly
I'll open the door and I'll let you in
and divil the one will hear us

So I went to her house in the middle of the
night when the moon was shinin clearly
She opened the door and she let me in
and divil the one did hear us

She took me by the lily white hand
and led me to the table
Sayin there's plenty of wine for a soldier boy
So drink it if you're able

She took my horse by the bridle and the bit
And she led him to the stable
Sayin there's plenty of oaths for a soldier's horse
ate it if you're able

Then she got up and she made the bed
and she made it nice and aisy
Then she rolled up the eiderdown
sayin soldier are you able

There we lay till the break of the day
and divil the one did hear us

Then I arose and pulled on me cap
saying darlin I must leave you

When will you return again
and when might we get married
When broken shells make Christmas bells
We might well get married

We were in the back of Mick Curran's Fleadh Express Bedford van. There was a trap door for watching the tarmac, and if things got claustrophobic you could always ride up on the roof rack for a spell. There was Mick, Donal, Francis, Tex, Brendan, Sean, Andy, Davoc, Óg and Peter around that day and we struck out for Boyle, Co. Roscommon for to fleadh for the Easter. Sally had come from Richmond in Surrey to visit Éire, and ended up on the floor of a railway freight carriage half full of black turf with Anne, Bridget and Catherine. We had two guitars and three tin whistles, one flute and a few dozen songs between us. Not a heap of money, either. The heavens opened and we were drenched and broke and miserable but young and in love with life.

There were two women in the corner of Grehan's pub, exotic moths dressed entirely in black drinking tumblers of raw whiskey and smoking Players full-strength. I'd never seen the like before and I've known them ever since and they're still as mad as then – slightly fading exotics. John Reilly sang 'Lord Baker' and purred as he paused every three verses to silk his throat with porter as he basked shyly in his new-found acclaim. Tony Grehan did tricks with the sweeping brush and his sisters silenced the pub with 'On the Galteemore Mountain So Far, Far Away'. We all fell in love and then fell around the place gambolling in the dark, fumbling and flustering in the early hours of the Sunday morning trying to get comfortable amid the turf and empty bottles, chattering, freezing and laughing manically for the jokes seemed so funny, and the crankiness of the lovemakers as they realised that the waggoners would never sleep and that their love could not be made. Andy Rynne sang this song maybe six times a night over the weekend and I've never been able to forget it since.

Returning from Fleadanna the music would resound in my head for days, echoing farther and farther away until, by Thursday, all that was left was a distant 'Dingle Regatta' on the old Clarke's whistle.

Row dill dum dee dil, row dill dum dee dill, rowdle dum dowlde dum diddle dum dee, and it was time to count the shillings again and tune up the box and take the road for Portarlington where I learned 'The Streams of Bunclody' in a hayshed that had a friendly pig and I bought a guitar from Ned Bulfin for £3 and Ructions Doyle tried to take it off me but Tommy McLoughlin said, 'Leave the chap alone, he's not doing any harm.'

Sweet Thames Flow Softly
by Ewan McColl

I met my love near Woolwich Pier beneath the big crane standing
And all the love I felt for her it passed all understanding
Took her sailing on the river flow, sweet river, flow
London town was mine to give her sweet Thames flow softly
Made the Thames into a crown flow, sweet river, flow
Made a brooch of silver town sweet Thames flow softly

At London yard I held her hand at Blackwall Point I faced her
At the Isle of Dogs I kissed her mouth and tenderly embraced her
Heard the bells of Greenwich ringing flow, sweet river, flow
All the time my heart was singing sweet Thames, flow softly
Limehouse Reach I gave her there flow, sweet river, flow
As a ribbon for her hair sweet Thames flow softly

From Shadwell Dock to Nine Elms Reach we cheek to cheek were dancing
Her necklace made of London Bridge her beauty was enhancing
Kissed her once again at Wapping flow, sweet river, flow
After that there was no stopping sweet Thames, flow softly
Gave her Hampton Court to twist flow, sweet river, flow
Into a bracelet for her wrist sweet Thames, flow softly

From Rotherhithe to Putney Bridge me love I was declaring
And she from Kew to Isleworth her love for me was swearing
Love it set me heart a-burning flow, sweet river, flow
Never saw the tide was turning sweet Thames flow softly
Gave her Hampton Court to twist flow, sweet river, flow
Into a bracelet for her wrist sweet Thames flow softly

But now alas the tide has changed my love she has gone from me
And winter's frost has touched my heart and put a blight upon me
Creeping fog is on the river flow, sweet river, flow
Sun and moon and stars gone with her sweet Thames flow softly
Swift the Thames flows to the sea flow, sweet river, flow
Bearing ships and part of me sweet Thames flows softly

Jack and Mavis ran a folk club in the Kingsway Hotel near Rochdale and I was the guest. My fee was £4 and the year was 1967. When my gig ended I was lorrying into a gansey of Thwaites ale when I met a quietly spoken Mancunian from Chadderton called Derek McEwan. He offered me a deal. I would move into his place in Rochdale where he ran a fish and veggie shop on Oldham Road. He gave me a three-sided bedroom and I drove a green-grocer's van around the estates of East Manchester. He also became my agent and friend and we lived a shambolic life together for two years. I'd get into Manchester market early and load up. Then back to the shop in Rochdale where I'd unload and re-pack the van for my housewives who were waiting for their spuds and whiting. I'd be back in Rochdale by midday when I'd clean up and go into the Morning Star, Oldham Road, for a gallon of ale and a game of dominoes. Come evening, Derek and I would scour the clubs of Lancashire trying to further my singing career (primary purpose) and meet as many women as we could (close second).

Derek got married once during our time together and had his reception in a Chinese restaurant in Middleton. I was his best man and he had a whip round to pay for the meal afterwards. We also drank his celery wine, which was a sober do for the brew was awful. Derek and I lingered in Rochdale for three months, but the bottom fell out of the vegetable van and we moved over the Pennines to Halifax. We travelled by night at speed. I learned this Ewan McColl song during this time. Derek had an eclectic record collection and this song was from one of McColl's radio ballads.

McColl's songs have always been far more popular in Ireland than in Britain. Across the water he would have been recognised as a radical artist and would be well known in various circles. But in Ireland, his work has been absorbed into the mainstream national repertoire. Many people would know 'Travelling People', 'Shoals of Herring', 'Go, Move, Shift', 'Dirty Old Town' without knowing or caring who wrote them.

When I recorded this song with Planxty in 1971 it was a minor hit. The Uileann pipes and harmonic sounded beautiful together and McColl's description of the Thames as a simile for love won many listeners' hearts.

Wave Up to the Shore
by Barry Moore

A daffodil is born and rises in the spring
It opens out its beauty to hear the cricket sing
But as quick as it does grow it decays away so soon
Before the summer sunshine has reached its golden noon

A stream it does rise in the mountains so tall
It swells into a river as gently it does fall
It meanders through country through city and through town
And in the boundless ocean the river it is drowned

On the seas the winds do rage and the waves grow so high
As they turn into white horses leaping towards the sky
But soon the waves grow gentle no longer do they roar
As they make their lonesome passage way up to the pebble shore

If I were like a daffodil so fair upon the ground
Or like a gentle river with its sweet and mellow sound
Like a wave up to the shore like a river into the sea
I'd lay down in my resting place contented I would be

When my brother recorded his first album *Treaty Stone* he asked me to produce it. Subsequent to that we have worked together on a number of recordings, both his and mine. Most recently we did a single together, a song of Barry's called 'Bogman': 'I'm a bogman, deep down, that's where I come from.' Occasionally we play together on stage and, when it happens, it is always spontaneous and I always feel really good doing it. At Carnsore Point we played until dawn, at Mother Redcap's I played bowrawn on 'I Need Love', at the Moorefield Club we did 'The Curragh of Kildare' at a Nancy Moore memorial concert that was also a benefit gig for Kildare Homeless. I also recall a wonderful night with the Centre for Independent Living, when we played together in the Royal Hotel amongst all our friends from the project.

It is strange for both of us, being brothers and doing the same thing. There have been times when it has been difficult, but the good times more than make up for any problems.

I've gained many listeners in Germany, Holland and America who come along to hear Luka's brother, and I'm sure it works both ways.

This is one of Barry's very early compositions. I recorded it in 1975.

Lanigan's Ball
Author unknown

In the town of Athy one Jeremy Lanigan
battered away till he hadn't a shillin
His father died and made him a man again
left him a farm and ten acres of ground
Myself to be sure got invitations
for the boys and girls I might ask
Being asked friends and relations
danced like bees around a sweet cask

There was lashins of drink wine for the ladies
Potatoes and cake there was bacon and tay
Nolans Dolans all the O'Gradys
courtin the girls and dancing away
Songs went round as plenty as water
the harp that once sounded thro Tara's auld hall
Nellie Gray and the ratcatcher's daughter
singin together at Lanigan's Ball

Six long months I spent in Dublin
six long months doin nothing at all
Six long months I spent in Dublin
learning to dance for Lanigan's Ball
She stepped out and I stepped in again
I stepped out and she stepped in again
She stepped out and I stepped in again
learning to dance for Lanigan's Ball

They were doin all kinds of nonsensical dances
All around in a whirligig gig
Julie and I soon banished their nonsense
out on the floor for a reel and a jig
How the boys they all got mad at me
for they thought the ceilings would fall
I'd spent six months at Brooks Academy
learning to dance for Lanigan's Ball

The boys were merry the girls all hearty
dancin around in their couples and groups

An accident happened Terence McCarthy
he put his boot through Miss Finnerty's hoops
She fell to the floor and cried holy murder
then sent for her brothers and gathered them all
Carmody swore he'd go no further
till he'd have revenge at Lanigan's Ball

Boys oh boys 'tis then there was ructions
I got a kick from Phelim McHugh
I replied to his introduction
kicked up a terrible hullabaloo
Moloney the piper was near gettin strangled
they leapt on his pipes bellows chanters and all
Boys and girls all got entangled
and that put an end to Lanigan's Ball

I was dwall-flunking with the Hull chapter of The Higglers. We were in an isolated field in the Beverly region of north-east Yorkshire. Dwall-flunking was a cross between tig, rounders, cricket and relivio and also involved gallons of ale. There was something quite pagan and nihilistic about this debauched field sport. Manic laughter, bearded, bellied, bra-less folkie alkies running debauched around the fields of Humberside – oh what a time we had. We had a wet cloth, a broomstick handle and a barrel of Cameron's Ale. I was in the midst of loving and lovable company. They shared everything with me, and ever since I've had a part of me lingering ghostlike around Humberside.

There was a ferry across the Humber which sold drink during the afternoons when pubs closed. Jim the Fish, Jo 90, Jules Pidd and myself put in a glorious afternoon going over and back, drinking rum and singing sea shanties. It was wild and it was funny and it was shocking. Other people were going about their daily lives, and to this day I can still recall their frightened looks as they encountered this bunch of young men drinking themselves stupid and laughing madly. At the time I did not know it but I was, of course, in the throes of early alcoholism. My life revolved around drink. I was starting to career out of control but I was able to do my work and, so long as I spent most of my time with like-minded people, the insanity of my drinking was less apparent to me.

There were great singers and songs in Hull. Mike Waterson taught me 'The Lakes of Ponchartrain' and 'Van Dieman's Land', and Brian and Sally Tozer taught me to dance to Led Zeppelin all night around the concrete pipes, and Ian Manuel sang Bothy ballads like 'Hymns to a Lost Time'. I used to sing 'Lanigan's Ball'.

Another night in the mid-Seventies I was crossing the Irish Sea homewards and I fell into the company of the singer Dermot O'Leary and his band The Bards. We sang heartily and quaffed mightily and Dermot and I were the last two left, for everyone fell by the wayside. We bonded on the high sea with brandy and song. He took a shine to 'Lanigan's Ball' and brought it home with him and subsequently topped the charts with his fine version of the song.

James Connolly
by Patrick Galvin

Where o where is our James Connolly
Where o where is that gallant man
He's gone to organise the union
That working men might yet be free

Then who then who will lead the van
Then who then who will lead the van
Who but our James Connolly
The hero of the working man

Who will carry high the burning flag
Who will carry high the burning flag
Who but our James Connolly all pale and wounded
Could carry high the burning flag

They carried him up to the jail
They carried him up to the jail
And they shot him down on a bright May morning
 And quickly laid him in his gore

Who mourns the death of this good man
Who mourns the death of this good man
Bury me down in your green garden
With union men on every side

They buried him down in yon green garden
With union men on every side
And they swore they would form a mighty union
Where Connolly's name would be memorised

13 May 1997

ast night I played in Southend-on-Sea. I had 685 people in an 1,800-seater.
It was a difficult night for I was not at ease with myself. The road crew was
not in top gear and I suspect there may have been a drinking session. At this

time I'm playing with Jimmy Faulkner and we are not as comfortable as we have been.

My audience are such good listeners. They are kind-hearted and they share my love of these songs and they recognise the music as being the kernel of our get-together. People of all ages and creeds and colours and persuasions join to hear their songs.

While these songs are in performance they belong to the air. No one cares who wrote them while I sing them, they belong to us collectively. Writers and publishers own copyright but the words are out there in the world vocabulary; where people think or speak, the words are floating back and forth. The notes that make the music are in cacophony everywhere, and sound is made from the first coo of a breast-fed babe to the last lonely whimper of a dying soldier.

Last night I saw the puzzled look on a young boy's face – he had come to hear 'The Shovel' or 'Joxer's trip to Stuttgart', and he was bemused by 'The Yellow Triangle'. Three women in the front row wished to hear 'Burning Times' and 'God Woman' and were confused by 'Lisdoonvarna' and 'Delirium Tremens'. This is a hard line to walk – some nights I find it so difficult to keep the ball at my feet. When I'm on song I am guided towards every nook and cranny of the hall, but when I'm off-key it can be a hard and lonely place to be.

I don't know where I first encountered 'James Connolly', but I had it long since recorded before I learned that it was written by Patrick Galvin, the Cork poet and writer. We have subsequently met.

I've heard Liam Weldon sing a version, and Eleanor McEvoy sang a great rendition at the unveiling of Connolly's statue outside Liberty Hall. I did a subsequent recording for an album celebrating 100 years of the Scottish Trades Union Council. The inclusion of this song caused anger among certain Scottish Trade Unionists who cared not that Connolly gave his life, living and dying, for all workers north, south, east and west. It was ironic uproar indeed, for Connolly was born in Edinburgh in 1869. He died in Kilmainham gaol in 1916, executed for his part in the Easter Rising.

The Curragh of Kildare
words by Robbie Burns, music unknown

The winter it is passed and the summer's come at last
And the birds they are singing in the trees
Their little hearts are glad but mine is very sad
For my true love is far away from me

And it's straight I will repair to the Curragh of Kildare
For it's there I'll find tidings of my dear

The rose upon the briar by the water running clear
Brings joy to the linnet and the bee
Their little hearts are blessed but mine is not at rest
For my true love is absent from me

A livery I'll wear and I'll comb back my hair
And in velvet so green I will appear
And it's straight I will repair to the Curragh of Kildare
For it's there I'll find tidings of my dear

All you who are in love and cannot it remove
I pity the pains that you endure
For experience lets me know that your hearts are full of woe
And a woe that no mortal can endure

Many have claimed both authorship and discovery of this beautiful Scottish ballad. Truth is it was probably written by Robbie Burns. In 1962 I discovered it in the Joyce collection. I brought it round to Donal Lunny and we worked in a chorus gleaned from the third and fourth line of verse three. If memory serves me, I gave the song to Mick Moloney in exchange for 'The Bleacher Lassie of Kelvinhaugh'. He subsequently recorded with The Johnstons and that wonderful version established the song in the national repertoire.

It was an earlier time. I was getting over the initial euphoria of my two-chord repertoire, 'Phelim Brady, the Bard of Armagh', 'The Jug of Punch' and 'Rosin the Bowe'. I was beginning to realise that there were songs beyond the ballad lounge, songs yet to be sung. I began to look for ballads that were lying dustily waiting to be rediscovered, tuned up and coaxed back to life. My new journey began to take me further afield and, one day, I discovered a book in the library in Newbridge – P.W. Joyce's collection of Irish music and songs. I gleaned a number of songs from this wonderful book – among them this jewel. This was back in 1962 and Donal Lunny and I worked it up into what it has become. Various ballad and folk bands have subsequently taken it to a million ears – one noted Irish singer even claimed to have written it, but Rabbie will ne'er be denied. Burns 'twas and Burns 'twill be.

P.S. I've just discovered that there is some doubt about Robbie Burns' authorship here. I can neither confirm nor deny at this time.

C.M. 10/11/99

Follow Me Up to Carlow
Author unknown

Lift McCahir Óg your face brooding o'er the old disgrace
That Black Fitzwilliam stormed your place and drove you to the fern
Grey said Victory was sure soon the firebrand he'd secure
Until he met at Glenmalure with Fiach MacHugh O'Byrne

Curse and swear Lord Kildare Fiach will do what Fiach will dare
Now Fitzwilliam have a care fallen is your star low
Up with Halbert out with sword on we'll go for by the Lord
Fiach MacHugh has given the word follow me up to Carlow

See the swords of Glen Imaal flashing o'er the English pale
See all the children of the Gael beneath O'Byrne's banners
Rooster of a fighting stock would you let a Saxon cock
Crow out upon an Irish rock fly up and teach him manners

From Tassaggart to Clonmore flows a stream of Saxon gore
Great is Rory Óg O'More at sending loons to Hades
White is sick, Grey has fled, now for Black Fitzwilliam's head
We'll send it over dripping red to Queen Lisa and her ladies

Here is a fierce song from the Wicklow mountains. Apart from its chilling imagery, this song contains an atmosphere and a mood which survives in the subconscious memory of many Irish people. They came from over the sea and took the land, raped and pillaged and murdered, and some chose to fight back.

Today, some of us still fight back in whatever way we can. The Collaborators frown upon this song. Better to forget these things, bad for business to sing of ancient battles.

I will not forget. I must forgive, but I should not forget.

12 May 1997, London
Arose at eight and pottered around looking at the morning and contemplating the day. Had a meeting at nine with my manager, Mattie Fox, and we discussed the emerging scenario with Warners *viz-à-viz* an upcoming compilation

album which has taken months of laborious work and deliberation. At one stage we were at the foot of the courtroom steps over this one, but we knew there were no winners in there apart from the lawyers. We are also seeking to retrieve my back catalogue to exploit it more actively. After this, we have a long discussion about developments in Vicar Street, our proposed new venue (with Harrie Crosbie, an acquaintance of old and primary partner in the venture). Overall, this meeting with Mattie lasted three hours, and I was fairly bunched after it and still I hadn't taken my guitar up.

At two, my assistant Dikon Whitehead and I leave by car for The Acoustic Café in the West End, where I am to do a promotional gig for the London Palladium Show. It is for an arts magazine programme called *Good Stuff*, which has an audience of five million (or so I'm told). They were a very good crew and took a lot of care with the shoot. I performed 'North and South' three times and they filmed it with one camera from different positions in the room. The cameraman was hot, as were the soundmen and the producer, and they made a very ordinary little bar look exceptionally well. I then did an interview with Davina McCall which was OK, but I've no idea how it will pan out.

Our driver is acting up a bit, but I think I can handle it. Then back to the hotel at six where I do an interview and then meet up with my boyhood friend of 40 years ago, Pat Paul McGowan. We go for a curry at Khan's in Westbourne Grove and he has a few beers and we talk about the good stuff of the last 52 years. Our mothers, fathers, brothers, sisters, homes, schools, lives, books, Van Morrison's out-takes, and we finally wind up with the fact that we are both blessed to have wives we love deeply and loving children who have become friends.

Back to my room at midnight where I hit upon two very good random movies on the box, a rare treat, and I gradually wind down to the bed where I put on the BBC World Service and fall asleep around three in the morning. Good, good day.

Section 31
by Barry Moore

Section 31 on the TV
Section 31 on the radio
Section 31 is a blindfold
Section 31 makes me feel cold

Who are you to decide what I should see?
Who are you to decide what I should hear?
What do you fear I cannot comprehend here?
What do you think that my reaction might be?

The silence in my ears, the darkness in my eyes
Heightens the fears, silences the cries
Of another brother taken in another act of hate
Of another family waiting for Heaven knows what fate

It was 1978 or 1979. I left Strandhill, Co. Sligo in a borrowed car and drove to Derry to do a concert for the Smash H-Block Campaign. I was booked to stay in a local hotel. The concert was sold out and was taking place in a tense and nervous city. At the end of the evening, I offered to drive some of the other musicians home. On the way back to my hotel, I was stopped at a road-block. They held me at the roadside for over an hour and played head games with me. They knew where I had been playing, who I had driven home, who had organised the concert, even the room number of my hotel. This would have been a regular occurrence for Northern activists but I found it to be a strange and frightening experience. These heavily armed and uniformed men treated me with aggression and pure hatred and I was scared. I got back to my room and lay there for a few hours listening to every creak and sound while I recalled the recent assassinations of H-Block activists. At about 3am I packed up and got out of there and I was relieved to get back to Sligo at breakfast time.

The banning of certain songs has, on differing occasions, both amused and angered me. I wrote a song called 'St Brendan's Voyage' which described, with humour, the travels of a sixth-century Kerry saint. It was banned by the

BBC simply because it mentioned the word 'Gibraltar'. The song itself had no political significance whatsoever. 'The Time Has Come' described the last meeting of the Hunger Striker Patsy O'Hara and his mother Peggy. I wrote it as a love song and it received a number of good plays on Radio Éireann. However, Eamon McCann reviewed the album and wrote of the substance of the song and (the same radio station) then banned it.

Other songs that I know to have been banned include 'They Never Came Home', 'Section 31', 'Back Home in Derry' and 'McIlhatton', the latter two simply because they were written by the late Bobby Sands MP and were thus deemed to be subversive. I was approached by a record label in Germany to do an album of songs that had been banned in Dublin and London, and I regret not having taken the opportunity.

Perversely, the banning of my songs has always served to heighten their popularity.

John o' Dreams
by Bill Caddick

When midnight comes and people homeward tread
Seek now your blanket and your feather bed
Home comes the rover his journey is over
Yield up the night-time to Old John o' Dreams

Across the hills the sun has gone astray
Tomorrow's cares are many dreams away
The stars are flying your candle is dying
Yield up the darkness to Old John o' Dreams

Both man and master in the night are one
All things are equal when the day is done
The prince and the ploughman, the slave and the freeman
All find their comfort in Old John o' Dreams

When sleep it comes the dreams come running clear
The hawks of morning cannot reach you here
Sleep is a river, flow on forever
And for your boatman choose Old John o' Dreams

I was doing a Midland club circuit in England in 1967. I had a 1956 VW Beetle, a Yamaha FG 180 guitar and a sleeping bag. Every night brought a new club, new friends and the possibility of hearing new songs. In Halesowen Folk Club (or was it Wolverhampton?) I heard the writer perform this song. I thought I recognised the music, and later realised that Henry Flanagan OP would have played it to me at Newbridge College.

I got the VW Beetle in Sheffield from a man called Harry. I paid him £50 and drove away as proud as a peacock. This was my second car, the first having been a 1963 Mini van, bought for £40 from a man called Ernie in Bury, Lancashire. The car became home, being used for transporting the act the length and breadth of the UK, but also being utilised as boudoir, dressing room, dining room, office, courting place, sitting room. I borrowed the purchase price from my Aunt Kathleen who was my mother's first cousin. Kathleen Sheeran (Ryan, Ashforth-Upton, Knowles) became my friend and confidante and was a truly extraordinary woman. She was an only child who was orphaned when her father, Joe Sheeran, was blown away at Ypres in 1917. He joined up in Slane along with the poet Francis Ledwidge, and together they fought and died with countless thousands in far-off fields. Kathleen was taken in by an aunt in Arbroath in Scotland. As a war orphan, the British State would provide her with an education, and the Arbroath aunt used this money to educate her own son and put Kathleen into service while still a child. Kathleen ran away to Glasgow, and the next twenty years are a mystery (to me), but she somehow ended up as Mrs Ryan and had a farm near Bury in Lancashire. Her next marriage found her the landlady of The Pack Horse Inn, Birtle, Near Bury, and she had become Mrs Ashforth-Upton. I first visited her here in 1960 when I came and worked the summer at this wonderful pub. She warmed to me, and we remained very close until she died in 1989. I used to play piano and sing, do the bottling, and I also fell in love with my third cousin, Terry, who was Kathleen's third daughter.

'John o' Dreams' is a special song for many people. These past twenty years I've performed it many times at services and funerals. In May 1999 I performed it with my son Andy and Donal Lunny at a funeral service commemorating the young life of Robbie O'Neill, a 25-year-old friend gone to rest. It is a great gift to be able to bring a little comfort to grieving parents by singing this beautiful song.

Hard Cases
by Johnny Mulhearn

You're in the pub at half past ten the money for the cure's all spent again
Trying to figure out who's carrying and where they'll be that day
Forget about the night before when you were flying for an hour or more
Move across to the cellar bar you'll be hoping that you'll find

One of them hard cases soft faces who grip you with their deadly smile
As the grip it tightens the grin gets slowly deeper
Beads of perspiration stand on your cadgulation
Till someone takes the pressure off and calls out for porter

Soon enough the tap runs dry and the afternoon goes slowly by
The barman looks on warily as your mates come drifting in
Someone says there's a session on The Pecker Dunne is back in town
Head across to the widows looking for the entrance fee

A woman you know buys you your last as the evening goes flashing past
Bridie is screaming as you're eying the slops behind the bar
The party crowd is gathering the banjo the fiddle and the mandolin

The cider flagon hunt is on
If you haven't got a tosser you can bring along a dozen of them hard cases

13 May 1997

This morning I talk with my good friend Brian Maguire who is far away in Mexico City. He is there to paint. I love his friendship and his art and I feel very good when I destroy him on the snooker table. We have never discussed it as such, but I feel that we collaborate in our work – certainly at my end of it – and I see music in his painting. I've grown to see the proximity of music to paint. I sometimes feel the beauty of poetry and I have been awestruck by sculpture, writers amaze me and actors move me to tears with their words and emotion and movement, but I feel at one with some painters. A brushstroke or a lump of colour can touch my heart in the same way as music from an instrument or a voice. The sculptor Henry Flanagan planted a seed in my young mind many years ago, and today I begin to know the fruits of comprehending the wonder of art.

But I am paranoid and suspicious of the word artist. I am a bit slow with people who write high-handedly about art: high art, low brow, naïve, native.

Here is a Mulhearn song as only he can write them. It is a unique song that brings us inside the daily life of a young alcoholic – still fit enough to do the music sessions and at day's end have the energy for partying and attempted courting, but all the time on the mooch, a sad life dedicated to cadging, scrounging and begging the price of alcohol to satisfy the terrible craving. There was a time when I used to see humour in this song, but not today as I realise it describes only too well that terrible imprisonment that some of us suffer, slaves to that which most people can enjoy at their leisure, but to which countless millions have become addicted.

15 May 1997, Philharmonic, Liverpool

I was really looking forward to this concert. A beautiful venue with the two cathedrals dominating the skyline outside, announcing their pompous splendour and total lack of humility. Wonderful buildings no doubt, but hard to find God in the disdain that flies from one massive citadel to the other.

On stage I found myself in a very strange place. The audience was welcoming, warm and very enthusiastic. Jimmy Faulkner and I played well but I was out of my mind in a very strange way. I could not focus on where I was, and the songs were out-of-body-like.

It is now the following day, 16 May, and I'm still in a different place. Very tired, and not too motivated for tonight's show in Blackburn. However, despite that, I give thanks to God for my voice and repertoire and the hands to play and the audience to listen.

'Ordinary Man'	'Nancy Spain'	'Quinte Brigada'
'Biko Drum'	'Back in Derry'	'Go, Move, Shift'
'Tim Evans'	'One Last Cold Kiss'	'North and South'
'Burning Times'	'Natives'	'Ride On'
'The Voyage'	'Sonny'	'The Time Has Come'
'Cliffs of Dooneen'	'Black is the Colour'	'Fairytale of New York'
'Welcome to the Cabaret'	'Lisdoonvarna'	'Delerium Tremens'
'James Connolly'	'Liverpool Medley'	'Missing You'
'Johnny Jump Up'	bowrawn solo	

Twenty-six songs performed at Liverpool Philharmonic in May 1997. This means my set ran to about two and a quarter hours. When I play such a long set it usually means that it took me a long time to settle down so I feel I've got to stay on longer to make up for the bad start.

I've often made the mistake of playing for too long. There is an optimum time for each individual concert. No two gigs are the same. Each audience has its own collective personality and the show must be tailored accordingly.

A concert to an audience of 3,000 people can be badly affected by one boor. Often, members of an audience will be too polite to deal with a tiny number of people who can be ruining their night. (There were many nights when I was the boor.) I think of the couple who may have saved to see a show, travelled a hundred miles, booked accommodation and tickets and looked forward eagerly to seeing a performance. Then they find themselves seated near some utter wanker who insists on being heard. For many years we have had a policy for dealing with trouble-makers. We give them their money back and ask them to leave. Then we invite them to a future show free of charge, provided they arrive in a sober state.

Away You Broken Heart You
by Philip Stewart

Away away you broken heart you
Leave my breast like a hollow cave
Stand me somewhere near the ocean
I will wait there wave after wave

Away away you broken heart you
Who can heal you when you're like this
There's no angel born in Heaven
There's no lover's healing kiss

Away away you broken heart you
Lose yourself in the darkest night
And if the stars can take your sorrow
Let them take it that's all right

Away away you broken heart you
Leave my breast like a hollow cave
Stand me somewhere near the ocean
I will wait there wave after wave

I became involved with this song straightaway upon hearing it. I worked for a number of years to find a way to sing it. It has always evoked a very strong feeling within me – a very clear picture in my mind when I sing it. It was also a very difficult song to record, nor have I ever been able to do it on stage.

Perhaps the sheer futility of the lyrics are simply too numbing to make live performance possible. I had a similar feeling come over me with 'Middle of the Island' but I persevered with that because in singing it I can focus positively on the cause of the song's event. In this case, however, the futility is unexplained and incomprehensible. Nevertheless, I am glad to have recorded this song as it has helped me to recognise some of my own past and to leave certain black places behind for today.

In my travels around the world I've encountered numerous people whose broken hearts were comforted and nourished by the healing power of words and music. A woman in New York travelled 80 miles to my gig in Queens because her late daughter had loved my songs. She got comfort from listening to the songs after her child passed away, and just wanted to hear them performed live.

A man in Yorkshire wrote to me about his wife and how the songs had helped her through illness. Two families in Limerick who lost their beautiful sons have followed the singer because their sons loved the songs. There are many other stories, too. Couples who met at gigs, subsequently got married and brought their children to gigs. I meet many people who have their own stories to tell and their own perspectives on the music.

I could not always have written about the work in this way, but now that I understand where the work comes from there is no ego involved. I am merely a conduit for words and notes that are sounded a million times each day around the world.

Without the power of God I cannot even move my tongue nor lift my little finger.

Sweet Music Roll On
by Graham Lyle

Down by O'Connell Street one summer's evening
I met a woman it was our first meeting
Crossed over the bridge and down to the river
By the strawberry beds I felt that I knew her
She called me her darling man

We spent a few hours, we drank a few glasses
We danced around the floor ignoring their glances
Everyone knew her name and they knew by my face
With a beer in my hand and my arm round her waist
She called me her darling man

The river runs deep
Sweet music roll on
Tho' the times are long gone
Sweet music roll on

Then came the morning and my boat was leaving
She smiled as she said to me no point in grieving
Every once in a while when I hear music playing
I remember her smile and I hear her voice saying

The river runs deep
Sweet music roll on
Tho' the times are long gone
Sweet music roll on

I was driving into Dublin one summer's evening in July 1972, in a VW van with my flowing locks and flares and clogs and I was well pleased with myself. Planxty was making a big noise with sweet music, and I had a grand bit of Nepalese hash in my póca that had lovely white veins of opium running through. I parked up my fine chariot and walked around Stephen's Green wondering where I'd go to sport. O'Donohue's or Toner's or McDaid's or Neary's or Keogh's or Sinott's or Rice's. I settled for McDaid's and made for Harry Street. Perched on high stools, I saw a woman I knew called Kay Finnegan, and sitting alongside her was the most beautiful woman I'd ever seen. Kay introduced me to Valerie Isaacson and my heart was beating loud within my breast.

Our first date was to a Planxty gig in a tent in Timahoe, Co. Kildare. That was 29 years ago, and today we are still together. We first lived in Sandymount in a single-room bedsit that we shared with Dan and Jim. These two men were from Seattle. They took lots and lots of acid and smoked the hash all day and all night 'MaryAnne'. They were most agreeable house guests and would cook and sew, shake and mow. Dan disappeared off the face of the earth, and Jim lives back in Seattle. We came home one night to find Jim hanging on to the electric meter. He had electricity flowing through and he was wired to the moon. He explained that he was connected through the electric grid to the Pacific and that he could feel vibrations from the west coast of America coming down the line to him in Sandymount, Ireland. It emerged later that he had, in fact, taken four tabs of pure acid, so connection with the Pacific was no problem.

Shortly after this we moved to Terenure and tuned in to Mountain, and Morrison, Dory Previn, Dylan and I began to listen to The Beatles. I was a late developer, and even though I lived in London and England right through the Beatles era, I was too busy at the folk music to pay any heed.

Valerie and I got married in James Street Catholic church on 19 December 1973. Valerie's bridesmaid was her sister, Sheila Isaacson, and Donal Lunny was best man. We had the early session in The Old Dublin Restaurant in Francis Street and, after a siesta, we had the larger session in The Grosvenor Hotel in Westland Row – long since demolished – where a row and a ruction soon began.

Soon we moved from Terenure to our first home in Inchicore, then to Coolcullen on the Castlecomer Plateau, then Garristown, Co. Dublin, then to Rialto in Dublin and finally to Monkstown, where we've been domiciled ever since.

Hughie Flint sent me this song and I sometimes sing it for it reminds me of that evening 27 years ago when I walked into McDaid's. Little did we know...

All I Remember
by Mick Hanly

I was lured by the rockin horse sweets and the boolabus fifty wild boys to a room
Sing lámh lámh eile the dish ran away with the spoon
Black shoes and stockings for those who say don't blue is the colour outside
God made the world, the snake tempted Eve and she died
Wild Christian brothers sharpening their leathers learn it by heart that's the rule
All I remember is dreading September and school

The priest in confession condemned my obsession with thoughts that I did not invite
As I mumbled and stuttered he slammed the shutter goodnight (goodnight to you too, Father)
Stainless as steel you know how I feel someone shoot me while my soul is clean
I don't think I'll last and my vow to abstain is obscene
Arch confraternity men to the fight raise up your banners on high
Searching for grace securing a place when they die

And they made me for better or worse
The fool that I am or the wise man I'll be
And they gave me their blessings and curses
It wasn't their fault it was me, just the one that you see

God kept a very close eye on me
Hung around my bed in the darkness he spied on me
Caught me in the long grass so often he died on me

Ballrooms of romance in Salthill and Mallow I stood like John Wayne by the wall
Lined up like cattle we wait to do battle and fall
You can't wine and dine her in an old Morris Minor ask her before it's too late
I danced on girls' toes and accepted rejection as my fate
Drink was my saviour it made me much braver but I couldn't hold it so well
Oh what a mess when I got sick on her dress it was hell

God kept a very close eye on me

7 September 1997

Last night I played a warm-up gig for a US TV show at Mother Redcap's Tavern in Dublin. This past ten years I've played here two or three times a year, usually benefit gigs and always sold by word of mouth. There have been memorable nights and great participation and order with sporadic outburts of mayhem and madness.

I opened with 'Away You Broken Heart You' and brought it into 'The Ballad of the Faithful Departed'. Working close with an audience really suits me and the last night they were dancing on me lap. Damien Dempsey came on and did a solid set and we did a song together. Juno came on and did 'Irish Ways and Irish Laws' and 'Strange Ways'. Her first song was superb, but I fucked up the second by being out of tune and setting an inappropriate pace. Eilish joined me for 'Singing Bird', and a new song she has written called 'Butterfly'.

'All I Remember' came from Mick Hanly backstage in Connolly Hall, Cork, circa 1980. The memories trawled up by this ballad are legion. Out there on the rim of sin and temptation waging war upon the pagan hordes, hands tied behind my back, collecting for the black babies. Gazing at my secret photo of Queen Elizabeth and trying on Mammy's lipstick in the mirror and wondering why my prick was stiff and what did it all mean when not even the prospect of everlasting flames could ease the sweetness of my venial sinning.

I served God at Mass where I became part of the Transubstantiation. I received the Host and swung the Thurible. I touched my dream-girl's breast in the Palace Cinema and learned about the facts of life above in the Gaeltacht of Gweedore where I got it all arseways as I fumbled in the dark with my fáinne.

The Rose of Tralee (Me and the Rose)
by C. Moore

It was five o'clock in the morning, I was only after getting off the Stena
I was heading down the North Wall minding my own business
When a voice behind me went 'Where are you going at this hour of the morning?'
I turned round and who was standing behind me only the Rose of Tralee
And she wearing a grand new blue Bean-Garda's uniform
(I thought for a minute that she was a Super)

'Hey Rose! How's it going, Baby? Last time I saw you was upstairs in The Tent
Down below in The Dome with Gaybo in the Pretty Polly tights and all the beauty queens
From Tashkent, Istanbul, Bangkok and Liverpool, how are you keeping?'
'Can you account for your movements?' said she to me
'Jasus Rose, there is no need to be like that. Movements is it?
I'll give you all the movements you want. You'd better sharpen your pencil
You're going to be a busy little woman. Christy has a memory like a supergrass
He can remember things that never happened at all

'The first thing I can remember is the seventh of May 1945 at the back of Donnolly's Hollow
It was the night before Pa Connolly drove the Roadstone lorry into the Seven Springs
And St Brigid started rolling out the Tintawn across the Curragh of Kildare
Then I woke up one morning, Rose, I was after getting conscripted into the Altarboys
I was ringing the bell and swinging the Thurible. The smell of the incense would remind you
Of the inside of an Arab's tent and no sign of Gaddafi nowhere'
'Ite Missa Est,' says Rose. 'Gloria Tibi Domine,' says I, for I love to hear a bit of Latin
It reminds me of the Old Tridentine. Sure the nine first Fridays never killed anyone

'The next thing I knew I was serving my time to be a cornerboy in the Curragh Camp
I was trying to teach the sheep to talk Irish, Cúpla Focal, Céad Míle Fáilte, Tiocfaidh Ár lá
Ah fuck you and your lá.
Then I got a job selling lambs balls to mushroom farmers that couldn't afford horse shite
One day I was walking across the Curragh of Kildare and I fell into an officer's mess
He was only home after six months in the LEB and the poor man was loaded
Then I met a fellow whose first cousin was married to a man whose sister's brother-in-law
Was going out with a girl whose grandmother used to fill hot-water bottles for Patrick Sarsfield
(Before the Battle of Clongorey). I had to go on the run

'I ran so fast that I ended up abroad in Paddington
Digging footings, scraping pots

Pulling cable, starting drotts
Boiling kettles, making tae
Digging deep, thrown away

'I was a disposable Paddy serving my time to be a co-pilot on a Kango hammer in Shepherd's Bush
I was doing 86 mph on a JCB down the Kilburn High Road
When the SPG flagged me down and held me under the PTA
Until I got away and went underground with the Green Murphy
Then one Thursday I was heading down the Hammersmith Broadway
And I met a man from Ballaghadereen in the County Roscommon
He was a demolition expert and Georgian houses were his speciality
"Any chance of the start?" said I "What would you know about demolition?" said he
"I've been known to demolish large bottles," said I "That'll do," said he

'Monday morning came and myself and Raymond Roland and Roger Sheelock and Liam Farrell
With Mairtín Byrnes and Tony Rohr we were painting a door
We gave it six coats and three coats more and that was just undercoat
The ganger was fond of a tune and Thursday never came too soon
We were getting four pounds a day and all we could eat
But it's an awful job trying to eat all day
Then I went looking for digs. Up the Chiswick High Road I knocked on the door
And this English lady came out and took one look at me
"Oooogh" said she "get away from my door there'll be no blacks nor Paddys getting in here."
So I let on I was a white South African
"O tar isteach" said she "Tá fáilte romhat a Buachall" She was a Mayo woman
"Come in outa that and make yourself at home but don't be blowing your nose in the blankets"

'Then I tried to join the British Army to better myself
I volunteered as a sub-contractor building houses with no doors or handles on them
"What ye bin doin' lately then, Paddy?" the recruiting officer said to me
"I was helping O'Brien to shift it, sir," said I "Spreading the toxic all over the Golden Vale"
I was helping Paddy Gallagher cover Stephen's Green in concrete
I was helping Sam Stephenson block all the daylight out of Dublin
I was taking the bends out of the Liffey for Dr Smurfit
I was counting the golden beans for Dr O'Reilly
I was doling out the diddley-eye for Dr Darragh
I was taking the sweetener out of the Greencore
And vacuum packing T-bone steak for Larry Maith an Fear'
"Oh you're overqualified for the British Army" said he
And he put me on the first Stena out of Holyhead. Total exclusion

'And here I am arriving home after eight years in exile. Aras Arís
This is some welcome for a returned immigrant. Céad Míle Fáilte my arse
With your pioneer pin and your fáinne and your white star for not cursing
It would be more in your line to give me a lift in the panda.' And she did

There I was in the back of the White Squad heading into town looking for an early morning house
There's Paddy Slattery 'You're welcome home, Christy' (big slate)
'Would you and your girlfriend like a drink?'
Well she took off her cap and in she went
'I'll have a brandy with a small drop of port,' said she 'I never drink pints when I'm on duty.'
Well she lowered it up, 'twas like throwing cold water into a barrel of sawdust
And no purse
'I'll see you tonight' said she 'and it'll be my twist.'

Well there I was, outside the GPO waiting for the most beautiful Kerry woman in the whole wide world
Here she comes, will you look at her, sashaying down the boulevard in her docs and her 501s
'Hey Rose! Over here!' 'What's on your mind big fellow?' (I was wearing my platforms)
'I wouldn't mind a bit of a dance.' So she took me to a disco in the Garda Club – Le Baton Rouge
Some spot. Wall to wall moustaches. Did you ever wonder what they do with all the hash?
'Twas like Woodstock – gay bikers on acid. Me and the rose we danced the night away
Five o'clock in the morning and she says to me 'Fancy coming back to my place, Lofty?'
Does a bear shite in the woods

Through Rathmines and Rathgar she got me siren going and the warning lights were flashing
Pulled in for two doner kebabs and the Leinster Leader
Back to her place two up two down. She pulled the cork out of the Blue Nun
And I got sick all over the Rottweiler
And then she put the music on
Daniel
'Oh then fare thee well sweet Donegal, the Roses and Gweedore'
'O! Rose', 'O! Daniel', 'Agh! Here.'
'I suppose the rasher sandwich is out of the question?'

I'll never forget the nights I was asked to sing this song at the Market Halle in Hamburg, and then in the Alte Opera in Frankfurt, and subsequently all over Germany. I'd close my eyes and head off on my boat and bike journey and the listeners would lift me far above the boards and we'd fly together in joy and sorrow. We laughed together and got sad together, for that's what the performance was all about, and they filled my heart with their emotions and exuberance and their enthusiasm filled the words and notes with new meaning and together we achieved something that I was so privileged to enjoy.

The song works differently in Ireland. Most listeners put their own slant on proceedings. I would like to take this opportunity to clear up the origins of this fine piece of *Erse*. (I have always taken erse to mean the Conqueror's Tongue as spoken in Bognia.)

My first encounter with Roses of Tralee was in The Dome Marquee in 1985. I had just finished a crazy performance in this tent. There were about 2,000 people there. Six orderly rows of beauty queens, their minders, local hoi-polloi, nervous parents and the odd parish priest and nun home from the missions. Behind this sedate seated audience lurked 1,500 lunatics on the drink. After the show I was taken to meet the beauty queens who all insisted upon kissing and cuddling my son Andy who still remembers the night fondly.

Then I was playing a concert in Boston a year later or earlier. Into my dressing room came the Rose of Tralee. She was absolutely stunning. She filled her Boston police uniform to perfection. She was tooled up too so there was no messing. She invited me back up to her place, to meet her family and fiancé and they invited me to sing at their wedding.

And then there was the night I was on the crossbar of Donal Lunny's bike. We had been playing the Olympia Theatre and we stayed in the Green Room till almost dawn. As we exited stage-door right we found that the limo had left, so we borrowed a bike and as we rode past Leinster House, Donal was pulled for having no light. The woman who took down our details was yet another Rose of Tralee (but there is never one at hand when you need one). I just had to write this song.

Recording this piece was a marathon endeavour and I recall attempting it on four different albums over a period of seven years. I tried every sort of way to get it down. I remember Donal Lunny trying to create backing tracks in at least three different studios. It all came to nothing in the end. I decided to give it one final blast in Sulaune Studio, Ballyvourney, Co. Cork. I had large boards containing all the lyrics, pauses, chord shapes and intervals mounted around me. I'd realised the only way to get it down was in one take and, exhausted after a week of trying, I decided to give it one final go.

Everything was set, I arose early and breakfasted and walked into the studio where Jim Donohoe, Roger Askew and Walter Samuel had everything switched on, primed and ready to roll. This, I had decided, was to be the final attempt, and away I rode with no bell on my bike.

Thirteen minutes later and we had a wrap. The problem was that I'd been performing this work live for about eight years, and in that time it had never developed a shape. I was constantly changing it (on the hoof) and it was quite unstructured, both in chords and segments. Such anarchy can work perfectly on stage, for in the mayhem and energy of a gig it is easy to paint over the cracks and faults and mishaps of the live performance. But in recording the piece, no such cosmetics are available and every flaw would sound gargantuan (to me).

That done, I brought in a number of musicians to add colour to various scenes. It was a long haul but I am still very pleased with the outcome. It is on the album *King Puck*.

The Dalesman's Litany
Author unknown

This version is from Denis Sabey of Bradshaw, Halifax, Yorkshire

It's hard when folks can't get their work where they've been bred and born
When I was young I used to think I'd bide 'mid the roots and the corn
But I've been forced to flee to town so here's my litany
From Hull and Halifax and Hell good Lord deliver me

When I was courting Mary Anne the auld squire he said one day
I've got no room for wedded folk choose to wed or to stay
I could not leave the girl I loved so to town we had to flee
From Hull and Halifax and Hell good Lord deliver me

I've worked in Leeds and Huddersfield where I've addled honest brass
In Bradford Keightley Rotherham I've kept me bairns and lass
I've travelled all three Ridings round and once I've been to sea
From Hull and Halifax and Hell good Lord deliver me

I've been thru' Sheffield lanes at night 'twere just like being in Hell
The furnaces thrust out tongues of flame that roared like the wind o'er the fell
I've sammed up coal in Barnsley pit with muck up to my knee
From Hull and Halifax and Hell good Lord deliver me

I've seen grey fog creep o'er Leeds Brig as thick as Bastille soup
I've been where folks are stowed away like rabbits in a coup
I've seen snow fall on Bradford Beck as black as ebony
From Hull and Halifax and Hell good Lord deliver me

But now my children all have flown to the country I'll go back
There'll be forty miles of heathery moor 'twixt me and the coalpit slack
And oft at night as I sit round the fire I'll think of the misery
From Hull and Halifax and Hell good Lord deliver me

In 1968 I had a cottage at Causeway Foot near Bradshaw on the outskirts of Halifax, Yorkshire. I settled in very well with the local people and I remember it as a particularly happy time in my life. There were good folk clubs in the area and many good musicians and singers. The George in Halifax, The Bradshaw Tavern, The Anchor in Brighouse, The Topic in Bradford, were all local. Leeds and Manchester were less than an hour away. I learned these verses from Denis Sabey and Alastair Cameron who ran the club at The Bradshaw Tavern every Sunday night.

I was very much a loner in those days. I lived in the old, damp, stone cottage at Syke Lane but spent most of my time on the road. Apart from gigging I was always well occupied with my other interests which included football at Elland Road, Rugby league at Halifax, and stock-car racing at Bellevue. I loved the cinema and I would travel to Manningham Lane for curry and hashish.

During these years I had friendships with many beautiful Yorkshire women but invariably they tired of my heavy drinking and unreliability. When they dropped me I'd always drift back to the hard-drinking gang.

Tell It To Me (What Put the Blood)
from the singing of John Reilly

Singing what put the blood on your right shoulder,
Son come tell it unto me
That is the blood of a hare Mama
you may pardon me

The blood of a hare never ran so red,
Son come tell it unto me
That is the blood of my youngest brother,
you may pardon me

What came between you and your youngest brother,
Son come tell it unto me
It was all for the cuttin of a hazel rod
that never will grow into a tree

What will you do when your daddy finds out,
Son come tell it unto me
I will lay my foot down on a ship's board
and sail far across the sea

And what will you do with your two fine children,
Son come tell it unto me
I'll give one to me mammy and other to me daddy
for to keep them company

And what will you do with your darlin wife,
Son come tell it unto me
She will leave her foot down on a ship's board
and sail right after me

Singing what will you do with your two fine horses,
Son come tell it unto me
I will take the reins from off their necks
no more they'll race for me

Singing what will you do with your woods and your lands'
Son come tell it unto me
I'll leave them there for the birds of the air
for to mourn and sing for me

10 August 1999

Last night I went to hear some music in The Tin Pub, Ahakista, Co. Cork. There was an ensemble of accomplished musicians playing good music. Towards the end of the evening a young woman began to play a tin whistle. She was unknown and unannounced, but after a couple of bars of music the entire pub fell into silence. Whatever spirit that was contained in her playing, it captured the imagination of the revellers. There were people there from many nations thronged in tightly, and we all were affected by this young woman's music. After a couple of rounds of the tune I recognised it as a beautiful variation of the old Liverpool sea shanty 'Sally Brown'. But this young musician from Bremen in Germany had imbued it with an atmosphere that stilled the night. She disappeared and no one knew her name or anything else about her.

John Reilly's songs have something of this quality about them. I've heard other versions of his songs that did not catch my ear, but when John sang them they always made an impression. All birdsong is beautiful but the sounds of the corncrake and the cuckoo and the lark ring out in the still air.

It has always been a pleasure to sing 'Tell It to Me'. I first recorded it on the 1975 album *Whatever Tickles Your Fancy*. Twenty-five years later, when I came to record *Traveller*, it was the first song I wrote down. There is a timelessness to this lyric. Every time I return to it I am imbued with the memory and spirit of John's singing.

Van Dieman's Land
from Mike Waterson

Me and three more went out one night into Squire Noble's park
We were hoping we might catch some game the night been proven dark
It being our sad misfortune they captured us with speed
And brought us down to Warwick Gaol did cause our hearts to bleed

Young men all be aware lest you be drawn into a snare
Young men all be aware lest you be drawn into a snare

It was about the fifth of March me boys at the court we did appear
Like Job we stood with patience our sentence to hear
Without jury bail nor witness our case it did go hard
Our sentence was for fourteen years straight away being sent on board

The ship that bore us from the land the Speedwell was her name
For full five months and upwards we ploughed the raging main
We saw no land nor harbour I tell you it's no lie
All around us one black ocean, above us one blue sky

About the fifth of August 'tis then we made the land
At five o'clock next morning they tied us hand to hand
To see our fellow sufferance filled me heart with woe
For there's some chained to the harrow and others to the plough

To see our fellow sufferance it filled me with despair
For they'd leather smocks and lindsey shorts and their feet and hands were bare
They tied them up two by two like horses in a dray
And the driver he stood over them with his Malacca cane

There was a female prisoner Rosanna was her name
For sixteen years a convict from Wolverhampton came
She often told her tale of love when she was young at home
But now it's rattling of her chains in a foreign land to roam

Come all of you young poaching lads and a warning take from me
Mark you well the story that I tell and guard your destiny
It's all about transported lads as you may understand
And the hardships we did undergo goin to Van Dieman's Land

When I first visited Hull in 1967, it felt like a fishing town. It was one of a number of northern towns that became focal points for me in my travels. Whenever I was booked to play there, I'd always try to make a week out of it, and I'd get other dates in the area – Beverley, Grimsby, Cleethorpes, Grantham – I'd play anywhere just to hang out in Hull.

When I played the Old Blue Bell there would always be singing through the night, and at one such session Mike Waterson sang this song and subsequently taught it to me.

There is something beautiful about the sound of a family of singers. I think of The McPeakes from Belfast, The Elliots of Birtly in Durham, The Beach Boys, The Stewarts of Blair, The Fisher Family, to name a few examples. The sounds of the Waterson family still live distinctly in my head. Like many others, I was deeply affected by hearing them sing. I can clearly remember the first time I heard them, even though it is 34 years ago. It was in The Hyde Football Club, near Manchester. There was a folk club there run by the Pennine Folk, and when The Watersons took to the stage I was mesmerised. Mike, Norma and the late Lal Waterson (RIP) with their cousin John sang *a cappella* for two hours; it was spellbinding and to this day it remains so.

The Lakes of Ponchartrain
from Mike Waterson

It was one fine March morning I bid New Orleans adieu
And I took the road to Jackson Town my fortune to renew
I cursed all foreign money no credit could I gain
Which filled my heart with longing for the Lakes of Ponchartrain

I stepped on board of a railroad car beneath the morning sun
And I rode the rods till evening and I lay down again
All strangers there no friends to me till a dark girl toward me came
And I fell in love with a Creole girl by the Lakes of Ponchartrain

I said my pretty Creole girl my money here is no good
If it weren't for the alligators I'd sleep out in the wood
She said you're welcome stranger from such sad thoughts refrain
For my mammy welcomes strangers by the Lakes of Ponchartrain

She took me into her mammy's house and treated me right well
The hair upon her shoulders in jet black ringlets fell
To try to paint her beauty I knew 'twould be in vain
So handsome was my Creole girl by the Lakes of Ponchartrain

I asked her would she marry me she said that ne'er could be
For she had got a lover and he was far at sea
She said that she would wait for him and true she would remain
'Til he'd return to his Creole girl by the Lakes of Ponchartrain

Fare thee well my Creole girl I never will see you more
I won't forget your kindness in the cottage by the shore
And at each social gathering a flowing bowl I'll drain
And I'll drink a health to my Creole girl by the lakes of Ponchartrain

When Mike Waterson taught me this song in 1967 he reckoned that, despite its geographical location, it must have some Irish connection – he felt it in his water. Anyway, I learned it from him and carried it back home where I recorded it with Planxty in 1975. The album was not a success but this song was subsequently taken up by many singers (notably Paul Brady and Liam O'Maonlaói) and it has since passed on into the national repertoire, so maybe Mike Waterson was right.

I have another song in a drawer somewhere called 'The Lakes of Old Ponchartrain'. I came across it in Toronto sung by a duo called 'Colm O'Brien and Mick Casey', who were well worth catching and I've admired them ever since. It was cold one night – having flown from Sydney to Toronto I had arrived in the wrong clothes. So Mick Casey gave me the coat off his back, for that's the kind of man he is.

Ten years later I was with the actor Tony Rohr from Carrick-on-Suir on a cold winter's night. He was playing at The Royal Court, London, and he was shivering so I gave him Mick Casey's coat and he hasn't put a foot wrong since.

I met Rohr in 1973 when we worked together in Edinburgh for eight weeks in a show called 'The Fantastical Feats of Finn McCool'. We've remained friends ever since – he listens to my work and I look at his and we move through our lives one in touch with the other. His late mother, Peggy Rohr, came to some London shows and always invited me home for supper. She'd enjoy a glass of something and every five minutes would cry out 'More sandwiches for Christy Moore!'

What connected me with this song was the wonderful line 'If it weren't for the alligators I'd sleep out in the wood'. I've often been in that situation but, so far, I've managed to avoid the alligators.

The Bleacher Lassie of Kelvinhall
from Mick Moloney

(incomplete version)

As I went out on a summer's morning
As I went out by the Broomielaw
It was there I met with a fair young maiden
Her cheeks like roses and her skin like snow

Lassie lassie why do you wander
All alone by the Broomielaw
Sailor sailor the truth I'll tell you
I've a lad of me 'ain and he's far awa'

It's seven long years since I loved that sailor
It's seven long years since he sailed awa'
Another seven I'll wait upon him
To be bleaching clothes in the Broomielaw

Lassie lassie you have been faithful
And true to me while I've been away
Our true hearts will be rewarded
We'll part no more from the Broomielaw

For many years now they have been married
They keep an alehouse in Kelvinhall
And the sailor laddies they come calling
On the bleacher lassie from the Broomielaw

I used to sing four verses of this in the early Sixties. I was dossing in Belgrave Square in Rathmines and I heard Mick Moloney sing it. Years later I discovered that The Broomielaw and Kelvinhaugh are situated in Glasgow and I heard more of the song in The Scotia Bar. The Scotia was the watering hole for local and transient musicians in Glasgow and it achieved notoriety within the ranks of folkies. It was the centre of activity for all us Raggle Taggles; songs were swapped, gigs were romanced and affairs commenced over pints of heavy, wee drams, jazz woodbines, Californian sunshine, golden speedballs and Polish vodka. We felt no pain.

I played at The Singing Jenny Folk Club in The Builders' Exchange, Huddersfield. 'The Bleacher Lassie' struck a chord with the barman who was a Polish expatriate. He invited me to stay on for a quiet drink. The pair of us lingered on sampling various flavours of Polish vodka; I sang and he began talking in Polish so I broke into Irish and next thing I knew it was eleven Thursday morning and I was out in Wood Street, Huddersfield confused and looking for my van. I had a gig that night in Halifax at The George and I also had a date with a charming beauty. I knew that I needed to sober up, but I simply could not.

Coming round by the Keighley Road my brakes failed totally. It was the end of my Volkswagon Beetle, but I still made the gig. The charming beauty did a runner.

Only Our Rivers Run Free
by Michael McConnell

When apples still grow in September when blossoms still bloom on each tree
When leaves are still green in November it's then that our land will be free
I wander her hills and her valleys and still through my sorrow I see
A land that has never known freedom only her rivers run free

I drink to the death of her manhood those men who would rather have died
Then to live in the cold chains of Bondage to bring back their rights were denied
Where are you now when we need you what burns where the flame used to be
Are you gone like the snows of last winter will only our rivers run free

How sweet is life but we're crying how mellow the wine that were dry
How fragrant the rose but it's dying how gentle the wind but it sighs
What good is in youth when it's ageing what joy is in eyes that can see
There is sorrow in sunshine and flowers and only our rivers run free

One night in 1969 I happened upon some great entertainment in Leeds. There was a concert in the Leeds Irish Centre featuring Liam O'Flynn on pipes, Cathal McConnell on flute and John Regan on accordion. When I got there the venue was hopping and I met many friends old and new. After the concert I went with the poet Pearse Hutchinson to the Regent Pub where the music continued through the night, then I blagged my way into the artists' billet. McConnell and I had hit it off and we sat up until dawn swapping songs. He sang me this beautiful song which his brother Michael had recently written. 'Only Our Rivers Run Free' was to become a big hit when I recorded it with Planxty two years later.

Thirty years on and I see this as the first of a trilogy of songs from different writers that express how I feel about the situation in the occupied six counties. The other two songs are: 'Irish Ways and Irish Laws' (1981) and 'North and South' (1996). There are many other songs which dealt with different aspects of the war, but these three are of particular importance to me personally.

'Only Our Rivers' was to travel around the world and it has been covered by many bands and singers. I have a number of other fine songs from the writer, one of which I hope to record. His songs are to be heard on a rare recording *The Songs of Michael McConnell* which I recommend, if you can find a copy.

Clyde's Bonnie Banks
Author unknown

By Clyde's bonnie banks as I lonely did wander
Among the pitheads as the evening grew nigh
I spied a young woman all dressed in black mourning
Weeping and wailing with many the sigh
I stepped up beside and gently addressed her
Would it help you to talk about the cause of your pain
Weeping and wailing at last she did answer
Johnny Murphy kind sir was my true love's name
Twenty-one years of age full of youth and goodlooking
To work down the mines of High Blantyre he came
Our wedding was fixed all the guests were invited
One fine summer's morning young Johnny was slain
The explosion was heard by the women and children
With pale anxious faces they ran to the mine
The news was made known when the bodies were counted
Three hundred and twenty-eight miners were slain

Mothers and daughters and sweethearts and lovers
The Blantrye explosion you'll never forget
And all of you good people who hear this sad story
Remember those miners who lie at their rest

I was wandering among the pitheaps of Wales, Lancashire, Yorkshire, Derbyshire, Tyneside, Lanarkshire looking for gigs, seeking sport, friendship, love, new songs, a new chord or a new verse for 'The Blackleg Miner'.

Thirty years on I get a warm feeling of recall occasionally marred by memories of the dark side. There were so many good things – the friendships which have endured the passing years, the performance skills that were honed in a thousand folk clubs: Whitehaven, Mirfield, Ashby de la Zouche, Bradshaw, Congleton, Denbeigh, Eccles, Falkirk, Grimsby, Hyde, Ilkley, Jarrow, Keighley, Lincoln, Macclesfield, Nether Edge, Ormskirk, Port Talbot, Queensferry, Redcar, Stevenage, Tynemouth, Uddington, Wrexham, Kings Cross, York, the Zetland. Endless couches, floor space, odd beds, warm beds, damp beds, sexy beds – you've got to get up early in the morning because the folk-club organiser is off to his day job and doesn't want hung-over folk singers left alone in his or her or our house to be raiding the fridge and reading the letters.

I'm stumped by this song. For once I have no recollection of hearing it or learning it or who wrote it. I recorded it in 1986 on the *Ordinary Man* album and in 1978 on the *Live in Dublin* album.

Spancilhill
Author Robbie McMahon

Last night as I lay dreaming of pleasant days gone by
My mind being bent on rambling to Ireland's isle did fly
I stepped on board a vision and I followed with a will
And I shortly came to anchor at the cross of Spancilhill

Delighted by the novelty enchanted by the scene
Where in my early boyhood so often I had been
I thought I heard a murmur and I think I hear it still
It's the little stream of water that flows down Spancilhill

To amuse a passing fancy I lay down on the ground
Where all my school companions they shortly gathered round
When we were home returning we danced with right good will
To Martin Moylan's music at the Cross of Spancilhill

It being on the 23rd of June the day before the fair
When Ireland's sons and daughters in crowds assembled there
The young the old the brave and the bold they came to sport and kill
There were curious combinations at the fair of Spancilhill

I went to see my neighbours to hear what they might say
The old ones were all dead and gone, the young ones turning grey
I met with the Tailor Quigley he's as bold as ever still
He used to make my britches when I lived in Spancilhill

I paid a flying visit to my first and only love
She is white as any lily and gentle as a dove
She threw her arms around me saying Johnnie I love you still
She is Mack the Ranger's daughter and the pride of Spancilhill

I dreamt I stooped and kissed her as in the days of yore
She said Johnny you're only joking as manys the time before
The cock crew in the morning he crew both loud and shrill
And I woke in California, many miles from Spancilhill

East Clare

I arrived in Tulla, Co. Clare, in September 1964. I hitched from Clonmel on a Sunday morning and three lifts later I was in Tulla for tea-time. The bank manager had booked me into lodgings with Miss Tubridy. The inside of the house had different shades of green on every wall and it was meticulously maintained. I carried all my worldly belongings in one hold-all bag and one guitar case. It was a time when guitar cases were uncommon and attracted curiosity from motorists who'd jam on in the hope that they'd snared a Clancy brother.

Next morning I checked into the National Bank, Tulla at nine and reported for duty. It was a two-handed office: me and a manager. It was like working in a prison cell. At first I thought that Tulla was the end of the world, but I was soon to learn that, after dark, interesting things began to happen.

The hotel was down the windswept hill. There were good card schools there where I quickly revealed my card-playing skills. Then, one night, the music started up and I ran up to the lodging house and came back with my beloved guitar. I was in.

Some weeks later I learned this song from John Minogue, who got it for me from the writer. I recorded it in 1971 and it has since passed into the national repertoire.

West Clare

When I go to West Clare I can see the music in the hills and stony fields. Today I look out upon the Sheep's Head and over Dunmanus Bay to Mount Gabriel and I can see many things: the beauty of it all, the bay, the beacons – as one man tries to quietly fish it another hungry man seeks to poison it. I can see God's work everywhere but I cannot see the music. In West Clare you can see the fiddle music, you can stand looking over a stone wall into a poor little field and it is there as plain as day. I saw concertina music on the square in Kilrush in 1964 and the vision never left me. Coming up from The White Strand in Milltown Malbay I met chanter music, and on the windswept Hill of Tulla (East Clare) I met the man that wrote Spancilhill. The music scarpered off the big fields of Meath and Kildare – there is no sign of it at all. I have seen it in Ahascragh too, and above in Ardara and you can plainly see the flute music in Fisher Street. You'd always have a better chance of glimpsing it around stony half acres, but seldom if ever on the ranches brimming with sleek shiny bullocks full of antibiotics and growth hormones. Show me a scrawny auld heifer unable for a bull and I'll show you a slow air with a slip jig traipsing after it. The combine harvesters have driven the music out of the John Hinde-coloured pastures where it has been forced to live in exile in libraries and museums. It needs the birdsong and the meadow to breathe, the wind through the furze, the distant corncrake in the meadow, the smell of the fair day.

Jasus, Christy, you're laying it on fairly thick there, but you never spoke a truer word. When Bono said, 'We'll have to get rid of the corncrake,' he knew exactly what he was talking about.

I think about the snobbishness and elitism that has always been part of the music world. Those unfortunates looking down their noses at 'lesser' souls and their popular songs. Those who retreat into the dark shadows and look out disapprovingly at music played for sport and fun and laughter. Fun is not cool, particularly if you never have any.

Ninety Miles to Dublin Town
by C. Moore

I'm ninety miles from Dublin Town I'm in an H-block cell
To help you understand my plight this story now I'll tell
I'm on the Blanket Protest my efforts must not fail
I'm joined by men and women in the Blocks and Armagh gaol

It all began one morning I was dragged to Castlerea
And tho' it was three years ago it seems like yesterday
Three days kicked and beaten then I was forced to sign
Confessions that convicted me of deeds that were not mine

Sentenced in a Diplock court my protest it began
I could not wear their prison gear I became a Blanket Man
I'll not accept your status I'll not be criminalised
That's the issue in the Blocks for which we give our lives

Over there in London how they'd laugh and sneer
If they could only make us wear their loathesome prison gear
Prisoners of War is what we are and that we will remain
The Blanket Protest must not end till our status we regain

I've been beaten round the romper room because I won't say sir
Frogmarched down the landing pulled back by the hair
I've suffered degradation humility and pain
My spirit does not falter your torture is in vain

I've been held in scalding water my skin with deck scrubs tore
Scratched and cut from head to foot and thrown out on the floor
Suffered mirror searches probed by drunken bears
I've listened to my comrades scream and sob their lonely prayers

Now with the news that's coming in the Protest must not fail
We've been joined by thirty women across in Armagh gaol
Pay attention Irish men and Irish women too
Show the Free State government their silence will not do

Tho' it's ninety miles from Dublin it seems so far away
It's like we're getting more support from the USA
Now you've heard the story of this living Hell
Remember ninety miles away I'm in my H-Block cell

In 1977 I received a communication from the H-Blocks in Long Kesh asking me to write a song in support of the men on the blanket. I went to visit Brendan McFarlane who was then OC of the Republican prisoners in the camp. It was my first time to Long Kesh and I felt nervous and intimidated. Subsequently I met the first Blanket Men to be released and I spent two days with Kieran Nugent, Fra McCann and Ned Browne. It was a harrowing time, for these three men had just come out from long stretches on the Dirty Protest. They were psychologically disorientated and finding it difficult to readjust. Despite that, they wanted me to have a precise view of what life was like for a Blanket Man.

When I had written the song I recorded it and released it independently. It was banned in Ireland but all 1,000 copies sold out immediately. It also featured on the subsequent album *H-Block*.

I began to spend more time in Belfast and Derry and other northern enclaves, and my experiences during the period very much shaped the thrust of my work for years to come. I began to support the armed struggle – to write and sing songs about the war. I was to learn many aspects about life under British occupation, under a sectarian police force, about the brutal effect that armed struggle can have on all its proponents, myself included.

17 March 2000
Today I live in hope of peace and fear of war. On the one hand so much has changed: the IRA ceasefire has held, the Free State has relinquished its aspirations for a united Ireland, 90 per cent of the island has expressed a clear desire for peace, yet we wrangle on endlessly. We need all the guns out of Ulster politics. I believe that the IRA will decommission in due course but not while the British Army, the Royal Ulster Constabulary and a large sector of the Loyalist and Unionist population are armed to the teeth – legally and otherwise.

Soldier Boys
by Wally Page

He's twenty-five and he's sick and tired
It's time to try the other side
Take the boat to Paradise
To sergeants and their men

He's never been to Dún na Rí
Nor combed the beaches after three
It's chips and beer and greenery
And comrades one and all

Till he signed and took the soldier's crest
A decent man in battledress
When bugles blow you do your best
For sergeants and their men

It's all for the roses
It's over the sea
It's all for the roses
Soldier Boys to be

He's way ahead second to none
With his Fabrique Nationali gun
Marching bands with Saxon blood
Sergeants and their men

They landed with the sinking sun
An invasion by the media run
They covered up and kissed with tongues
Sergeants and their men

But the phantom gunner danced the end
Battered human bodies bled
They butchered us we butchered them
Sergeants and their men

It's all for the roses
It's over the sea
It's all for the roses
Soldier Boys to be

But a flower of love grows on his grave
Forgotten soon the cowards and the brave
The coldest hate still lives today
For sergeants and their men

Wally Page sang this song for me in his music room in Dublin and I was instantly smitten by the emotion it evoked. Although he explained to me his vision which was deeply personal I've always managed to hang on, albeit unwittingly, to my own personal interpretation.

It's of another time and yet it's of today; it's of another place and yet it's right beside me. I did not write these words, but they describe exactly times and places and people who are deep within me. It is the mark of good work when it can encompass us all.

I love to hear Wally sing.

I joined the army in 1960 and soldiered for two years in the FCA. I camped in Kilkenny and learned to square bash around the wet canteen. I began to develop low self-esteem, for no uniform could follow my contours. We drank Time ale on draught at 1s 7d a pint, and danced with beautiful Kilkenny women in the city centre dance hall where Private Mangan got off with a pair of twins who hadn't got a tit between them but they were smashers. I was a sharp shot on the range, always ahead of the posse. Corporal Flannery showed me how to access large bottles of Guinness from the NCOs' mess, and things began to look up. My hearing is fine, please God.

Farewell to Pripyat
by Tim Dennehy

'Twas a Friday in April 1986 the day that our nightmare began
When the dust it rained down on our buildings and streets and entered our bedrooms at noon
Touched the glass and the trees, bicycles, cars, beds, books and picture frames too
We stood around, helpless, confused, nobody knew what to do

At two o'clock Sunday the buses arrived, a fleet of a thousand or more
We were ordered to be on our way not knowing what lay in store
Some of our citizens fled in dismay and looked for a good place to hide
When four o'clock came and the last bus pulled out 'twas the day that our lovely town died

And the shirts sheets and handkerchiefs crack in the wind on the windowledge withering plants
And the Ladas and Volgas are parked by the door and the bikes in their usual stance
Our evergreen trees lie withered and drooped they've poisoned our once fertile land
And the streets speak an awful silence nothing stirs but the sand

A visit back home is so eerie today a modern Pompey on view
To see all the old shops and the Forest Hotel and the Promyet Cinema too
The mementoes we gathered are all left behind photos and letters and cards
The toys of our children untouchable now toy soldiers left standing on guard

So fare thee well Pripyat my home and my soul this sorrow can know no relief
A terrifying glimpse of the future you hold your children all scattered like geese
The clothes line still sways but the owner's long gone as the nomadic era returns
The question is black and white blurred into grey the answer is too easy to learn

Tim Dennehy's path and my path have converged, usually around Milltown Malbay or Mullagh where he dwells with his family. In this song he takes the biggest of big stories and reduces it to its basic elements. There is no talk here of faded idealism, of bribery and corruption, of power-hungry officials and idiotic power play. Rather, it describes this holocaust in its simplest form and it is awful.

I have found it next to impossible to do this song live because of its horrifying landscape and the fact that we are so powerless in the face of such an evil process. Recording it fulfilled a need within myself to mark this cancerous event in the history of mankind: we have not heard the last of Chernobyl. Long after the living memory of the Nazi holocaust has begun to fade from everywhere except the libraries and history books, people will still be trying to live with the horror of Chernobyl as it lingers on for ever.

Plane Crash at Los Gatos
by Woody Guthrie

The peaches are in and the crops they lie rotten
The oranges are stacked in their creosote dumps
They're driving us back to the Mexican border
It takes all of our money to go back again

Farewell to my friends goodbye Rosalito
Adios mes amigos Jesus é Maria
You won't have a friend when you ride the big aeroplane
All they will call you will be deportee

Some of us are illegal and most are not wanted
Our work contracts and we must move on
The six hundred miles to the Mexican border
They drive us like outlaws like rustlers like thieves

My father's own father he crossed the river
You took all the money he made in his life
My sisters and brothers worked in your fruitfield
Rode in your trucks till they lay down and died

The skyplane caught fire o'er the Los Gatos valley
Like a fireball of lightning it plunged to the ground
Who are those friends lying round like dead leaves
The radio said they were just deportees

They died in your hills they died in your valleys
They died in your mountains they died on your plains
They died neath your trees and they died in the bushes
Both sides of the border they died just the same

It was a Wednesday night in 1967 and I arrived at St Clare's Folk Club in Victoria Avenue, Manchester. The McPeake family from Belfast were performing and as always they were simply uplifting. The club was run by a couple of renegade priests – Philip and Fritz – and it was always a guaranteed night of good music and crack. I heard a singer called Tony Downes sing this song and it was one of my first introductions to Woody Guthrie.

I frequented this club and I was often called upon to do a spot. It was at venues like St Clare's that I began to develop my acting and to hone a personal style of performance. Watching musicians like The McPeake Family, Packie Manus Byrne, Harry Boardman and a host of others, I would pick up new songs and watch their chords and listen to their introductions and absorb the communicative skills that could be employed to gain attention from an audience.

Packie Manus Byrne now lives back in his native Ardara, Co. Donegal. He has spent his long life traversing the roads and playing his music, telling his stories. Many's the night in the Sixties he took me back to his room in Ardwick Green, Manchester and gave me food and lodgings, taught me a song or the turn of a tune; he was a good friend to me.

The Dusty Diamondtina
by Hugh McDonald

The faces in the photograph are fading
I can't believe he looks so much like me
For it's ten long years today since I left from Cork Station
And I won't be back till the drove is done

For the rain never falls on the Dusty Diamondtina
A drover finds it hard to change his mind
The years have passed and gone like the drays from old Cork station
And I won't be back till the drove is done

It seems like the sun comes up each morning
Sets me up then takes it all away
Dreaming by the light of the campfire at night
Ends with the early light of day

I sometimes think that I'll go back to Sydney
It's been so long and it's hard to make up your mind
For the cattle trail rolls on and the fences last forever
And I won't be back till the drove is done

This song came in the post. I suspect that my version of the song has developed to be at variance with the original. Unfortunately I no longer have the author's original recording to check it out.

Each post brings a new batch of albums, CDs and tapes. They come from all over the world and people send them for different reasons. Mainly, they come from writers seeking to get their work recorded, but also from people seeking a comment for their sleevenotes, people seeking to play support on concerts, young acts looking for a recording deal or a manager or *anything*, people sending me their work because they feel it is similar to or influenced by my own.

These past ten years I've had to stop responding to unsolicited material – it is simply too time absorbing and sometimes leads to awkward situations. Some years ago I received a particularly awful song from a woman in Kildare. I instantly binned it for it was unsolicited and *dire*. Six months later I received a solicitor's letter demanding that the tape be returned. I ignored that as well.

I do, however, try to listen to as many unsolicited songs as possible because it has been my experience that many gems lie hidden inside the tape mountain. I also remember the time when I would always send my own work to Pete Seeger and Ewan McColl and how grateful I was if I got a reply.

This song came in the post.

The People's Own MP
by Bruce Scott

How many more must die now how many must we lose
Before the island people their own destiny can choose
From immortal Robert Emmet to Bobby Sands MP
Who was given thirty thousand votes while in captivity

No more he'll hear the lark's sweet notes upon the Ulster air
Or gaze upon the snowflake pure to calm his deep despair
Before he went on hunger strike young Bobby did compose
The Rhythm of Time, The Weeping Wind and The Sleeping Rose

He was a poet and soldier he died courageously
And we gave him thirty thousand votes he was the people's own MP

Thomas Ashe gave everything in 1917
The Lord Mayor of Cork McSwiney died freedom to obtain
Never a one of all our dead died more courageously
Than Bobby Sands from Twinbrook the people's own MP

Forever we'll remember him that man who died in pain
That his country north and south be united once again
To mourn him is to organise and build a movement strong
With ballot box and armalite with music and with song

Galway turned out to have a very vocal anti-Republican element in the Seventies and Eighties. I remember being taken aback at the way people turned on me – some of them very abusively – because of my support for the Blanket Men, the No-wash Protesters and the Hunger Strikers. Certain friends began to give me a wide berth while others were confrontational and extremely critical.

There was a 'Smash H-Block' concert in Leisureland, Galway. I travelled down alone, having been assured that local musicians would turn up to play in support. Only one man turned up – the late Micky Finn. He joined me on stage and, not only did he play beautiful music, he also donated all the day's takings from his work as a busker.

It was a difficult time for people who supported the prisoners, for to do so was to be marked down by the Secret Police and, in many instances, to be subsequently harassed and intimidated by the anti-Republican zealots. Your phone could be tapped, your house searched, your workmates intimidated – it was a hard time for many people.

This is what happened in the Republic – in Ulster it was a very different story. H-Block activists such as John Turley and Miriam Daly were murdered for their humanitarian concerns and activities.

The Scariff Martyrs
from Mrs Murphy of Tulla, Co. Clare

The dreadful news through Ireland has spread from shore to shore
Such a deed no living man has ever heard before
The deeds of Cromwell in his time I'm sure no worse could do
Than them Black and Tans that murdered those four youths in Killaloe

Three of the four were on the run and searched for all around
Until with this brave Egan in Williamstown was found
They questioned him and tortured him but to his comrades he proved true
And because he would not tell their whereabouts he was shot in Killaloe

On the twelfth day of November the day that they were found
Sold and traced through Galway to that house near Williamstown
They never got a fighting chance but were captured while asleep
And the way that they ill-treated them would cause your blood to creep

They hackled them both hands and feet with twines they could not break
And brought them down to Killaloe by steamer on the lake
Without clergy judge or jury on the bridge they shot them down
And their blood flowed with the Shannon convenient to the town

After three days of perseverance their bodies they let go
At ten pm the funeral passed through Ogonnolloe
They were kept in Scariff chapel for two nights and a day
Now in that place of rest they lie kind people for them pray

If you were at the funeral it was an awful sight
To see four hundred clergymen and they all dressed up in white
Such a sight as these four martyrs in one grave was never seen
They died to save the flag of love the orange white and green

Now that they are dead and gone I hope in peace they'll rest
Like all young Irish martyrs, forever among the blest
The day will come when all will know who sold their lives away
Of young McMahon and Rogers, brave Egan and Kildea

Teddy Murphy ran the pub at the top of the hill in Tulla where he lived with his new bride and his mother. One evening, he asked if I'd bring the guitar over and sing a song for his mother. She then sang this song to me, and told me of how she had attended the funeral of the Scariff Martyrs, and I can still see the picture she painted for me.

I subsequently sang this song for many years. Gradually, some of the lyrics began to sound mawkish, but today, as I reflect upon them, I realise that they expressed exactly how Mrs Murphy felt and that the song should be reproduced as she sang it.

The Old Triangle
by Brendan Behan

A hungry feeling came o'er me stealing and the mice were squealing in my prison cell
And the auld triangle went jingle jangle along the banks of the Royal Canal
To start the morning the screw was bawling get up ye bowsie and clean your cell
The screw was peeping Skinner Mac was sleeping and he was dreaming of his girl Sal
In the female prison there lie seventy women and it's in there with them that I'd like to dwell
The moon was shining the sun declining Skinner Mac was pining in his prison cell
And the auld triangle went jingle jangle along the banks of the Royal Canal

Everyone in Ireland has sung or heard this song. It is sometimes presented in a sentimental manner, which misses the point. When I think of prison I think of the harsh reverberation of steel on steel, steel on concrete, keys banging into locks, shouting voices, whistles, loud television, blaring volume, each sound loud and sharp in an awful cacophony.

My own experience of incarceration is limited to being detained for minor misdemeanours. Drunk and disorderly, possession of cannabis, failing the breathalyser. The longest I've spent in a cell to date is 36 hours and it was absolutely dreadful. I was frightened, alone, threatened, powerless and whenever I hear or sing this song I have no romantic or sentimental illusions about The Auld Triangle.

I have visited many prisons principally as an entertainer but sometimes to see friends. I've performed in Mountjoy, St Patrick's, The Women's Prison, Arbour Hill, Wheatfield, Dundrum, Portlaoise and Limerick. I've also visited Long Kesh and Manchester's Strangeways.

Many prison gigs remain vividly in my mind. My first performance in The Women's Prison in Mountjoy was pure anarchy and mayhem. The audience was only interested in having a bit of crack and a good laugh and fuckin' eejit me was trying to be a serious folk singer. I blew it. Next time in there (two years later) I was ready for the madness and gave as good as I got and we all had a ball. The best backing vocals I've ever encountered were in The Women's 'Joy and I wanted to stay the night.

One gig I did on the Provo landing in Portlaoise Prison was recorded on a ghetto-blaster. I came across bootleg copies in Canada and America. The quality was dreadful but the atmosphere was captured. I recall the late

Dominic McGlinchey being at this gig. I was not allowed to perform on his landing and the Provos invited him to their show and he attended. This would have been a significant event within the prison.

Because of segregation and logistics it could take five or six separate performances to cover every prisoner in Portlaoise or Mountjoy. The atmosphere would be different on every landing and could vary from emotional and enthusiastic to cynical and withdrawn. Everyone has their own way of doing their time.

I will never forget playing for the HIV-positive men in The Base of Mountjoy. It was an emotional occasion and I have never been given such a heartfelt welcome as I received from those men that evening. We sat together for an hour and I sang my fucking heart out for them and they knew it and they let me know that they knew it. A number of them were old friends from The Meeting Place ten years earlier.

On another occasion I played to one prisoner. I had covered the prison and he was the only one left. He was in isolation. When I entered his bleak and lonesome cell he pulled *The Christy Moore Songbook* from under his pillow and asked me to sing 'Ninety Miles'. He was a young lad who had suffered an extremely violent childhood. His life was in utter chaos yet he welcomed me into his cell and I'll never forget him. His name was Anthony Cawley.

The highlight of any prison gig is getting musicians from the audience up on stage. It always makes for a great finale for prisoners love to see one of their own up there giving it a good lash with the visiting 'celebrity'.

Easter Snow
by C. Moore

Oh the Easter snow
It has faded away
It was so rare and beautiful
And it melted back into the clay

Those days will be remembered
Beyond out in the Naul
Listening to the master's notes
As gently they did fall
Oh the music
When Seamus he did play
But the thaw came on the mantle white
And turned it back into the clay

He gazed at the embers in reflection
Called up lost verses again
Smiled in roguish recollection
While his fingers gripped the glass to stem the pain
When knocked upon his door would open
With a welcome he'd bid the time of day
Tho' you came when the last flakes had melted
While it lay upon the ground you stayed away

Séamus Ennis came to do a series of gigs in the north of England, and I offered to put him up and drive him to his venues. It was my first time to meet him – I believe it was 1968. He was not in the best of health, and was particular about what he ate. But, God love him, I think it was the drink was the problem.

I don't believe he was at ease performing in folk clubs, and he was not on top of his game. He always remembered our time together, and never let an opportunity pass without thanking me for the bit of hospitality I extended him.

I can only describe Séamus as a giant of Irish music, song, language and folkore. I have heard some recordings of his piping that were made when he was in his prime; he was a true master of his instrument.

Val and I were living in Garristown, Co. Dublin, and Séamus was living nearby in the Naul. I visited him there and he was not in the best of form. We spent long hours together and he talked endlessly about music and songs, but we were both drinking and not all of our talk made much sense. He criticised me strongly for the use of bad language. He detested the sound of it and, indeed, he set me thinking. He tried to give me songs, but we never quite managed to stay focused.

He ended his days a lonely man.

They all showed up for the funeral.

Luke Kelly
by Mick O'Keeffe

The years have passed the time has flown since first I saw you there
With feet apart to the music moved your head of curly hair
The spotlight shone in colours bright reflecting on your face
The music notes soared sweet and clear, the spirit of your race

Your songs told tales of peace and joy, of sorrow and of love
The power and passion of your voice soared heavenly above
And from the inner soul there came emotion in each song
You stirred the hearts of many Luke when you sang of right and wrong

The humour of those laughing eyes was shared in full with all
You sang songs that filled the hearts that filled the music hall
The ecstasy and joy was felt in chorus clap and cheer
When that son of Éireann took the stage, the King of Balladeers

I saw you sing a hundred times a thousand songs or more
I still can clearly hear your song tho' your time with us is o'er
Fond memories are all we have when we think of you today
Your name we'll always honour Luke, we're glad you passed this way.

L uke Kelly was an original and completely unique singer. His legend lives
on and although it continues to grow, his status is thoroughly deserved.
His voice could fill a concert hall or silence a bar-room. The passion of his
singing attracted me to him and it was a privilege for me to have known
him. He helped me and encouraged me and subsequently we became friends
who met occasionally.

I got to know him in 1969; we met only occasionally, usually with bevvy
on. We sang together once or twice, notably in Teac Furbo, Spiddal, Co.
Galway when Planxty and The Dubliners played a week together in that
slaughterhouse of porter and crack. The first time we met was in Salford,
Lancashire, where The Dubliners were recording a TV show in a pub called
'The Two Brewers'. He picked me from the queue (attracted by the guitar
case) and we chatted and he took me on in. I ended up spending the night

with The Dubliners in their hotel, and next morning he was gone when I woke. That was the way things were.

Luke introduced a style of singing into Ireland. Like myself, he was deeply influenced by the Revival singers in Britain, and by their repertoire. He incorporated that into the Dublin ballad singing style that he had created and introduced us to a form of singing that is heard today all over the world.

The Travelling People
by Ewan McColl

I'm a freeborn man of the travelling people
Got no fixed abode with nomads I am numbered
Country lanes and byways were always my ways
I never fancied being lumbered

In the open ground we could stop and linger
For a month or two for time was not our master
Then we'd pack our load and be on the road
Nice and easy no need to go faster

I've known life hard and I've known life easy
And I've cursed the nights when winter winds were storming
But I've danced and sung through the whole night long
Watched the summer sun rise in the morning

We knew the woods and the resting places
And the small birds sang when winter time was over
Then away I'd jog with my horse and dog
They were good old days for the rover

All you freeborn men of the travelling people
Every tinker, rolling stone and gypsy rover
Winds of change are blowing old ways are going
Your travelling days will soon be over

I recently uncovered a copybook that listed my repertoire in 1968. It contains almost 200 songs and of those there are only 30 that I would sing today. I was surprised by these statistics for I had no idea that so many songs were lost to me. There were some whose titles I do not even recognise: 'The Dosser's Lament', 'The Dublin Barber', 'A Nice Little Free State', 'The Lucky Elopement', to mention but a few.

This song of Ewan McColl's has been ever present in my repertoire since I first heard it sung by the man himself. It was a chart-topping song in Ireland in the late Sixties when recorded by The Johnstons.

The Boy from Tamlaghduff
by C. Moore

As I walked over the Glenshane Pass I heard a young woman mourn
The boy from Tamlaghduff she said is ten years dead and gone
How my heart is torn apart this young man to lose
We'll never see the likes again of young Francis Hughes

For many years his exploits were a thorn in England's side
The hills and glens became his home it was there he used to hide
Often when surrounded he'd quietly slip away
Like a fox he went to ground kept the dogs of war at bay

Francis and three volunteers were coming around the pass
When they were confronted by a squad of SAS
The volunteers gave all they had till Francis took two rounds
He gave the order to retreat and wounded went to ground

The UDR and RUC came with their tracker dogs
In their hundreds hunted him across the farms and bogs
When he was too weak to move they captured him at last
And from the countryside he loved they brought him to Belfast

From Musgrave Park to Crumlin Road then to an H-Block cell
He went straight on the blanket then on hunger strike as well
Altho' his weapon had been changed to a blanket from a gun
He wielded it courageously as the hunger strike begun

As his young life ebbed away we helplessly looked on
On the twelfth of May the Black Flags lay in 1981
Deep mourning around Tamlaghduff has turned to burning pride
Francis fought them every day he lived and fought them as he died

As I walked over the Glenshane Pass I heard a young woman mourn
The boy from Tamlaghduff she said is ten years dead and gone
How my heart is torn apart this young man to lose
We'll never see the likes again of young Francis Hughes

In order to write this song I met Francis' parents in Bellaghy and spoke to them at length. I also spoke to his sister in Belfast. I received the go-ahead to meet volunteers who had served with Francis in the Irish Republican Army. I was taken to a house in the Republic where one volunteer (still on active service) gave me precise details of Francis' capture, and also of his exploits. He was a very highly regarded soldier amongst his peers, for his courage, ingenuity, bravery under fire, for disguise and sheer audacity.

I wrote the following notes after meeting a volunteer who had soldiered with Francis:

Francis had little or no life outside the struggle. He had a consuming passion that his people should not have to meet foreign soldiers in their townlands. He was a country lad who volunteered to join the IRA after receiving a beating one night at a British Army checkpoint.

Francis was well received among all age groups. He was a serious man with a sense of humour. He would never be threatened by the presence of the enemy, no matter how close. His brazen approach towards enemy units often meant that he passed through roadblocks that were set up to look specifically for him. As a soldier he was exemplary, and his example and leadership instilled many around him with the same qualities that were his – total commitment and a fearless desire to win the war.

His life as a soldier was without pause during his last three years. Unlike others, he was never off duty and forsook normal life as we know it completely. His lifestyle became nomadic and he was always on the move. One pleasure he allowed himself was céilí dancing, which he loved. He was 5'11" and strong and sturdy and was a good mover. The story of his last two years alive gives a clear picture of the man – big Frankie Hughes.

Frankie and a comrade were moving towards a safe house and were in the townland of Fallea between Maghera and Dungiven. They were challenged by eight enemy soldiers, whereupon they took instant action which they claim eliminated some three or four of the enemy (one was admitted to). During the exchange, both Frankie and his mate were wounded. Though wounded in the lower right leg, his mate ran like fuck and the Brits left standing took after him but he escaped. While his mate was being chased Frankie, badly wounded, crawled away. He was finally captured some 24 hours later in bushes where he was tracked down by the trail of blood he left behind him. He was taken to Musgrave Hospital where he spent nine months recovering. He was then remanded to Crumlin Road. After a period on remand he was charged and convicted of murdering a British soldier and given life. He went straight on to the Blanket (H5). After two years he volunteered for the first Hunger Strike and was finally chosen for the second.

While in Musgrave and Crumlin Road, Frankie was a thorn in the side of his interrogators, who described him as the 'worst cheeky bastard' – a fair compliment.

The thought that he would have to make the ultimate sacrifice was often with him and never caused him difficulty. He simply abhorred the forces of occupation and sought to defeat them constantly.

Blackjack County Chains
by R. Lane

I recorded this song for the album *Voyage*.
It did not make the cut but was subsequently
re-mixed and released on the album
Smoke and Strong Whiskey.

It has not been possible for me to include this lyric,
as is the case with 'Tribute to Woody', 'I Pity
the Poor Immigrant' and 'One Last Cold Kiss'.
I would like to add that I totally respect whatever
positions writers take with regard to their own work.
I feel privileged to have been able to sing and record
the songs and I can ask for no more.

It would be a good point at which to reiterate
my gratitude and respect to all those writers
who made it possible for me to include their songs
in this book.

2 July 1999

March 1998 was a time of great change. I had to cancel a lengthy Irish tour, all of which had sold out. This was a very difficult decision to make, for I knew the disappointment it was going to cause to those tens of thousands who had taken the trouble to book seats. I was also very much aware of the problems it would cause all those involved in the tour – the promoters, the venues, the booking agents, the publicists and most of all my own manager and his staff. It is difficult to set up a tour and get it up and running, but cancellation brings a whole different set of logistical problems, not least of which is getting people their money back.

However, I simply had no option. I had had a complete mental breakdown which left me unable to hold a guitar or think about a song, never mind do a gig. In December 1997 I returned from a three-month tour of Australia and New Zealand with some club dates in New York on the way home. I arrived feeling tired, but five days later I simply cracked up. It was a terrifying experience, for my mind went into a strange spin and my emotions were completely awry. Mental turmoil came on me in waves and I withdrew into a dark corner. I was put into hospital for tests and they knocked me out for a week. I came home on Christmas Eve 1997 and I was a complete wreck. Friends tried to help me but I could not respond. Val was the only one I could relate to but Andy, Juno and Pádraic helped me as best they could. Brother Barry was also a pillar of strength, as were all my family.

I have been blessed with a doctor, Patrick Nugent, who also became a valued friend. He took me under his wing and went inside my head and helped me to put the pieces back together again. I also learned about the power of prayer, that when my mind was leaving me the one thing I could do that helped me focus was to pray. My prayer was in the form of talking to my Daddy who, though he died in 1956, came back into my life during this crisis.

Slowly I began to get some peace of mind again. Val and I went to Cork to try to make some plans and pick up the pieces.

The first big decision was the tour. Then I had to withdraw from The Vicar Street Project – a Dublin venue which I was involved in the planning and building of. This was to have been the realisation of a dream of mine but sadly it had become my nightmare. Today it is Dublin's premier music venue but I have settled for being a singer.

Finally, I needed to dismantle the *modus operandi* which had evolved over the previous fifteen years but was no longer required. I had no idea what the future would hold, but even as I began to recover I knew that my touring days were over. If and when I was to play again it would be at a different pace.

New Galway Races
by C. Moore

There's Bethlehem and Cheltenham and there's Lourdes and Limerick Junction
A trip to Medjugorge or a rub of the extreme unction
Good people climb Croagh Patrick with serenity on their faces
Others find salvation below at the Galway Races

There's clergymen dressed up like men and models home from London
'Whallup and hows she cutting John', 'Begod sure only middling'
There's gamblers there with wads of notes going mad to gamble
Na boys isteach as Inverin there just to take a ramble

Helen Lucy smells the mattress reviews the hairy bacon
Sez Mickey Finn to Galligan 'Hey Peter what ye taking'
Shish kebabs Kinvara crabs as people stuff their faces
Some couldn't ate to save their lives at the Galway Races

It's there you'll see gentility and sheep dressed up like mutton
Double barrelled names with more airs than auld melodeon
The talk is all of tillage of silage and con acre
I tell ye scraws and bottoms would be closer to the mark sir

Sir John Mucksavage Smythe is there with Smurfits and O'Reillys
Owners and trainers, stable boys and jockeys
With silk around their arses getting up on rich men's horses
Not to mention wives and daughters and marriages and divorces

There's pontoon and twenty-five and savage games of poker
There's them who'd bet their lives on two flies walking up the wall sure
Wise men from the east making eyes at go-go dancers
Ministers of state accepting drink from terrible chancers

They're under starter's orders now Ted Walsh anticipating
Billy Burke is up on Santa Claus she'll surely take some batin'
Necks are craned eyes are strained there's fear upon the faces
Agony and ecstasy below at the Galway Races

Salthill after dark is like Sodom and Gomorrah
People doing things tonight they'll regret tomorrow
Folk and trad they're disco mad Karaoke and set dances
People who've seen better days looking to take their chances

When I was sixteen I travelled to the Galway Races with my friend and neighbour John Flood. It was 1961, he had a Mini and I had a tent. We had £15 a man, enough to set a mill going with my two shinbones stuck in my pocket and my head stuck under my arm. As soon as we hit Salthill we got the tent up and struck out for O'Connor's ballad lounge where Christy O'Connor was Master of Ceremonies and the crack was 90. Flood somehow arranged it for me to get up and sing and I scored heavily with 'Rosin the Bow' and 'The Jug of Punch'. We pulled two fine models from Wexford and the Galway Races were looking up.

Next day we met up with a Moorefield contingent that included Jim McDermot, Ba Dowling, Doggy Anderson and Harry Fay. The rum and black was flying and Flood was getting anxious for he'd got a tip from Kevin Bell for the 3.30 and we had planned to have a good punt, but I had other notions and horses and jockeys were not among them.

We never made it out to Ballybrit but we backed a few winners and then, almost twenty years later. . .

It was bigger than Woodstock
In Ballybrit down in Co. Galway
With Fr Mick, Bishop Eamon, Cardinal Sin
Pope John Paul the Second came flying in

He kissed the Holy Ground
Young people of Ireland – I love you

Such an air of celebration
Half a million people dancing in the rain
In a great new church for the young
Where everything was clearly black and white

He kissed the Holy Ground
Young people of Ireland – I love you

His Holiness came here and spoke it plain
Nailing his colours to the mast
He walked across the women
And Fr Mick, Bishop Eamon and Cardinal Sin
went home fulfilled

We all kissed the Holy Ground in a cloud of smoke
Young people of Ireland – I love you

The Singer
by Patrick Nugent

I'm not what I seem on the outside
Not the riches, the glory, the fame
I am more than my public perception
I'm not just a face and a name
I'm more than a maker of music
I'm less than a weaver of dreams
I burn with my own fire inside me
The singer is more than he seems

I'm a singer of songs for the silent
I sing them the best way I can
I share all my soul's special secrets
But remember I'm also a man

You fans feel the furious fingers
You tap to my foot on the ground
You thrill to the throb of the bowrawn
And you soar on the waves of my sound
But you don't see the singer's discomfort
As round in the rhythms you sway
For the music that mellows your memories
Is a part of me given away

I pour out the power of your passions
I flood out your blood with my pain
You burst with my pride in our country
So I strum it again and again
But the magic is more than the music
If you think that it's not then you're wrong
The singer's the voice of the people
But the singer is more than his song

I'm a singer of songs for the silent
I sing them the best way I can
I share all my soul's special secrets
But remember I'm also a man

I've never gotten round to singing this song. Patrick wrote it specially for me and I include it here to honour my dearly departed friend. Over and above his skills as a GP he had a deep insight into the human condition and he had a particular love and understanding for the weak ones in his care.

For most of my life as a performer I always maintained that the work was so pleasurable that it could not be difficult. I used this theory to fool myself. Patrick pointed out to me the pressures and pitfalls of my occupation and I believed him. He spoke of the pressure of trying to fulfill people's expectations night after night, of trying to reach the lofty heights I felt were necessary. When I tumbled Patrick put me together again.

Goodnight, Doc.

Hey! Ronnie Reagan
by John Maguire

You're so cool playing poker with death as the joker you've got nerve but you don't assure us
With your paranoid vistas of mad Sandinistas and the way you're defending Honduras
We'll dig shelter holes when we've bargained our souls as for Pershing and Cruise we shovel
While the myth of our dreams turns to nightmares from the White House back to the hovel

Hey Ronnie Reagan I'm black and I'm pagan
I'm gay and I'm left and I'm free
I'm a non-fundamentalist environmentalist
Please don't bother me

Since the Irish dimension has caught your attention I'm asking myself what's your game
Have you shed any tears these past fifteen years or is that just a vote-catcher's gleam
Your dollars may beckon but I think we should reckon the cost of accepting your gold
If you get your way what a price we will pay, what's left when freedom is sold

You'll be wearing the Green down in Ballyporeen in the Town of the Little Potato
With your arm around Garret you'll dangle your carrot but you'll never get me to join NATO
I've watched you for years amid laughter and tears acting out your games of deception
Despite what you see there's no welcome from me and I firmly oppose your reception

There was a terrible frenzy when that man came here. He and his wife and his entourage epitomised all that is unpalatable about America. They came here and pushed everyone aside, walked upon our ways and trampled upon our culture purely for photo opportunity. All the bogshites and charlatans had a field day on this occasion of gross crassness and bad taste.

To an extent the same atmosphere prevailed for the visits of J. F. Kennedy and Bill Clinton, but somehow both these men appeared to have a love for and an empathy with the people of this small island.

At the time of the Reagan visit I would not have been a big fan of Irish Special Branch, but nevertheless I was pisssed off by the manner in which the US police came in and literally shoved our men aside. I recall seeing large helicopters flying across Munster one day, and there was an eerie discomfort at the huge invasive presence in the country.

Babies were kissed, lounges got a coat of paint, toilets got paper and Garret giggled and fawned.

The island of saints and scholars, and gamblers and arselickers – if we must have special armed police, at least let them be our own.

Good Ship Kangaroo
from Mrs Elizabeth Cronin, Macroom, Co. Cork

Once I was a waiting man who lived at home at ease
Now I am a mariner that ploughs the stormy seas
I always loved seafaring life I bid my love adieu
I shipped as steward and cook me boys on board the Kangaroo

I never thought she would prove false or either prove untrue
As we sailed away from Milford Bay on board the Kangaroo

Think of me oh think of me she mournfully did say
When you are in a foreign land and I am far away
And take this lucky thrupenny bit it will make you bear in mind
This loving trusting faithful heart you left in tears behind

Cheer up, cheer up my own true love don't weep so bitterly
She sobbed she sighed she choked she cried 'til she could not say goodbye
I won't be gone for very long but for a month or two
And when I return again of course I'll visit you

Our ship it was homeward bound from manys the foreign shore
Manys the foreign present unto my love I bore
I brought tortoises from Tenerife and ties from Timbuktoo
A China rat, a Bengal cat and a Bombay cockatoo

Paid off I sought her dwelling on a street above the town
Where an ancient dame upon the line was hanging out her gown
Where is my love she's vanished sir about six months ago
With a smart young man who drives the van for Chaplin Son & Co

Here's a health to dreams of married life to soap suds and blue
Heart's true love, patent starch and washing soda too
I'll go into some foreign shore no longer can I stay
With some China Hottentot I'll throw my life away

My love she was no foolish girl her age it was two score
My love she was no spinster she'd been married twice before
I cannot say it was her wealth that stole my heart away
She was a washer in the laundry for one and nine a day

Somewhere along the line I came to possess a recording of Mrs Cronin's beautiful singing. She had a unique sound, a beautiful voice combined with perfect diction and her singing in English was wonderfully coloured by the inflections of her native tongue. I simply love the way this woman sings.

For me, the song itself is the kernel. If my mind becomes focused on the pictures the song creates, I believe that my voice will follow. Next up is the texture and rhythm of the accompaniment. This is vital to get right, for if it is off-key or unsuitably rhythmic, my mind will focus on these flaws rather than the work. Then there is the timbre of the voice to be used. I have not actually counted, but there are many different vocal approaches that perhaps only the singer can define.

Lastly comes the frame for it all. The audience is more than a frame; in my own case I only get down to it when I have an audience to work with. What this may indicate I will leave to the psychoanalysts, but I've never been able to completely lose myself in a song in my workroom or a studio.

In the workroom I'm very aware of the sounds around the house, children coming from school, Val keeping the home together, phone or fax, birds or dogs or cats in the garden. In the studio I'm just disrupted by everything around me. But in the live arena, 95 per cent of the time I am completely at one with the work.

I recall once receiving severe criticism for my singing of 'Good Ship Kangaroo'. It was from a man highly regarded in music circles as a custodian and performer of the tradition. I was particularly stung by his words, but today I am more assured about my work. I have never claimed to be a traditional singer of the old songs. I am in the revivalist camp, for I was not at the famine, nor 1798, nor 1916, I never took the King's shilling nor bought tortoises in Tenerife. I now see that some of the staunch fundamental traditionalists would prefer the work to die with the old singer. I am happy today that this wonderful song has been heard and enjoyed by thousands around the world who, like myself, have felt the warmth and joy of Mrs Elizabeth Cronin's beautiful music.

So ye lords and ladies of the high ground get down off your horses and enjoy God's gifts.

Whiskey In the Jar
from The Clancy Brothers

As I was goin over the Cork and Kerry mountain
I met with Colonel Packenham and his money he was counting
I first produced my pistol then produced my rapier
Saying stand and deliver for I am a bold deceiver

Musha ring dum a doo dum da
Whack fol de daddy O
Whack fol de daddy O
There's whiskey in the jar

He counted out his money and it made a pretty penny
I put it in my pocket and brought it home to Jenny
She sighed and she swore she never would deceive me
But the devil take that woman for she never could lie easy

I went up to my chamber all for to take a slumber
I dreamt of gold and silver and sure it was no wonder
But Jenny drew me pistols and filled them up with water
And sent for Captain Farrell to be ready for the slaughter

Early the next morning before I rose to travel
On came the special horsemen and likewise Captain Farrell
I first produced me pistol and then produced me rapier
But I couldn't shoot the water so a prisoner I was taken

If ever you go hunting in the morning bright and early
Through the hills of Dublin or the mountains of Tipperary
Keep one hand on your pistol and the other on your money
And keep your eyes well peeled for that darling sporting Jenny

I've not sung this song in public for 35 years but I love to sing it at home to myself. It transports me back to an earlier time:

Like a stranger in this world I was lost and in a rage
Heading down a dead-end street seeking centre stage

Until I heard Liam Clancy sing and I listened for a while
For the first time in my life I felt like I was home and dry

In 1961 Ireland was ultra Conservative and extremely Catholic. The Church had its wet paw stuck into every aspect of my life and it felt like it was crawling all over me. I heard this music and I wanted it. It became my vehicle of escape. It would carry me away down the road from priests, Brothers, nuns, sins, confessions, first Fridays, fast, total abstinence, on down to a place where the good music was made.

In the early-morning houses and the late shebeens
We sang our songs and played our tunes and planned our crazy schemes
In the arms of gentle women and the hearts of lonely men
I learned about the warmth of love, the cold of fear and pain

Along the way I began to hear the old singers, to be introduced to the bigger songs. Down past the fun and frolicsome ballads I came to the spirit songs, the mystical verses of John Reilly, Joe Heaney, Bert Lloyd and the heavenly voices of Jeannie Robertson, Belle Stewart, Norma and Lal Waterson, Elizabeth Cronin.

I followed old-time singers and listened to their songs
I learned to vamp the jigs and reels and rhythm the bowrawn
The guitar was my passport, the sleeping bag my home
Always heading down the road to learn another song

Thirty-seven years later I still love deeply the work itself – the words and notes and pictures painted in the singing.

I got well sucked into the maelstrom of the business. It probably began in 1972 when I received a large cheque for the album *Prosperous*. The arse was out of my trousers and I was living hand to mouth, albeit in a most enjoyable way. I began to rub shoulders with people from the music business, and I was beginning to understand the machinations and even to see things from the business point of view. I have encountered good and bad people in music, but I've never met one industry person who had the deep understanding or love of the work that many players have.

Within the parameters of the music industry, for every artist at work there is a legion of bureaucrats – management staff, road crew (sound, lighting, drivers, security, merchandise), agents, promoters, venue staff, studio staff, recording company staff, PR company staff, and all these good people have an interest, to a varying degree, in the outcome of that person's work.

A profile of the artist is developed; it is shaped by the work itself and coupled with the image the various agencies feel would be most beneficial. Artists can end up in a very lonely place if they are fed self-interested platitudes by the people surrounding them. Lines such as 'You are a blue-chip act', 'Artist at the height of your powers', 'Performing like a true champion', 'Your performance is like a meal from a great chef' – all this auld shite will eventually take its toll.

I never met Bob Dylan but I sang with Pecker Dunne
And when we drank Lough Éireann dry we went looking for Lough Dan
The crack was good in Cricklewood but 'twas better in Athboy
When Maggie Barry called me up for The Wild Colonial Boy

Green Island
by Ewan McColl

The island lies like a leaf upon the sea
Green island like a leaf new fallen from the tree
Green turns to gold as morning breezes gently shake the barley bending the yellow corn
Green turns to gold there's purple shadows on the distant mountains sun in the yellow corn

They came in their longships from lands across the sea
They came in their longships they saw the land was green
Wind in the barley, trout and salmon leaping in the rivers sun on the yellow corn
Leaping ashore they slaughtered those who laboured in the barley scything them down like corn

The longships sailed away and new invaders came
With longbow and lance bringing death in England's name
With sword and with mace they went raping through the fields of barley, plundered the yellow corn
Crop followed crop and prospered in the killing fields of barley, harvest of new young corn

Marching down the years the men of war they came
With bombs assassins bullets CS gas and guns
Ghosts from the past are chasing shadows through the fields of barley hiding in the yellow corn
Nine hundred years they've tried to trap the wind that shakes the barley and the sun in the yellow corn

The island lies like a leaf upon the sea
Green island like a leaf new fallen from the tree
Green turns to gold as morning breezes gently shake the barley bending the yellow corn
No force on earth can ever trap the wind that shakes the barley nor the sun in the yellow corn

Still the rape goes on. Roisín McAliskey is released and there is uproar from the Conservative and Unionist ranks. No matter the lack of evidence, for any taig will do.

It's a long long way from Clare to here
All right Paddy, don't forget your shovel
Irish pigs
Send the paras into the Bogside and sort the savages out
Building up and tearing England down

Terry Waite, Gareth Peirce, Sister Clarke, Michael Mansfield, Jeremy Corbyn
Margaret Thatcher
Our wildness misconstrued as dysfunction

Ewan McColl and Peggy Seeger sent me this song and shortly afterwards
Ewan died. I took great care in recording it for it meant a lot to me that he
would send me a song.

The Hackler from Grouse Hall
Author unknown

I am a roving hackler lad that loves the shamrock shore
My name is Pat McDonnell and my age is eighty-four
Beloved and well respected by my neighbours one and all
On St Patrick's Day I used to stray round Lavey and Grouse Hall

When I was young I danced and sung and drank strong whiskey too
Each sheebeen shop that sold a drop of real auld mountain dew
With poitín still on every hill the Peelers had no call
Round sweet Stradone I am well known round Lavey and Grouse Hall

I used to go from town to town for hackling was my trade
None can deny I thought that I an honest living made
Where e'er I'd stay by night or day the youth would always call
To have the crack with Paddy Jack, the hackler from Grouse Hall

I think it strange how very much the times have changed of late
Coercion now is all the row with Peelers on their bate
To take a glass is now alas the greatest crime of all
Since Balfour placed that hungry beast, the sergeant from Grouse Hall

This busy tool of castle rule he wanders night and day
He'll take a goat all by the throat for want of better prey
The nasty skunk he'll swear you're drunk tho' you've had none at all
There is no peace around the place since he came to Grouse Hall

'Twas on a pretence of this offence he dragged me off to jail
Alone to dwell in a cold cell my fortune to bewail
My hoary head on a plank bed such wrongs for vengeance call
He'll rue the day he dragged away the hackler from Grouse Hall

He'll run pell mell down into Hell to search for poitín there
And won't be loathe to swear on oath he found it in Killikere
He'll search your bed from foot to head sheets blankets tick and all
Your wife undressed must leave the nest for Jemmy from Grouse Hall

Come old and young clear up your lung and sing this little song
Come join with me and let them see you all resent the wrong
While I live I'll always give a prayer for his downfall
When I die I don't deny I'll haunt him from Grouse Hall

Poitín me darlin', whiskey the life of me, stick to the cratur, the rare auld stuff, the best of friends and enemies, my life's blood.

Many eulogies have been written and many the praise been sung. In retrospect, despite many's the helpless laugh and loud guffaw, I think it could be best named as the Devil's own water. Far from being the stuff of life, I'd say the balm of death be closer to the mark. By all means rub greyhounds and dose cattle or rub it in the child's scalp after bathing in a cold draughty house, but as for drinking it . . .

Even with the purest tincture the first swallow could be fiery enough. But once the first and second charge were swallowed it got easier after that and, before long, a fellow could be climbing the walls of the Fillmore West in Bray, Co. Wicklow, or could be locked into the filthy dressing room of Caesar's Palace in Bunclody or lobbing bottles from the sixteenth storey of a London hotel or watching the scians flashing out in Inverin. It could remove warts and life itself, and still we sing on and on about it.

On yonder hill there's a darlin' little still with the smoke curlin' up the sky
By the smoke and the smell you can plainly tell that there's poitín me lads nearby

I had some fine highs, but they were never worth the lows that followed, nor the close shaves involved. Tony Murray gave us a gallon for a wedding present and we drank it all, too. God rest you Tony, you distilled a pure drop.

St Patrick Was a Gentleman
Author unknown

St Patrick was a gentleman he came from dacent people
He built a church in Dublin town and on it put a steeple
His father was a Gallagher his uncle was a Grady
His aunt was an O'Shaughnessy and his mother was a Brady
The Wicklow hills are very high so is the Hill of Howth sir
But there's a hill much higher still much higher nor them both sir
On the top of this high hill St Patrick preached his sermon
He drove the frogs into the bogs and banished all the vermin

There's not a mile of Erin's Isle where dirty vermin mustered
But there he put his dear fore foot and murdered them in clusters
The toads went pop and the frogs went hop slap dash in to the water
And the snakes committed suicide to save themselves from slaughter
A hundred thousand reptiles blue he charmed with sweet discourses
And he dined on them in Killaloe in soups and second courses
Where the blind worms crawling in the grass disgusted all the nation
Right down to Hell with a holy spell he changed their situation

No wonder that them Irish boys should be so gay and frisky
Sure St Pat he thought them that as well as making whiskey
No wonder that the saint himself should understand distilling
For his mother kept a sheeben shop near the town of Enniskillen
Was I but so fortunate as to be back in Ulster
I'd be bound that from that ground I never more would once stir
For there St Patrick planted turf and cabbages and praties
Pigs galore, mo grá mo stór, altar boys and ladies

17 March 1997

Once again it comes around – always a day for flashbacks. If Patrick came to Ireland today the poor man would have his work cut out, for today's serpents are a lot more slithery than those of fifteen centuries past. If he had tried to banish them today, the saint would end up in the cooler, he would be ridiculed and charged with protecting his Authors, he would face assassination and certainly would be banished from the Catholic Church, which would be busy honouring Rupert Murdoch on the one hand and trying to protect Pope Pius XII from charges of total complicity with Nazism on the other.

It's 25 years since I uncovered this old song. I recorded it in 1979 and it's well known today. This past week I've seen quotes from it throughout the media. Traditionally, it was a great day for drowning the shamrock. The poor man must have a sense of humour, for we honour him with a day of drunkenness and debauchery. Catholics travel from all over the world to get drunk here in his name.

I recall a TV show in Melbourne on St Patrick's Day in the Eighties. I was sharing a table with the Irish ambassador, a Mr Sharkey from Derry. I sang 'The Time Has Come' and 'Back Home in Derry'.

I remember a Paddy's Day in the Sixties when I was charged and convicted of drunken driving. The day was going quite well until I began accepting lethal cocktails of champagne laced with brandy – then I offered to give a one-armed retired British army colonel a lift home. I drove straight into the arms of the Lancashire constabulary and the colonel disappeared on me.

Once I Had a Love
Author unknown

I once had a love and I loved her so well
I hated all others who spoke of her ill
Now she's rewarded me well for my love
She's gone to be wed to another

I saw my love down to the church go
And the bride and bride's mother made a fine show
I followed after my heart full of woe
To see my love wed to another

I saw my love she sat down to dine
I sat down beside her and poured out the wine
I drank to the lass that would never be mine
For she's gone to be wed to another

The men of the forest ask it of me
How many strawberries grow round the salt sea
I answer them back with a tear in my eye
How many ships sail in the forest

Dig me a grave and dig it so deep
Bury me in it to take a long sleep
Cover it over with flowers so sweet
Maybe in time I'll forget her

It all seems so long ago. Singing this song I was living in a time of innocence. The big questions of the day were the lift home or the lie down or the entrance fee.

I moved to Manchester in 1967. From Silver Crescent in Gunnersbury, West London, to 48 Alexander Road, Moss Side. It was through the kindness of The Grehan Sisters that I moved, as they offered to introduce me to the circuit of clubs in Lancashire. I shared a bedsit with their brother Tony, who was a true eccentric and, among other things, an inventor, songwriter, psychic and downright total head-the-ball. But he made a wonderful flatmate for no two days were ever the same.

The man who managed the house also dealt hash on the side. At age 22 I had an intense dislike of hash – I saw it as somehow dangerous. Sixteen pints and a bottle of vodka was masculine and much more in order. Within a year I had changed my mind about hash, grass, speed, acid, mescaline and, subsequently, cocaine.

I spent my days wandering around Manchester, practising my songs and trying to wangle a few bob here and there. I did odd bits of work in jobs as varied as building with Wimpey, box jumping in a waste-paper factory off Oldham Street, cold-meat portering for Lewis of Piccadilly and bar work in the Pack Horse Inn at Birtle, near Bury. However, as soon as I could survive from music I threw away my cards and off I went. I could survive then on £10 a week, so if I got three gigs I'd be fine. The clubs I played at first were The MSG, Crown & Anchor, Mike Harding's club in Blakeley and venues run by Frank Duffy, Harry Bradshaw, Tony and Arthur, Jack, Mavis and The Valley Folk in Bury. And then I began to move out to Leigh, Bolton, Hale, Congleton, Ashton, Openshaw, Hyde – and the fee was going up to £6 or £8 a night.

Off to Sea Once More (Shanghai Browne)
Author unknown

When first I landed in Liverpool I went upon the spree
My money at last I spent it fast I got drunk as drunk could be
When my money it was all spent it was then that I wanted more
A man must be blind to make up his mind to go to sea once more

Once more boys once more
To go to sea once more
A man must be blind to make up his mind
To go to sea once more

As I was walking thru Liverpool I met with Angeline
She said to me come home with me and we'll have a cracking good time
When I awoke it was no joke for I was all on my own
My silver watch and my money too and all of my gear was gone

A boarding master picked me up his name was Shangai Browne
I asked him would he take me on and he looked at me with a frown
The last time that you sailed with me you never chalked no score
I'll take a chance, give you an advance, and send you to sea once more

So I shipped on board of a clipper ship bound for the Arctic Sea
Where the cold winds blow mid the ice and the snow and Jamaica rum would freeze
And worse to bear I'd no hard weather gear for I'd spent all my money on shore
It was then that I wished that I was dead so I'd go to sea no more

Sometimes we're catching the big sperm whales sometimes we're catching none
A twenty-foot oar stuck in my paw and pullin the whole day long
When the daylight's gone and the night comes on I rest upon my oar
Boys oh boys I wished I was dead or snug with the girls on shore

Come all you bold sea-faring boys who listen to my song
When you come off them long long trips I'd have you not go wrong
Take my advice drink no strong drink don't go drinking with them whores
Get married instead sleep in your own bed and go to sea no more

I was in love with a woman but she turned me upside down and inside out. I met her at a folk club in Palmer's Green in London. She was sitting in the third row with a big head of curls. So I asked her to fly away to Jersey with me the following day, and she did. We had a lovely honeymoon, but then my love and drinking became too much and she went off on me and fell in love with a junkie and I kept chasin her and she stole me fuckin heart for a couple of years so I drank me head off anyway.

23 March 1998

It's 32 years later and I'm in a vacuum-like space. This morning I'm dominated by fear and anxiety which is a sure sign that I've taken back the controls. I don't have my work obsession to distract me from the reality of my powerlessness over people, places and things. I can take hold of the briar of financial insecurity and torture myself – I can only day-dream about work for I do not know how or when or where to begin. Of course, we have decided to go slowly, step-by-step through the maze that the past has created and when that image yields up the hard facts of our situation then, perhaps, we will be able to see the path on which to walk.

Talk Shows

Singing on live talk shows is a terrible fate. The audience is frozen to the chair, totally freaked by the possibility that their dials will appear on the box. They keep one totally disinterested eye upon the performance, the other obsessed eye on the monitor. There is justice in this. When I appear on chat shows I am totally prostituting my work in order to sell units for me and a record company, or seats for me and the promoter. I am using my God-given talents for Mammon. This might be different if it's a tribute show or an issue show, where I may be genuinely using my work and talent to pay my respects to, say, Paul McGrath or, perhaps, to oppose a nuclear power station in Ireland.

Shows to remember would include the anti-nuclear *Late, Late Show*. I was on the verge of the DTs. I had odd shoes on and my keks were not the best. I was just at the end of a five-day jag in Galway and I was in bits. I had been travelling with Mick Coogan from Castlecomer and I made up verses for the song on the journey to Dublin. I performed two songs: 'Nuke Power' and 'The Workers Are Being Used Again'. Monday's *Irish Independent* carried the banner headline 'Taoiseach's wife slams folk singer'. My nerves were rattled when I met 'Scoop' Glennon in Buswells, so I had a few large gin and tonics before he interviewed me.

Sullivans John
by Pecker Dunne

Sullivans John to the road you've gone far away from your native home
You're gone with the tinker's daughter all along the road to roam
Sullivans John you won't stick it long till your belly will soon get slack
You'll be goin the road with a mighty load and your tool box up on your back

There is a horse fair in the county Clare in a place they call Spancilhill
Where my brother James got a rap of a hames and poor Johnny they tried to kill
They loaded him up in an auld ass and car all along the road to pass
Saying bad luck to the day that I went away to join with the tinker band

I met Kate Coffee with her neat baby behind on her back strapped on
She'd an auld ash plant all in her hand to drive her donkey on
Enquiring at every farmer's door as on the road she'd pass
As to where she'd get an auld pot to mend or where she might swap an ass

Sullivans John to the road you've gone far away from your native home
You're gone with the tinker's daughter all along the road to roam
Sullivans John you won't stick it long till your belly will soon get slack
You'll be goin the road with a mighty load and your tool box up on your back

In the winter of 1998–99, I played one frame of snooker with 'The Whirlwind' Jimmy White. He was giving an exhibition against local hot-shots in Sallynoggin, Co. Dublin and I was wheeled out as token-local-celebrity fodder. It was a gloriously mad evening and a number of the audience had been oiling themselves nicely in preparation. Jimmy destroyed his first five opponents and then my turn came. I was very nervous as he broke off and dispersed the reds all over the table. I potted a difficult red and followed it with a beautiful pink. I missed my next red and Jimmy sipped his half of lager, put down his Benson & Hedges, strolled nonchalantly around the table and cleared it with a 134 break.

As a token of my awe and admiration, I gave him a rendition of 'Sullivans John'. I've never recorded or gigged this song but I like to sing it on certain occasions.

Snooker is an important part of my life. I play mainly with my son Andy and the painter Brian Maguire. Please allow me to record that, in the Premier Snooker Club, Dun Laoghaire (run by Eugene Hughes, a contender), on Friday 14 January 2000, I scored my first 50. It was towards the end of a tense best of 11, and we were poised on 5–5. Then it happened. Red-black-red-black-red-brown-red-pink-red-blue-red-black-red-black. Thankfully it was with an opponent who understood the significance of the event. We put our cues down and sat in wonderment.

I could only liken it to winning the talent competition in The Palace Cinema, Newbridge in 1955 when I was ten years old and I went out on stage and sang 'Kevin Barry' and the crowd went wild. I was bitten. Or the time I scored a try for Newbridge in 1960 in the Schools Cup, and for Corinthians of Galway against Clontarf in 1965, or the goal for Moorefield against Round Towers in 1963 (the list is not endless).

I used to love hard physical training and playing, but today I settle for singing 'Sullivans John' and playing snooker. I've even let go of ever propping (at no. 3) for the Irish XV.

Rocky Road to Dublin
Author unknown

In the merry month of June all from my home I started
Left the girls of Tuam sad and broken hearted
Saluted my father dear kissed my darlin mother
Drank a pint of beer my grief and tears to smother
Then off to reap the corn leave where I was born
I cut a stout blackthorn to banish ghost and goblin
In a brand new pair of brogues I rattled o'er the bogs
Frightened all the dogs on the rocky road to Dublin

One two three four five
Hunt the hare and turn her
Down the rocky road and all the way to Dublin
Whack fol doll de dah

In Mullingar that night I rested limbs so weary
Started by daylight next mornin bright and early
Took a drop of the pure to keep my heart from sinking
That's the Paddy's cure whenever he's on for drinking
To see the lassies smile at me curious style
Laughing all the while 'twould set your heart a-bubbling
They asked if I was hired the wages I required
I was bloody well tired of the rocky road to Dublin

In Dublin next arrived I thought it such a pity
To be so soon deprived a view of that fine city
Then I took a stroll all among the quality
My bundle it was stolen in a neat locality
Something crossed me mind, I should look behind
No bundle could I find upon my stick a-wobbling
Enquiring for the rogue said my Connacht brogue
Wasn't much in vogue on the rocky road to Dublin

I soon got out of that my spirits never failing
Landed on the quay just as my ship was sailing
The captain at me roared said that no room had he
When I jumped aboard a cabin he found for Paddy

Down among the pigs I played a few slip jigs
Danced some hearty rigs the water round me bubblin
Then at Holyhead I wished myself was dead
Or better far instead on the rocky road to Dublin

The boys of Liverpool when we were safely landed
They called me a fool I could no longer stand it
Me blood began to boil my temper I was losin
When poor old Ireland's isle they began abusing
Hurrah my soul sez I shillelagh I let fly
Some Galway boys close by they saw that I was hobblin
Then with loud hurray joined in the affray
Quickly cleared the way for the rocky road to Dublin

Hackneyed and chainsawed in a thousand Irish bars morning, noon and night from Kaiserslautern to Warnambool this song has survived the test of time and persistant abuse. I've no idea who wrote it or when, but to me it's almost Joycean in its glorious use of English as we speak it.

This is an epic journey from Galway to Holyhead, reminiscent of a few journeys I made myself from Kildare to London in a time before ferries and flights when a fellow would hitch to Dublin and then down the North Wall to take the cattle boat to Liverpool. The cheapest passage was 8/-, and a bunk could be had for half a dollar or five bob, if a fellow needed such extravagance. There were great nights on those old cattle ships – I recall one evening when the captain went around with the hat for a collection for The Grehan Sisters and myself. There were songs and rows and love-making and drinking on the high sea and there's many a one got off the boat not sure whether they were coming or going. . .

Go on and sing the song. Give it everything you've got, never mind the shapes, your career, your manager, agent, roadie, publicist, accountant, lawyer, driver, security, caterer, doorman, ticket collector, engineer, tape op, sound man, light man, monitor man, humper – just sing the song for yourself to warm your own heart.

Singing for money can be a bad thing.

Spanish Lady
Author unknown

As I went out by Dublin City at the hour of twelve at night
Who should I see but the Spanish lady washing her feet by candlelight
First she washed them then she dried them all by the fire of amber coal
In all my life I ne'er did see a maid so sweet about the sole

I asked her would she come out a walking and went on till the grey cocks crew
A coach I stopped then to instate her and we rode on till the sky was blue
Combs of amber in her hair were and her eyes knew every spell
In all my life I ne'er did see a woman whom I could love so well

But when I came to where I found her and set her down from the halted coach
Who was there with his arms folded but the fearful swordsman Tiger Roche
Blades were out twas thrust and cut never a man gave me more fright
Till I lay him dead on the floor where she stood holding the candlelight

So if you go to Dublin City at the hour of twelve at night
Beware of the girls who sit in their windows combin their hair in the candlelight
I met one and we went walkin I thought that she would be my wife
When I came to where I found her if it wasn't for me sword I'd have lost my life

I have no recall as to where or when I encountered this song, but it was in my earliest repertoire. I also feel that I may have written some lines, but I can't figure out which ones.

I first came to Dublin in the early Fifites. During my childhood I spent most extended school holidays with my maternal grandparents Jack and Ellie Power. Jack was from Hayestown and Ellie was a Sheeran from 'The Cotton Mills', both townlands being in the region of Yellow Furze – near Navan, Co. Meath.

Jack Power was a farm steward for Sir Alexander Maguire at Ardmulchan, near Navan. He left that job after my mother suffered what would today be described as sexual harassment in the workplace. Next, he managed a farm for M.J. Gleeson Esq. of Sheffield, who owned a large farm at Loughlinstown House, near Dunboyne, Co. Meath. Then Jack and Ellie moved to Weston, near Celbridge, where he managed a farm for Mr Gleeson which was subsequently taken over by the Department of Agriculture, which still runs 'Backweston' today.

Jack was a great man for cowboy films, and he took me to Dublin many Saturdays in his old black Ford Prefect. He and I would visit the Adelphi, Metropole, Carlton and Savoy cinemas to marvel at John Wayne, Audie Murphy and Stewart Granger. Doubtless Grandfather also had time for Ava Gardner, Lana Turner and Bette Davis, but they were of no interest to me in the early Fifties. (As time passed this began to change – I began to notice things about the girl next door, physical differences, intriguing items of clothing, the eroticism of lipstick and then there was that picture of the young Queen. . .)

In those days, Jack would park outside the cinema in O'Connell Street and we'd saunter in and have two Knickerbocker Glories before the programme began. Heading back to Weston, the Ford would inevitably pull up at the Ball Alley House in Lucan, and Jack would mosey up to the bar and leave me in the car with endless bottles of lemonade and bars of chocolate. He'd have bottles of stout for the crack, and gin for the kidneys and then out he'd come at nine or ten with his hat well back on his head and head home to Ellie to face the inevitable music.

He was an avid wireless man, and a dreadful smoker – he died during a fit of coughing after lighting the first Sweet Afton of the day. It was in front of my sister Terry; he was around 62 at the time. Ellie never recovered from his death, and took to the bed. She taught me how to back horses, and I spent many hours in bed with her as she told me of her childhood and stories from the Boyne and all her fantasies about her beloved son Jimmy, who was the apple of her eye. He died alone in Birmingham, smothered by being spoiled, God rest them both.

Foggy Dew
from Jack Power
Hayestown, Navan, Co. Meath

As down the Glen one Easter morn to a city fair rode I
There armed lines of marching men in squadrons passed me by
No Fifes did hum nor battle drum rang out their dread tattoo
But the Angelus bell o'er the Liffey swell rang out in the foggy dew

Right proudly high over Dublin Town they hung out the flag of war
It was better to die 'neath an Irish sky than at Suvlas or Sudelbar
And from the plains of Royal Meath strong men they came hurrying through
While Britannia's huns with her long range guns fired Hell through the foggy dew

The bravest fell and the sullen bell rang mournfully and clear
For those who died that Eastertide in the springtime of the year
To and fro in my mind I go I kneel and I pray for you
For slavery fled oh rebel dead when you fell in the foggy dew

'Twas Britannia bade our wild geese go that small rations might be free
But their lonely graves are by Suvlas waves or by the fringe of the great North Sea
Had they died by Pearse's side or fought alongside Cathal Brugha
Their graves we would keep where the Fenian sleep 'neath the shroud of the foggy dew

Back through the glen I rode again and my heart with grief was sore
For I parted then with gallant men I never would see more
And to and fro in my mind I go and I kneel and I pray for you
For slavery fled, oh rebel dead when you fell in the foggy dew

My lovely grandfather used to whistle and sing this song. Jack was a fine, well-built, straight, athletic man. He worked all his life for English millionaire absentee landlords. He adored his beautiful daughter (Mammy) and loved his exiled son. He went to Mass every Sunday, and that was about the size of it. Ellie stayed in bed most days, but got up in time to have a splendid fry on the table when he came in, always bringing a little gift.

Once, they sent me to Lucan to get a Mass said for some dead person. Ellie gave me a blue ten-pound note and a Mass card. The priest signed the card and kept the £10. I was eleven and I did not know what to do. In those days, a Mass cost 10/- to £1. Jack was earning about £13 a week. The fucking bastard of a priest kept the tenner. God forgive him.

Bold Fenian Men
from Ellie Power (née Sheeran), late of Cotton Mills

It was down by the Glenside I met an old woman
Plucking young nettles she ne'er heard me coming
I listened a while to the song she was humming
Glory oh glory oh to the bold Fenian men

When I was a young lad their marching and drilling
Awoke in the Glenside sounds awesome and thrilling
I can still hear them now amidst all my wild dreaming
Glory oh glory oh to the bold Fenian men

Some died on the hillside some died mid the stranger
And wise men have told us their cause was a failure
But they loved dear old Ireland and never turned traitor
Glory oh glory oh to the bold Fenian men

I passed on through the glen God be praised that I met her
Be life long or short I will never forget her
We may have good men but we'll never have better
Glory oh glory oh to the bold Fenian men

The Holy Ground
From the wireless, author unknown

Farewell my lovely Diana a thousand times adieu
We're going away from the holy ground and the girls we all love true
We will sail the salt sea over and we'll return for sure
To see again the girls we love and the holy ground once more

Fine girl you are
You're the girl that I adore
And still I live in hopes to see
The holy ground once more

Now I am salt sea sailing and you are far behind
Love letters I will write to you with the secrets of my mind
The secrets of my mind my love you're the girl that I adore
How I long to hold you in my arms and kiss your lips once more

Now the storm is raging and we are far from shore
And the good old ship is tossing about and the rigging is all tore
And the secret of my mind my love you're the girl that I adore
And still I live in hopes to see the holy ground once more

Now the storm is over we are safe and well
We will go into some public house and we will drink like Hell
We'll drink strong ale and porter and we'll make the rafters roar
And when our money is all spent we will go to sea once more

In 1963 I travelled to Dublin with Turlough McGowan to hear The Clancy Brothers and I heard this song. Turlough McGowan was the eldest brother of my best friend Pat McGowan, who lived six doors down the Moorefield Road. Pat and I knocked around together mainly between 1954 and '58, occasionally 1959 and '63, and again in more recent years. We did a lot of things together. Once, we boxed the heads off each other in a makeshift ring with proper gloves, much to the merriment of his three older brothers and their pals. Turlough left home around 1957 and went to London, coming back later as the first real Teddy Boy we'd ever seen. Later, he returned to life in Newbridge and spoke about Flann O'Brien and Behan and Joyce and he sold insurance and had a great style with porter and a cool high-stool attitude. He returned to London in the late Sixties, came back to Ireland briefly in the Nineties, and then back to London again. He walked out of his door in 1996 and has never been heard of since.

Friday, 3rd April 1998
Yesterday I made an announcement to the press to try to set the record straight. Despite all my efforts, they still did their own thing. At no time did I mention retiring, but the Irish media have retired me. However, I am resting and that is all. While I take time out, I will attempt to disengage from the mighty. I have willingly gone along with the assembly of the forces that drove the monster that my career has become, now I need to untangle it all.

I read today how Dorothy Parker once commented about writers producing anything from a little trickle to a mighty torrent. I produced a little trickle that was marketed like a mighty torrent. My strength has been in the act of live singing.

Tim Evans
by Ewan McColl

Tim Evans was a prisoner down in his prison cell
And those who read about his crime condemned his soul to Hell

Go down you murderers go down

For the killing of his own dear wife and murder of his child
The jury found him guilty and the hanging judge he smiled

Tim Evans walked around the yard and the screws they walked behind
He saw the sky above the wall but he knew no peace of mind

The screws they came to his cell and they hammered on his door
Get up you dirty murderer the screws at him did roar

The governer came to his cell with the chaplain by his side
Sayin your appeal has been turned down prepare yourself to die

They took Tim Evans to the place where the hangman did prepare
They tied the rope around his neck with the knot behind his ear

A thousand lags were screaming and bangin on their doors
Tim Evans didn't hear them he was dead forever more

They sent Tim Evans to the drop for a crime he did not do
Dr Christie was the murderer, the judge and jury too

I had been singing the old songs, listening to traditional singers, copying their styles and learning their verses. I heard Woody Guthrie sing about 'Sacco and Vanzetti', I heard Ewan McColl sing 'Tim Evans' and these men turned me on to the possibility of my work becoming modern and relevant. Their work encouraged me to write my own songs, to give my version of the news. While I still love to sing of Lord Baker and Little Musgrave, I like to intersperse them with stories of today's events, of eco-warriors and sacred mountains, of Veronica and Rory.

My own life's experience has been greatly enhanced by singing these songs, my imagination fuelled by the vivid imagery of the words and the encouraging prop of a gallon or two of good ale. I could be deep-sea whaling, fighting for the King of Spain, making love to the King of Turkey's daughter, meeting the Pope in Knock, and I never even had to get my hands dirty. I've done enough labouring work in my earlier existence to understand that these same songs romanticise the dreadful boredom and savage work involved in many of the jobs I've sung about. It's one thing to sing 'McAlpine's Fusiliers' on a stage of a Saturday night – another to be out on some God-forsaken site on a Tuesday morning frozen to the bone with some neuck of a Mayo gangerman shouting in your face because you can't get some clapped out dumper started.

There is something wonderful about a folk club full of folkies singing sea shanties (Wey-hay-roll & go) of a Tuesday night in Cheshire, or a bunch of McColl groupies marching into Havana on a Saturday night in King's Cross.

I love it.

Dark-Eyed Sailor
Author unknown

As I went a walking one evening fair
It being the summer to take the air
I spied a female and a sailor boy
And I stood to listen, and I stood to listen
To hear what they might say

He said young girl why do you roam
All alone by yonder lea
She heaved a sigh and the tears did roll
For my dark-eyed sailor, my dark-eyed sailor
He ploughs the stormy sea

He said you must drive him from your mind
Another young man you surely will find
Love turns aside and it soon grows cold
Like a winter's morning, like a winter's morning
The hills are white with snow

She said I'll not forsake my dear
Altho we are parted for manys the year
For gentle he was not a rake like you
To induce a maiden, to induce a maiden
To slight the jacket blue

One half of the ring did young William show
She ran distracted in grief and woe
Sayin William William I have gold in store
For my dark-eyed sailor, my dark-eyed sailor
He has come home again

There is a cottage by yonder lea
This couple live there and do agree
So maids be true when your love is at sea
For a stormy morning, a stormy morning
Brings on a sunny day

I went to Bill Leader's house in Camden Town in 1968 and recorded three songs with a view to doing an album for the Transatlantic label. Subsequently, Bill came to Ireland in 1970 with a Revox tape recorder and two microphones, and we recorded the *Prosperous* album which featured this song.

It was a magical time. The music was fresh and it sparkled. Every day brought new fun as we rollicked around Pat Dowling's pub and then up to Rynne's cellar to lay down another track. I remember going to Dublin to look for a concertina player who could not be located. But I did come across Kevin Conneff, the bowrawn player who joined us for a track. We came across Clive Collins – a nomadic English fiddle player – and he came down and jammed for a few days.

In so far as I can recall, the mood around the recording was one of joy. I was jubilant to be playing with Donal, Andy and Liam and their enthusiasm showed the feelings were mutual. I came to the album with an open mind and no expectation nor ambition apart form the making of the record itself. When I think of all the recording that has been done since, none has ever achieved the same feelings of fun and crack. There has been lots of good music created and played, but seldom have we laughed so much.

I remember a club in Leeds in 1968–69 run by Bob and Carol Pegg. They subsequently formed a band called Mr Fox. It was ever so earnest and the music was deep and meaningful and the audience was highly intelligent and took its 'Folk' very seriously indeed. I loved to play this kind of club occasionally. Quaff a good sup of beer and get up there and give long, meaningful and made-up introductions – the longer they lasted the better.

I suppose it was all part of a growing desire to be all things to all people – as this grew within me I became quite besotted with people-pleasing and could dive into any company. Perhaps I was deluded into thinking I got away with it, as I drank with a broad cross-section. Priests, whores, pilots, armed detectives, gangsters, millionaires, paupers, jockeys, soldiers, journos, poets, authors, deep-sea divers, stars, and many who did not know their occupations – nor did it matter, just so long as they supped their stuff and got on with the business at hand.

The Old Man's Song
by Ian Campbell

At the turning of the century I was a lad of five
My father went to fight the Boers, he never came back alive
My mother had to bring us up no charity did she seek
She rubbed and scrubbed and scraped along on seven-and-six a week

At the age of twelve I left my school and went to get a job
With growing kids my ma could do with the extra couple of bob
I knew that longer schooling would have stood me better stead
But you can't afford refinement when you're struggling for your bread

When the Great War started I did not hesitate
I took the Royal Shilling and went to do my bit
We fought in blood and sweat and mud three years or thereabouts
'Til I copped some gas in Flanders and was invalided out

When the war was over and we'd settled with the Hun
We went back to civvy street we thought the fighting done
We sought to earn our wages but we were out of luck
Soon we found we had to fight for the right to go to work

In '26 the General Strike found me upon the street
By then I had a wife and kids their needs I had to meet
The brave new world was coming and the brotherhood of man
But when the strike was over we were back where we began

I struggled through the Thirties out of work now and again
I saw the Blackshirts marching and the things they did in Spain
I brought me kids up decent and taught them wrong from right
But Hitler was the man who came and taught them how to fight

Me daughter was a land girl she got married to a Yank
My son he got a medal for stoppin one of Rommel's tanks
He was wounded near the end of the war and convalesced in Rome
He married an Eyetie nurse and never bothered to come home

Me daughter writes me every week a cheerful little note
About the coloured telly and the other things she's got
She's got a son a likely lad he's just turned twenty-one
Now I hear he's been called up to fight in Vietnam

Now we're on the pension and it doesn't go too far
Not much to show for a life that's been like one long bloody war
When I think of all the wasted lives it makes me want to cry
I don't know how we'll change things but by Christ we'll have to try

'The Old Man's Song' is one of two songs in my repertoire from the pen of Ian Campbell (the other being 'The Sun is Burning'). Through staying with Ian's parents in Birmingham I befriended Bob Cooney from Aberdeen. Bob was a lifelong socialist and also a veteran of the Spanish Civil War. Despite our age difference, Bob and I hit it off and he took me to a number of political gatherings in the mid-Sixties. I got to meet Communist Party members in different parts – I particularly recall houses in Grimsby, Lincoln and the West Country. Fine, comfortable households owned by professional people who also happened to be Communists. Marx and Lenin on the wall, *The Morning Star*, 'Granma' in the lavatory and sparrows' legs in garlic and the finest claret on the table. The manifestos were leather-bound and confined to mahogany bookcases safely under lock and key. I rode into these gatherings on Bob's coat-tails. I always enjoyed the hospitality but seldom understood the dialogue. Monday morning Bob and I would head for the station and get back to our lives.

For many years I've been an avid collector of my own bootlegs. There are two categories. Firstly there are the fraudulent copies of official albums. These have been duplicated with varying success but would seldom pass muster for the sleeves are usually flawed and badly reproduced. I have a small number of these items, one cassette copy of *The Christy Moore Collection* purchased by a friend in Thailand for five dollars. There was a good counterfeit copy of *King Puck* given to me by a friendly detective who held one back after a raid in Dundalk, Co. Louth, when hundreds of thousands of various CDs were confiscated. Another came after a raid on a record retailer in Dublin who was about to release a live Planxty album without the band's authorisation.

The second category of bootleg is of more interest to me. These are the tapes of concerts I've done in my travels. The producers somehow manage to record live shows – then back to their bedrooms to get duplicating. The sleeves are basic, usually full of mis-spells and wrong titles and the quality of the recordings is often shite. Although the music industry is very opposed, I like them. I've enjoyed purchasing *Christy at the Trip to Tipp.*, *Christy at Finsbury Park*, *Christy at Glasgow Green* out of vendors' suitcases on O'Connell Bridge or Grafton Street.

Liffeyside
Author unknown

I am a poor auld Dublin man and my age it is fifty-three
I work away and draw my pay and I spend my money free
I have a wife and family my pleasure and my pride
I love to take them rambling down by the Liffeyside

How often do my thoughts go back to days of long ago
When Jane and I were courting on the banks of Pimlico
When a one-and-one cost four pence with vinegar and salt
And a couple of coppers bought for you a glass of glorious malt

All down the Coombe and Patrick Street we'd stroll on a Saturday night
Where the ballad singers sang so sweet and the stars they shone so bright
'Twas there I met my darlin Jane and asked her to be my bride
On a Saturday night when the stars shone bright down by the Liffeyside

The cowheel and pigs trotters and the plates of steaming peas
Those smells so sweet perfumed each street of the ancient liberties
Then we'd sit and rest with friends the best and the hours were never long
With a good auld jar in Gilligan's Bar and a rousing Irish song

Fare thee well ye days of old when all of us were young
When the best of drink flowed freely round and the best of songs were sung
Mid friendship and good company pleasure flowed full tide
We'll never see the likes again down by the Liffeyside

What is the point of lying about it? What ties up my tongue? Why must I get knotted up until my heart aches with the frustration of not knowing – fear of being found out even when there are no lies told. Anger boiling up and feeding those mad, mad feelings of frustrated uselessness. Not being able to ask for help – refusing to look God in the face for fear of having to let go of all this insanity.

Drink ten drinks and be in a dirty snug in some arsehole kip and sing this song to some old drunks and feel their acceptance like a warm glow – feel at home with the alcohol coursing through the system within and fellow stupid fuckers nodding in agreement as we all assure each other that we truly understand and that no one cares outside the death circle – we'll spend it together and when the money is all spent you look around and everyone is gone and you're on a strange street in a nameless town and I am scared now but something always turns up. . .

> Who was minding me?
> The auld Fine Gaeler.

> I came to a V in the road
> at Great Yarmouth
> afterwards in Piccadilly
> in Muckross (after Harrods)
> in the toilet of The Meeting Place
> and in Red Peter's flat

I came to many vital junctions, any one of those ignored paths could have led to the final destruction,

> a drunken gun to my head in 1968 in Manchester
> more vodka and Bacardi
> out of sight out of mind
> shoot me you bastard or fuck off – you and your gun

> I saw him five years ago driving a Rolls Royce
> with a box maker in the back

Musha God Help Her
By Pierce Turner

Musha God Help her, she's in an awful state
She's got that husband fella's run away
A teenage daughter in the family way
And she can't pay her bills to nobody

Poor Mrs Donoghue out there by Ballynew
She used to be a king from Davitt Street
All of them were spotless in their parents' home
Till she got married to that animal

According to all accounts they never go to Mass
He's with that young one out in Ballyhack
She don't have a stitch across her back
But she can well afford to drink

I really don't know what's to become of them
All the street is up in arms at them
They make more noise than an army
When she starts throwin all the cups at him

I really wouldn't mind if they were friendly
But they never say hello to nobody
You'd really think that they were somebody
It makes me laugh you know at the back of it all

Music played for the love of music. Music played for the money. Music played for kudos. Music played for ego. Is it folk or is it art or is it rock and roll, acid house or Céilí, does anybody know?

I saw a man play for an hour, then put his fiddle down and weep unashamedly before his listeners, who shuffled uncomfortably, many of them not understanding.

I saw a man in a wheelchair backstage at a festival in France and he wept and wept because the music had touched his heart and opened the sluice gates to his tears. Everywhere I go I see people who feel the music in the way it is meant to be felt.

Tuesday 5 May 1998

How many friends does one make in a lifetime? What constitutes a friend? I have ten thousand acquaintances, and it is difficult to focus when an entire population knows something about me.

You went too deep into the well, the bucket was hitting the bottom but still I drank and drank like a mad thirsty demon – thirsting for acclaim, roars of approval, the eyes looking up full of awe and wonder, hearts touched by the words and voice that God had given. But the singer soon forgot and fed his foolish ego.

Today, at this moment, I have gratitude.

Thank you.

Leaving of Liverpool
Author unknown

Fare thee well to you my own true love
I am goin far away
I am bound for California
and I hope that I'll return some day

So fare thee well my own true
and when I return united we will be
It's not the leaving of Liverpool that grieves me
But my darling when I think of thee

I am sailing on a Yankee clipper ship
the Davy Crockett is her name
And Burgess is the captain of her
and they say she is a floating Hell

Oh the sun is on the harbour love
and I wish I could remain
For I know it will be some long long time
before I see you again

For much of my life I've been transient. Always leaving can become a way of life and the next town always promises a new buzz. I loved to sing the leaving songs.

5 May 1998
You should write a book, some people say and, sometimes, when it suits me, when I'm trying to explain what I do with my time, I'll say 'I'm writing a book.' Book me bollix. I don't have a book in me. With regard to a biography, for me there is nothing extraordinary about my life. Val and I have produced three beautiful children and what we have together is extraordinary and wonderful. The work is different. Places, trains, hotels, restaurants, venues, managers, agents, publicists, roadies, engineers, accountants, secretaries, A & R-ists, lawyers, barristers, studio moguls, photographers et al are extraordinary people in their own right but the work done is nothing special. What is

extraordinary is when God's gifts come into the work, when people play instruments in unison and harmony and God's music is perceived and the voice is uttered and blends in. I go on and on about this. Today I'm feeling ill at ease. I'm dis-eased in my mind and not so well in my body either. I've no idea what ails me and all I can do is to pray for peace of mind – that I might not have this uncertainty, nor be worrying Val who I know is concerned by my demeanour.

There is no choice today except to live in my reality. I cannot take a pill, lift a drink, smoke a joint, run away on a tour. I'm here alone, just now, with my reality and my total dependence on God alone.

Streets of London
by Ralph McTell

Have you seen the old boy walking the streets of London
Picking up newspapers wearing worn-out shoes
In his eyes the light has died he's living on the other side
Yesterday's paper telling yesterday's news

Have you seen the old girl who walks the streets of London
Dirt in her hair and her clothes in rags
She has no time to stop for talking she just keeps on walking
Carrying her home in two carrier bags

In the all-night café at a quarter past eleven
There's the same old boy sitting there alone
He's looking at a world inside an empty teacup
Each cup lasts an hour and he wanders off alone

Have you seen an old boy walk the streets of London
Memory fading like the D-Day ribbons that he wears
In a winter city the rain shows no pity
One more forgotten hero, in a world that doesn't care

So how can you tell me you're lonely
And for you that the sun don't shine
Let me take you by the hand and walk you through the streets of London
I'll show you something that'll make you change your mind

It was at a club somewhere in Manchester that I first met Ralph. The club was run by Rai Birnes and his wife Maureen. Afterwards I was invited back and Ralph and I began a friendship which continues to this day. Back then he was a £15-a-night act working every night, while I was still at the £3–£5-a-gig stage and taking anything I could get. Next time I went to London Ralph introduced me to his manager (and brother) Bruce May, who had some interesting pointers for me with regard to my set. He was quite blunt (and absolutely correct). He told me I should take myself more seriously and that I was selling myself short, so bad was some of my material. There was some talk of his managing me, but that came to nothing, although he did introduce me to Michael McDonagh who was then a fledgling manager and I seem to remember him getting me a few dates.

Like every other young singer around in those days, I sang this song for a while but never as part of my set, always as an encore, for it got the whole room singing.

Those rooms were great places. They came in all shapes and sizes with audiences ranging from 25 up to 100, but seldom larger. PA systems were few and far between, so none of us had mike technique.

In those early days my music had little or no political edge to it. I was apolitical with regard to movements and causes, and in general found it all very boring. I was more inclined towards Hell-raisers and wild party-makers than Trotskyists or Marxists. There were clubs that had political leanings, like McColl's, Ian Campbell's, Cleethorpes, Glasgow Folk Centre, Nottingham – in these venues I could easily busk a political gig and get away with it. But I was always aiming for a good time and I would be more interested in getting close to the beautiful women in the front row than having my ear bent by some Fidelista about the sugar crop or the good ship Granma. But all interests were conditional on a mutual love of alcohol in whatever form you like.

As the Civil Rights Movement gained momentum in Belfast and Derry, I began to encounter sympathisers around the UK. These varied from Republicans to a variety of communists, some of whom had bizarre attitudes to Northern Ireland and the emerging struggle for civil rights.

1969

It was just after dawn in Mixenden in Halifax, Yorkshire. I was living in a two-bedroomed flat in a 13-storey tower block. There was Derek McEwan and I, Hamish Imlach and Red Billy from Glasgow, Dave Shannon, Sam Bracken and Fíona from Belfast, and maybe five or six others, all sleeping soundly.

There was a loud knocking on the hall door and I opened it to a clatter of detectives who had a warrant to search, which they proceeded to do. When they saw a mountain of musical instrument cases in the hall their little hearts must have leaped for joy. As they went from room to room they came across some unpretty sights – all they found was a bunch of folkies sleeping it off. My name had shown up in a Republican notebook in Glasgow, and they were checking it out.

Twenty years later I had a similar experience, this time with Free State special police, and it was more chilling for they came into our family home in Dublin. It was a dark time in Ireland for there had been some particularly heinous violence and kidnapping and, once again, a wider and wider net was being trawled until the home of every known sympathiser was raided.

Blackwater Side
Author unknown

One evening fair as I took the air down by Blackwater side
While gazing all around me an Irish lass I spied

All through the first part of the evening we rolled in sport and in play
Then the young man arose and gathered his clothes singing fare thee well 'tis day

That's not the promise you made to me when you lay on my breast
But you made me believe with your lying tongue that the sun it rose in the west

Go home go home to your father's garden go home and cry your fill
And think on the sad misfortune you brought on by your wanton will

There's not a girl in all the country so easily led as I
When fishes they fly love and seas they run dry love it is then I will marry aye

This song reminds me of my early days when I sang purely for the love of it.
Tommy Potts played special music. He once told his nephew Séan that music should never be played for money. I understand the meaning of this. Once the lucre comes into it certain factors are liable to come into play.

In my own case I still vividly recall the wild joy of singing years ago at the Fleadh Ceol in Scariff. Everywhere music was swirling through the air and then a song could still everything for a spell, touching the hearts of many before pausing and ending and making way for the reels to rollick once more.

My first fee was ten shillings from Peggy Jordan in The Embankment in 1964. Then £3 and a crate of stout in the Town Hall, Newbridge. In 1965 I got £5 from Paddy Fitzgerald in The Collins Hall, Clonmel, which was savage cabbage as I was on £7 a week in the bank. Then I went to England and began to do it for love and money. On and on it went, getting more and more into the business of music.

Thirty-two years on I am blessed in that my music has made me a lot of money, and I love the songs more deeply than the cash. In the past, I surrounded myself with many people whose livelihoods were dependent on the mass appeal of the music. I, too, became more interested in the success than in the song.

(I've tried betimes to join a session where music is being played for its own sake. I try and sit in but I find myself becoming the focus of attention rather than the session itself. Sometimes the other musicians can resent this and I totally understand for they just want to make their music without some drunk demanding that *I* sing 'Lisdoonvarna'.)

Kevin Barry
Author unknown

In Mountjoy Jail one Monday morning high upon the gallows tree
Kevin Barry gave his young life for the cause of liberty
Just a lad of eighteen summers yet there is no-one can deny
As he walked to death that morning he proudly held his head on high

Just before he faced the hangman in his dreary prison cell
British soldiers tortured Barry because he would not tell
The names of his brave comrades and other things they wished to know
Turn informer or we'll kill you Kevin Barry answered no

Calmly standing to attention as he bade his last farewell
To his broken-hearted mother whose sad grief no-one can tell
For the cause he proudly cherished this sad parting had to be
Then to death went proudly smiling that his country might be free

Another martyr for old Ireland another murder for the Crown
Whose cruel laws may crush the Irish but can't keep their spirit down

Lads like Barry are not cowards from their foes they will not fly
Lads like Barry will free Ireland for her cause they'll fight and die

From my youngest days I remember the imagery this song created in my mind. Years later when I was shown the gallows in Mountjoy they were totally unlike what I had imagined. Kevin Barry occupied a special place in my mother's heart (she named her last child Kevin Barry Moore), and because of the way she sang this song Kevin Barry has always been special to me.

As a boy when I sang it at Feiseanna and at concerts in Newbridge and the Curragh the same pictures ran across my mind. I felt emotion long before I knew anything about the long struggle for Irish Independence. When I came to learn about the centuries of strife and war in Ireland, my feelings had long since been stirred by young Kevin Barry.

So much murder, torture, madness and mayhem with protagonists and victims on every side. Cynical politicians in the main with a few sincere voices in their midst shining like beacons from the parliaments of puff and bluster. Young idealists, cute hoors, crazy psychopaths, spin doctors, devilish clergy.

Kevin Barry, Bobby Sands, Mairéad Farrell prepared to die for their ideals while Charlie Haughey, Ray Burke, Pádraic Flynn and Liam Lawlor claim membership of a Republican party.

The Jug of Punch
from Austin O'Donnell

It was one pleasant evening in the month of June
When those feathered songsters their notes did tune
A small bird sat on an ivy bunch
And the song he sang was the jug of punch

Toora loora loo, toora loora lay
Toora loora loo, toora loora lay
A small bird sat on an ivy bunch
And the song he sang was the jug of punch

What more diversion can a man desire
Than to be seated by a snug coal fire
Upon his knee a pretty wench
And in his hand a jug of punch

If I were sick and very bad
And was not able to go or stand
I would not think it all amiss
To pledge my shoes for a jug of this

The doctor fails with all his art
To cure an impression upon my heart
But if life was gone to within an inch
What would bring it back but a jug of punch

But when I'm dead and in my grave
No costly tombstone will I crave
Just dig a grave both wide and deep
And place a jug of punch at my head and feet

Bridget Dowling was my father's mother. She was one of three children who grew up on the Dowling farm at Barronstown, Milltown, Newbridge. As a boy I heard the older people talk of her beauty as a young woman. When she was twenty she was married off to a bank manager from

Newbridge called Christopher S. Moore. He was also a farm owner and horse breeder as well as being 40 years her senior. I presume the reason for the marriage was that Christopher Moore's land had adjoined the Dowling land, so as well as getting a beautiful young bride he was also joining two fine farms in wedlock.

My father Andy was born to this marriage in 1915, and in 1919 his father the bank manager died. For the young widow, life in Newbridge became a trial and she found her financial affairs hard to handle, so bad decisions were made. She also found motherhood very difficult and, God love her, she was not great at showing love nor affection (she had possibly not known too much of it herself). My daddy was sent to various boarding schools from the age of five until he was 18. The Bower in Athlone, a convent school between Naas and Kilcullen called Kilashee, Willow Park and, finally, Blackrock College. He had little or no experience of family life.

I remember Bridie well as she lived until 1964. She was always a cold, aloof woman and I have no memory of her face ever smiling. When my parents married she refused to attend the wedding as she felt that Daddy was marrying beneath him! The irony of the outcome is that Nancy nursed the three elder Dowlings to their painful and prolonged deaths with love and compassion.

When Bridie Dowling died she was buried in her family grave, as she had expressed a wish not to be buried with her husband and son.

We have two family plots in Milltown graveyard. All the Dowlings for 200 years are in one, and Christopher S. Moore is in the other, along with the remains of Daddy and the ashes of Mammy.

What more diversion can a man desire
Than to sit him down by an ale-house fire
Upon his knee a pretty wench
And on the table a jug of punch

In 1954 the Moore farm was divided by the Land Commission and given to migrant families from Kerry and Mayo; they became good neighbours. Nancy tried to hold on to the Dowling farm but, eventually, was forced to sell in 1969. It was bought by a religious order.

The Ballad of Eamon Byrne (died 25 November 1982, aged 19)
by C. Moore

In the buildings up in Foley Street young Eamon Byrne was born
Life was rough you grew up tough and learned to hold your own
The only time the rich heads came was at election time
Like most of those around him young Eamon turned to crime

The first time he was taken in he was eleven years of age
Locked up in St Laurence's a puppy in a cage
In and out of nick in Loughan House he spent two years
There he learned a brand new trade and forged a new career

Before he died young Eamon Byrne was fearful for his life
Who was trying to stitch him up who held the carving knife
If it was accidental as the State does claim
Let there be a full enquiry for his killing was a shame

Some unanswered questions have always bothered me
How come the Gardai knew his name before the robbery
How come twelve armed policemen lay in wait that day
Could they not have arrested him, not blown him away

Have we dispensed with Justice, has our system broken down
Have we got executioners on the streets of Dublin Town
Such a veil of secrecy surrounds that fateful day
'Tho ranks are closed the questions posed will not fade away

I wrote this song and performed it once in The Belvedere Hotel, Dublin to raise funds for this young man's funeral. There were many police around the street outside the function and a few of them harassed and jeered me when I left the hotel.

I'd long forgotten this ballad but the recent killing of John Carthy in Abbeylara brought it back to mind. The circumstances were completely different for John was not involved in any crime but nevertheless he was shot down mercilessly by highly armed, highly trained but yet unskilled State troopers.

Paddy on the Road
by Dominic Behan

I've won a hero's name with McAlpine and Costain
With Fitzpatrick, Murphy, Ashe and Wimpey's gang
I've been often on the road on my way to draw the dole
When there's nothing left to do for Sir John Laing
I used to think that God made the mixer pick and hod
So that Paddy might know Hell above the ground
I've had gangers big and tough tell me tear it all out rough
When you're building up and tearing England down

In a tunnel underground a young Limerick man was found
He was built into the new Victoria Line
When the pouring gang had past sticking through the concrete cast
Was the face of little Charlie Joe Devine
And the ganger man McGurk big Paddy ate the work
When the gas main burst and he flew off the ground
Oh they swear he said 'Don't slack, I'll not be here until I'm back'
Keep on building up and tearing England down

I remember Carrier Jack with his hod upon his back
How he swore he'd one day set the world on fire
But his face they've never seen since his shovel it cut clean
Through the middle of a big high tension wire
I saw auld Bald McCall from the big flyover fall
Into a concrete mixer spinning round
Altho' his life was spent he got a fine head of cement
As he was building up and tearing England down

I was on the hydro dam the day that Pat McCann
Got the better of his stammer in a week
He fell from the shuttering jam and that poor auld stuttering man
He was never ever more inclined to speak
No more like Robin Hood will he roam through Cricklewood
Or dance around the pubs in Camden Town
But let no man complain Paddy does not die in vain
When he's building up and tearing England down

So come all you navvies bold who think that English gold
Is just waiting to be taken from each sod
Or that the likes of you and me could ever get an OBE
Or a knighthood for good service to the hod
They've the concrete master race to keep you in your place
The ganger man to kick you to the ground
If you ever try to take part of what the bosses make
When they're building up and tearing England down

This was the title song of my first album recorded in London in the autumn of 1968.

My big ambition had been simply to record an album. I felt that to get my work on to vinyl would be a great achievement. With three years of touring under my belt, I recognised that to be a 'recording artist' would attract higher fees and would raise my profile a lot. I could make the jump from being an £8-a-night act to the dizzy heights of £20–25 a gig. The fact of having an album was much more important than the material on it. I performed for Dominic Behan like a puppet; I'd have recorded 'Liverpool Lou' in Norwegian to make this album. Folk clubs usually had raffles, and if the guest artist had an album on the prize list it seriously affected the way the audience (in, say, Mexborough or West Hartlepool on a cold Tuesday night in November) would view the act. 'I mean, he must be good – he's got an album.'

I still recall the euphoria I felt when I got hold of my first copy of *Paddy on the Road*. I went to visit the singer Noel Murphy in Shepherd's Bush and we gave it a spin. I was walking on air, I was 24 and I was on vinyl – what more could a singer desire?

Cricklewood
Words by John B. Keane

Cricklewood Cricklewood
You stole my youth away
I was young and innocent
You were old and grey

Come all you true born Irishmen and listen to my song
I am a bold buck navvy and I don't know right from wrong
Of late I've been transported from Ireland's holy shore
My case is sad my crime is bad I was born poor

If you are born poor me lads it is a shocking state
The judge will sit upon your crime and this he will relate
I find the prisoner guilty and the law I must lay down
Let him be transported straight away to Camden Town

Take him down to Cricklewood and leave him in the pub
Call the barman landlord then propose him for the sub
Leave him down in Cricklewood mid mortar bricks and lime
Let him rot in Cricklewood until the end of time

I arrived in London in 1966 with my guitar and a sleeping bag. I tried busking but to little avail. I then tried singing in some Irish pubs where this song always went down well. I was making no headway until I met a musician one night in The College pub in Harlesden.

Raymond Roland hailed from Loughrea, Co. Galway, but lived in Willesden when I first met him. He played the accordion in an exciting and original way and lived for family, music and crack. I met him in the White Hart pub in Fulham Broadway where he played nightly with Liam Farrell and various guests that could include Mairtín Byrnes, Roger Sherlock, Michael Dwyer, Johnny Bowe and many other musicians on their way through. I started visiting his gigs with my guitar in 1966, and after a while Roland gave me the 'start': I would sing a few songs while the band took a break. Roland also played Sunday mornings in the Willesden Junction Hotel with Stevie Loughlin. Then Sunday night he played for a céilí in the Quex Road Irish

Centre in Kilburn. This band featured an eccentric electric violin owner who also possessed a PA system. As well as these regular gigs he also would do one-offs and one such was a wedding in Cricklewood.

He invited myself and a fiddle player called Jim Power to be his band, and we struck up at two in the afternoon. I've no recollection of the wedding group but the party was soon in full swing and everyone was sending drink up to the podium. God knows but we were a strange trio for none of us were much good at backing the strays that get up at weddings. But as soon as Roland hit the reel button all shortcomings were forgotten. He was a wild buck and a great character. I often stayed with himself and Rose, who always extended hospitality and never turned me away no matter what condition I was in.

Other musicians on the circuit then were Festy Conlon, Paddy Taylor, Kevin Taylor, Finbar Dwyer, Maggie Barry, Michael Gorman, Sean Maguire. This was all a very specific scene. It had nothing to do with folk or showband, but stood on its own. Occasionally, Roland would get booked for a folk club, but the session atmosphere and the studied listening always unhinged him and he never took to this circuit.

Around this time I began to drift into the folk-club circuit and I was shortly to move to Manchester and throw in my lot with the folkies. However, I've always kept in touch with the London trad scene, which to this day has a unique flavour, very different to, say, New York or Sydney, Dublin or Galway.

James Larkin
Author unknown

In Dublin City in 1913 the boss was rich and the poor were slaves
The women working and the children hungry then on came Larkin like a mighty wave
The workers cringed when the bossman thundered seventy hours was their weekly chore
They asked for little and less was granted lest getting little they'd asked for more

Then came Larkin in 1913 a labour man with a union tongue
He raised the workers and gave them courage he was their hero and a worker's son
On came Larkin in 1913 a mighty man with a mighty tongue
The voice of labour the voice of justice and he was gifted, he was young

It was in August the bosses told us no union man for them could work
We stood by Larkin and told the bossman we'd fight or die but we'd never shirk
Eight months we fought eight months we starved we stood by Larkin through thick and thin
But foodless homes and the cryin children broke our hearts and we could not win

When Larkin left us we seemed defeated the night was dark for the working man
Connolly came with new hope and counsel his motto was we'll rise again
In 1916 in Dublin City the English army burnt our town
Shelled the buildings shot our leaders the harp was buried beneath the Crown

They shot McDermot and Pearse and Plunkett they shot McDonagh Ceannt and Clark the brave
From bleak Kilmainham they took their bodies to Arbour Hill to a quicklime grave
Last of all of the seven leaders they shot down James Connolly
The voice of labour the voice of justice gave his life that we might be free

The Scotia Bar in Glasgow was the watering hole for an exotic troupe of people and I took to it instantly. On my early visits there I befriended Freddie Anderson, Mick Broderick, Billy Connolly, Danny Kyle, Arthur Johnston and a bevy of Scotland's sons and daughters. Hamish Imlach took me in first time, which meant I had an instant coterie of friends there. Arthur Johnston taught me this song.

The year was 1967 and I was still relatively naïve about sectarianism. In Glasgow however, I began to understand how deeply the sectarian divide ran between the Prods and Taigs. I went to my first Celtic game and was astonished to hear the songs they sang: 'Kevin Barry', 'Off to Dublin in the Green', 'On the One Road'. . .

We went for an after-hour drink in The French Club in Glasgow and I chose to sing 'James Larkin' when my turn came. A skirmish ensued when other drinkers objected to one Fenian bastard singing about another. Another night, in a club way down the river, I was physically abused for singing rebel songs and suffered a similar fate in a hotel up-country in Perthshire where the landlord objected strongly to my repertoire. All this was pre-1969 when things were quiet enough on the home front but in Glasgow and other Scottish towns the hot waters of sectarian strife were bubbling along nicely, waiting for the gates to open.

Tuesday 7 July 1998

These past few days I've been back in touch with the world of the music business. Last night I spoke to a man who told me he could deliver The World. If I felt like doing a world tour he promised to make me a very rich man. The conversation alone unsettled me. It was very much like cattle-dealer talk. I believe this man could deliver, but I feel a bit of distance now between myself and those attitudes to this work that I do. It was all about exploitation of a commodity. This man and his cohort are highly successful in the world of music promotion, but I think I am very rich today to be at home with my family, wanting for nothing. I must strengthen my resolve not to be attracted and then seduced by promises of fame and wealth. Let us keep it simple.

26 January 1999

Another tribunal, another day in Dublin Castle. Another envelope full of forgotten money. These fellows were so busy collecting money that they find it very difficult to remember the details of when and where or from whom. Shaking down builders is very different from giving them the nod and the shook-down gambler has come home to roost. It keeps our minds off Sellafield, mortgage culture, armaments, tax avoidance, rich laws, poor laws, army deafness, heroin, guns, bishops, prostitutes, petrol, cancer, art, promiscuity, confession, blow-jobs, no jobs, three jobs.

I Wish I Was in England
Author unknown

I wish I was in England
In France or even in Spain
Wherever dwells my own true love
To hold her near again

Long time I've been rovin
In country and in town
But never in my rambles met
A maid of such renown

Until I met my true love
On the slopes of Knocknashee
Her long hair in the howling wind
Blowing wild and free

My true love she did promise me
Some land with ambling kine
And on her ample pasture land
To build a mansion fine

Oh but then my love she left me
And wandered far away
And I've been searching for my love
Full long and manys the day

So I wish that I was in England
Or wherever she might be
So I could hold her in my arms
And together we would be

16 May 1998

All those hours spent dreaming of distant lands. My imagery fuelled by movies or songs or books or the faces of absent friends and all those new friends waiting to be met. Dream on, dream on and escape the now, look to tomorrow, back at yesterday, but never live in the now.

The sun shines down on Moulnaskeaha. The distant bay is calm between the Sheeps Head and Goleen. The birds are full of it – dear God, let it be here, let me find it here for it is here that I must be.

The option is to fly off to Sydney or New York or Paris and the first thing I'll meet upon arrival is myself, warts and all, and soon, within hours, I'll remember that it's not far, far away but it's always within.

I'll be walking down a lonely street in Wooloomalloo, all round me men will be shuffling for butts, sitting staring vacantly at walls, looking at me, looking through me with total apathy, not even bothered to ask for a smoke or a dollar or a drink. Into the Matt Talbot Hostel, I'll feel like an intruder, like a ghoul tourist. But I'll go on, I'll find the room, I'll get the message, I'll go back out into the day. Stepping over near-corpses, I'll walk up the steps around by Darling Harbour and I'll return to my five-star hotel, into my suite and I'll give thanks – there but for the grace of God go I.

Lock Hospital
Author unknown

As I was a-walkin down by the Lock Hospital
Cold was the mornin and dark was the day
I spied a young squaddie wrapped up in white linen
Wrapped up in white linen and cold as the day

So beat the drum slowly and play the fifes lowly
Sound the dead march as you carry him along
Cover him over with a bunch of white roses
So no-one will notice as we pass them by

Father and mother come sit you down by me
Sit you down by me and pity my sad plight
My body is injured and badly disordered
All by a young lover my own heart's delight

Get six of my comrades to carry my coffin
Get six of my comrades to carry me on high
And let every one hold a bunch of white roses
So no-one will notice as we pass them by

Over his headstone these words were written
All you young lovers take a warning from me
Beware of those women who roam through the city
The girls of the city were the ruin of me

The first time ever I dropped acid was in Manchester after playing a gig in The MSG. There was a fellow called Barney and a team of men and women who chatted me up after the gig and I liked the gimp of them. We all piled into a Bedford van and headed out towards Oldham. On the journey these pills were passed around and I dropped one and washed it down with what was maybe my tenth pint of Newky Brown. We got back there and stopped at a Chinese takeaway – something began to happen there that ended twelve hours later. I spent six hours in a wardrobe listening to a radio. All my favourite songs kept getting played, interspersed with wonderful news breaks. My first trip on acid was not horrid at all, but some time during the course of my eighteen hours in that house in Oldham I got scabies and discovered that the radio in the wardrobe had not worked for years.

I ended up some time later in the Lock Hospital, known as the pox hospital. This was my second visit. Ten years earlier I was working at EMI Records in Hayes, Middlesex. It was a terrible hot job – I perspired fiercely all through the twelve-hour shifts and I got a dreadful sweat rash. This provoked a vicious blister on every follicle around my groin area. Of course, I assumed I had the galloping-knob-rot and took myself off to the Lock. Not at all, my good man, sez Dr Khan, and sent me off with a bottle of pills – but I was worried at the time.

I think I'll sing this song again; its time has come around once more.

Hey Sandy
by Harvey Andrews

Hey Sandy hey Sandy
Why are you the one
All the years of growing up
Are wasted now and gone
Did you see them turn
Did you feel the burn
Of the bullets as they flew
Hey Sandy hey Sandy just what did you do

The sun was hot and the air was heavy and the marching men came by
You stood at the door and you watched them pass and you asked the reason why
The sound of steel from the jackpot heel came pounding through your head
Your reason is past they're come at last with the message of the dead

At the college square they were standing there with the flag and with the gun
And the whispered words as the young ones stirred is why are these things done
And the air was still with a lonely thrill of now the hour is near
And the smell of sweat was better yet than the awful stench of fear

Did you throw the stone at the men alone with their bayonets fixed for hire
Did you think that they would kill no-one did you scream as they opened fire
As the square ran red and your bloodstains spread and the darkness round you grew
Did you feel the pain did you call the name of the man you never knew

I have no idea where I heard this song or the previous one. With most songs I have a clear recall of where I first heard them, of getting the words, of the general atmosphere that was around, but my memory fails me here.

I grew up on the edge of the Curragh Military Camp. There were always soldiers in my life. My father was in The Free State Army when I was born, having spent the 'Emergency' years in the Third Infantry Battalion. My godfather, Mick Higgins, was a high-ranking officer. As a young boy I knew many young army officers who had flats around our home. Outside the environs of home I came into contact with many soldiers: Tommy Cullen,

Pete Madden, Frank O'Shea were the men who ran the Curragh Swimming Baths and who taught us how to swim competitively. Jack Cullen was the coach in the Newbridge Boxing Club – he was a sergeant from Kildare Barracks. Woodner Quinn was a great tenor who encouraged me to sing and was one of the leading lights of the Dominican choir. For four summers I spent endless days cycling to and from the Curragh pool preparing for swimming galas. One of my sporting highlights was winning the Newbridge Cup in 1959 for the Under-14 50-yards freestyle, where I barely beat Paul Hyland on the touch. Paul was the leading swimmer in Kildare and won many national titles. It should be said that he was swimming backstroke in the freestyle event, so he was at a great disadvantage.

When my music and drinking career began it was often back to the Curragh again. The only place a drink could be had of a Good Friday was in the camp, but you needed a good military contact to gain entrance. I had a guitar and a small bunch of ballads and that was my entrance fee. The various messes and wet canteens were the scene of manys a happy Good Friday. The butcher Farrell quaffed his pint and with frothed lips announced, 'Lads, this is not Good Friday, it's Great Friday!' My cousin Paddy Power stood on the table amidst bottles, glasses and ashtrays and gave a fine rendition of 'The Patriot Game'.

My first true love was a girl from the camp. We spent many's the hour in The Furze at Donnolly's Hollow, or the soldiers' cemetery or the Sands Picture House; all of those hours are remembered in the warm afterglow of puppy love.

All my army camp activities were peaceful.

Cold Blow, Rainy Night
from Mike Harding

Me hat is frozen to me head
Me body is like a lump of lead
Me shoes are frozen to me feet
From standing at your window

Let me come in the soldier cried
Cold blow and the rainy night
Let me come in the soldier cried
I'll never come back again oh

Me father's working down the street
Me mother the bedroom keys do keep
Me door and windows all do creak
I cannot let you in

Then she came down and let him in
And kissed his ruby lips and chin
They went back upstairs again
And the soldier won her favour

Now you've had your way with me
Soldier won't you marry me
No my love that never can be
So fare thee well forever

Then he got up out of the bed
And he put his hat upon his head
She had lost her maidenhead
And her mammy had heard the jingle

Then she cursed the rainy night
Cold blow and the rainy night
Then she cursed the rainy night
That ever she let him in

I first sang this song with Mike Harding in The Golden Lion, Blakeley, Manchester in 1967. He taught me chords and harmonies and brought me to his home and put me up for manys the cold, rainy night. Both Mike and his wife Pat became my patrons for they fed me and housed me when I was a struggling folk singer.

Seven years later I was a bit short of material for the third Planxty album and Mike's song came to mind and we did a grand version of it.

It was a difficult time. Donal had left the band to be replaced by Johnny Moynihan, who was a leading force in the revival of Irish music in the Sixties. Johnny has a great ear and is particular in his delivery and eccentric in his approach.

After Donal had departed, the band was different. In fact, I believe that the original spirit that existed for the first two years of the band was never again recaptured. We became a disjointed bunch. There were many tensions within the band: money was scarce, I was weary of singing the same auld shite and I was drinking and drugging too much. Not a happy time for anyone.

Later, in the Seventies, the original band got together again with additional members and recorded some very good music. But the spark that lit the early years was a bit diminished.

In recent years the four original members of the band have gotten together annually. We've broken bread, had great fun and even played some music. We've discussed various possibilities, made plans, swapped tapes and then off into the night on our separate ways.

Maybe we should leave good enough alone. Leave the legend to grow in peace. Then again, it would be fun. . .

11 June 1999
Twice in recent weeks I've heard young people sing the praises of this album. I took it down and listened. It is ageing very well. I sang this song again and it was a grand reunion. I'll do it more often.

Little Drummer
Author unknown

One fine summer's evening both gallant and gay
Twenty-four ladies went out on the quay
A regiment of soldiers soon passed them by
A drummer and one of them soon caught his eye

He went to his comrade and to him did say
Twenty-four ladies I saw yesterday
And one of them ladies has my heart won
And if she denies me I'm surely undone

Go to this lady and tell her your mind
Tell her she has wounded your poor heart inside
Tell her she has wounded your poor heart full sore
And if she denies you what can you do more

Early next morning the drummer arose
Dressed himself up in the finest of clothes
A watch in his pocket a cane in his hand
Saluting the ladies he walked down the strand

He went up to her and he said pardon me
I'm the young drummer who caught your eye
Fine honoured lady you have my heart won
And if you deny me I'm surely undone

Get off little drummer what do you mean
For I'm the lord's daughter from Ballykisteen
I'm the lord's daughter I'm honoured you see
Get off outa that and stop makin so free

He put on his hat and he bade her farewell
Saying I'll send my soul down to Heaven or Hell
With this pistol that hangs by my side
I'll put an end to my dreary young life

Launch of the *H-Block* album on 15 September 1980 at The Brazen Head, Dublin. With me are Brian O'Buaill, Piaras O'Dubhaill and Kevin McConnell.

Friendly secret policeman in Ballyfermot, the day that Bobby Sands died, 1981.

The Baggot Inn, Dublin, 1983. With Keith Donald, Mick Hanly, and Donal Lunny.

Backstage with Rory,
God only knows
where or when.

Nancy and choir at Lansdowne Studio, recording *Unfinished Revolution* album (1987).
BACK ROW: Donal Lunny, my sisters Eilish and Anne. FRONT: Andy, Nancy, myself, Barry (with son Robbie), and Terry.

With Donal Lunny and Tony Rohr at The Royal Albert Hall, 1987.

With Ronnie Drew and Shane McGowan at the *Late Late Show* in 1987.

With Martin Doherty at the Sydney State Theatre, 1988.

'The Parade of Innocents', Dublin, 9 December 1989, calling for the release of the Birmingham Six.

Singing with Sinéad O'Connor at the Nelson Mandela Concert, Olympia Theatre, Dublin, 17 July 1989.

Our gang at home in Dublin, summer 1990.
With Juno, Val, Pádraic, Andy.

Dr Patrick Nugent (RIP),
my good friend,
GP, and counsellor.

With Paul Hill and Andy at
the London Fleadh, 1990.

A RARE SIGHTING OF
DINOSAURS AT PLAY
COULTER'S CASTLE, NOV. 1999

Surprise 50-something birthday party for Billy Connolly, in Bray, Co. Wicklow, 1999.
LEFT TO RIGHT: Jim McCann, Billy, myself, Paul Brady, Ralph McTell, Ronnie Drew, Phil Coulter and Shay Healy.

With Bono. Looking for corncrakes, 1999.

With Gay Byrne on the last *Late Late Show*.

Come back little drummer don't take it so ill
I do not want to be guilty of sin
To be guilty of innocent blood for to spill
Come back little drummer I'm here at your will

We'll hire a car and to Bansha we'll go
There we'll be married in spite of our foes
For what can be said when it's over and done
But I fell in love with the roll of your drum

I was so short of inspiration for the third Planxty album that Andy Irvine gave me a dig out by suggesting this song. When I sang this with Planxty, I could sense the audience glazing over, starting to shuffle and yawn, wondering if they'd be out in time for a few pints. I've not had that feeling these past years. It is vital for a singer to be aware of the audience's reaction to the work. Long bouts of applause and adoration are easily defined, but it's a great asset to be able to feel the early signs of collective boredom. Invariably in a crowd of thousands, there will be defectors as there will be those there under protest. More than once I've seen the new spouse partner of a long-term follower looking up at me bemusedly, wondering what all the fuss is about. Yawns are stifled, the watch is consulted and bad vibes emanate while their partners bop enthusiastically to 'Lisdoonvarna' or 'The Rose'. However, collective boredom can be more difficult to detect, and I thank God for the antennae given me to cope with this. I've seen other artists ploughing on oblivious or unconcerned as the audience dies with tedium. I suppose in some cases total boredom can be confused with respect, such as 'They must really respect my work so much that they feel it would be inappropriate to react.' Bollox! They are fucking well traumatised with the numbing dreadfulness of self-satisfied, smug indulgence. The elitists see failure as some kind of success.

Planxty in Italy

Two Fiat vans and one Ford Transit in convoy. First up, a Ford Transit driven by Brian (Fumes) O'Flaherty from Boyle in Co. Roscommon with Matt Molloy map reading. Next came John (Half Shaft) McFadden and Leon Brennan, both from Donegal, in the gear truck. Bringing up the rear, a van-load of folk stars out from Ireland: Christy Moore, Donal Lunny, Andy Irvine, Liam O'Flynn, Sean Cannon – support (now playing for The Dubliners), Lofty (Kevin Flynn) – manager, Nicky Ryan – sound engineer. Before Italy we had performed in France, Germany, Switzerland, Holland, Austria, Britain and Ireland. It was an arduous tour and when we saw Chianti we knew it was time to hang loose. We painted the Via Venita, hung out with exiled poets, a crowd of couples who came to Rome to be married in their hundred by the Pontiff. Christ Almighty but there were terrible hangovers in Italy. I must have gotten a bad plate of pasta. (They never stop boasting about their mothers' spaghetti – I much prefer the way Val makes it.)

'The Good Ship Kangooroo!' shouts Luigi and we playing an outdoor concert in Mussolini's back garden to 5,000 wonderfully warm, welcoming Italians who could hear little or nothing for the PA was minimal. The vino flowed, the chillums reddened, the lovers danced and how we laughed and how we cried.

Little Mother
Author unknown

Hey little mother what's in your bag
Chocolates and sweets

Hey Mr Postman what's in your bag
A note from your beloved

Hey Mr Tailor what's in your bag
The finest wedding dress

Hey Mr Harvester what's in your bag
Solitude and death

Valerie and I and Andy were living in Coolcullen, Co. Carlow. We had dropped out to become self-sufficient in the country. The only things I managed to grow were onions and marijuana. Christ, we had thirteen pounds of grass and three pounds of that was prime. It was a special spot and we connected well with our wonderful neighbours.

I got a letter from Norway offering me some gigs in Bergen. I was managing myself at the time, so it was easy for me to convince the act to go. I drove from Kilkenny across England and took a ferry to Norway. Arriving into Bergen after a very drunken voyage, I was greeted at the dockside by the promoter. Straightaway things felt a bit odd. The gigs were not quite what I had expected. The promoter was also a singer, and part of his plan was that he and I would record 'Liverpool Lou' together in English and Norwegian. This was the first I'd heard about it. There was only one thing to do – I went on the piss. They tell me that drink is an awful price in Norway. . .

Anyway, I split from the promoter for a couple of days and left him practising 'Liverpool Lou'. When I eventually returned – hours before gig time – the vibes were absolutely brutal. It was a delicate situation. He was a big fucker and he was angry and I was alone in Norway and I was rattling from drink. There was only one thing to do.

Oh Liverpool Lou, lovely Liverpool Lou

After the show, which I don't recall, I went to the home of an Irish woman called Bridget Woods for a bit of a party. She played an album from a Norwegian band which featured this song. I listened to it most of the night. It was all a long time ago.

The Least We Can Do
by Gerry Murray

The least we can do
is make the world a better place
Not just for a few
but for all the human race
To end wars and quarrels
make John Lennon's dream come true
To build a new set of morals
it's the least we can do

Show some love and compassion
when people are feelin low
Make it not just a fashion
that may come and go
Bring an end to oppression
it imprisons the truth
And be free with your expression
it's the least we can do

Follow his rainbow deep
into the evenin sun
Pray that its colours
will together blend as one
Seek and we may find
the dream he loved to pursue
A peace for all mankind
it's the least we can do

Gerry Murray from Charlestown, Co. Mayo sent me this good song. He is a diverse writer of plays, books and poetry. In his spare time he runs a lovely pub, and he and his wife rear a young family.

Mayo has always been a unique county in which to perform. Such mad venues, full of excitement and danger. The Beaten Path was a huge drinking emporium miles from anywhere. I would always perform there before a showband. My concert would end, the bars would open and, chairs gathered up, 1–2–3 and away we go. I would come off stage in a lather to find the band togging off in the dressing room, Susan McCann or Philomena Begley putting on the war paint before facing up to a late night dance.

The Midas Club in Ballyhaunis was built up by Paul Claffey whom I first encountered when he, aged 14, promoted a Planxty concert and did a good job on it. The Midas was like a large asylum with bars (for drink) on every wall. The first time I played there we sent posters that clearly stated 'Concert at 9pm'. At 11pm the hall was completely empty, and at 12 midnight it was full. Mayo people came to concerts when they were ready. Cows milked, children washed, confessions made, sufficient pints drunk and then we'll go and see your man – when *we* are ready.

The Traveller's Friend in Castlebar has undergone as many changes of direction as myself. I first played there on Christmas Eve in 1973, when it was barn-like and cavernous and almost empty. In 1996 I played there again and it was full for six nights. Another year in between, I did a guest spot for a song contest and went on stage very drunk, having travelled down by train with the actor Eamon Morrissey and drunk bottles of stout non-stop from Kingsbridge to Castlebar. Pat Jennings has booked me to play there on numerous occasions and I never know what to expect.

Then there's the Sound of Music in Glenamaddy, O'Hara's in Foxford, some dreadful kip in Ballaghadereen, Pearls in Ballina, along with The Georgian Rooms and Beleek Castle. Achill Island on New Year's Eve after the chicken and chips. I did not get on stage until 2am. Sweet God, a venue in Ballinrobe where coffins were stored in the dressing room.

Mayo has always been a great county for live music, and has produced many eccentric and distinguished impressarios, from Father James Horan to Paul Claffey and Andy Creighton.

'Oh take me home to Mayo.'

Among the Wicklow Hills
by Pierce Turner

Singer's Lyrics

The autumn evening filled with copper shades
I see the bird's neck in the frame
A figure walks into the sunset
Someone goes past suspended in the air
Takes more imagination
When everything's remote control
It's just a case of
What's on the far side of the road

Tell everybody
I'm going away for ten years
I'm going to wander
Among the Wicklow Hills

The travelling children in their Sunday clothes
Lost on the corner of the street
Fat Gypsy lady smacks the window pane
A farm dog gets out on the motorway
Takes more imagination
When everything's remote control
It's just a case of
What's on the far side of the road

Tell everybody
I'm going away for ten years
I'm going to wander
Among the Wicklow Hills

Author's actual lyrics

Spring still paints fire escapes with copper shades
Radios rap and screech like trains
A figure floating through the sewing set

Some guy walks past suspended by the sky
Takes more imagination
When everything's remote control
For me it's just a case of
What's on the other side of closed

Tell everybody
I'm going away for ten years
I'm going to wander
Among the Wicklow Hills

New Ireland glue child in his Sunday jeans
Stuck to the corner of the street
Fat Gypsy lady smacks the window pane
A farm dog gets on to the motorway

I like the way Pierce Turner sings. He walks up on the table tops, dances between ashtrays and glasses as the women peek up the leg of his trousers and he lets on not to notice. He has lived in New York since he was only a chap and he is totally unaffected by it, with the model still dripping off of him. He comes home often for the weekend, jumps off the 747 for Wexford and he don't even have time for the lag for he do hit the ground running, straightway sending in a high ball to Nicky Rackard or Tony Doran or Super Sub, depending upon the mood he's in.

I played in the Opera House in Wexford one night and a bat went mad. It's a dangerous name to give four walls and a roof – Opera House – probably needs a bit of bingo to knock the edges off.

What is it with people who go to opera? Why all the fur coats and tuxedos and jewellery – *what is it?* We went to hear Pavarotti in the Royal Dublin Society and it was a right gathering – talk about fur coats and no knickers. Corporate boxes, business boxes, dirty boxes. Yer man disappeared for a feed after every song. He took more bows, every song was treated like a complete concert, such a palaver. The conductor did a fair bit of shaping too – I was exhausted watching the two of them. Now don't get me wrong – the man has an incredible voice and is truly a wonderful artiste. But a few more songs and a few less exits and entrances would have suited this listener.

My only experience of ballet was *Swan Lake* in San Francisco. One of the

Russian companies. I couldn't keep my eyes open – I left at the interval and went back to my hotel where I couldn't sleep a wink.

San Francisco is a mad fuckin' city. I met a coke dealer there. Sold me great gear for half nothin, and then insisted that we continuously chop from his stash. It was the purest. He nearly broke my heart. Drove across the bridge to do two shows in Sausalito. Travelled with a doctor and a novelist in a sweet American car. Got to the gig in a little club with lots and lots of local wine and weed and more coke. Back across the bay to the doctor's house. Madness, madness. The behaviour was building towards the heart attack.

Eventually got to bed at eleven next morning with two shows to do that night at the Great American Music Hall. I woke up early afternoon with the complete horrors. Mild DTs coupled with coke hangover, body and brain under heavy pressure; I had no idea how I was going to do a show, never mind two. I got to the venue and began trying to nurture the body, mind and nervous system back into a shape. A couple of gin and tonics, a Valium, then sip a few white wines and, as show time approaches, a large G and T and a couple of lines of the marching powder.

The first show was very difficult, lots of Fleadh cowboys and cowgirls. A few Newbridge ex-pats who couldn't get in (both houses full) broke down the stage door and encountered the crowd-control engineers.

The second show was mellow and laid back – or so it seemed at the time.

Remember the Brave Ones
by Barry Moore

Remember the brave ones with the blackened face
Digging the trenches for the human race
Remember the brave ones with sandy eyes
Storming the beach head hear the battle cry
Mow them down

The European fields and the coastal sands
Ran wet and warm where warriors had spilled
The Christian sacrifice must never happen again
The search began to find a cleaner way to kill

Remember the brave ones who flew the skies
Dropping their gifts down on the passers-by
Deliver to London and to Dresden town
Let the buildings and rubble be their sleeping gown
Blow them up

The European fields and the coastal sands
Ran wet and warm where warriors had spilled
The Christian sacrifice must never happen again
The search began to find a cleaner way to kill

Remember the brave ones when the button is down
In an office in Moscow or Washington
And the faceless features of a child unborn
To a civilisation that wouldn't learn
To forget the brave ones and let them lie
Let their death moan be a warning cry
Of a battle that burns up like a million suns
Where there are no heroes and there are no brave ones

We're heading towards the second Moving Hearts album. Rehearsals have
become very difficult. We are becoming entrenched in our own ideas.
Some members are suffering from a lack of confidence, while others

amongst us are becoming stronger and are also having to carry a heavier burden.

We were still making great live music but tiring of the repertoire. It was next to impossible to get new material into the set. Anyway, we forged on and got the second album together, which featured this song from Barry. I feel this song was a turning point. I loved the excitement in it and the imagery it brought to mind, but my voice could not carry it. I was having to pitch it just too high in order to suit the pipes. I began to feel out of my depth; Donal and Declan and Eoghan were becoming embroiled in chord games. I'd witnessed this a decade earlier when Donal and Andy did the same thing with Bill Whelan on the sideline.

There are times when I feel curtailed by my limited musical knowledge; I have no theory and cannot read, I can play eight chords and three scales and sing two and a half octaves. I would love more dexterity on the fret boards. However, there sometimes can be a downside to bags of theory and buckets of chords – the substance can be forgotten. In the rush to use all knowledge at all times, the simple plot can be lost and the song or tune can be encumbered with unnecessary notes in unsuitable chords. Occasionally, I encounter musicians who know many of the chords but can carefully choose the few simple notes that are the most suitable ones. Such musicians create the magic moments.

No matter how complex the pattern, nor the dexterity upon the frets, nor the notes per second, nor the demented diminished, it matters not a whit if the heart of the player is not involved with the substance of the work. Too often I've seen good players seduced by their technique into abandoning the core, leaping around frivolously, decorating everything to the extent that the simple piece of music is lost.

On the Run
by Jessie Farrow

You poison my sweet waters you cut down my green trees
And the food you feed my children is the cause of their ill disease
Our world is slowly falling and the air is not fit to breathe
And those of us who care enough we've got to do something

Our newspapers they're just having us on
They never tell us the whole story
They just put our young ideas down
I was just wondering if this was the end of our power and glory

I worked in your factories I studied in your schools
I lingered in your prison in your unemployment too
I can feel the future trembling as the word gets passed around
If you stand up for what you believe in be prepared to be shot down

What will you do about me
What will you do about me

I feel like a stranger in the land where I was born
I live like an outlaw always on the run
You've got me always on the run

Your soldiers break the laws you make you don't put them behind bars
Most of what you teach them to do is against your very own laws
We are fugitives from injustice we are going to be free
Plastic bullets and internment don't do the things we need

I know that you are the stranger now but my time will soon come round
You keep adding to my numbers as you shoot my people down
I can feel the future trembling as the word gets passed around
We will stand up for what we believe in we are prepared to be shot down

Declan Sinnott taught me this song. He recognised it as one I would love to sing, and that would be ideal for the Moving Hearts to tear into. He was spot on. I've repeatedly tried to find a way of doing this solo but, so far, without success.

When I began to run downhill I found it hard to stop; until I reached the bottom I was running all over the shop. Gigs, causes, parties, meetings, strikes, drugs, tours, after hours, rehearsals, gigs, banks, tax man, sheriffs, crack merchants, up and down, on and on the merry-go-round never having time to stop and take a good look at what was going on.

Perfect. Diseased.

I went to see an all-Ireland semi-final in 1951. In the old Hogan stand my father threw me in the air. It seemed like five minutes before I landed back in his arms and it was brilliant. Steak and onions and gravy and him telling me to look at the green lights on the wireless so he could give Mammy a kiss. Then Kildare matches and Moorefield matches, Meath matches, Railway Cup finals and I started going to race meetings. Daddy took me to Lansdowne Road and I saw Jackie Kyle, Noel Henderson, Cecil Pedlow, I saw A.J.F. O'Reilly, Andy Mulligan, Ronnie Kavanagh. When I saw Gordon Woods grind Ray Prosser I wanted to be a prop forward and I still want to play for Ireland. Race meetings, bottles of stout, ten shillings each way on Santa Claus at 18–1. Billy Parkinson was my racing guide and we took refreshments with Prince Monolulu and met Billy Burke in The Harp in Kildare. My granny was in love with Lester and he often brought home the bacon. Boxing tournaments in the town hall: I supported Irish champions and got to meet the heroes, Joe Cox, Mousie Connolly, Colm McCoy, Henry Peacock, Fred Tiedt, Harry Perry – sport all the way. As soon as I hit London I went straight to Craven Cottage to see Johnny Haynes and Jimmy Conway. Later I visited every premier division ground except The Dell, and got into many lower division grounds. I followed speedway at the Shay in Halifax, and stock cars in Bellevue. I saw Best-Charlton-Law-Stiles-Crerand-Foulkes-Aston-Dunne-Stepney many's the Saturday, and also hit Maine Road and Gigg Lane frequently. Caught rugby league at Rochdale and Halifax and went to see professional wrestling once – not a sport at all and the audiences were really dodgy too. Along the way I've looked at baseball, Aussie rules, greyhound racing, motor racing, motor cross, hockey, Wimbledon tennis, handball, road bowling.

I love sport. To watch the protagonists and their followers is to see a side of the human species that just turns me on big time.

I'd probably travel to watch two flies race up a wall.

Metropolitan Avenue
by Noel Brazil

First days in the loft I thought I might live
New faces new streets
No cash in the hand was making me think
What now what's coming next
That's not to say I wasn't welcomed
I was welcomed I was taken in
I took the bait when I was hunted
I was wretched I was freezing

Metropolitan Avenue
Standing tall in the winter snow
I'll be back to you before I go

Don't run like a dog I know how it feels
Without heat without love
Ran free in the park like Jekyll and Hyde
Me and Pete me and Pete
Up half the night unwilling witness to some stranger's feud
Deep underground I hear the notes of some old gambler's blues

Metropolitan Avenue
Standing tall in the winter rain
Will I ever see your face again

This rose will never blossom now
It needs light shining on its back
This road will never take me out
I've been stopped in my track
There goes the night
And now the dawn begins to filter through
I took the bait when I was hunted, I was wretched
Didn't know that I was failing you

Metropolitan Avenue
Standing tall in the winter sun
I'll be back with you before I'm done

I've tried to introduce this song into my set a hundred times but I've always faltered. The words always spirit me off to New York and Amsterdam. I first heard it sung into my ear in Grogan's.

Grogan's Pub 1972
Music and smoking drugs were not allowed. There were off-duty pimps and brassers and robbers and thieves, poets, actors, dossers, chancers, saints and spoiled priests with actresses, but you could not sing nor smoke ganga.

Except one Saturday night when all hell broke loose. We were gathering for a party in Upper Rathgar and the lunatics were assembling from all sides. I had my guitar under a bench for safekeeping and I had a hash pipe and lots of top-shelf ganga. One thing led to another and before we knew it Sally Brown was making the rafters roar and the hash pipe was cooking brightly. There was total hilarity, it went completely over the top but no one was hurt. Nothing like it happened again – in Grogan's, that is.

Twenty-five years on and the place looks the same. Hardly any of the faces that I knew are to be seen; two have survived inside the counter, but the outsiders have fallen by the wayside – some to better things and others to nothing at all. Every seat is still occupied and the buzz is as it was. Drinking patterns are generally the same, and groovy new drinks have not made much impact. John Jordan's ghost still sits in his alcove and Paddy O'Brien's still dances attention in that special way.

I wore it like a badge of honour, being an accepted member of the clientele. To come in and sit down and your name and poison to be known, to be able to get a bit of a slate, to get phone messages and to be asked 'How is herself?' All part of the wonderful game. The mad, mad game of pub life, chasing the warm glow, that glow that comes but once and brings on the chase that ruins us.

Mad Lady and Me
by Jimmy MacCarthy

Among the walls and ruins of the horrid civic stone
I walked without a lover for my older bones
The sun was strong in going down it was a dreamlike day
It's there I met the trinity it's there I heard them say

And she said bye bye Momma
Goodbye Brother John
Fare thee well ye Shandon bells
Ring on ring on

She leaned and leaned much closer and hugged them all goodbye
Her mother cried don't go my love sure we all must by and by
A drunken tongue said leave her off she'll drive us all crazy
She turned around and saw my face and both of us was she

Up and down the limestone wall then down the granite steps
She threw herself into the stream with a splash and no regrets
Side stroke swimming midstream throwing kisses to the crowd
And everything was silent and the sky had not one cloud

We were swimming out in the sunset
We were swimming out to sea
Swimming down by the Opera House
The mad lady and me

This is another unique song from the work of Jimmy MacCarthy. I have no idea what inspired it yet his words always remind me of women I have encountered – women whose lives made a lasting impression on me. Jimmy knows nothing of these particular women yet every time I sing 'Mad Lady and Me' his words paint their pictures.

Bejasus and she was mad all right. Her parents married her off to an auld fellow. The couple consummated the cold affair and she bore him a son whereupon he died, leaving her an unloved and unloving young widow and single mother. In the town she was the bank manager's young widow, renowned for her wealth and beauty; she soon lost both. Her son was my father.

●

By Jesus she was mad all right. Her father raped her for eight years, beat her black and blue, broke her jaw and her nose, left her scarred and broken. She lived in Hell in the midst of a tight-knit Roman Catholic community. I never met her, I only heard her story.

●

Jesus Christ but was she mad. Orphaned at four, she was sent to Scotland to an aunt who viewed her as unwelcome child labour. Her father's demise in Ypres entitled her to an education. Aunt used the money to educate her own child. At fourteen she was put into service in Glasgow. At sixteen she ran away to make her own way in life. She found it impossible to show or accept love but I loved her very much.

●

Mystic Lipstick
by Jimmy MacCarthy

She wears mystic lipstick
She wears stones and bones
She tells myth and legend
She sings rock and roll

She wears the chains of bondage
She wears the wings of hope
She wears the gown of plenty
Still finds it hard to cope

Croí ó mo croí your heart is breaking
Your eyes are red your song is blue
Your poets are underneath the willow of despair
They have been lovers of your sad tune – lovers of your slow air

And though they say how it hurts you
And sing the book of your heart
Oh sweet black rose how they've loved you
And it's hard to, but they do, Éire they do

She keeps fools for counsel she keeps the wig and gown
The cloth and bloody warfare, the stars stripes and crown
And still we pray for a better day now God willing it's for the best
But I've just seen the harp on the penny with a dollar on her naked breast

It is at the end of Europe. The last rock. This island of mine is my body and
blood. I come from here. My mother, my two grandmothers, my four
great-grandmothers all took the waters, ate the produce, breathed the air of
Ireland. Dunmanus Bay, Moulnaskeaha, Liffey water, Barronstown, Seven
Springs, Moorefield, Boyne Valley, Yellow Furze, Lough Reagh, Athlone,
Hayestown, Waterford, Cotton Mills, these are where my roots lie.

My spiritual home is the townland of Barronstown, at the foot of the Hill
of Allen, four miles west of Newbridge. Milltown church and cemetery is
where my paternal family and the ashes of my mother mingle with the dust
of all the old neighbours.

I can feel it as soon as I arrive in the environs of the home place. The body relaxes as the eye takes in the familiar landmarks, Allen, the water tower, the college clock, the Liffey, the Curragh Plains. Then, when I begin to see familiar faces and shapes I remember days long gone – at school with him, danced with her, delivered groceries to them, played football, sang in the choir, courted, fought, loved, hated, prayed, laughed with and cried with. Irish ropes, cutlery factory, Sandersons, Bord na Móna, Tintawn.

I've spent more of my life in Dublin by now. Our house in Monkstown is my home and the spot where I feel rested. But this city will never be my home place for I don't know its nooks and crannies, I've no bolt holes nor neighbours in the emotional sense.

You go to a wake, sit around to talk and hear the adults share memories and comfort the grieving with assurances that everything will be all right, sure God is good. Or you go in and laugh your hole off on the way home from school; we got shagged out of a few wakes, I suppose it was laughing out of fear. Some auld neighbour you'd see pottering about and there they are just skin and bone and are they in Hell or in Heaven, in Limbo or in Purgatory?

Maybe they're just under the bed waiting for us to clear out and give them a bit of peace.

Maybe.

Rosin the Bow
from Liam Clancy

I've travelled this wide world all over
now to another I go
For I hear that there's good quarters waiting
to welcome bold Rosin the Bow

To welcome bold Rosin the Bow me boys
To welcome bold Rosin the bow
I hear that there's good quarters waiting
To welcome bold Rosin the Bow

When I'm dead and laid out on the counter
A voice you will hear from below
Saying send down a hogshead of whiskey
To drink with old Rosin the Bow

And get a half dozen stout fellows
and stack em all up in a row
Let them drink out of half-gallon bottles
to the memory of Rosin the Bow

Get this half dozen stout fellows
and let them all stagger and go
And dig a great hole in the meadow
and in it put Rosin the Bow

Get ye a couple of bottles
put one at me head and me toe
With a diamond ring scratch upon them
The name of old Rosin the Bow

I feel that old tyrant approaching
that cruel remorseless old foe
And I lift up me glass in his honour
take a drink with old Rosin the Bow

Hash, grass, LSD, mescaline, speed, peyote, cocaine, opium, heroin, Valium, Rohypnol, psilocybin, Californian sunshine, golden balls, and the odd drink thrown in for sport.

Babycham, Guinness, Time, Smithwicks, Phoenix, Macardles, Celebration, Harp, Carlsberg, cider, scrumpy, keg, bitter, mild, brown, Sauternes, Chablis, Riesling, Champagne, Muscadet, Blue fuckin Nun, Amarillo, Black Tower, Mateus, Paddy, Jameson, Powers, Bushmills, Hennessy, Martell, Courvoisier, Hine, Remy Martin, Jack Daniels, Wild Turkey, poitín, Gordon's gin, De Kuypers, Cork dry gin, Tullamore Dew, Tullamore whiskey, Celebration Cream, Winter's Tale, Sandeman port, Armagnac (and a leg), Tequila.

Sulphate, powders, pills, Major, Carrolls, Camels, Marlboro, Disc Bleu, Gitanes, Samson, Drum.

Never the needles, the smack only a few times, always inadvertently.

Schnapps, ouzo, retsina, Appel Korn, Glenfiddich, Glenmorangie, Australian White, Yates Special Red, Baileys, light and keg, Watneys and Double Diamond, Strongarm, Thwaites, John Willy Lees, Smith, Tetleys, Boddingtons, Old Peculiar, barley wine, Tony Murray's drop, Davoc Rynne's, brown and mild, black and tan, Tia Maria, Campari, Angostura bitters, Pernod, pastis, Ricard, Anis, Harvey Wallbanger, Bloody Mary, Fidel Castro, brandy and crème de menthe, Irish coffee, daiquiri.

And this is only the stuff I can remember in ten minutes without stopping to think.

I've not had the obsession for eight years and the compulsions are now few and far between – the odd time, in despair, I would momentarily entertain the thought of getting right out of it. But, with God's help, this would soon pass.

I would still have the capacity to get right out of it on work. Work, work – the be-all and end-all. I could be in the company of my loved ones and be thinking about some sound check in a kip in the arsehole of beyond – what will I open with, will the PA arrive, will O'Brien show up and ruin the night? Christ, is it any wonder my family sometimes take me less than seriously.

Smirnoff, Cossack, cherry brandy, Blue Star, Newky Brown, Tzar, Bacardi, Kiskadee, Navy Rum, Stinger, Black & White, Dimple, Haig, Highland Cream, Bass, Worthingtons, milk stout, McEwans, Chartreuse, sangria, Slibovitz.

A ball of malt, a hair of the dog, a commencer, one for the road, a nightcap, just the one, a tincture, a wee drop. One drink is too many, a thousand drinks would not be enough.

Tribute to Woody
by Bob Dylan

I regret that I am unable to include
the lyrics of this song which I recorded
on the *Prosperous* album in 1970.

Here Dylan pays an early tribute
to some of the players who influenced him
in his early life, men like Woody Guthrie,
Cisco Houston, Sonny Boy Williamson
and Leadbelly – men who 'came with
the dawn and were gone with the wind'.

The melody is devised from an earlier
Guthrie song '1913 Massacre'. I've never
heard Dylan's original version but learned
the song from Tony Small of Galway
in Finsbury Park in 1968.

I arrive in town. Know nobody so it is perfectly safe. Off the train and saunter out of the station to find a suitable bar to gain my bearings. It is 1pm so I'll just eat a smidgin of hash to get the ball rolling. Two or three pints of cider to loosen up for the afternoon. I'll check where the gig is and leave my guitar in safety while I set out to the public baths for a good soak and shave, get myself feeling brand new as the hash spreads throughout warmly, making the world seem like a happy place to be. Well scrubbed, in stage shirt and clean gear I seek out the rogan josh not later than 5pm.

Back to the gig around seven, meet the Johnny and do the usual weighing up, getting to know you, getting to know all about you; enquire as to where the skipper may be (floor or sleeping bag), suss out the drinking habits, then reconnoitre the audience as they gather. Dressing rooms are non-existent so I mingle among the audience.

Maybe a familiar face from some previous encounter, mostly nods and winks as I get nervous in public, but sometimes odd friendships fall into place.

In a club on Teeside I met Jock. He'd come to England to get away from knife law in Glasgow, but not before he'd received matching scars on each cheek and a few others for good measure. He talked all the time about warfare and fighting but was a lamb at heart.

Vicki was a madame in Yorkshire who had a weakness for folk music. She was sad and lonely, no matter how hard the others tried to accept her into their company. She was badly marked by her occupation.

Ian was on the drug squad and always had a good stash. Joe was a city gardener and grew top-quality grass at his work in Lincoln.

I was on the run around Britain, trying to escape, run, run, run and everywhere I went I found new families to join.

In Finsbury Park I heard Woody Guthrie. In the midst of druggy, drunk mayhem I heard this song. I was ready for Woody for my heart was almost broken. I'd been doing some hard travellin, I was looking for love, but I was looking from inside a bottle.

Sliab Gallion Braes

Author unknown

As I went a-walking one morning in May
To view yon yon mountains and valleys so grey
I was dreaming of old Ireland all a-going to decay
And the flowers that grow around you bonny Sliab Gallion Braes

How oft in the morning with my dog and my gun
I roamed through those valleys for sport and for fun
But those days they are all over and I must go away
So farewell unto you bonny Sliab Gallion Braes

How oft in the evening with the sun in the west
I roved hand in hand with the girl I love best
But the joys of youth are vanished and I am far away
So farewell unto you bonny Sliab Gallion Braes

It was not the want of employment at home
That caused us poor exiles from Ireland to roam
But those tyrannising English landlords they would not let us stay
So farewell unto you bonny Sliab Gallion Braes

I remember singing this song on board an oil rig. I worked with a Texan who loved to borrow my box and sing 'Streets of Laredo' and he always asked me for 'Gallion Braes'.

It was 1966. I got off the chopper and made my way to the office. I got my two weeks' wages for labouring as a roustabout on the Orion oil rig in the North Sea – £175 for fourteen days at twelve hours a day. I signed on for another two weeks and was told to be back in seven days. Into Great Yarmouth we decided to go for a few drinks before going our separate ways.

A man can drink a lot after fourteen days on an oil rig.

I was back in the office next morning looking for an early start and I got on the first chopper back out – another fourteen days ahead and a terrible hangover to boot. I had spent the lot in one night – a roustabout could have many friends in Great Yarmouth in 1966.

On the Orion life was tedious and hard. It was very much work, eat and sleep. There were no recreational facilities and the living quarters were very cramped. It was next to impossible to find time and space to play music but on my last trip I encountered the Texan. He was a company man and had his own cabin. He asked me round with my guitar and we swapped a few songs. I sang 'Sliab Gallion' and he sang 'Pretty Boy Floyd'.

Pretty Boy Floyd
by Woody Guthrie

Come gather round me people a story I will tell
About Pretty Boy Floyd the outlaw Oklahoma knew him well
It was in the town of Shawnee on Saturday afternoon
With his wife beside him in the truck as into town he rode

There a deputy approached him in a manner very rude
Using vulgar language that his wife overheard
Pretty Boy grabbed a log chain the deputy grabbed a gun
In the fight that followed he laid the deputy down

He took to the woods and the mountains by the Canadian River shore
Pretty boy found a welcome at many a poor farmer's door
He took to the woods and mountains and led a life of shame
Every crime in Oklahoma was added to his name

There's many a starving farmer the same old story told
How Pretty Boy paid their mortgage and saved their little homes
More speak about a stranger who came to beg a meal
And underneath the napkin left a twenty dollar bill

In the town of Shawnee on a Christmas day
There came a car filled with groceries and a message that did say
You say I am an outlaw you say I am a thief
But here's a Christmas dinner for the children on relief

As round the world I travel I see all kinds of men
Some will rob you with a six-gun some with a fountain pen
But as round the world I travel and round the world I roam
I've yet to see an outlaw drive a family from their home

Can music change the world? Well, it certainly changed mine. It took me around Kildare as a boy to sing on various amateur stages, in choirs and light opera. Then, in my teens, to Fleadhs and festivals and ballad lounges around Ireland. In my twenties it took me all over Britain, in my thirties around Europe to Berlin and Hamburg and Paris and Rome and Bergen and Vienna, in my forties to Sydney and Melbourne and New York and San Francisco and here I am, in my fifties, getting back to basics and music is still changing my world and since my world is part of the world – music *can* change the world.

Many of the songs I've sung have changed my world. This music is primarily for myself. So long as I do it for myself to soothe this soul, this troubled heart, this crazy head then, and only then, is there a chance that it will reach you.

If I do it primarily to reach you, if I sing, write, record primarily for the listener, chances are I cannot become emotionally involved with the work. My tears will be crocodile tears, my laughter canned – I will be like a puppet dancing to the strings of industry and mammon.

Dunlavin Green
Author unknown

In the year of one thousand seven hundred and ninety-eight
A sorrowful tale the truth unto you I'll relate
Of thirty-six heroes to the world they were left to be seen
By a false information they were shot on Dunlavin Green

Bad luck to you Saunders their lives you sold away
You said a parade would be held on that very day
The drums they did rattle and the fifes they did sweetly play
Surrounded we were and quietly marched away

Quite easy they led us as prisoners through the town
To be shot on the plain we then were forced to lie down
Such grief and such sorrow in one place was ne'er before seen
As when the blood ran in streams down the dykes of Dunlavin Green

There is young Andy Ryan he has plenty of cause to complain
Likewise the two Duffys who were shot down on the plain
And young Mattie Farrell whose mother distracted will run
For the loss of her own darling boy her eldest son

Bad luck to you Saunders bad luck may you never shun
That the widow's curse might melt you like snow in the sun
The cries of those orphans whose murmurs you shall never sheen
For the loss of their own dear fathers who died on the green

Some of our boys to the hills they have run away
Some of them have been shot and more have run off to sea
Michael Dwyer of the mountain has plenty of cause for the spleen
For the loss of his own dear comrades who died on the green

T he story of this song still hurts me today. I've been to Dunlavin and I've stood where the blood flowed in streams. Dunlavin is very close to my home place. When I sing the names I see faces that I seem to remember.

It was a local slaughter. The anger lives on in my veins and I find it hard to dissolve it. I'll keep trying to forgive but I'll never forget.

Scallcrows
by C. Moore

Sunday morning page to fill
Gather grist to grind the mill
Find a pot to dip the quill
Sacrifice all candour

Attracted by the lure of stars
To lurk around expensive bars
Seeking rumours swapping jars
With pimps and ponces

Sunday morning hear the sound
Of hungry scallcrows circling round
Seeking prey that must be found
To satisfy the hunger

With pointed beaks as sharp as knives
Tearing strips off people's lives
Buzzing like bluebottles
Among the dead and wounded

All this writing about a life in music, playing, recording, travelling, drink-ing – I've purposely left out the most important part of my life. My family.

When I perform I give you everything I've got – I give you my best shot, my heart and all my emotions are weaved into each performance. The life I share within this family is a different story. It is not mine to give – it is ours.

I have always been reticent and I've refused downright at certain times to discuss family. I've resented the sleazeballs who've crossed the line. There is more than enough in the work to write about. Take the last album but one. It contained work on: racism, God's sexuality, Bloody Sunday, the Lie, alco-holism, violence/inner rage, paedophilia, Seamus Heaney, the BBC, the poli-tics of meat, Mullaghmore, the peace process, Rory Gallagher, and still they look for the tabloid story.

Take my work, take my words and music, take my performance and disseminate it any way you like. There is enough grist there to grind your mill.

All these words are out there on everyone's lips, all these notes are sung a million times each day by God's creatures; it comes through this simple head of mine and I sing it because I love to sing.

These gifts given to me I will gladly share.

The Night Before Larry Was Stretched
from Andy Rynne

(incomplete)

The night before Larry was stretched the boys they all paid him a visit
A bait in their bags too they fetched and they sweat in their gobs till they riz it
For Larry was ever the lad if a boy was condemned to the squeezer
Would fence all the duds that he had to treat an auld friend to a sneezer
And moisten his gob before he died

The boys came crowding in fast they drew all their stools round about him
Six glimps of the porter were placed for he wouldn't be well waked without them
When one of us asked would he die without having duly repented
Sez Larry that's all in my eye and first by the clergy invented
To gain a fat bit for themselves

Then I'm sorry poor Larry sez I to see you in this situation
And blister my limbs if I lie I'd have soon it had been my own station
A chalk on the back of the neck is all that Jack Catch cares to give you
And mind such trifles a feck for why should the likes of them grieve you
And now boys come tip us the deck

The cards being called for they played till Larry found one of them cheatin
Quick he made a hard rap at his head for this lad was easily beaten
So you'll cheat me because I'm in grief be the Jasus if that be your reason
I'll have you to know you damn thief that your crack and your jokes out of season
And I'll throttle your knob with me fist

The clergyman came with his book and spoke to him so neat and so civil
Larry tipped him the Kilmainham look and tossed his big wig to the devil
Then Larry he raised up his head and taking a sup from the bottle
He cried like a baby and said the rope will soon round my neck throttle
To squeeze my poor windpipe to death

So moving these last words he spoke we all vented our tears in a shower
For my part I thought my heart broke to see him cut down like a flower
On his travels we watched him next day and the hangman I thought I could kill him
But Larry not one word did say until he came to King William
When his collar grew horribly white

When he came to the gallows at last he was tucked up so neat and so pretty
The rumblers jogged him off his feet and he died with his face to the city
He kicked too but that was all pride for soon you could see 'twas all over
Soon after the rope was untied and at dark we waked him in clover
And sent him to take his ground sweat

It was always meant to be. I feel I am withdrawing back into myself. I am retreating more and more into aloneness. Can I make the break from all the shoddy artifices of successful showbusiness? Can I retrace my steps back to the core of the work? Have I come too far into the culture of personality? Am I addicted to fame and the turning of heads? Can I handle the journey back to anonymity where both the work and I could breathe easily without the weight of expectation?

Fear is a lack of faith. If I spend each day consumed by fears for the future I am losing out on all the good, beautiful, positive things that surround my life today. The path onwards will be revealed provided my eyes are open to see.

Avondale
by Dominic Behan

Have you been to Avondale
Or lingered in her lovely vale
Where tall trees whisper all low the tale
Of Avondale's proud eagle

Where proud and ancient glories fade
Such was the place where he was laid
Like Christ was thirty pieces paid
For Avondale's proud eagle

Long years that green and lovely glade
Has nursed Parnell her proudest Gael
And cursed the land that has betrayed
Avondale's proud eagle

I recorded 'Avondale' in 1969. It was written by Dominic Behan, who produced my first album.

We left Dominic's house at 3am. We had run out of drink. We walked a
few blocks and he knocked up the local off-licensee who came down in his
dressing-gown and seemed neither surprised nor annoyed with our late call.
We got two bottles of Bacardi, a couple of dozen stout and twenty Hamlet
cigars – then back to Domo and Josephine's gaff for more of the same. I
liked this man. I'm sorry I fell out with him, but it was all down to my drinking and fucked-up thinking.

Many years later I stood beside him in Grogan's; we were both drinking
large gin and tonics and were well on it but not drunk. In our stupid stub-
bornness we both refused to acknowledge the presence of the other – it was
the last time I saw him alive and I deeply regret not having embraced him.

'You'll never be as good a man as your father.' 'If you're half the man your
father was. . .' 'Your Daddy was a wonderful man.' 'You are the man of the
house now, you must take care of your mother, brothers and sisters'.

These are some of the phrases that shaped my young head. There was a
legacy of expectation that I knew I could never fulfil. Today I understand it a

little better. I accept my father's life as being short and very difficult. I hardly knew him at all, but I love him very much. I think I know a little of his demons, maybe I have a slant on his hurt and dis-ease.

Now I try and understand our children. God knows I don't want to hurt them in any way, but I know that sometimes my behaviour is not all it might be.

4 September 1998

Will it ever change? I cannot rest on the laurels earned these past years. I'm chasing a new sound again; it is long overdue. I've been chasing the same sound for a long stretch and I snapped it with *Graffiti Tongue*. It's time to move to a new space or to pack up. Some refreshment is needed and it may be coming on. I've laid down a few tracks with Leo Pearson, and I like the shape it is taking.

I visited my school friend Ronnie Nolan today in St James' Infirmary; as we sat and talked I noticed so many young men with cancer and leukaemia. Ronnie has been a tower of strength and inspiration this past year, but as I left the ward today I felt numbed by the youth of many of the cancer victims. Why, oh why do we continue on this road to ruin? Our food, air, water, all to be polluted in the names of progress, economic boom or greed and avarice.

Landlord
by Jim Page

Here he comes looking for the rent
Greedy yellow eyes and his tongue all bent
Padlocked pockets bad luck nose
Sniffing round my doorway going thro my clothes

Hey landlord why do you treat me so cold
Ye got a mortgage on my body and the deeds of my soul

I've a run-down room with a two-way roof
That man's a thief and I've got the proof
He likes to take he doesn't like to give
I pay him rent to have a place to live

Hey you I know you well
You run a rock and roll tavern in a greasy hotel
You misuse a lot of people you're such a greedy man
I've got to wear gloves when I touch your hand

Oh how could you treat me so cold
Ye got a mortgage on my body and the deeds of my soul

You go sneaking around to see what you can see
You unlock doors where you've got no right to be
Your eyes are weak you tell lies
Some day somebody is gonna get wise
And you'll get evicted out on the street
No food in your belly no shoes on your feet
You'll walk around from door to door
No-one will want to see you anymore

You'll wake up down here on the street
Bricks and mortar lying round your feet
Treat me cold now cold as you please
Come next winter you are going to freeze

My landlords and landladies have been a mixed bunch.

From lodging houses to bed and breakfasts, bedsits to digs, flats and apartments, rough kips and five-star hotels, I've encountered every sort of landlord and lady and a few others besides. In Annie Kehoe's of Clonmel, I became part of a family for eighteen months and, 40 years on, the bonds created still remain. In Chiswick, a Mayo man evicted me in 1966 because I would not go to Mass. In 1961 in Southall, also West London, Mr Khan gave me my first bowl of curry, while in Lancashire I earned my keep by driving the landlord's vegetable van.

Landlords and ladies come in all varieties. A few take in lodgers or guests out of loneliness or to gain a few extra shillings, but the vast majority are hungry individuals who move around their dilapidated properties conniving misery as they work out new methods to hold on to the deposits of their unfortunate tenants.

In 1963 I arrived home to my lodgings in Grosvenor Road, Rathgar, to find my two joint landladies distraught. Their beloved cat had been killed on the road and they asked me to dig a grave. That done, they coffined their mog in a shoebox and, as I laid it to rest, they wept bitterly and recited a decade of the Rosary. My charity was recognised at rent time.

I had a room above a pub in Pearse Street, Dublin. When it was time to move on, I really needed my deposit back. I had everything in order except the bed which was broken but I'd concealed the damage. The landlord came to inspect the premises. He counted the spoons, checked his furniture and fittings and, when he had decided everything was in order, he sat on the bed to write me a cheque. He ended up arse over tip on the lino and my deposit disappeared up in smoke. Oh ye Gods.

Carrickfergus
from Jake McDonald

I wish I was in Carrickfergus
Only for nights in Ballygrand
I would swim over the deepest ocean
Only for nights in Ballygrand
But the water is wide and I can't swim over
Neither have I the wings to fly
I wish I could meet a handsome boatman
To ferry me over my love and I

And in Kilkenny it is reported
There's marble stone there as black as ink
With gold and silver I would support her
And I'll sing no more till I get a drink
I'm drunk today and I'm seldom sober
A handsome rover from town to town
But now I'm sick and my days are numbered
Come all you young men and I'll lay me down

When I returned to Ireland in 1971 to join Planxty it was a joyful home-coming. I moved into a house in Sandymount – my belongings were a guitar, a sleeping-bag, a few clothes and a 1963-model Jaguar car.

We drove to Cork to play support to Donovan. This was our first major gig – prior to this we'd been playing pub and club dates.

Donovan was a big star and was doing an Irish tour to celebrate his moving to Ireland. He had an Irish band and an English road crew. We were left very much to our own devices – we did not have a sound engineer and Donovan's engineer showed little interest in giving us soundchecks.

At the City Hall in Cork the audience had come to hear Donovan – very few had ever heard of Planxty, but that night we came around the bend. Half-way through our set the crowd suddenly took to our music and the excite-ment was infectious for we reacted to their enthusiasm and turned in a mighty set.

We were on our way.

19 July 1998

Looking at a performance from The Albert Hall on the BBC, I was struck by the presence of a huge choir and a full orchestra and solo singers. I was knocked by the enormity of it all, the huge sound of the orchestra and the resounding of the massed voices. I thought about singing 'Someone to Love Me' *a cappella* in that same venue and I got a flashback to the night, to the feeling as I stood alone in front of many thousands and this simple song came through me and stilled the night – just like 'Carrickfergus' had stilled me 35 years earlier.

Someone to Love Me
from Joe Heaney

I wish I had someone to love me
Someone to call my own
Someone to sleep with me nightly
I'm weary of sleeping alone

Meet me tonight in the moonlight
Meet me when we can be alone
I've a fine story to tell you
That I'll tell by the light of the moon

If I had the wings of a swallow
I'd fly far over the sea
I'd fly to the arms of my true love
And bring her home safely with me

If I had ships on the ocean
I'd line them with silver and gold
I'd follow the ship that she sails in
My darling is eighteen years old

(from a different source)

If I had the wings of an eagle
O'er those prison walls I would fly
Fly into the arms of my darling
In there I would stay till I die

Meet me tonight in the moonlight
Meet me when you are alone
In this dreary cell I am pining
I'm weary of being alone

Joe Heaney was one of the great Irish singers. He sang in the Sean-Nós style and for many was the leading exponent of this old traditional way of singing.

I met Joe a few times in the Sixties. We did not know each other very well, but I always got a good welcome from him. We met once in a Liverpool lodging house and once on a train somewhere in the UK. Our other meetings were in O'Donoghue's pub in Dublin.

Many years later I was visiting the house of Martin and Lyn Doherty in Maroubra, New South Wales. Lyn told me how Joe had been a guest in their house when he was performing at the Sydney Opera House. As a token of his gratitude, he gave Lyn this song before leaving.

I have not been able to trace anyone who has ever heard Joe sing this song. I suspect it was a very special song for him and that he never sang it in public. That he taped it for Lyn was probably a sign of his gratitude for the hospitality extended to him.

I have recorded this song on a number of occasions, but never to my complete satisfaction. One version was used as the B side of a single. God willing I will record it properly some day.

I used to perform it live and once or twice it felt the way Joe did it on Lyn's tape. I'd love to get it right for it is one of those songs that has raw emotion deep within it, but it is not easily mined.

St Patrick's Arrival
Author unknown

You heard of St Dennis of France he never had much for to brag on
You heard of St George and his lance how he murdered the heathenish dragon
The saints of the Welshmen and Scots are a couple of pitiful pipers
And might just as well go to pot when compared to the patron of vipers
St Patrick of Ireland my dear

He sailed to the Emerald Isle on a lump of a paving stone mounted
He beat the steamboat by a mile which mighty good sailing was counted
Says he the saltwater I think has made me unmerciful thirsty
So bring me a flagon to drink to wash down the mulligrubs burst you
Of drink that is fit for a saint

He preached then with wonderful force the ignorant natives a teaching
With porter washed down each discourse for says he I detest your dry preaching
The people in wonderment struck at a pastor so pious and civil
Exclaimed we're for you me old buck and we'll heave our blind gods to the devil
Who dwells in hot water below

This finished our worshipful man went to visit an elegant fellow
Whose practice was each afternoon to get most delightfully mellow
That day with a barrel of beer he was drinking away with abandon
Says Patrick it's grand to be here I drank nothing to talk of since landing
Any chance of a drink from your pot

He lifted the pewter in sport believe me I tell you it's no fable
A gallon he drank from the quart and left it back full on the table
A miracle everyone cried and all took a pull on the stingo
They were mighty good hands at the job and they drank till they fell yet be jingo
The pot was still full to the brim

Next day said the host 'tis a fast day and I've nothing to ate but cold mutton
On Fridays who'd make such repast except an un-Christian-like glutton
Says Pat stop this nonsense I beg, you're only raw maishin and gammin
When the host he brought out the lamb's leg St Pat ordered it turn into salmon
And the leg most politely complied

You've heard I suppose long ago how the snakes in a manner most antic
He marched to the Co. Mayo and ordered them into the Atlantic
Hence never use water to drink the people of Ireland determine
With mighty good reason I think for St Patrick has filled it with vermin
And snakes and other such things

He was as fine a man as you'd meet from Fairhead to Kilcrumper
Under the sod he is laid let's all drink his health in a bumper
I wish he was here that my glass he might by art magic replenish
But since he is not what bad luck my auld song must come to a finish
For all the drink it is gone

The words of 'St Patrick's Arrival' are a mystery to me. I don't recollect their coming or from whence they came. I married the lyric to the melody of 'The Night Before Larry Was Stretched' with some slight variation, and I recorded it on the 1978 album *The Iron Behind the Velvet.*

The film-maker Thaddeus O'Sullivan used the song in his early work *On a Paving Stone Mounted.* He filmed a performance I gave of the song at The National in Kilburn in 1979. *On a Paving Stone Mounted* makes occasional appearances at film festivals – I last saw it about twenty years ago.

Subsequently I did some work with Joe Comerford when he was preparing to film *Reefer and the Model.* I worked on the dialogue and did some screen tests but it came to nothing and the part of Reefer went to Ian McElhinny. My last communication with the film world was when Jim Sheridan offered me a good part in his 1996 film *The Boxer.* I declined, and when I went to see the film I was well pleased for the part was superbly played by a bona fide actor.

Foxy Devil
by Joe Dolan

When I was young and handy in my prime
In taverns I would sit and bide my time
It's there I met your company I'd sit and drink my fill
It's there that you took hold of me I think you've got me still

You're the foxy devil when you like
You set your mind at ease and then you strike
You set my head a-reeling you make me shout and sing
Memory flees I get no ease until I have a drink

Whiskey in the morning or night
Gives strength to sing and dance to love and fight
So despite misfortune I'll take you as you are
The best of friends and enemies the best I've known by far

You're the crafty rogue and that's for sure
For your company there is no cure
I've squandered all my money the best years of my life
On your charm despite the harm, the suffering and strife

Joe Dolan taught me his song as we drank a bottle of Jameson in Craughwell, Co. Galway and waited for the bacon to boil. We wrestled on the floor between verses and then all went quiet for a long spell and Joe began to paint pictures. I opened an exhibition of his paintings in Longford in 1984 and I've hardly seen him since.

The artists that have really turned me on include Brian Maguire, Liam O'Flynn, Donal Lunny, Andy Irvine, Annie Briggs, Norma Waterson, Martin Carty, Patrick Collins, Henry Flanagan, John Reilly, Frances Tomelty, Catherine Byrne, Mike and Lal Waterson, Tommy Peoples, Steve Cooney, Pádraic O'Keeffe, Declan Sinnott and Jimmy Faulkner. These are a few of those who have chillled me and uplifted this heart of mine.

This earth is so beautiful, yet this beauty is now threatened by the human species, this arrogant lot who justify every rape and pillage so long as it is for the good of 'mankind'. Every now and then I encounter a special person or a true artist and there is a small glimmer of hope that maybe, just maybe, the power of goodness will blossom and expand hand in hand with the power of God, and maybe we will survive.

The lorry-load of pigs, the plastic in the hedges, the factory farming of our fellow animals, the salmon cages, the chickens in their millions, the awfulness of it all, cancer, insanity, dysfunction, poison, murder, hatred, facism. Alzheimer's helps us forget.

Where has the love gone?

Where is the compassion and understanding?

Who cares anymore?

Do I?

Morrissey and the Russian Sailor
Author unknown

Oh come all you true born Irishmen, wherever you may be
I hope you'll pay attention and listen unto me
I'll sing about a battle that took place the other day
Between a Russian sailor and gallant Morrissey

It was in Tierra Del Fuego in South America
The Russian challenged Morrissey these words to him did say
I hear you are a fighting man you wear the belt I see
Indeed I wish you would consent to have a fight with me

Up spoke Johnny Morrissey with heart both brave and true
I am a valiant Irishman that never was subdued
I can whack the Yankee the Saxon, Bull or Bear
In honour of old Paddy's land the laurels I'll maintain

They shook hands and walked around the ring commencing then to fight
It filled each Irish heart with joy to behold the sight
The Russian he floored Morrissey up to the eleventh round
Wid Yankee, Saxon and Russian cheers the valley did resound

A minute and a half he lay before he could arise
The word it went around the field he's dead rang out the cries
But Morrissey recovered and rising from the ground
From that up to the eighteenth the Russians he put down

The Irish offered ten to one that day upon the grass
No sooner said than taken and they covered all the cash
They parried away without delay up to the twentieth round
When Morrissey received a blow which brought him to the ground

Up to the thirty-second round 'twas fall and fall about
Which caused them Yankee tyrants to keep a sharp lookout
The Russian called his seconds to pour a glass of wine
Begod sez Johnny Morrissey this battle will be mine

The thirty-seventh ended all when the Russian smelt a fart
When Morrissey with a dreadful blow struck the Russian on the heart

They sent for a physician to open up a vein
The doctor said 'Tis useless, he will never fight again'

Our hero conquered Thomson, the Yankee clipper too
The Benica boy and Shepherd he also did subdue
Let us fill a flowing glass and here's a health galore
To noble Johnny Morrissey who came from Templemore

The circus is over. I have resigned myself from the ring. No more ballads on the high-tension wire. If and when I return to live performance it needs to be with a new set and new music.

15 October 1998

Today I realise that I have regained my life. I am blessed with many gifts in life but for years my head has been dominated by work and by the nuts and bolts of being a very regular performer. Today there was to have been a meeting that would have brought me back into that negative mindset. Thankfully, however, a few blips came across the screen which indicated to me that extreme caution would be required, so I cancelled the meeting.

(We went to the opening of *The Phantom of the Opera* at the Point on Tuesday. Subsequently I made two decisions. I will never again attend a gala opening, nor will I ever again don a suit. Fuck the limo, fuck the suit and let's go to the pictures.)

22 October 1998

The natives got drowned in the deluge on the way to the cabaret to hear the fairytale. Yer man in the vest and him sweatin like fuck. The lights and the sound and one little baldy auld fella makin all that racket and the way he deals with hecklers – it's a show in itself.

The night I met The Clancy Brothers, Glasgow, 1986

It was in the Seventies, I was in some TV studio in Scotland. I cannot recall precisely what area of my work was involved but what remains clearly in my mind is the fact that The Clancy Brothers were on the show. It was my first time to meet Paddy and Tom, I'd previously met Liam and Bobby. These guys were my Beatles and to meet them was an exciting enough prospect; to be on the same show was dreamtime. I sat with Tom for a while and he spoke of some of my work and how he particularly liked 'John O'Dreams'. This was a defining moment for me. I've never dwelled on the 'importance' of the work, for in a world like this art can never be important. But it can be vital. These Clancy men were vital to the development of modern Ireland and certainly they helped me to cast off the shackles of conservative Catholicism and to break free from the terrible dark sentence that Mother Church had read out for me. The ideals of cold-prick De Valera were melted away by the arse-kicking sounds of the balladeers from Carrick-on-Suir via Greenwich Village. The lads had crossed the Atlantic and along with Makem discovered the wealth of culture that lay untapped until awoken by the American folk revival. I certainly needed these winds of change to rattle me off my pot of safe, middle-class, fucked-up and frustrated bank-clerk-ship of mundanity with its pension at the end of 45 years of blind subservience. The Clancys whispered revolution in my ear and I stood up and sang 'Fuck youse all the whole fuckin' lot of youse. I'm outa here and shove yer bank up your holy arse.' Thanks lads.

Joe McCann
by Eamon O'Doherty

Come all of you fine people wherever you may be
I'll sing of a brave Belfast man
Who scorned Britain's might tho they'd shoot him on sight
And they shot down Joe McCann

He fought for the people of the markets where he lived
In defence of the rights of man
But the Undercover crew told the soldiers what to do
They shot Joe McCann

In a Belfast bakery in the August of the year
When internment was imposed throughout the land
Six volunteers from Belfast held 60 soldiers at bay
And their leader was Joe McCann

He had no gun so he started to run
To escape them as manys the time before
One bullet brought him down as he lay on the ground
They shot him ten times more

He fought and he died for the people of this land
The Protestant and Catholic working man
He caused the bosses fear and for this they paid him dear
When they murdered Joe McCann

I was going walkabout in Sydney, filling in a day, looking at lives and soaking up the new world for all I was worth. When a fellow is not drinking and drugging he gets to do the simple things, to suss out Wooloomaloo, hit the parks and the walks and the churches and arcades, go down the lanes and up the high steps and never feel lonely in daylight, only when the sun goes down and when the homeless have nowhere to turn except in.

As can happen when out in a strange town, I've sometimes just happened upon the venue in my walkabout. As I came down the street towards the Sydney State Theatre, I became aware of a pavement artist and I'm always drawn to this transient artwork so I headed over. I was tickled to find my old mush smiling up at me from the NSW sidewalk. The artist was Gary Palmer from Belfast and we've been in touch ever since.

These paintings on the pavements are so like songs in the night. I am intrigued by this medium and love to observe. There never seems to be any hard sell, barely any awareness even of the observer. Lost in chalk and creation.

I recorded 'Joe McCann' in 1976. I sang it in Ballymurphy one night and it was not at all appreciated. Sections of the audience had to be restrained from coming up on stage for instant dialogue. Joe McCann was a soldier, but internecine warfare had tarnished his image in the Provo heartlands and some Free State balladeer was not going to sing his praises just anywhere. I learned my lesson. Joe McCann has followed me around the world and I still hear his name called out in distant places.

The song was written by Eamon O'Doherty, late of Derry and the last 40 years living in Dublin. He is a sculptor of many national monuments, a one-time painter and portrait artist, flute player, opponent of Aosdána, raconteur and architect. He wrote this song after Joe was shot dead in a gun battle with British paras in the markets area of Belfast.

17 August 1997
After Omagh
Who will sing The Patriot Game tonight?
What great Republican hero parked this car?
Where do we go from here
As the blood of innocents
Flows down the streets of Omagh Town?

Suffocate
by Noel Brazil

Paddy maintains we're all yellow inside
Gunsmoke got him no mistake
Says he wants to get his car on the road
Can't even locate the brakes
He'd give his kingdom for a drink he would
Sell his mother like he sold his blood
Waiting for his dole satisfied him
Paddy couldn't even learn how to swim

But you go crazy if you think about it
So you don't think about it
You suffocate

Backs against the wall
Let the building fall
It may not be the perfect life
But it's better than none at all

Eighteen beats twenty-one you bet
It's just a gag John no sweat
The old man says he needs a hand
And the neighbours only ever want cigarettes
Drinks in the evening
Everybody is emigrating
Or planning for it anyway
Oh sure it's all just the same auld thing

Come out of your Celtic twilight kids
Join the bums down here by the bank
We're all having a rare aul' time
Put another drop of juice in the tank
Rise there Paddy rise
Forget about your stupid pride
Oh the state of us
What the hell is happening

You promise your mother, your wife, your daughter, yourself that it will never happen again. An hour later you are sitting there, the panic has been quelled and the jitters ironed out. You've got a Major cigarette burning and a full glass and a tinkle in your pocket and a voice in your head telling you that this is where you belong. This is where my friends are – the only ones who really understand. The other soldiers begin to arrive and the previous night's jigsaw put back together. The quiet hum of nerve engines getting serviced and memories getting jolted. It's starting to loosen out a bit now and any plans for the day are becoming unlikely. A guffaw from the lounge, a pair of cawphoos from the snug, put them up again there Paddy like a good man and the barometer is now visibly rising. It's time for a mosey. I'll head over to O'Donohue's to see if there are any legends in town. I'll try Doheny and Nesbitt's for a plate of beef or Toner's for a bit of art. Cheese and mustard goes well with a bottle of stout and, well-nourished, we might try a large Gordon's with tonic, ice and lemon. Thoughts in the afternoon turn towards evening. This was the best time – slip into a decent gents for a good duck in the sink, finger-brush the teeth and clear the lungs. Approve the visage in the mirror without ever remembering that from here on the day goes downhill.

18 September 1998

Nancy is six years dead today. She'd probably be 80 if she'd lasted, but God knows she'd had enough. All our mothers are unique and Neans de Paor was no exception. I used to have a medal she won for singing in 1935, and this version of her name was on the back. Well Neans, my darling, I miss you still but only in the physical; I miss your laugh, the way you called me Son or Chris (never Christy), sometimes 'Christopher, don't be bold.' I could spend a happy day with you today but I've got your spirit in my heart tonight and your blood in my veins and these limbs and bones were nourished by your very essence.

Messenger Boy
Christie Hennessy

I'm a messenger boy
Bringing my love to you

I'm going to saddle up my old grey mare
Ride through the night without a worry or a care

I see a light in her bedroom
And I pray to God that I'm not here too soon

Two big dogs and a man shouts who goes there
I've ridden through the cold and the wind and the rain
And the frost and the snow
And I'm in love
And I do not feel the pain

I'm a messenger boy
Bringing my love to you

3 October 1998, A Basket of Messages

I've decided to take another year off from gigging. Recording would appear to be on the horizon and less distant. There is some new music in the air and it feels good. As time passes I realise more and more how obsessed and strung out I became with the Christy Moore circus. So many nights I was putting out so much that I could have cracked. The family knew it but I was too proud and hard to have heard them, even if they'd tried to tell me.

4 October 1998

Today I wish to write about my super-nev. Donnaca Rynne is 27 years old. Since birth he has borne cerebral palsy with courage and good humour. Two years ago he was diagnosed as having Multiple Sclerosis. As if the one illness was not enough to bear, Donnaca has been saddled with another heavy burden to bear. I've just spoken to him – mainly about life and music but also about his new frame and possible new wheelchair. We always laugh and joke and he has some good insights into my work and also shares deeply about his own problems, but never to the exclusion of others. Today he is my hero. In the entire extended family there are two serious physical illnesses and he has both of them. It has occurred to me that of all the members of the extended family, no one would shoulder these burdens with such courage and goodwill as this wonderful young man – Donnaca Rynne my super-nev.

5 October 1998

Then there would be the nights when the voice could travel anywhere the song took it, a song you could have sung 3,000 times but this time it's like you're hearing it for the first time. I could close my eyes and travel off on the song carpet, forgetting about the roomful of listeners, about the off-stage world – leaving it all far behind I'll dream of Turkeyland, Bucklesfordberry, Seven Springs, or wherever the movie would take me.

No doubt about it

I was getting out of it.

●

6 October 1998

Donal Lunny is once again my neighbour although we seldom meet. My earliest recollections of him are from childhood; even then he was a cut apart. We never did the same thing until the ballads came along. We connected through guitar – he played one and I got one and he taught me the three-chord trick. Moving on a few years, there was a very brief band called Rakes of Kildare, so brief as to be unworthy of further mention. He was moving into the Dublin scene and I was getting the early semblance of a repertoire, based very much on collections like Joyce and O'Lochlainn. When I came to Dublin he was becoming a recognised player around the scene. We set up room together in Pearse Street. I moved on but we always kept in touch. Through my three bank years, 1963–66, our paths crossed in Prosperous, Newbridge and at music sessions. When I went to England we kept in touch with very occasional correspondence. When time to record *Prosperous* came I contacted him first, and then it was on into Planxty. I was rattled when he told me he was leaving, and soon afterwards I left the band myself. Then it was Planxty again and Moving Hearts. After that he produced *The Time Has Come*, *Ride On*, *Ordinary Man*, *Unfinished Revolution* and *Voyage*.

We were doing a tour together in 1988. I thought it was going well. Out of the blue Donal told me his feelings, which were very different from mine. It was a very painful time. We parted for a number of years until we did some pre-production work on an album in 1991–2. When Mother died this album was aborted – I decided to go a different road. I presumed that Donal knew I was going a different way, but he did not. He heard about the recording and was not pleased. Thus began another period when we were out of sorts. I hated these periods for I value his friendship.

Later, Donal invited me to sing at his father's funeral. This meant a lot to me – Frank Lunny was a good friend to our family and I was honoured to be asked. Today we are more in touch again, but for obvious reasons it is not like 25 years ago, or even fifteen years ago.

Recently, I have recorded a song with Donal for a forthcoming retro album that he is putting together. He also played on three tracks of my *Traveller* album.

He is, without doubt in my mind, the main man in Irish music.

Dunnes Stores
Author unknown

Close your eyes and come with me back to 1984
We'll take a walk down Henry Street to Dunnes department store
The supermarket is busy the registers make a din
The groceries go rolling out and the cash comes rolling in

Mary Manning is at the checkout and she's trying to keep warm
When a customer comes up to her with a basket on her arm
The contents of their basket Mary's future was to shape
For the label clearly stated 'Produce of the Cape'

I can't check out your oranges missus you'll have to put them back
For they come from South Africa where white oppresses black
I'd have it on my conscience and I couldn't sleep at night
If I helped support a system that denies black people's rights

Our union says don't handle them it's the least that we can do
We fought oppression here for centuries we'll help them fight it too
The managers descended in an avalanche of suits
And Mary was suspended 'cos she wouldn't touch the fruits

Dunnes Stores Dunnes Stores Dunnes Stores
With St Bernard better value beats them all

Her friends were all behind her and the union gave support
They called a strike and their pickets brought all Dunnes stores to a halt
No-one would tell the bossman what he bought or sold
These women are only workers, they must do as they are told

Dunnes Stores Dunnes Stores Dunnes Stores
With St Bernard better value beats them all

The messages came running from all around the world
For such concern and sacrifice, courage brave and bold
When fourteen months were over ten women and a man
Had helped to raise black consciousness all around the land

Clery's in O'Connell Street wouldn't sell South African shoes
Bestman sent all their clothes back, Roche's stores their booze
Until all South Africa goods were taken off the shelves in Dunnes
Mary Manning was down in Henry Street, sticking to her guns

I've always enjoyed singing on picket lines, whether they be the big high-profile pickets or the small unnoticed protests by individuals. In the Seventies, for a period, I was so wired that I'd almost be out looking for pickets to support. Some stay clearly in the mind. There was a cement strike in the Seventies. There was a meeting at the GPO – well supported and with good orators tempers were starting to rise. I was about to sing my 'No Scab Concrete' number when a lorry-load of English-produced cement was spotted driving down the other side of O'Connell Street, the British driver blithely unaware of the terrible predicament that was about to befall him.

In a flash, someone was across O'Connell Street and under the lorry (stopped at Abbey Street lights). Knowing what to cut he immobilised the truck and all the demonstrators were up on the lorry and, before the Gardaí could charge, most of the scab cement was dumped on Europe's finest thoroughfare and I never got to sing the song.

I recall other GPO rallies; 'No to Europe', 'Anti H-Block', 'Bobby Sands MP' (RIP) are three that come to mind.

Take It Down
Author unknown

Take it down from the mast Irish traitors
The flag we Republicans claim
It can never belong to Free Staters
They have brought on it nothing but shame

They have taken our brave Liam and Rory
They have murdered young Richard and Joe
Their hands with these foul deeds are gory
In performing the work of the foe

We stand with Séan and with Fergal
With McGrath and Russell so bold
We'll break down the English connections
And win back the nation you've sold

Leave it to those who are willing
To uphold it in war or in peace
To the men who're prepared to do killing
Until England's foul tyrannies cease

I used to sing this song. I think I heard Johnny Morrissey doing it in 1964. I hadn't got a clue what it was about nor what drew me to it. It is a blood-thirsty song written during a cruel time in our recent history when, subsequent to British withdrawal from Bognia, we began to slaughter each other at an awful rate. The civil war politic is still festering. I encountered it recently during a Cork City by-election. I was 70 miles away from the constituency but I listened to civil-war bickering in a pub on election night. Young men talking about Blueshirts and Republicans as if Mick Collins had just left the room. God blast the lot of 'em and their bullshit. It would be more in their line to discuss the destruction of their bay or the slaughter on their roads by drunken drivers, or the corruption that exists all around us today.

I'd close my eyes and sing this song in an English folk club and I would be Dan Breen for three minutes. As the alcohol buzzed through my veins and 60 puzzled folkies listened on, I would be lying in ambush in the Galtee Mountain waiting for a convoy of Black and Tans or Auxies, but then I'd reach the last chorus and it would be time for me to sing 'The Wild Rover'.

Sam Hall
by The Parnell Folk, author unknown

Oh my name it is Sam Hall, chimney sweep, chimney sweep
Oh my name it is Sam Hall, chimney sweep
Oh my name it is Sam Hall and I've robbed both rich and small
And my neck will pay for all when I die when I die
And my neck will pay for all when I die

Oh they took me to Coote Hill in a cart, in a cart
Oh they took me to Coote Hill in a cart
Oh they took me to Coote Hill and 'twas there I made my will
For the best of friends must part, so must I, so must I
For the best of friends must part, so must I

Up the ladder I did grope, that's no joke, that's no joke
Up the ladder I did grope and the hangman pulled the rope
And ne'er a word I spoke, tumbling down, tumbling down
And ne'er a word I spoke tumbling down

As I recall this song I recall a time. I was trying to be part of a blossoming scene and it was so very hard to get a foot in the door. There was a lot of elitism and snobbery at work, and a lot of people eagerly guarding their own little patches. At the time I felt very inferior to many of the singers and musicians, and today I realise that many of those people were quite at their ease when others felt uncomfortable in their august company. Looking back now, I wish them all well, God love them, for their selfish stance has often led them into cold, unfulfilled cul-de-sacs. The generous spirits are still at one with life today, still moving around singing and playing with warmth and generosity, while the cold ones navel gaze in angst and frustration.

8 October 1998

Father dear, it's 42 years today since you were taken from us. I still see your smiling face and the pucker on your lips when you whistle and the Brylcreemed black hair and your nails and your smell and I've just remembered sitting on your knee all those years ago. Today I am twelve years your senior and I still have the benefit of your guiding hand. Thank you for all your recent help – you are a wonderful father and I will always love you.

Sweet Carnloch Bay
Author unknown

As winter was brawling o'er high hills and mountains
And dark were the clouds o'er the deep rolling sea
I spied a wee lass as the daylight was dawning
She was askin the road to sweet Carnloch Bay

I said 'My fair lass, I surely will tell you,
The road and the number of miles it will be
And if you consent I'll convey you a wee bit
And show you the road to sweet Carnloch Bay'

Here's a health to Pat Hamill, likewise the dear lassie
And all you young ladies who're listening to me
And ne'er turn your back on a bonnie wee lassie
When she's asking the road to sweet Carnloch Bay

There was a time all right. Traffic was sparse. It didn't matter very much which direction the next car was going, a fellow could thumb whatever came along. Naas, the Curragh, Athgarven or Allenwood, it mattered not a whit; sometimes further out to Rathcoole or Kilcock or Baltinglass or even distant Portarlington just so long as I got well away from this one-horse town where every hoor and hoor's melt knew me seed, breed and generation and where my thirst could never be quenched in peace and solitude without some shaggin' latchicoe enquirin' after my mother and tellin' me what a great man my father was and I'd never be fit to lace his boots. The guitar was well wrapped in a horse blanket and was a great aid to gaining transport, for it was a time when to carry a guitar was quite exotic – indeed it was revolutionary and dangerous. In them days guitars were few and only played by fellows who maybe didn't go to Mass and, while their long-term prospects weren't great, there was a fair chance that you'd knock a good night out of them, and where there was ballads there would often be after-hours and loose porter.

I've travelled this wide world all over
And now to another I go

I'd never been farther than Marlborough (aka Portlaoise), but once the song started my fancy knew no bounds. I could be heading down the streets of Laredo singing 'Red Sails in the Sunset' while 'Tom Dooley' or 'Sixteen Tons' were always good items when the glass needed refilling. Get them singing and the publican would soften, for singing can be thirsty work and now closing time looms and it's time to seek the lie down. 'Did you ever sleep under a bush, Angela?' 'Well can I be your bush tonight?'

There's no business like show business and if you bussed all them bar-room republicans to Ballymena at closing time, Ulster would be full of hang-overs in the morning.

I never met Shan Mohangi, but I once spent three days with Prince Monolulu in The Standhouse and he never once had to put his hand under his gansey. Paddy Leahy was buying all round him and if you didn't finish your drink you were liable to get a smack in the mouth. Kathleen Anderson was trying to talk sense into me and I was checking out Darky Prendergast's form for he had a hot two-year-old going in Baldoyle the following Saturday, and Monolulu (by now) wasn't at the races. We went looking for bed and breakfast. We were turned back at Fetherstonaugh's gate so we struck out for Fr Moore's Well and got good hospitality at Lily-the-Pinks for I had a dozen stout and Prince Monolulu could have had anything under his toga. Joe Jackson was in the corner getting himself outside two bottles of brandy and telling me how he gave her the two barrels (hence the twins). Last I heard was 'Get up them stairs Biddy till I make a propellor out of your arse,' and sure I never saw the good man since for it was a single-storey dwelling.

Next day Mick Monahan rode a winner over seven furlongs and myself and Billy Parkinson were on her. We had a decent bet and we headed for The Harp Bar to spread the largesse about. We got back to base around closing time and Joe Doyle brought us to his cold room where Mixer sang while Jimmy Barry sliced the ham.

There was a time all right.

Unquiet Grave
from Frank Lunny Junior

Cold blows the wind oe'er my true love's grave
Soft fall the drops of rain
I never had but the one true love
in the cold clay she lies slain

I'll do as much for my true love
as any young man may
And I will lie upon her grave
for twelve months and a day

The twelve months and a day being o'er
a voice came from the deep
Saying who is that who sits upon my grave
and disturbs me from my sleep

'Tis me 'tis me your ever true love
who sits upon your grave
All I seek is one kiss from your cold lips
one kiss is all that I crave

You crave one kiss from my cold lips
but my breath is earthly strong
Take one kiss from my cold clay lips
and your life will not be long

Go sit in yonder garden green
where once we used to walk
The sweetest flower that ever grew
has withered to a stalk

The stalk it withered decayed and died
so must our love decay
You must seek contentment my love
'til death takes you away

It was one of those wild nights in Davoc Rynne's cellar. Pipes were howling as old accordions wheezed, bows were hopping across fiddles as saliva dripped from concert-pitch timber flutes, the rhythm section was in ecstasy for this was Heaven. There was no shortage of porter and the odd tincture of poitín came around to revive flagging participants. Frank Lunny sang 'Unquiet Grave' and stilled the cavorting as we all focused on the lover's broken heart. A guitar chord came in gently behind the singer and a furtive fiddle chanced it and found the right note. We were all caught by the spirit of this lonesome song.

Years later I was booked to play in The Forum, East Kilbride. It was a small folk club holding maybe 50 listeners. When I sang this song something happened and once again we were all in the midst of the lover's pain. I was to perform there many times and 'Unquiet Grave' was always requested and the audience would sing it with me and it was a unique experience.

May 1999

Today I am mixing some music at Digital Pigeon in Ringsend. It is thirty years since my first album and how this world of recording music has changed. The main difference is that today I feel the power in my work. Without this power that opens the voice, tunes the ear, directs the words, echoes the notes, creates the air, shines the light, I could not craw like the sickest crow. In those days, when I thought it was all down to me, I was carrying a burden that was too heavy – I was seeking acclaim, fame and fortune. Today, I am celebrating the gifts that God has given me and I have no great expectation to burden the process.

It was so difficult to make an album in 1968. There were so many bouncers to pass before getting to record. Recording studios were big buildings owned by powerful recording companies and patrolled by various ruthless and sometimes corrupt agencies, all of whom fed off the creative output of musicians and singers. There were publishers lurking around dark alleys waiting for the next innocent to devour. These vultures are less prevalent today, but their likes are still about although harder to spot now for they wear different clothes and hide behind different disguises. In earlier days they had little need to conceal themselves.

In 1999 there is no big deal in the recording process. Studios are now a series of small black boxes that become cheaper by the day. Anyone can record now and the stuff is there to prove it. Fellows buy guitars on Monday, and then record the album on Tuesday. There are lorryloads of shite being produced every day, but there is no harm in it. The recording process is now safely in the hands of the people who make the music, and while the multinational giants hold the world to ransom, at least we have the power and the means to sing about it.

I'm looking at my first article in *Melody Maker*. The head on me! I wanted to look like a navvy and to sing like a navvy. I had my first publicity shot done on top of the Pennines as the M62 was being constructed above Halifax. It was a strange mindset. I was 24, I was making my first album and I was positioning my persona in the midst of construction. But that was where I felt comfortable, just so long as I wasn't on the shovel. Let me sing about shovels, but don't ask me to drive one.

Rocks of Bawn
Author unknown

Come all you loyal heroes wherever you may be
Don't hire with any master till you know what your work may be
Don't hire with any master from the clear daylight til the dawn
For he'll want you rising early to plough the rocks of Bawn

My shoes they are well worn and my stockings they are thin
My auld coat sure it's threadbare now and I'm leaking to the skin
But I'll rise up in the morning from the clear daylight to the dawn
Then I will be able to plough up the rocks of Bawn

Me curse attend you Sweeney for you have me nearly robbed
You're sitting by the fireside with your feet upon the hob
You're sitting by the fireside from the clear day light till dawn
And you know you'll not be able to plough the rocks of Bawn

Oh rise up there lovely Sweeney and give yer horse some hay
And give him a good feed of oats before you start the day
Don't feed him on soft turnips take him down to your green lawn
And then you might be able to plough the rocks of Bawn

I wish that the Queen of England would write to me in time
And place me in a regiment all in me youth and prime
I'd fight for Ireland's glory from the clear daylight till dawn
And I never would return again to plough the rocks of Bawn

Where are the Rocks of Bawn? Who is Sweeney? Maybe Sweeney could crush the rocks with his tongue if only he could find the Jizz. Take a cold, cold day and put yourself snug in the corner with your arse on the bench and your toes well roasted. Now there's beet to be mangled and animals to be tended, hedges to be trimmed, fences to be mended, doors to be re-hung, the haggart to be tidied, cartwheels that need greasing and expectations to be fulfilled. Sweeney would rather dream of Camden Town or Kalgoorlie, Croke Park or the Bronx where the girls would be winking and the porter flowing freely. Joe Burke would tear into 'The Bucks' and Sweeney could send money home and pay to have all that work done.

Here we are now in Ireland, Mother Ireland. We have exported our Buacaills and Cailíns for centuries. We've sent them away, far away and we've expected them to find work and refuge in the four corners of the world. We've sent our brothers, nuns and priests to preach the gospel of love. Now we've been given the opportunity to show love and compassion and welcome to refugees fleeing famine and terror and our response is absolute in its lack of love.

Citizens of Ireland are attacking helpless refugees. Irish hard-chaws are beating up immigrants. Civil servants are quoting false statistics and fuelling racial hatred and paranoia. The Church, in the main, is silent. We are being dehumanised in our rush to ride this Celtic tiger. In our hunger for Mammon we have lost our good nature – we kick out at 'knackers and niggers', we have neither charity nor compassion and we will certainly devour ourselves in our frenzy.

Streams of Bunclody
Author unknown

Oh the streams of Bunclody they flow down so free
By the streams of Bunclody I'm longing to be
A-drinking strong liquor in the height of my cheer
Here's health to Bunclody and the lass I love dear

The cuckoo is a pretty bird, it sings as it flies
It brings us good tidings, and tells us no lies
It sucks the young birds' eggs to make its voice clear
And the more it cries cuckoo the summer draws near

If I was a clerk and could write a good hand
I would write to my true love that she might understand
For I am a young fellow who is wounded in love
Once I lived in Bunclody, but now must remove

If I was a lark and had wings and I could fly
I would fly to yon arbour where my true love she does lie
I'd fly to yon arbour where my true true love does lie
And on her fond bosom contented I would die

'Tis why my love slights me, as you may understand
That she has a freehold and I have no land
She has great store of riches, and a large sum of gold
And everything fitting a house to uphold

So fare you well father and my mother, adieu
My sister and brother farewell unto you
I am bound for America my fortune to try
When I think on Bunclody I'm ready to die

I first heard this song in O'Donohue's which for many years was the best-known pub in Dublin. It was the Mecca for singers and musicians who arrived in the city. I made my first visit there around 1963 and it reeked of character and musical anecdotes. There was a poet in each snug and every second stool was home to some luminary or other. For an eighteen-year-old with three chords and new sandals it was heady stuff, to be rubbing shoulders with real folkies. You'd see Joe Heaney, Ronnie Drew, Peter Mulready – three men who spring to mind. Or could it be Garech Brown swanning around or the Boston Kennedys or The Clancy Brothers might be in town, and behind it all were Paddy and Maureen O'Donohue whose pub, purely by chance, became Ireland's premier music house. I sat in awe there and listened to Ted McKenna, Maeve Mulvanney, Mick McGuane, Jessie Owens, Anne Byrne who would have been there regularly.

Gradually I began to fit in there a bit and started to bring my guitar along. After months of listening I was asked 'Do you play that or do you just carry it around?' Ted McKenna got me to sing my first song in O'Donoghue's in about 1963. Around three years later I was home from Overseas Balladeering when Maureen asked me for a picture for her wall of fame and I felt I had arrived. Thirty years later that picture is still there, and I go in once every five years to check it out.

The Kerry Recruit
Author unknown

About four years ago I was digging the land
With my brogues on my feet and my spade in my hand
Says I to myself what a pity to see
Such a fine strapping lad footing turf in Tralee

Wid me toorim mi neaa me toorum mi na
Wid me toorim mi nure im mi nure im mi nya

So I buttered my brogues and shook hands with my spade
And I went to the fair like a dashing young blade
When up comes a sergeant and asks me to 'list
Arra, Sergeant a grá put the bob in my fist

O! Then here is the shilling, as we've got no more
When you get to headquarters you'll get half a score
Arra, quit your kimeens, ses I, Sergeant goodbye
You'd not wish to be quartered, and neither would I

And the first thing they gave me it was a red coat
With a wide strap of leather to tie round my throat
They gave me a quare thing I asked what was that
And they told me it was a cockade for my head

The next thing they gave me they called it a gun
With powder and shot and a place for my thumb
And first she spit fire and then she spit smoke
Lord, she gave a great lep and my shoulder near broke

The next place they sent me was down to the sea
On board of a warship bound for the Crimea
Three sticks in the middle all rowled round with sheets
She walked thro' the water without any feet

When at Balaclava we landed quite sound
Both cold wet and hungry we lay on the ground
Next morning for action the bugle did call

And we got a hot breakfast of powder and ball

Sure it's often I thought of my name and my home
And the days that I spent cutting turf, och mavrone
The balls were so thick and the fire was so hot
I lay down in the ditch, boys, for fear I'd be shot

We fought at the Alma, likewise Inkermann
But the Russians they whaled us at the Redan
In scaling the walls there myself lost my eye
And a big Russian bullet ran off with my thigh

It was there I lay bleeding, stretched on the cold ground
Heads, legs and arms were scattered all around
Says I, if my mama or my cleaveens were nigh
They'd bury me decent and raise a loud cry

They brought me the doctor, who soon staunched my blood
And he gave me an elegant leg made of wood
They gave me a medal and tenpence a day
Contented with Sheela, I'll live on half pay

In Ireland we call it the FCA; England has the Local Defence Force, and most uncivilised countries have their own version. It's like boy scouts with drink and guns. In the 35 years since I turned in my beret, the FCA has probably become a lean, mean killing machine. But in my day it was a different story. I joined for one reason only – two weeks' summer camp with wages.

I've always had a difficult shape to cover with cloth, but my army uniform was the most undignified outfit I've ever encountered. As always, a person with my girth should, in tailor's terms, be six foot four inches tall, so much of my life has been spent getting trousers taken up. No matter what I did with my uniform, I always felt like shite. But I had to get to that summer camp. I joined my platoon in Newbridge College where the two corporals were mean, miserable hoors gits. And then the sergeant would arrive and he was a jumped-up little bollix of a power freak, but all three paled when our officer breezed in from Pluto. This guy was something else. He viewed his miserable schoolboy platoon as his own and he lived out every fetish and fantasy upon our ill-clad backs. Long marches, square bashing, weapon training and cruelty were the order, but we suffered it all to get to camp.

My short stint in army life gave me a little insight into what career soldiers must endure. This was not the Foreign Legion by any means, but suffering was part of the preparation – for camp. Then it was summer.

We loaded up into an army truck and off to war on the dance floors of Kilkenny. The pint of beer was 1/8, it was brewed in Kilkenny – Phoenix on draft. And then to the Carlton Ballroom to hear Prince Vince with his rubber-hose medley. During the day we contorted ourselves with war games, but once we walked through those gates all the suffering was forgotten. We were sixteen-year-old killing machines with money in our pockets and auras of Old Spice to protect us.

When I was confined to barracks, or drew guard duty, the Wet Canteen was the place to go. It was a bleak bar but the drink was cheap – 1/5 for a large bottle and there were good nights put in.

I only survived one summer, but its memories have brightened my life and when I run across old comrades we go back again and visit our 'army years'.

God save Ireland from invasion.

Little Beggarman

Author unknown

I am a little beggarman and begging I have been
For three score or more down the little Isle of Green
I'm known from the Liffey way down to Killaloe
And the name that I go by is Auld Johnny Do
Of all the trades a going sure beggin is the best
For when a man is fired he can sit down and rest
Beg for his supper when he's nothin left to do
Except to slip around the corner with his auld rig-a-doo

I slept one night way down in Curraghbawn
'Twas a wet damp night and I slept till the dawn
Holes in the roof and the rain was comin through
And the rats and the cats they were playin peek-a-boo
Who should I waken but the woman of the house
With her white spotted apron and her calico blouse
She began to frighten when I said How do you do
Don't be afraid m'am, it's only Johnny Doo

Over the road with me pack on me back
Over the road with me big heavy sack
Holes in me shoes and me toes peepin through
Sing skidderi dill doodle dam it's only Johnny Doo
I must be going to bed it's getting late at night
In goes the fire and out goes the light
Now you've heard the story of me aul' rig-a-doo
Goodnight and God be with you sez aul' Johnny Doo

In 1967 I made my way across Cheshire to Congleton in my fine VW Beetle which was my pride and joy. I sought out the Cheshire Cat public house where the Union Folk Club was held every Monday night. At opening time I entered the premises and introduced myself to the landlady as the evening's 'turn'. I sat into the tap room and fortified myself with a pork pie, a Scotch egg and a saucer of pickled onions for there was a long night ahead. The resident band and the audience began to drift in. The Union Folk were a solid, part-time band and they wore red shirts and black leather waistcoats. Their repertoire was mainstream, popular folk and they had a lovely rapport with their home crowd. They would warm the audience and then present me on to the floor for my first set. There was no stage, I simply stood at one end of the room and began to sing. My first set could have been: 'Galway Roses', 'Verdant Braes', 'Rocky Road', 'Follow Me up to Carlow', 'Curragh of Kildare', 'Spanish Lady', 'Calton Weaver', 'Unquiet Grave', and my second set: 'Jim Larkin', 'Belfast Brigade', 'Kevin Barry', 'Dark-Eyed Sailor', 'Tippin' It Up', 'Sam Hall', 'Seth Davey', and then I'd always finish with the 'Little Beggarman'.

By the end I'd always be soaked in sweat and as there were never any dressing rooms I had to try and cool off in the midst of my crowd, who were now clambering around in what had become a room full of happy people recently unfettered from the discipline of being an audience. I'd try and dry off and change as surreptitiously as possible, and then the priority was to sort out bed-couch-floor, or love nest if I was lucky. That done, there was the fee to collect and the carry-out to organise.

Monday night was not the best night for partying, but in Congleton they never shirked and we'd bale back to some gaff or other for more of the same.

Tuesday mornings in Cheshire were never great for me, fully clothed in my sleeping bag, stiff and sore trying to piece together last night's fun. Get the engine started, scrub the grinders and hold the hot head under the cold tap, examine the wardrobe for the least offensive and then adieu to Congleton and where am I tonight? It could be Alnwick or Prudhoe or Hebburn, I'd point the Beetle, clear my throat and be off – Chorlton-cum-Hardy here I come.

Three Drunken Maidens
Author unknown

There were three drunken maidens came from the Isle of Wight
They started to drink on a Monday never stopped till Saturday night
But when Saturday night it came me lads still they wouldn't get out
These three drunken maidens they pushed the jug about

They had woodcock and pheasant they had partridge and hare
Every kind of dainty no scarcity was there
They drank ten pints a piece me lads and still they wouldn't get out
These three drunken maidens they pushed the jug about

Then in came the landlord he was looking for his pay
And a £40 reckoning these girls were forced to pay
They had £12 a piece me lads, still they wouldn't get out
These three drunken maidens they pushed the jug about

Then in came Bouncing Sally with her cheeks as red as a bloom
Move up my jolly sisters and give young Sally some room
And I will be your equal before the evening's out
These three drunken maidens they pushed the jug about

Where are your feathered hats young maidens brisk and fine
They've all been swallowed up me lads in tankards of good wine
Where are your maidenheads young maidens brisk and gay
We left them in the alehouse it's there they'll have to pay

Planxty's first hit single – number five in the Irish charts and we never looked back. I was all hairs and flares and we were up and down the roads of Ireland like commercial travellers.

Andy Irvine got the song from Maddy Prior who recorded it with Steeleye Span. Liam O'Flynn added 'The Dublin Reel' and we had an exciting piece of music. Some nights we'd play it twice or three times, for the gigs were most un-concert-like and we'd be competing with cash registers, calf dealers, United Irishman sellers, town commissioners, sex maniacs, bank robbers, engaged couples and those under the influence of mind-altering substances, and not all of these good people had come to hear 'serious' musicians being precious about their work. But, sure, we all need to make a few bob for them substances don't come cheap.

On The Blanket
by Mick Hanly

The truth comes as hard as the cold rain
On my face in the heat of a storm
The stories I'm hearing they shock me
To believe that such deeds can go on
You can starve men and take all their clothing
You can beat them up till they fall
You can break the bodies but never the spirit
Of the men on the blanket

The truth should be told so I'll tell it
It all began five years ago
Kieran Nugent refused to be branded
And refused to wear prison clothes
They threw him in naked to H-Block
And spat out their filthy abuse
And left him awake till the cold light of day
With only a blanket

England your sins are not over
The H-Blocks still stand in your name
And tho' many voices have cried out to you
It is still your shame
And if we stay silent we're guilty
While these men lie naked and cold
In H-Block tonight remember the fight
Of the men on the blanket

For four years this man and his comrades
In shameful conditions did lie
From Dublin indifference and silence
From London contempt undisguised
Tho' life to these men was precious
A hunger strike protest began
To try to move the hearts of the tyrants who keep
The men on the blanket

How angry the March winds were blowing
As Prisoners of War made their call
With deals and false promises broken
How many more young men must fall
The people have raised up their voices
The world cries for justice in vain
To end the cruel fortune and the lives to regain
Of the men on the blanket

Tonight as I stand here in Sligo
My heart filled with sorrow and shame
In mourning for Martin Hurson
His body laid out in Tyrone
This young man had so much to live for
His dying must not be in vain
As we stand here tonight remember the fight
Of the men on the blanket

August 1999

Eighteen years later and the guns are cocked but silent. Our national news is dominated by the lies and corruption of some politicians. Endless tribunals slowly unravel what we always suspected – the coercion of big business and politics, of banker, builder and ruler with the Church quietly in the background giving us their cynical God line while they try to cover up their own current and historical sins of cruelty. Martin Hurson died in agony and, eighteen years on, David Trimble and John Taylor may be about to talk to Gerry Adams and Martin McGuinness. Outside the door lurk the mad killers of Omagh and the Orangemen swarming to march down the Garvaghy Road. Who murdered Rosemary Nelson? I simply assume that collusion exists between the police and the perpetrators.

While the peace process inches forward, the RUC remains sectarian and bigoted. As long as they are allowed to remain entrenched in their historically biased attitude to policing, there never will be decommissioning and why should there be?

As I sit in this quiet Cork valley today I feel no need to hold arms for I do not feel threatened in any way by my neighbours or my police force. I sincerely believe that decommissioning will not be a problem when all the people in Northern Ireland feel protected by their constabulary.

House in Carne
by Jim 'Doc' Whelan

My name is Nuke Power a terror am I
I can wreak destruction on land, sea and sky
Your minister says that I'll do no harm
He locks me up in his house down in Carne

Toora loo toora lay
I can cripple and maim, cause death and decay

He'll have me well guarded by night and by day
With soldiers on land and with sailors at sea
But he cannot tame me or keep me down
By locking me up in his house down in Carne

Such a beautiful country I see all around
Where people and flowers and fishes abound
I'll change the whole picture in ten seconds I warn
If he tries to lock me in his house down in Carne

I'll poison your children I'll strangle your dog
I'll kill every creature on land, sea and bog
I'll devastate Ireland from Killarney to Larne
If he tries to lock me in his house down in Carne

When we arrived on the site at Carnsore Point in 1978 it was a wild and beautiful place. We had decided to focus our anti-nuclear campaign on the land where the Electricity Supply Board were planning to site a nuclear power station. Martin Ronan gave us permission to use his land despite much local opposition. We had no idea how many people would arrive as we set to work. On Monday it was a clear site with no amenities except sun, wind, sea and grass. Volunteer workers from far and near began to arrive and, slowly, a skilled workforce began to assemble. A small, wind-powered generator gave us our first night light, as the stage was built the site was planned out, and two men undertook to design and build a toilet system that worked admirably. We got water from two sources and also built some large tanks to store it. Kitchens were planned and built and we got marquees from Co. Galway. There were constant meetings as problems arose, and decisions needed to be made hourly as the site evolved. It was an exciting time in my life, to witness people power and be part of it. A broad collective of diverse people using their varied skills and talents collectively in pursuit of a common ideal – a nuclear-free Ireland.

We organised a medical centre and patrols to watch the coastline which had the potential to be dangerous. There were play areas for children, washing areas, car parks, food tents, advice centres, and the whole site was lit at night by generators. We decided to corral the burger and chip vans off-site and this was difficult. We had no funding apart from what we raised ourselves, yet by the weekend we were ready to roll.

Ten thousand people turned up and the weekend was a glorious success. The best of Irish music performed at this free gathering, there was poetry, theatre, dance, performance artistes and more and more music. Everyone got fed and no one was hurt. There was little or no drunkenness and only one incident that required police assistance. By the time the festival was over, we had thousands of recruits into the anti-nuclear movement and had set in place 22 groups around the 32 counties. We also decided to form a roadshow that subsequently visited eighteen centres around the country, consolidating the various groups that had formed at Carnsore.

Come Tuesday and the clean-up began. My last memory of Carnsore is of a line of 50 to 60 people on their knees going across the site picking up every matchstick of litter, so when we closed Martin Ronan's gate on Friday the site was as we found it. A bit battered and bruised, perhaps, but nothing that nature could not endure.

'No nuclear power – that's what the people say.'

Grannie's Dustbin Lid
by Joe Mulhearn

As I was climbing into bed at my grannie's side
I looked out the window the Brits they had arrived
The house was surrounded they smashed the front door in
They'd come to take away the lid of me Grannie's bin

She opened up her window she clambered down the spout
Soon her bin was rattling to call the neighbours out
She took out her whistle and blew away like hell
And soon we heard an echo as her neighbours blew as well

Scream bang shout
Rattle up a din
Let the soldiers know me girls
The Brits are coming in
Rattle up your bin lid
Beat the message out
Get your rhythm going
Whistle bang shout

A soldier came up the stairs, a rifle in his hand
She kicked him with her button boots as down the hall she ran
Up came another one his medal for to win
But all he got upon his knob was the lid of me grannie's bin

The music rose like thunder as the bins and whistles played
The army soon retreated they knew they'd overstayed
It wasn't made of silver it wasn't made of tin
But once again it saved us all, the lid of my grannie's bin

The English have the radio, the telly and the press
To all sorts of fancy gadgets they've always had access
From Pettigo to Bellahy from the Bone to Castlefin
The only way to spread the news is the lid of my grannie's bin

Helicopters, night sights, infra-red, Saracens, Timoney Tanks, CS gas, rubber bullets, snatch squads, special powers, Diplock courts, interrogation centres, torture techniques, spies, unlimited weapons-ammunition-training resources, British army, RUC, UDR, in their tens of thousands, Land Rovers, hi-tech communications, forts, barracks and. . .dustbin lids.

Which side are you on, which side are you on?

The women who beat their dustbin lids announced the arrival of Operation Motorman, the beginning of Internment, movement of snatch squads, the death of Bobby Sands.

Which side are you on, which side are you on?

They saw their fathers and husbands and sons, their daughters and mothers and sisters harassed on the streets by squaddie bully boys armed to the teeth, lifted and beaten and interned, batoned and kicked.

Which side are you on, which side are you on?

They travelled in crowded vans to internment camps where they suffered discomfort and insults to visit their loved ones.

And they fought back defiantly with dustbin lids.

Jesus Christ and Jessie James
by Brian Moore

Will you come and listen to the story going round
How our Lord and Jessie James rode into Belfast Town
They stopped for a drink they stopped for a meal
Drinking whiskey, drinking wine they were feeling mighty fine
As they rode into Belfast through the hills of Ligoniel

Not a word was spoken as they travelled on their way
Until they came to the falls and Jessie he did say
God I haven't felt so good since I robbed the Glendale train
Our Lord he raised his head, turned to Jessie and he said
I never thought I'd see the likes of Calvary again

They rode past the burnt-out motorcars and the tangle of barbed wire
In a city built upon a swamp and baptised by fire
Our Lord was going to bless the place but a bullet pierced his hand
As the blood came trickling down turned to Jessie with a frown
Looks like the old stigmata is infectious in this land

Our Lord was riding a donkey, Jessie James was riding a mare
And they rode past the army tanks and never showed a care
Jessie on his fiddle played the victory at the Boyne
Jesus put his guitar down turned to Jessie with a frown
I don't think you should play that tune when we're passing through Ardoyne

On the top of Divis Mountain there stands a lonely tree
And children passing by there they stop and bend a kneee
And men with hidden guns they make a silent vow
That the riots will stop the day the soldiers go away
Leave our Lord on Calvary and Jessie hanging from the bough

Here is a song that offended almost everyone. I've always loved it since hearing it on an album by The Men of No Property. The imagery appeals to me – my vision of Jesus is that he'd be more likely to hang out with Jessie James than Charlie McCreevy; I think he'd spend more time in Ardoyne than up the Antrim Road and we'd more likely find him with Peter McVerry than with the Primate of All Ireland.

It's all so mixed up and my head got so confused. Excommunication is a confusing phenomenon. They'd have you believe that it is Christian to keep your head down and say nothing. Good Christian, keep quiet, only open your gob to confess and receive. 'Preach the Word of God.' God does not need words; what Word anyway – the word of the wind, the sun, the water, the word of the innocent child, the source of mystery? Is the word of Bishop Comiskey the Word of God or is the word of the suffering child the Word of God? Does God live in a palace or a hut?

Blessing the guns, blessing the planes, blessing the destroyers, excommunicating the rebels. Blessing the occupiers, excommunicating the occupied. . .

The Crow on the Cradle
Author unknown

The sheep's in the meadow the cow's in the corn
now is the time for a child to be born
He'll cry for the moon and he'll laugh at the sun
if it's a boy he'll carry a gun
And if it should be that our baby's a girl
never you mind if her hair doesn't curl
With rings on her fingers, bells on her toes
and bombers above her wherever she goes

Sang the crow in the cradle

Your Mummy and Daddy they'll sweat and they'll save
Build you a garden and dig you a grave
Oh hush-a-bye baby why do you weep
we've got a pill that can put you to sleep
Hush-a-bye baby the black and the white
somebody's baby was born for to fight
Hush-a-bye baby the white and the black
hush-a-bye baby is not coming back

Bring me a gun and I'll shoot that bird dead
That's what your Mummy and Daddy once said
Oh crow on the cradle what shall I do
That is the question I leave unto you

I performed this song with The Early Grave Band on the Anti-Nuclear Roadshow which toured Ireland in 1978. We played thirteen cities and towns. The purpose of the tour was to commence or consolidate autonomous groups around the country and to follow up the first Anti-Nuclear Festival with a focal point to nourish the seeds sown at Carnsore Point.

We played Newbridge, Kilkenny, Waterford, Wexford, Cork, Tralee, Limerick, Galway, Sligo, Derry, Belfast, Dundalk and Dublin. We had 22 personnel and each performance was, in theory, to be funded by the host town.

Tralee was a problem for we only drew a handful of supporters to the CYMS Hall. One local activist explained the small crowd was because the gig was free and that Kerry people were always suspicious of something for nothing. Cork was electric and the crowd were full of enthusiasm. So much so that the actor who played Minister for Energy in the play was assaulted – Fergus Cronin played the part so convincingly that certain Leesiders could not contain their anti-nuclear zeal. The unfortunate actor had to be rescued from the angry mob and carried to the bus where he was coaxed back to life by the rest of the cast and emerged brand new for the second show.

Mrs McGrath
Author unknown

Now Mrs McGrath the sergeant said
Would you like to make a soldier out of your son Ted
With scarlet coat and cockade hat
Now Mrs McGrath wouldn't you like that

Mrs McGrath stood by the shore
Waiting for her son for seven years or more
'Til she saw a ship sailing into the bay
Here's my son Ted now Musha clear the way

Captain dear where have you been
Have you been sailing on the Med-it-tare-i-in
Have you got news of my son Ted
Is the poor fellow living or is he dead

Then up came Ted without any legs
Walking on a pair of wooden pegs
She kissed him a dozen times or two
Mother of God sure it can't be you

Were you drunk or were you blind
When you left your two fine legs behind
Or was it walking on the say
Took your two fine legs from the knees away

No I wasn't drunk and I wasn't blind
When I left my two fine legs behind
But a cannon ball on the fifth of May
Took my fine legs from the knees away

Oh Teddy McGrath the widow cried
Your fine legs were your mother's pride
Them stumps of trees won't do at all
Why didn't you run from the cannon ball

And if I had you back again
I wouldn't take the shilling the sergeant paid (I wouldn't let you go to fight the King of Spain)
I'd rather have me son as he used to be
Than the King of France and his whole navee

In 1963 we were all getting turned on together. Start up this song and strum the only guitar for miles around; the whole room fell into the story and before the third chorus men who'd never sung a note were ready to join The Clancy Brothers. Word soon spread about the ballad sessions and people flocked to hear the many bands and groups and singers who emerged.

These songs began to paint vivid pictures of our past. They had survived centuries of damnation; sneered at, banned and denounced, all we had to do was sing them once and they sprung back to life as if they'd never been locked away. Their revival was a turning point in our history and culture. They turned our heads and we began to look at where we were and who we were and many of us loved what we saw.

I began to dig deeper and what lay dormant was exhilarating; I found songs that touched me deeply and singers who sang them with sincerity.

The Meeting of the Waters
by Thomas Moore

There is not in this wide world a valley so sweet
As that vale in whose bosom the bright waters meet
Oh! The last rays of feeling and life must depart
Ere the bloom of that valley shall fade from my heart

Yet it was not what nature had shed o'er the scene
The purest of crystal and brightest of green
'Twas not her soft magic of streamlet or hill
Oh no it was something more exquisite still

'Twas that the friends beloved of my heart were near
And they made every scene of beauty more dear
They could feel how the best charms of nature improve
When we view them reflected in those whom we love

Sweet Vale of Avoca how calm could I rest
In your bosom of shade with the friends I love best
Where the storms that we feel in this cold world should cease
And our hearts like the waters be mingled in peace

Long before I discovered the real songs I encountered the likes of this song. Then, when I went for the singing lessons and the elocution, this song was on my shortlist when I performed publicly as a boy soprano. Don't forget your shoes and socks and shirt and tie and all. Hands by my side and my socks tight up to my knees and my little spirit harnessed to sing a Thomas Moore ditty. These were the parlour songs sung stiffly by the corseted classes gathered around pianos aping their betters. God save us all, but wouldn't they have been better off if they'd loosened their gussets and danced a set around the kitchen floor or sung a bar of a song that might have stirred some emotion locked deep away inside them.

The Armagh Women
by Margaretta D'Arcy

In Black Armagh of the Goddess Macha
Last February in the grey cold jail
The governor in his savage fury
Came down to break the women's will
Forty jailors my forty jailors
From the hell of Long Kesh come down
And help me break these Irish women
Who will not respect our English Crown

Forty jailors put on their armour
Strapped on their helmets took up their shields
Then they beat the Armagh women
Thinking they could make them yield
Three days he kept them locked in darkness
Locked in filth hard to believe
When he unlocked them he was so conceited
He thought he'd broken them to yield

If you have suffered, the Governor said
It never happened it was just a dream
Come out come out obey my orders
But the Armagh women would not move
They swore they'd never give in to the Governor
They swore that they would break him down
Until him and his jailors were locked in prison
By the women of Armagh Jail

And there they remain these warrior women
Locked and bound in Armagh Jail
They hold the Governor and his warders powerless
The Armagh women won't concede
Women of Ireland understand your power
Women of Ireland stand up and declare
Side by side we'll stand together
And tumble down their grey cold jail

I heard Geraldine King, the fine singer from Inishbofin, sing this song. She taught it to me and I believe it was written by Margaretta D'Arcy who resides in Galway. I performed it once in The Conway Mill, West Belfast. It has an ancient feel to it. It describes a time in the Armagh women's prison when the Governor tried to smash a protest in support of the Blanket Men in Long Kesh.

Whiskey, You're the Devil
Author unknown

Oh whiskey you're the devil, you're leading me astray
Over hill and mountains and to Americay
You're sweeter, stronger, dacenter, you're spunkier than tay
Oh whiskey you're me darling, drunk or sober

Well now me boys we're on for marching
Off to Portugal or Spain
The drums are beating, banners flying
The devil a home we'll come tonight

Love fare thee well
With me skiddery eye dill do dill dump ee da
With me skiddery eye dill do dill dump ee da
Me right fol tooraladdy oh
There's whiskey in the jar

The French are fighting boldly
Men are dying hot and coldly
Give every man a flask of powder
His firelock on his shoulder

Says the mother do not wrong me
Don't take my daughter from me
For if you do I will torment you
And after death my ghost will haunt you

You sing about it and you drink it and you start to believe it. Whiskey from a thousand different bottles. The finest of liquor to the cheapest hard tack, from Redbreast to raw poitín, single malt to Yates rotgut and on and on we went. From the top of the highest mountain I roared in speculation only to wake up seconds later on a cold, cold floor. What town is this, where is my box, did I fall or was I struck.

I look at ads for hard liquor and I still cannot believe my eyes. Slim models and beautifully dressed young men conversing seductively over whiskey on glinting ice. Would you ever ask me bollix. That message is wasted on me, advertising agencies who ply these dangerous pictures should visit lock-up wards and drying-out units. What about wet brains and road carnage and wife beating and delirium tremens.

The Gresford Disaster
Author unknown

You've heard of the Gresford Disaster
Of the terrible price that was paid
Two hundred and sixty-two colliers were lost
And three men of the rescue brigade

It occured in the month of September
At two in the morning that pit
Was wracked by a violent explosion
At the coal face where gas lay so thick

A short while before the explosion
The shot firer Tomlinson cried
If you fire that shot we'll be all blown to Hell
And no-one can say that he lied

The firemen's reports are all missing
The records of forty-two days
The colliery manager had them destroyed
To cover his criminal ways

Down there in the dark they are lying
They died for nine shillings a day
They've worked out this shift and it's now they must be
In the darkness until Judgement day

Well the Lord Mayor launched his collection
To help the poor children and wives
The owners have sent some white lilies dear God
To pay for the poor miners' lives

Farewell to our wives and our children
Farewell to our comrades as well
Don't send your son down the dark dreary mine
They'll be damned like the sinners in Hell

I understand why many people today do not want to hear these songs. Why bother, don't I have enough troubles of my own? Put on 'Waterloo' for Jasus' sake and give us a break from your lamenting – Christ almighty I came out to be entertained. All of these attitudes are valid and I've no problem with them.

I sing these songs for they satisfy me. I want to pay my tribute to those who died and, in remembering the dead of Gresford, Trimdon Grange, Ludlow, Artane, I picture in my mind the work practices that exist today, the owners and bosses who still take short cuts. As I sing, I hope that maybe some one listening might see the error of their ways.

Hands Off the GLC *(For Ken Livingstone)*
by C. Moore

I first arrived in London back in 1963
In all my travels round the world 'tis a favourite place for me
In Camden Town and Cricklewood I've had the curtain call
And once or twice I did a turn up in the Albert Hall

Invited by the council upon this royal stage
To do an anti-racist gig myself they did engage
Since I arrived in London I'm very sad to see
Maggie and her boot boys trying to sink the GLC

Pavarotti sings in Finchley for the well to do
James Galway plays for millionaires on board the QE2
Covent Garden caters for the fur coats and the Whigs
But the GLC will try to see that the unemployed have gigs

Racing out in Goodwood, yachts at Maidenhead
Boating at Henley all you need is lots of bread
Keep the fun all for themselves that's what the Tories do
But the GLC will try to see there's fun for me and you

Denis Thatcher for Lord Mayor, young Mark collects the rates
Maggie Thatcher will be Queen when the Queen she abdicates
Cruise at Hyde Park Corner plastic bullets in Southall
The paras back from Crossmaglen dig in around Whitehall

I was invited by the Greater London Council to do a number of concerts in
The Great City. There was a memorial concert for the Tolpuddle Martyrs
in Battersea Park in 1984, and an anti-racism concert in The Royal Festival
Hall in 1985 which I recall specifically because the staff pulled the power
plug on me. The audience called long and hard for an encore and when they
refused to leave I decided to go back out. This angered the uniformed stage
crew who blacked out the hall. My tour manager Jim Donohoe came front-
of-stage with a torch and lit me up as I sang 'James Connolly' to 1,500 people

with no amplification. I wrote this little ditty for this particular concert; it caused us all to have a lighter moment in the midst of Maggie's mayhem.

Jim was to repeat the torch exercise maybe half a dozen times over seventeen years, notably in Salthall, Galway, during a lightning storm, in Malahide, Dublin, during a power cut and in another nameless venue during a riot.

Hey! Paddy
by Wally Page

From Rotherhithe in London to Bethnal by the Green
Paddy worked the buildings with the pick and shovel squad
Friday nights he'd always end up drinking with the lads
The craic was mighty with the navvies from the sod

There's a hooley on for Jimmy he's the gofor on the site
(They) lifted him for sleeping rough they gave him forty days and nights
He's out again and crouching beside 'got ye's' fire for heat
Drinking billy after billy-can of charcoal tea

Hey! Paddy Hey! Paddy where have you been Paddy
Hey! Paddy where have you been (hi ho)
Hey! Paddy guess what we're taking you in Paddy
Hey! Paddy where have you been (hi ho)
Fol de doll de dairy do

Jimmy sang the rebel songs Paddy sang them too
Till the Rasta man from Trinidad whispered them the news
Listen to me my good friend this warning take from me
The cops are lifting Paddy bastards from across the Irish Sea

Sitting in a cafe down the King's Cross Road
Drinking cappucino on a bellyfull of beer
His head was only lifting he had twenty minutes left
For another cup of coffee and another cigarette

Lousy Monday morning on the tube Paddy read the rag
They were looking for a photo fit he was the one they lagged
The coppers lifted him and took his photo for the files
And they kicked him in the bollix just to make him smile

Wally Page wrote this ballad – I've been trying unsuccessfully to record it for ten years but I do have one live version of it sung in The Rialto, Derry at a Bloody Sunday memorial gig in 1993. I sang it beside 'Scapegoats' and it was a memorable performance for Johnny Walker (of the Birmingham Six) was in the audience.

I also tried to sing it in the Hammersmith Odeon when Paul Hill and Gerry Conlon came to the concert three nights after their release – the emotion was so high that night that the entire audience simply stood and applauded the two innocents for minutes on end. It was their night.

Bless this Guitar
by Peter Cadle

I've taken this road and I've chosen this view
The place is familiar the feeling is new
This old church lies in ruin from the wind and the rain
And I'll rest my guitar on the stones that remain

Bless this guitar
To reach out
And touch who we are
Bless this guitar

From the mountain the sea looks as calm as a pool
The evening is welcome the night is cool
I'll sit here for a while with the breeze in my hair
While the kestrels above are riding the air

Greeks and Romans have stopped to look over the bay
Byzantine Travellers have passed on their way
Here and there now and then stones have slipped from the wall
And these are the changes this place can recall
I've loved this wild place its smells and its sounds
Been here as long as the stars all around
I know the path well I'll find my way back
Just one more late Traveller on this ancient track

I've never been too far from my guitar these past 40 years. I hate to travel anywhere without an instrument, for a guitar means many different things to me. Foremost, it has been my soother. To sit quietly in a cool corner and play an old song or strum a favourite tune has calmed me down a thousand times. Often, alone late at night in some hotel kip a thousand miles from home, I've sat quietly looking out across a strange city and I've caressed my box and sung some ancient song. I've taken my guitar to weddings, christenings and funerals for experience has taught me never to be caught without it.

One of the great joys is to sit with a bunch of singers and pass the box around. In my younger days the guitar opened many doors, and got me many lifts to strange places and into curious situations. Then it has been the tool of my trade. I've leapt on to stages and strode out holding my guitar high beneath the spotlight before hammering out the opening chords of 'The Deluge' or 'Welcome to the Cabaret'. Then to gently pluck a lonesome minor chord and sing quietly out into the night, the simple notes reverberating across the stalls up into the highest balconies, the old verses bringing us all together one more time.

Bless this guitar.

Andytown Girl
by C. Moore

I see the image of your face
But I cannot hear your voice
Even tho' your lips are moving
Your sweet lips they are moving
Now I see you laughing
But I cannot hear your voice
Even tho' your eyes are shining
Your eyes forever shining
You are playing in the sand
But I cannot hear your voice
And I see you dancing
As you do your Irish dancing

When you were behind those prison walls
I could not hear your voice
But you told me of your dreaming
And I know what you were dreaming
I saw how you were taken
And I could not hear your voice
But I knew you weren't complaining
You were not one for complaining
I saw your hands joined in communion
But I could not hear your voice
I know you took a beating
But you never will be beaten

Mairéad Farrell once wrote to me asking would I write a song for her and her comrades, which I did ('On the Bridge'). One day I saw her walking down a sandy beach; shortly afterwards she was executed in Gibraltar. I tried to write a song for her. When I saw a film about her life and death I wrote down these images gleaned from a silent family film shown on her documentary and from *Death on the Rock*.

I've never performed this song.

Joe Doherty
by C. Moore

I thank you for the privilege of singing on your stage
Of visiting your country and the welcome that you gave
I don't wish to abuse it but one thing I'd like to say
Joe Doherty is still locked up in a New York jail today

There's many in for murder, remanded on appeal
Behind barbed wire and concrete, iron bars and steel
Here is a man who's never once been charged with any crime
Does anybody understand why Joe's still doing time

With respect to Mr Thornburg please may I call you sir
Joe's papers have been on your desk a thousand days and more
Why must US Justice be subsumed by Thatcher's plan
To extradite and persecute another Irishman

Six times faced extradition, six times Joe has won
Judge Sprizzo ruled in '84 leave this man alone
Between Washington and London the game of chess goes on
Bishops, castles, kings and queens and Joe Doherty is the pawn

I stand here in the shadow of the Statue of Liberty
I thank you for listening to my songs and the welcome you gave me
As I leave the shores of America may I suggest to you
Joe Doherty has done nothing that George Washington did not do

Joe Doherty is an Irish Republican who was arrested in America and held
for ten years while Britain sought to extradite him back to stand before a
Diplock court. Eventually he was extradited back to Long Kesh in 1993, and
subsequently released in 1997. He now works with a Republican ex-prisoners'
group in the New Barnsley area of Belfast.

I wrote and performed this song while in the United States. OK, so I took
some liberties, but I was in America, it's a big place, I only had two weeks,
Joe was down for years on end – I needed to cut myself some slack, get the
song finished in time for the show.

Moorefield
by C. Moore

Come all you loyal Moorefield fans who've suffered down the years
Put down your pints hang up your boots and dry up all your tears
Here's an auld come-all-ye written specially for you
Of how we won the championship of 1962

'Twas a damp and dirty Sunday but in history it's gone down
John Joe Murray stood at the Pinkeen Bridge as the Rags rode into town
Famous for their fighting men and for Dan Donolly's arm
Moorefield women prayed their husbands wouldn't come to harm

For saving goals or gripping pints you need a steady hand
Our keeper Dinny Craddock had the finest in the land
In front of him at fullback was his cousin Skinner Behan
Whose family played for Moorefield long before the Sarsfields came

The corner backs they used to train in Neeson's every night
Jim McDermot on the left and Fido on the right
Joe Moran in the middle and Dave Stapleton half back
Jimmy Cummins on the other flank resisting each attack

God rest you smiling Paddy Moore gone back to West Kildare
From Carbury to Croke Park you plucked balls from the air
With faithful Doggy Anderson forever by your side
These two marauding Moorefield men struck terror far and wide

Now I'll recall the forward line Ray Clinton from Mayo
Our Captain Toss McCarthy who left Suncroft years ago
And Jimmy Dowlin or the Ba, pure Moorefield to the core
He treated backs like Tintawn as he nailed 'em to the floor

Top o' the right was Johnny Gibson the quiet fisherman
On the left was Narky Farrell of the famous Reddy Clan
A special place lies in my heart for the hero of the day
He knew the good times and the bad, our hero Harry Fay

This song was written rapidly before a concert in the Moorefield Gaelic Athletic Association Club in 1989. I've never touched it since but, despite all its flaws, it marks a specific and important time in my life.

To the south side of Newbridge lies my homeland of Moorefield. It originally took its name from Moore the Landlord (no relation). The Moorefield GAA Club was part of my birthright; my father played for and was deeply involved in the club. For those who've not experienced it, it is difficult to understand the depth of emotion that can result from such involvement. It is not like rugby or golf or snooker or cricket or soccer. In my experience it runs deeper; it is tribal. At the other end of the town lies the Sarsfield GAA Club, and there has been bitter rivalry between the tribes for over a hundred years now. I've heard and seen this rivalry erupt a thousand times in my lifetime, once as far away as New South Wales at a concert in the Sydney State Theatre where Moorefield and Sarsfield expatriates engaged in verbal banter at my concert. I've heard it in San Francisco and London and I've seen it erupt violently from time to time in dancehalls and down drunken lanes in the early hours.

The last 30 years has seen a softening in most quarters. Newbridge people are more transient now. People have intermarried and moved up and down the town. My own sister Terry now lives in the heart of Sarsfield and could not have better neighbours, but the rattle of sabres is never too far away. Sarsfield's has been the more successful club by far, at senior level, whilst Moorefield has been the better club in the younger divisions. With some, on both sides, the bitterness remains deep and vicious. I know men who detest me deeply for one reason only: 'He is a Moorefield man.'

I played at Juvenile, Minor, Junior and, on a few occasions, Senior level for the club. One of my proudest moments was scoring a goal for the Seniors versus Round Towers, but I was still taken off at half-time when Toss McCarthy arrived late from work.

When my father died in 1956, my mother always maintained the strong link and presented the club with 'The Andy Moore Perpetual Trophy' which is still played for every year.

Galway to Graceland
R. Thompson

She dressed in the dark and she whispered amen
She was pretty in pink like a young girl again
Twenty years married and she never thought twice
She sneaked out the door and crept into the night
And silver wings carried her over the sea
From the west coast of Ireland to West Tennessee
To be with her sweetheart she left everything
From Galway to Graceland to be with the king

She was humming Suspicion it was the song she loved best
She had Elvis I love you tattooed on her breast
When she landed in Memphis her heart beat so fast
She dreamed for so long now she'd see him at last
She was down by his graveside day after day
Come closing time they would pull her away
To be with her sweetheart she left everything
From Galway to Graceland to be with the king

They came in their thousands from the whole human race
To pay their respects at his last resting place
But blindly she knelt there and told him her dream
And she thought that he answered for that's how it seemed
They they dragged her away it was handcuffs this time
She said my God man are you out of your mind
Don't you know that we're married see I'm wearing his ring
I came from Galway to Graceland to be with the king
I came from Galway to Graceland to be with the king

I remember going to see Richard Thompson play with Fairport Convention in the Free Trade Hall in Manchester in 1968. It was an eye-opener for me and the band sowed a seed that sprouted years later in both the Christy Moore Band (1975) and Moving Hearts (1981). He is one of the sublime musicians. I loved his electric playing and subsequently his writing, acoustic playing, singing and stage persona. Along with Martin Carthy, Nick Jones, to name but two, he is an influence on many and a great artist.

I know the woman in this song. I've met her in many guises. It could be a simple or even an obsessional devotion to some icon that brings on the singular purpose that can dominate a life. Some artistes experience disturbing devotion from hordes. Personally, I've encountered a small number of people whose interest in my work went beyond the norm. That said, I realise that my own interest in the work surely has been obsessional betimes, so why should I find it strange in others? Nevertheless I have been disturbed on occasion when I've encountered troubled people who have attached excessive importance to the work. I've been accused of being a 'saviour' and 'one who understands' and 'I've lived for your work', and I usually run and hide. A woman in New York told me, 'When I hear you sing it's like a shot of political heroin.' It was backstage at the Brooklyn Academy of Music and I recall feeling ill afterwards.

This opens up the question again of the validity or importance of the work. This song is important in that it addresses the peculiar phenomenon of a particular obsession. Selfishly, my own work is validated by its importance to me, but on a broader scale it has acted as a useful focus for many people. The work has upset many people who have been unsettled by the content, it has made people laugh heartily at recognising obvious situations, and I've felt deep emotion sweep across manys the room. While many critics round the world have lauded the work, some closer to home have an almost hateful aversion to it and I think I understand where it comes from.

I am of the Bog and of the town and of the city and of the Catholic Church and of the GAA and of the Rugby club and of the Traveller and of the Protestant and of the Branchman and of the bank robber and of the Provo and of the Free State Army man and of the child in Granard and of the priest and of the pastor and of the holy nun and of the Buddhist monk.

I know a little bit about many things and I know very little about most things; I've lost my veneer of self-importance, or at least I am working on it.

So if you hate my work, don't worry about it – there's plenty of alternatives around for you to enjoy.

St Patrick's Dance in San Fernando
by Colm Gallagher

I'm so happy now St Patrick's Day is over
And all the paper hats are thrown away
And all the plastic paddies have gone back into clover
But I know that they'll return another day

I bought a ticket to a dance in San Fernando
I watched the happy faces turning grey
Growing weary of the folklore beards and banjos
Too proud to please the people when they play

Long ago at a fleadh in Ireland
I saw a man sit awkwardly and shy
Afraid to even loosen up his collar
As his voice soared like a swallow through the sky

At the grand St Patrick's dance in San Fernando
There were dignitaries there of every kind
I heard that the proceeds went for ammo
So I got drunk and had a right good time

I haven't yet decided who I'll marry
Or if anyone would marry me at all
But if I do I'll go to San Fernando
Me and my wife we'll have ourselves a ball

Here's another song from Colm Gallagher who gave me 'The Reel in the Flickering Light' and has written a fine body of unique songs. I've not yet managed to record or perform this song, but I want to include it because of the many things it describes and the diversity of its verses, and yet they hang together.

The first verse could be anywhere at any time. St Patrick's Day 1959 in Co. Kildare, or Paddy's Day 1993 in California. We now have St Patrick's Week in Dublin, where American Paddywhackery has been re-imported to the power of ten and Temple Bar is covered in a lava-like crust of vomit.

The dance in San Fernando starts off well enough but soon the beer begins to flatten and the whiskey goes sour in the belly or mad in the head. The banjo reverberates painfully at midnight.

I think back to years ago and that man singing 'Graceful Swallow'; he was truly a quiet and conservative man, but when he closed his eyes and sang his heart out he carried us all across the heavens, if only for a fleeting glance. . .

They were all there early on: Congressmen pressing the flesh and Lord Mayors nodding and winking, and then the hat went round and it was full of big notes and nobody said a word, everybody knew but nobody said.

So I just said nothing, I got drunk and with a top-shelf stagger I made my way home and if I don't crack me nut off someone's gable I'll be back again next year – older, more cynical and ready for more punishment.

Stall the Digger Sham
by C. Moore

As the moon shone down along the old Rhine valley
Two sham chuckies from the Falls were on the gin
In de authentic Irish pub down Gooter Strasse
They fought about whose turn it was to get them in
Bridie from the Bogside got abusive
As her dander with the Schnapps began to rise
She tore into two Free Staters out from Galway
Where were you on Bloody Sunday Bridie cried

So stall the digger sham, tell Einstein to go easy on the water
I'm outa here as soon as I can raise the fare
Trying to keep the best side out on German porter
Waiting for the dust to settle over there

In Ludwigsberg Dieter flipped out on the cocaine
As Gráinne gave him hardstick down the hall
She battered his machismo something brutal
Till Dieter roared in German Fuck yiz all
Pascal from Ardoyne was fantasising
And humming Irish ways and Irish Laws
Until Dieter struck the nut on Pascal's dentures
Another poor auld martyr for the cause

The Dubliners were playing in The Stadthalle
One cold November night in East Berlin
When Roisín was introduced to Wolfgang
Straightaway she took an awful shine to him
She got romantic when John Sheehan played the Coolin
She got frisky when Ronnie went to sing
But when Barney struck up the mason apron
Roisín knew she would commit a mortal sin

I wrote this song during my last German tour in 1996. The tour itself was a
great success and all the gigs were full except for Mannheim and Köln

which were near enough to being sold out. I was travelling with my tour manager Jim Donohoe and the promoter's rep, who also drove, was Martino Glandsmann. The only difficulty with the tour was the sequence of cities, for we were constantly on the autobahns criss-crossing Germany and retracing the same routes time and again. I've always suspected that promoters take some secret delight in breaking the bollix of unfortunate touring acts. I have a vision of Karsten Jahnke throwing darts at the German map to plan tours. In Australia it gets worse. On more than one occasion I've done Sydney–Perth–Sydney, a round trip of 6,000 miles and been expected to do a show each night. I recall a Planxty sequence that read London–Edinburgh–Brighton–Sheffield, this at a time when we were travelling through the nights in a Ford Transit.

All the stuff in this song happened over a few nights of that German tour, with some embellishment in the last verse. There is nowhere in the world quite like Germany to tour, and it is with deep sadness that I realise once again that I'll probably not play another gig there.

Goodnight Dieter, Heinz, Klaus, Antonio, Karsten, Martino, Girly, Barbra, Gudrun, Martha, and most of all to Abi Wallenstein. (If you happen to hear Abi busking in Hamburg, do give him my love. He is a Palestinian Jew who sings the blues. He is a main man.)

Panhandlers of Ireland
Author unknown

It was in a pub down in Galway
Outside there was sleet and hail
I was sitting well in by the fireside
Drinking a grand pint of ale
When in through the doorway there stumbled
A travelling crony of mine
I stepped up to the counter
And ordered two glasses of wine

He said he was tramping since daybreak
Through the wind and the storm
He chanced to step into this alehouse
Hoping the auld kip might be warm
Many miles we had travelled together
And journeyed in search of the jar
We had many happy reflections
And the two of us perched at the bar

We talked all about Connemara
Reminisced about old Donegal
Of the times we had plenty of money
And the times that we had none at all
How we ran away from Tramore Races
Hiked to the fair of Ballinasloe
How once we drank too much poitín
Above in the county Mayo

We went over the haybarns and skippers
The dosshouses the simons and spikes
And once when we cycled round Kerry
On a pair of brand-new stolen bikes
We spoke of the hobos and beggars
The knackers and cuckoo tramps
And the time that we ate the raw turnips
And ended up with stomach cramps

We drank a health to the Garda Siochána
Above in the sweet town of Kells

When we stole the barrel of porter
And they locked us up in the cells
From Dublin to Waterford City
Not to mention the town of Loughrea
Or the time that we got Sullivan drunk
And the damage he did the next day

We talked about so many places
Too many to put down in print
And before the day it was over
The pair of us were truly skint
It was in that pub down in Galway
The pair of us stood up to go
To panhandle the towns around Ireland
Evermore travelling on to and fro

Our son Andy was but an infant. Val and I were on the road in search of sport. We drifted down to West Clare, the year was 1976 and we called in to McGanns of Doolin. Tommy and Tony were both at the helm and without so much as a blink Tommy invited the three of us to stay as long as we liked. A wild-looking man came into the bar and him and I struck up well. He was a fair man to shift it, but his health was waning and he carried a bottle of some stomach emulsion which we quaffed frequently to keep the acids at bay. I never got to know his name, but that night he was called 'The Hacksaw'. He gave out this recitation and sent it to me later. I never saw him again after.

We pulled out of Doolin two days later. Many moons passed and I received a note from The Hacksaw which contained this fine version of 'McAlpine's Fusiliers':

Did your mother come from Kerry or sweet old Kiltimagh
There's plenty of eggs and bacon in the kip below the town
For timbering and shuttering we'll give three ringing cheers
For Dan McCann is the handyman in McAlpine's Fusiliers

Have you heard about our regiment who came from Inis Fáil
How we drove the Mersey Tunnel and the banks round Ebbw Vale
For the heavy shillings we had plenty of volunteers
Sure we picked the best and sacked the rest in McAlpine's Fusiliers

You may walk along the banks where you will plainly see
In our moleskins and our navvy boots our uniformity
The graft is tough and we're all dog rough we have no dreads or fears
'Tis for the pub we'll get the sub in McAlpine's Fusiliers

Have you heard the stories of our famous ganger men
The bull-nosed Tacker Reddy, the ferocious Darkie Finn
But for one Joe McGeever give three hearty cheers
He's the foremost sergeant major in McAlpine's Fusiliers

Here comes all the hayboys with their fancy shirts and suits
They're ashamed to don the moleskins, the Yorks or navvy boots
We'll make sure they go the distance like we have done for years
If they can dig it out they'll get the shout with McAlpine's Fusiliers

Now it's 23 years later and The Hacksaw is still on the move and to the good. Tommy McGann went on to do great things in Boston but died tragically while at home in Clare last year. He was honoured posthumously in the Boston Paddy's Day parade and the city has named a square after him. He was forever helping newly arrived immigrants to find work and accommodation and was a great source of employment to hundreds of Irish musicians, this one included. To top it off, he was a lovely man and I'll not forget him.

My building site career was not extensive but left a mark upon me. This song touches a heartstring, it romanticises a hard and dangerous industry where only the strongest and hardiest could survive. Many's the life was ruined in this industry, yet there is something almost romantic in these songs.

I suppose it was such an awful life that, fuelled by the comforting drink, we had to make light of it.

First Hunger Strike Song
by C. Moore

What put the blood on your hands iron lady
What put the blood on your hands
Is that the blood of a hawk or a dove
No that's the blood of a man

Is that the blood of Tom McKearney
From the town of Moy
His family murdered, lifted, beaten
Are you going to let him die

Please give me news of Brendan Hughes
Who hails from the Falls
Like his brother Joe, like his brother Tony
Are you going to let him die

What are you doing to Tom McFeely
His wife and family in Co. Down
His father died from your torture and beatings
Are you going to put him down

Is that the blood of young John Nixon
From the county of Armagh
For eight years now you've harrassed him
Will you let him waste away

On Bloody Sunday Ray McCartney
Watched the paras come to town
Saw them slay Jim Wray his cousin
Will you let him too go down

This song was performed once outside the General Post Office in Dublin in October 1980. A great crowd had gathered to support the men who had commenced a hunger strike in Long Kesh prison. They were demanding political status.

I recall the occasion clearly. I was very nervous for although I'd sung out-side the GPO before, this was a dangerous time. Men were on hunger strike and people's lives were at stake. The level of police harassment was impossi-ble to understand; they seemed to target the defenceless. I felt that the behav-iour of sectors of the police force at the time of the Eighties' Hunger Strike was reprehensible and, twenty years on, many citizens have still not forgot-ten.

The behaviour of ministers was even worse. It appeared to me that the families of the second batch of hunger strikers were treated with cynical dis-dain by the Irish Government.

Thatcher had Fianna Fáil in her arse pocket.

Margaret Thatcher
by C. Moore

She placed her hand upon the lieutenant's shoulder
Honoured him for his attack upon Goose Green
Whispered in the ear of the ship's captain
Who scuppered the Belgrano and one thousand men from Argentine
The beast that she let loose upon the Falklands
Stalks from Stamford Bridge to bark around Brick Lane
Sink the Argies was the war cry in the Eighties
It will come back to haunt us all again

Her hand held the key that locked the prison
Where Carol Richardson lay innocent of crime
Teenage woman fitted up and pronounced guilty
Lady Thatcher simply let her do her time
Loved, revered and toasted by her cronies
As they smiled upon the spoils of her regime
Suave sophisticated guiltless criminals
At her beck and call time and again

Her handiwork wreaked havoc on the Mersey
Brought hunger on to Teeside and the Tyne
There was ten per cent employment in the Bogside
Five per cent in Ballymurphy and Ardoyne
From these wastelands she created
Young men coaxed into regiments to train
To maim, to kill, live out her murderous fantasies
And carry out her orders on Goose Green

Thatcher's work is still clear to be seen on both sides of the Irish Sea. The greed and avarice that prevailed in the British economy during her reign is still at large as the monstrous Celtic Tiger runs riot around this island. The cities are marked by a sky lined with cranes, while out in rural parts many are demented by the grant culture. It's as if the illness that was rampant in the City of London has travelled like rabies in all directions – more, more, more for me and fuck the sick and needy.

When I saw her recently take tea with Pinochet and laud him for his support during the Falklands War, I thought that perhaps the poor lady might be totally mad. But that would be to trivialise her absolute danger to us all.

I sense her spirit in Garvaghy Road, Brick Lane, Soho, Hungerford, Harrods, and anywhere where greed is seen to be good or violence the answer.

Ballindine Eviction
by C. Moore

As I rambled abroad by Kilsheelan
The river meandered on down
To my right lay the Comeragh mountains
To the left of me sweet Slievenamon
Where the fishermen cast on the waters
And the apples are pressed into wine
Where the cows return slowly to pasture
Through the fields that surround Ballindine

I marvelled at nature's abundance
In Tipperary so rich and so rare
I drunk deep from the well of springwater
And filled my lungs with fresh air
When I came to John Hanrahan's homestead
On the land around Ballycurkeen
I lay down in the wildflower meadow
And dreamt a mysterious dream

I dreamt of a curious eviction
Unlike the evictions of old
No sign of a redcoat or bailiff
'Twas much more pernicious and cold
On the air came a colourless vapour
And the fields fell silent and still
As I lay in that wildflower meadow
Dreaming on Hanrahan's Hill

When I awoke I was frightened
It was time for me to go home
As I made my way towards Cluan Meala
I came upon Merck, Sharpe and Dohme

I n 1963, during my first National Bank posting to Cluan Meala or the Vale
of Honey (which the English translated into Clonmel – a word that means

absolutely nothing), I got to know the land round Kilsheelan. The smell of apple cider was often in the air where between Slievenamon and Castle de la Paor, I spent manys the happy hour.

Twenty-five years later I eavesdropped upon two scientists talking about their good day's work. They had flown into Ireland from far-flung laboratories, and were giving testimony in a court case involving a chemical giant and a local farmer whose herd was mysteriously dying.

I performed this song once.

The Phone Tap Squad
by C. Moore

Fragment

Be careful when you're talking on the phone
Don't assume that you're together all alone
Wires get crossed and rights get lost along the line
The phone tap squad they can be listening all the time

Should they get wind that you have ceased to go to Mass
Or if you are anti-coursing pro-divorce
If you say you'll meet your date at the GPO
The phone tap squad will mark it down and away you'll go

Should you mention you have voted for Sinn Féin
They'll mark you down for holidays on the Curragh Plain
If they should hear that you're opposed to nuclear war
The phone tap squad will mark your chart in Templemore

I was recording a show for television at the National Stadium and I stuck in these few lines for sport. I was paranoid in those days. I imagined that my phone was tapped, that our house was watched, that my movements were logged. Once or twice I even fantasised that detectives were following me. Silly me.

A fool told me about a file on me and another fool told me I was on a police list in Templemore.

This song was never transmitted, but years later I was approached by a secret policeman enquiring whether I had ever recorded the song about 'The Phone Tap Squad'. He had been on the squad and had heard about the song and would love to hear it.

So, here you are, Officer.

Veronica
by C. Moore

In the broad daylight of a summer's day
On the Cork to Dublin motorway
Suddenly the singing birds
Were startled in their song
In the quiet of that moment
Our world went out of kilter
In that split second
Veronica was gone

But you will never silence her
Your story will be written
Her spirit won't rest easy
Until the job is done
With boots and fists you broke her bones
When you gunned her down at home
As soon as she was able
She faced you up again

You who made the phone call
You who took the message down
You who hired the hitman
You who hatched the plan
You who drew the money down
You who paid it over
You who remains silent
You are guilty everyone

As you lurk around your fortress in secrecy and furtiveness
You'll always be reminded of her smiling face
As you crawl around the darkness of your criminal insanity
Forever on the lookout for another hiding place
You try to count your friends you ponder on your enemies
Recalling the whereabouts of your treasure trove
But when it's time to write your final will and testament
You'll understand what goes to make a legacy of love

Veronica Veronica Veronica, warrior woman
Veronica Veronica Veronica, I offer you this song

We were out on Cape Clear Island. Val had gone to the Co-op, the children were scattered around. I was working on this book and in the background I had Radio na Gaeltachta playing quietly. There was a news flash. In the distance I only recognised two words – Veronica Guerin. I knew straight away that there could only be one reason for this woman to make a news-flash item. I switched over to the national radio station and my fears were confirmed. Veronica had been murdered. I wrote the first two verses that same afternoon, and the third verse some weeks later. I am trying to record it.

One Hundred Miles from Home
by Johnny Duhan

One hundred miles from his home
Through the lonely city he does roam
Looking for a place to lie down
Somewhere he can call his own

Where he can lay his head down
Where he can relax his wrinkled brow
Where he can dream of his home town
Where he can feel his troubles drown

But when he wakes up
And takes his first look
At his tattered surrounding
When he awakes
As his dream breaks
He asks himself how can I survive
Another day of being alive
'Til the evening comes

One hundred miles from his home
He has got nothing of his own
His clothes are torn and he's forlorn
He's got no friends he's all alone

When he gets out of bed
Each morning that's his greatest dread
A grey fog is filling up his head
Sometimes he wishes he was dead

I've been visiting this song for fifteen years now but we've never quite settled together. I performed it for a brief spell when touring with Donal
Lunny in 1988. I have a rough recording of our performance in the Cork
Opera House, but despite the quality it is a good version of the song. Watch
out for the boxed set.

It is a song that does not look well on paper – it needs the music to bring it to life. Johnny Duhan's recording was featured on a limited edition 'Big Issues' tape which I produced in 1994 when I was patron of the *Big Issue* journal in Ireland.

Boys of Mullaghbawn
Author unknown

On a Monday morning early as my wandering steps they did take me
Down by a farmer's station his meadow and green lawn
I heard great lamentation that the wee birds they were making
Saying we'll have no more engagements with the boys of Mullaghbawn

I beg your pardon ladies, I'll ask you this one favour
I hope it is no treason on you I now must call
I'm condoling late and early my heart is nigh on breaking
All for a noble lady that lives near Mullaghbawn

Squire Jackson is unequalled in honour or in favour
He never turned a traitor nor betrayed the rights of man
But now we are in danger from a vile deceiving stranger
Who has ordered transportation for the boys of Mullaghbawn

As those heroes crossed the ocean, I'm told the ship in motion
Stood up in wild commotion as though the seas ran dry
The trout and salmon gaping as the Cuckoo left her station
Saying fare thee well old Erin and the Hills of Mullaghbawn

To end this lamentation we are all in consternation
None cares for recreation until the days do dawn
For without hesitation we are charged with combination
And sent for transportation from the Hills of Mullaghbawn

It is almost impossible to comprehend anymore – the importance that songs had in earlier times. Today I am bombarded by so much information every waking hour but, in living memory, people gathered around the light and heat of an open-hearth fire and drank in the story and music of a new song. The longer the better for it broke the night, lit up the evening and the singer was always a welcome visitor.

In my own lifetime I sat at such a fire with my Granny Moore, Grand-Auntie Annie and Grand-Uncle Frank. The lamp would be trimmed low to save paraffin and the wireless only switched on for the Angelus and news.

Those large, heavy glass batteries had to be carried to town for a recharge so there was a value put on the power contained and it would not be wasted on banalities. They would sit around the burning turf and talk about the condition of the hens, pigs, calves, cows, bullocks, horses; the progress in the garden of the spuds, carrots, turnips, onions, mangels; the depth of the water in the well, the clamp of turf; when to kill the pig, shoe the horses, bull the cow, trim the hedgerows, go to the bog, mow the meadow; talk about the wild white cats and the robins, corncrakes, cuckoo; plan a fresh thatch, whitewash the house, give a day here, get a day there.

I cannot recall where I learned this song, nor can I visualise any other singer's rendition. I began to sing it in the mid-Sixties and I've always been moved by its deep emotion and vivid landscape.

It is a good day for me when I'm able to sing a song and I don't forget the days when I was unable. Mr Michael Bowen Sr of Rathoora, West Cork, told me, 'There is no such thing as a bad day until you can't get out of bed.'

Croppy Boy
Author unknown

'Twas early early all in the spring
The pretty small birds began to sing
They sang so sweet and so tunefully
And the song they sang was sweet liberty

'Twas early early last Thursday night
The yeoman cavalry gave me a fright
The fright they gave me was my downfall
I was prisoner taken by Lord Cornwall

'Twas in his grand house that I was held
And in his parlour that I was tried
My sentence passed and my courage low
When to New Geneva I was forced to go

As they led me through Wexford Street
My own first cousin I chanced to meet
My own first cousin did me deny
And the name he gave me was the Croppy Boy

As I was walking up Wexford Hill
With grief and sorrow I cried me fill
I looked behind and I looked before
And my poor mother her hair she tore

Farewell Father and Mother too
My sister Mary farewell to you
If ever I chance to return home
I'll sink my pike in some yeoman's bones

At this very moment, one thousand years ago, this millennium started and now, as I sit here in this new aluminium, I pray that the slaughter will end.

This morning I hear President Clinton asking Hollywood to curb its violent output. Last night his planes dropped bombs on Kosovan civilians. Irish

Gypsies are in the midst of a bloody feud between two families, they are murdering each other in the graveyard and in the caravan. Our brave heroes up north are burning children to death or putting bombs in English shopping centres to take their war to Warrington – Irish soldiers blowing up English shoppers, just like Kosovo, a war where only innocent civilians become victims. The soldiers are either at 30,000 feet or on their way back to Ireland.

It is my simplistic and uneducated opinion that there is an inevitable conclusion to the journey our race is taking. As we, collectively, become less spiritual and more removed from that which sustains us, unseen and distant forces gain more and more control over every aspect of our environment. In my lifetime we have come a long way. Fifty years ago, all the food produced was for local consumption. Fifty years on *all* food is produced solely for profit. Our world is falling into the hands of the producers of armaments, oil, food, cars, aeroplanes, tobacco, drugs, communication and other powerful lobbies. These new emperors also control the media, who lie in any way necessary to hold their position, and to tell the truth is more than their jobs are worth.

God only knows what this has to do with the Croppy Boy. 'It was early early all in the spring.'

Ford's Siamsa Cois Lee
by C. Moore

Welcome good people to Ford's siamsa cois lee
To Leo Sayer, Don McLean, The Wolf Tones and me
And one whom I must mention and praise before the Lord
Three cheers for our sponsor, hurrah for Henry Ford

Eighteen forty-seven was the year it all began
John Ford left Ballinascarthy his fortune for to win
He set sail for America like many round that time
As the anchor was hauled up the Shandon bells did chime

John Ford's grandson Henry Ford came back across the sea
Starting building cars and tractors on the banks of the Lee
With a leg up from George Crosby Henry got on well
He churned out his motor cars to the sound of the Shandon bell

Dollars flowed in millions for over sixty years
In '81 a thousand men built 30,000 cars
Henry started thinking it is time to go
For labour was much cheaper in the Gulf of Mexico

Ignoring this loyal workforce their families and fears
Henry Ford turned Judas after sixty-seven years
On a Friday in July of nineteen eighty-four
As the Shandon bells did gently chime Henry slammed the door

Henry sold his workers out for the sake of a few bob more
Now he thinks this sponsorship will even up the score
Cork people love their music, of that there is no doubt
Fords can sponsor all they like but they locked the workers out

There's many a Leeside family who would be here today
If they had not lost the right to work and earn their pay
As we enjoy our siamsa let us strike this final chord
We'll crawl from Cork to Donegal
Before we'll drive a Ford

I wrote this with a view to performing it at Ford's Siamsa Cois Lee in 1985. This was an annual, one-day event which drew huge crowds to a football stadium in Cork every summer. It was known as Siamsa Cois Lee until Ford shut its Cork Motor Plant and sacked its workforce, whereupon it became Ford's Siamsa Cois Lee.

Word got out that I'd written this song – I'd performed it on the Friday night at the Wexford Inn in Dublin – and there was opposition to it and I was lobbied not to sing it. I decided I would go ahead.

I walked out on the stage and I was confronted by total mayhem. There were 50,000 people there and I was totally thrown, for this was not the sort of festival crowd I'd previously encountered. It was like a field of madness. To try and perform a new ditty would have been absolutely futile, so I pulled out my bag of hits and with head down and knobs to the right, I went for it.

Henry Ford was off my tiny hook!

Ford is still at it. This year I went to an arts awards evening sponsored by Ford and the *Independent* newspaper. The stage was dominated by a Ford motor car which the firm's mouthpiece described as 'a work of art'.

The Two Devines and Breslin *Charlie Breslin, David and Micheal Devine*
by Donal O'Kelly

Shoot out the streetlights
Shoot out the streetlights
And soldier D obliged
Two five-round bursts of tracer bullets
Flashed across the night

Five o'clock in the morning
On a hill outside Strabane
One hundred and seventeen rounds were fired
And not one shot returned
The two Devines and Breslin
Were riddled full of lead
Twenty each to the body
Then one to the head

The two Devines and Breslin
To the final court were led
Twenty each to the body
Then one to the head
Soldier D stood confident
Unnamed with covered face
Gibson led him gently on
And declared there is no case

Shoot out the streetlights
Shoot out the streetlights
Soldier D obliged
Two five-round bursts of tracer bullets
Flashed across the night

I did not know these men nor their families nor friends. I accept that they
were IRA volunteers and that whatever took them across the fields in the
dark hours was IRA business. These men were described in Dublin, London
and parts of Belfast as terrorists. The forces mounted against them were

awesome. Two powerful governments and all their PR machinery, one of the mightiest armies in the world backed up by a highly sophisticated, armed and partisan police force. Yet this mighty 'law and order' collective could not arrest (I would say capture) these three volunteers. It was quicker and 'cleaner' to execute them on the hillside than to bring them for trial.

These words were written by Donal O'Kelly and I came across them in Spanish Point, County Clare. In the hardback edition of this book I inadvertently assumed authorship until my mistake was pointed out to me. I wish to thank the author for his generosity of spirit and his understanding of my error.

7 May 1998

Birthdays. Fifty-three of them. This one's all the better for being at home. Amongst the family instead of amongst the world of strangers, many of them unmet friends. But it's lovely to lie in one's own bed on this day.

It was a revelation once I got over the taste of it. Around 1960 I managed to keep a few bottles down and the buzz began. Shyness began to recede and elation and madness to take its place. A year later I tasted Jamaica rum and blackcurrant, which would do the job rapid. Bang in a few of them before closing time and the world was there for the taking. A fellow could go to Dreamland and listen to Brendan Bowyer, or Lawlor's Ballroom and dance to the Paragon Seven. I could drink with men who knew my father and marvel at their memory of him.

She became my friend early on. I could meet her anywhere, anytime and she was always happy to comfort me – if she put her arms around me I'd fill up with warm woozie feelings which wiped away all fear and hurt and shyness. I even forgot that I was terrified of physical violence and went so far as to fight myself on a few occasions.

Wrestling in the dirt in Prosperous over a woman. Beaten at Esher in Surrey over another man's wife. Hammered in Wales for a rebel song. Smashed up in Rochdale by John Haig. But next morning I'd always go back to my friend and she would soothe my aches and pains.

Today, at 53, I've lived without her for nine years. Without her fog enveloping me I've come to feel reality. The reality of love and goodness. The reality of fear and responsibility.

Kilkenny Doll
by C. Moore

I did not write this story did not make up this song
I put a tune to a news report to sing it won't take long
It happened in Kilkenny as Christmas time did fall
A policeman claimed a Tinker woman stole a baby doll

The doll was valued fifty pence a gift for Santa Claus
The woman swore the bill was paid that she never broke the law
They dragged her to the wagon laden down with hefty men
Charged her at Christmas time with stealing fifty pence

The judge came to the session in his fine big motor car
Renowned for his no-nonsense ways regarded at the bar
He heard the evidence of the guard and the Tinker woman too
He even heard her small son swear that Mammy paid for the doll

When the judge had heard enough he soon made up his mind
My job is to protect good folk from people of your kind
He handed down the sentence he upheld his law
He gave her Christmas in Mountjoy for a ten-bob baby doll

Such a savage sentence for such a trivial crime
Did he have to lock her up and it being Christmas time
Most people have forgotten Kilkenny Court that day
That Tinker woman, that baby doll, and that Judge —

When we lived in Kilkenny in the mid-Seventies, our attention was often drawn to local newspaper reports of the courtroom antics of Judge —. Renowned for his pronouncements on the local circuit, he provided much fodder for both local and national journalists. One moment he could elicit guffaws of laughter from his audience, the next he could reduce the less fortunate to tears. He was known to tear strips off young Gardái who might not be presenting their evidence properly, and he was capable of humiliating counsel for prosecution and defence alike. But, most of all, he was renowned for his barbarity (my word) when dealing with sectors of society that did not meet with his approval.

I once stood before him while offering bail for a man in Waterford Court. This particular man would have appeared before the Judge regularly, but he was nevertheless entitled to bail. The judge turned on me. He was disparaging about my clothes, my hair and beard, my demeanour, and expressed incredulity that one such as I could be a musician. 'What nature of musician could you possibly be, Mr Moore?' he taunted me, before answering his own question. 'Some pub musician no doubt.' I must admit that he scared me that day and I was not even on a charge.

I performed this song once. It was on the fringe of the Kilkenny Arts Festival in 1978 and yes, it was in a pub.

God's Truth
by C. Moore

Way back in 1974 I was twenty-eight years old
I met a woman, fell in love and we got engaged and married
Way back in 1974 Billy Power went to prison

In 1976 our first child was born, I was
Present at the birth, a joyous experience
To see a beautiful and healthy baby boy
Come into the world
In 1976 Hugh Callaghan began his third year in prison

In 1978 we had our loving daughter
We called her Juno after the Goddess of Love
Each time I see her I'm filled with love
In 1978, Dick McIlkenny, the father of loving daughters
Began his sixth year in prison

In 1983 we had our second son and lost
our second daughter
We had each other to comfort and love and hold
We shed tears together
In 1983 Paddy Hill was alone, in solitude
Beginning his ninth year in prison

In 1986 we bought our house, our family home
My wife, me, our three children, my wife's father
Our dog, his cat all together under one roof
In 1986 Gerry Hunter began his twelfth year in prison

In 1989 my loving mother reached her seventieth year
All our family came together and it was a day of love and happiness
In 1989 Johnny Walker spent his fifteenth year in prison

Sixteen years down our different roads
And for my six fellow countrymen – nothing has changed
A change of category may rest guilty consciences
But for the innocents nothing has changed

Even their gaolers know that they're innocent

Even prison governers know that they're innocent

Even bishops and cardinals know that they're innocent

Even thieves and whores know that they're innocent

Even the IRA know that they're innocent

Even the British Army know that they're innocent

Even the RUC know that they're innocent

Even the West Midlands Police Force know that they're innocent

Even we all know that they're innocent

God's Truth

What Price Justice
by Dick McIlkenny 18 November 1989

What price justice for the innocent locked up in prison cells

What price respect and peace of mind for those who know and will not tell

What price the horror of the beating the torture and the cries

Of honest men who in terror signed perverted statements filled with lies

What price hunger and deprivations threats with guns and growling dogs

Of minds now blank and wandering as if lost within a fog

What price the cries of wives and children of families torn apart

Whose moans and wails of anguish come from deeply wounded hearts

What price the long lost years filled with loneliness and pain

And the longing to be held in loving arms again

What price the loss of love and joy of children all now full grown

And left without a father now with children of their own

What price for honesty and truth for dignity restored

For the innocent to be set free, exonerated, recompensed, back in society once more

What price what price

On 18 November 1989 I performed a concert at the Wembley Conference Centre in support of The Birmingham Six Campaign. In 35 years of gigging I was never so ill before a show. I had a temperature, an inflamed throat and a croaky, husky voicebox. Yet once I hit the stage and saw 2,000 people gathered to demand the release of six innocent men, their energy lifted me out of my sickness and the adrenaline took over. Dick McIlkenny sent 'What Price Justice' out and asked me to read it to the gathered friends.

The second piece, 'God's Truth', I prepared on the journey across to London.

Weela Weela Waile
Author unknown

There was an auld woman who lived in the wood
Weela weela waile
There was an auld woman who lived in the wood
Down by the river Saile

She had a baby three months old
She had a penknife long and deep
She stuck the penknife in the baby's heart
There were three hard knocks came a knocking at her door
There were two policemen and a man

Are you the woman that killed the child
I am the woman that killed the child
They took her away and put her in the Curragh (second time in jail)
They put the rope around her neck
They hung the woman 'til she was dead
The moral of the story is
Never stick a penknife in the baby's heart

I heard it on the radio recently that a Dublin man got four years for torturing two babies in his home – one his own child and one his stepchild. There is a world of bad news on the airwaves, but this particular item caused me distress and anger.

When I was a young singer this was regarded as a fun song – why, I will never know. Ronnie Drew sang it, but as I recall he did not sing it with humour. It became popular nationwide and I've heard it at manys the session. It is a macabre and disturbing song – I cannot find its origin or history, but I still sing it occasionally and there is a young audience today who hear it differently. They've been exposed to a lot of dark music and view it with interest rather than the hilarity with which it was viewed in my day.

In 1999 we acknowledge most of the sickness in our midst while in the Sixties the Thought Police were brushing many of our sins and sicknesses underneath the carpet. 'What happens in the family should stay in the family' was one of the mantras I remember; 'Such things are best left alone' was another.

Juice of the Barley for Me
Author unknown

In the sweet County Limerick one cold winter's night
With the turf fires a-burning I first saw the light
And the dirty auld midwife went tipsy with joy
As she danced round the floor with her slip of a boy

Singing bainne an bó is an gaibne
It's the juice of the barley for me

When I was a young lad of ten years or so
With my turf and me primer to school I did go
To that dirty old classroom without any door
And Brendan my teacher dead drunk on the floor

I was never too good at the learning or thinking
But I soon was as good as the teacher at drinking
Not a wake nor a wedding for five miles around
But myself in the corner was sure to be found

One Sunday the priest read my name from the altar
Saying you'll end up your days with your neck in a halter
You'll dance in the jigs between Heaven and Hell
His words they did scare me the truth now I'll tell

Early next morning as dawn it did break
Down to the vestry the pledge for to take
And there in that room sat the priests in a bunch
Round a big roaring fire drinking tumblers of punch

my additional lyric:
Dancing the jigs between Heaven and Hell
Surely not if you drink the top-shelf stuff
What about the Tia Maria ads
If only Jesus had turned the water into milk
Just like his mother
A better miracle altogether
But not for the powdered milk brigade

Lying bastards
Destroying cultures
Demeaning customs
Hypnotising innocent minds
Desecrating the beautiful union of mother and child
To sell their crap

H earing this song again, euphoric recall of earlier times, footloose and fancy free, heading into Thurles with my banjo on my knee, lowering the sparkling cider down my gullet until it began to bite, Jesus Christ I've never felt better, all my inhibitions sliding away, sure I'll sing that song again, I'll stand up on the counter and I'll sing like I've never sung before, my God but you're a beautiful woman, I could sing for you all right, it goes on and on, trawling up glorious memories of wild reels and heavenly voices and sweet, sweet companions. But euphoria never recalls black eyes, grazed knuckles, dark cells, cold floors, empty pockets, chest pains, palpitations, shivers and shakes, dark lies, never, never, only the tears of laughter and the night-long empty love-making.

The Gander
from Willie Clancy

It being one evening of late as I strayed and rambled through fields
Where oft times I've wandered in haste and very quick speed
I was going to a freak where rakes and factions do meet
There would be drink and strong tea, hot cake, and things that were sweet

The evening been freezing indeed and it was very cold
With corns in my heels, me boys, and cramps in my toes
I thought it no harm to warm my shanks by the fire
Thinking Myra and her daughter they surely would me admire

The teapot came round from the spout we got stuff very strong
Auld Myra said spake or make the verse of a song
Auld Bill in the corner was cursing and swearing with fright
For his gander was stolen and roasted last Saturday night

This gander was old he was noble both sturdy and strong
He never grew cold altho' he lived very long
His feet and his legs were as yellow as the gold that does shine
And his gob it would bore an inch board in a very short time

I've travelled Killarney Kilgarvan Kanturk and Kenmare
Down around by Cork Harbour I was dealing in turkeys and geese
But in all of my rambles and travels I never did see
The likes of Bill's gander for grandeur and audacity

The girls that all came were game and looking for breed
They'd heard of the name and the fame of Bill and his geese
They'd measure this fine gander's legs with a carpenter's rule
And they never would leave till they saw the fine length of his tool

It was the winter of 1964 when I arrived into Milltown Malbay, Co. Clare. A
wet Sunday night, I sought out my accommodation and eventually dried
off in the warm house of Mrs Downes. It was a music house and, seeing my
instrument, I was indeed made welcome. Having travelled from East Clare I

was cold and famished but the landlady soon banished all hardship with a hot dinner and a warm, dry bed. Nourished and replenished I enquired about music and she directed me across the street to the house of Tom and Maisie Friel and it was there that I met Willie Clancy for the first time. Willie was a legendary Uileann piper but was also much loved for his humour and his singing – that night he sang this fine song and asking me to sing 'Liverpool Lou' he accompanied me with the pipes.

Along with Séamus Ennis, Joe Heaney and Sean Maguire, to name but three, Willie was one of the great Irish musicians of his generation. These highly skilled exponents of their instruments also understood and had access to the soul of the music. They could still the loudest night with a slow air or quiet song. They carried the tradition and the emotion in their playing and it has been a great privilege to encounter them and to have known them.

Maguire, of course, plays on. Since I first met him in Jarrow, Tyneside in 1968, our paths have crossed occasionally and never without fun. Despite various setbacks Sean bows on, knocking sparks from his beloved violin.

Then too I sang with Maggie Barry in Harlesden, vamped with Joe Burke in Slough as we supped brandy and crème de menthe, accompanied Felix Doran one Sunday morning in Salford, sat in with Festy Conlon in Camden Town and rattled a bowrawn with Matt Molloy in Ballaghaderreen. All these memories, all these songs and dances. What a life I'm having.

The Bord Na Móna Man
by C. Moore

She spent seven days creating the world, the sun, the moon and the stars
Then the Plough, the Milky Way, Jupiter and Mars
Then she opened up her ribcage and pulled out a little man
She left him out near Tullamore that's where it all began
As to why she picked the short grass God only knows
Life began for the little man without a stitch of clothes
Go forth says she and multiply, God Mam and I will begod
What better place to start the race than below in Dowlin's bog

At the edge of Tankardgarden he built a lonely cell
Where he contemplated Limbo, Purgatory and Hell
Being a lonely celibate he found it hard to sleep
All he had for company was jockey boys and sheep
When he had converted Moorefield, Raheens and Narraghmore
He set sail down the Liffey 'til he came to Balitore
Where he broke up the bordellos and smashed the poteen stills
Introduced the fear of God around the sandy hills

Now there's not a corner of the world where the bogman can't be found
Where the pagan's thought the earth was flat he showed them it was round
Taught them how to flagellate themselves when he rang the bells
He exorcised auld cultures and banished them to Hell
When the bogman went out fishing he terrorised the trout
To make the natives buy his catch on Friday's meat was out
He ate sheep's eyes on Sundays mashed mangels through the week
On holy days he gently braised sheep's balls in buttermilk

Way back in the Sixties when the world was facing ruin
The East and West were neck and neck to be first on the moon
When the yankee left his module to walk the lunar land
Who was there to hold the ladder but the Bord Na Móna man
In the Russian revolution it's a well-known fact
It all began in Allenwood when the bogman he got sacked
Joe Stalin left Rathangan set sail for Leningrad
Where the turf was good and black and the porter wasn't bad

512

He opened up the Klondike and blazed the Yukon Trail
Crushed graves in California before Columbus had set sail
He drank tea on top of Everest before Hillary was born
Blindfold up the north face and backstroke around the horn
While John Bull conquered half the world with a mighty sword and gun
Paddy colonised the planet with the music and the song
Having ruled the world and ruled the waves it must be hard to take
Sunset at the empire Paddy singing at the wake

And don't you know he's a whore to go once he gets his foot half in the door
He's as sound as a bell he'll work like hell hire him if you can
I hear tell he's great and you'll never beat *The Bord Na Móna man*

This song preceded 'God Woman' by ten years. I wrote and re-wrote this ballad and even tried to record it on many occasions. It never quite gelled, nor did its progeny. Still, I've got a fascination with these words. They are so vivid for me and all the pictures are of my life. Maybe this song is not over yet.

I've recently recorded a song with my brother Barry (aka Luka Bloom) called 'I'm a Bogman'. For decades I've quietly suffered derogatory comments about bogmen, culchies, turf mould, bogger stuff and much more of the same; quietly and with dignity I've listened to city dwellers mouth their guff. I've just called up my sweet memories and transfixed within their beauty – the noise of suburban harangues passed over me like wisps of cloud on a summer's day, almost unnoticed.

I'm a bogman, deep down – it's where I come from.

Abbeville
by C. Moore

There's a better way of doing things
That's for sure
Instead of closing down hospitals
Putting VAT on food
Doing U-turns designed specifically
To keep lying MEPs
In Brussels jobs

I kind of half trusted you
In the last run-up
I gave you my number two
On the evidence of eye contact
And one sincere gripping handshake
Over a cup of tea in your house
We spoke of 'The Stardust' and 'Section 31'
The arts and the future
And although we spoke about it
We never actually called it
The war in the North

Later you called on Paddy
To shine the headlights of Cúchulainn
'The full fuckin' headlights Paddy
You're on fuckin' dim'
To say the least, I found it odd
But I was sucked in by your eccentricity

There is a better way of doing things
That's for sure
It's time to clear out the attic
And bring the lot of you to the Oxfam shop
Where you will hang on hooks
Ignored and sneered upon by those you ignore today

I was playing a concert in Malahide. Charlie Haughey was An Taoiseach of the day. A few days before the gig I received an invitation to visit our Prime Minister's house, which lay in the vicinity of Malahide. It was a Sunday afternoon and after I finished my sound check and rehearsal I was collected and driven to Abbeville.

I remember an imposing entrance with uniformed and armed police around. When we got to the house Mr Haughey met me at the bottom of the steps and told me it was an honour to have me in his home. Into the house and up more steps (as I recall) surrounded by busts in alabaster, maybe even marble. Through some passageways and into a complete and fully stocked authentic and mahogany pub. (I thought, why in the name of Jasus am I off the drink?) There were three other men in the room but Mr Haughey took me to one side and we spoke quietly for an hour. He then showed me some paintings – much Irish art, contemporary and earlier, hanging everywhere – I could have taken more time to gaze upon it all. When it was time to go he showed me Cúchulainn, and away I went to do my bit for Charlie's subjects.

Meeting Haughey like that was an incredible experience. I did feel like a troubadour summoned to the court, yet when we talked it was very much on a one to one. Haughey was curious about my work, my life and background, parents and grandparents, it was very much the sort of conversation I'd have with any Irishman I'd meet in Auckland or New Jersey. I recall it was the week when members of Fianna Fáil had defected to form the Progressive Democrats.

Many years on, and Mr Haughey's life is in ruins. Revelation upon revelation comes tumbling out as all the old pigeons come home to roost. If I was playing in Malahide tonight I'd probably knock him up and see if the kettle was on.

Don't Get Me Started
by C. Moore

Don't get me started unless you're going to let me finish
Otherwise we'll all end up wondering what we're missing
Like the day I nearly got a ride off Darky Prendergast
But I couldn't make the eight stone seven
So I sat in with the rest of them
And tore strips off everything that moved
Oh the warm begrudgery of it all
But even that small pleasure is now denied

Hey bollocky bishop, mind your own business
Tend your flock of sheep and leave the rest alone
Don't concern yourself with my eternal prospect
But rather, look into your own
Now that your commander's staff of infallibility has woodworm
And you stumble on your path of confusion
Keep out of my affairs
I know your game for once I lived beneath your spell
Until I came unto the use of reason
And began to fathom out what you are all about
Were Jesus to come back here today
We'd all get short shrift

Hey there you member of Parliament
Mr, Mrs, Ms, Master, Sir, Lord, Senator, Jo, Joanne
How is your old veneer
Your suit, costume, front, shine, coiffure, edifice
Sliding roof, façade, PR job, gleam, glint, glamour
Lickarse, kickarse, grovel
Butter wouldn't melt in your mouth
It wouldn't get time
Now I don't want to generalise, Generalissimo
But I saw your carry on with Reagan
And when that Israelite warmonger came over
You honoured him with your posse of 28 outriders
Astride my motorbikes with little bags and white flags

Like soldiers coming home from the LEB
Needing frenchies and divorces getting border duty, bank duty and duty free

On the run, on the dole, on the blanket, on the mattress
On your wits, on your nerves, on sufferance and pity
The great divide, all for me and none for you
I am not an artist, I am a clown
I love everybody and hate no-one at all

Here is a song I wrote for the Eurovision but it failed at the weigh-in, it being ugly and overweight and that was only at the post office.

I played the Eurovision in the Eighties. Planxty did the interval spot with a piece called 'Timedance'. Bill Whelan was in Planxty at the time and he went on to write the music for Riverdance. The Irish Ballet Company danced to our music and the whole affair was very classical but indeed lacked the sparks that were to fly from Flatley's feet ten years after, as he and Jean Butler gave birth to a new genre.

We agreed to do the gig when our A & R woman convinced us that we'd be huge. Six hundred and fifty million people watch the Eurovision, she cried, and we relented. All 650 million went and put on the kettles when we appeared – Flatley, where were you?

Good Ship Granma
by Ewan McColl

The good ship Granma lies at anchor in the harbour
Waiting for the evening tide to bring high water
It's bound for Cuba she must go across the Gulf of Mexico
And the Caribbean ocean
She's carrying a human cargo eighty-three good companeros
Each one burning with determination to be free

Against Batista the Fidelistas
Courage was their only armour
As they fought at Fidel's side
With Che Guevara

The fire lit on that Cuban beach by Fidel Castro
Shines all the way to Terra del Fuego
Sparks are blown upon the breeze men rise up from off their knees
When they see the night is burning
It blazes up in Venezuela, Bolivia and Guatemala
And lights the road that men must go in order to be free

Ten days out from Mexico these companeros
Landed on the Cuban beach Los Colerados
And Fidel said this year will see our country and its people free
Or else we will be martyrs
We've only guns enough for twenty the enemy has arms a-plenty
Meet him and defeat him and he'll keep us well supplied

Five weeks later in the Canyon de la Rio
The people's army numbered eighteen companeros
Hungry, weak but unafraid they're learning revolution's trade
In the high Sierra Maestra
In the mountains winds are blowing bearing seeds of hope and sowing
Crops in Cuba's earth that marks the birth of victory

En companeros Americanos
For a people's free America
Fidel has shown the way
With Che Guevara

They fought their way across the peak of El Tourquino
Joined by peasant bands and men from Santiago
They faced Batista's tanks and trains drove them back down into the plains
From the high Sierra Maestra
They drove the gangsters from Los Villas straight across the Cordilleras
Santa Barra fell to Che Guevara and was free

In 1967 I befriended a number of Communist Party members and through them met many fine fellow Travellers both in and out of folk clubs throughout Britain. As was the case then, and as is the case now, I was always totally ignorant of political theory and dogma. I know nothing of the different philosophies of Marx and Engels, Trotsky, Stalin or Lenin. I wouldn't know my Che from my Mao but I've always known the difference between a greedy boss and an exploited worker.

This particular song I encountered in a house somewhere around the English west country. A Communist yank was the host and a group of us were invited along for a weekend. I was riding in on the coat-tails of Bob Cooney, a veteran of the Spanish Civil War. It was a difficult visit for me for I knew nothing about the main topic of conversation, mainly an animated and heated discussion about the theoretical aspects of the struggle of the proletariat. I did notice, however, that they appeared to be going around in circles at times and that their arguments were littered with Party-speak. I've always been more at home with activists than theorists, the former are most important in any struggle but the latter are essential. Anyway, there was plenty of food and drink and no shortage of good whiskey so I played my part.

While there, I first heard this wonderful song of Ewan McColl's. I've been trying to sing it for years. I managed it once or twice in 1969 but never since. Upon re-writing the lyrics for this project I have vowed to sing 'Good Ship Granma' in the new millennium – God willing!

The Ridge and Coolcullen Brigade (March 1943)
Author unknown

Come listen good Christians and Pagans likewise
To a tale of West Carlow the snow and supplies
When the farmers determined to break the blockade
They recruited the Ridge and Coolcullen Brigade

There were twenty plough horses with saddles and sacks
And a score of real cowboys astride on their backs
With a Panzer division on shovel and spade
In advance of the Ridge and Coolcullen Brigade

Tom Comerford was first with Jack Neill to the rear
Mick Sheeran in charge on Harry Smith's mare
As they rode through Old Leiglin each buacaill and maíd
Waved a hand at the Ridge and Coolcullen Brigade

They rattled through Leighlin and never drew rein
'Til they came within sight of the Barrow's back drain
Going in by the brewery the horses all neighed
For the thirst of the Ridge and Coolcullen Brigade

They drank at the fountain and fed in the town
People thought they were a circus broke down
Down Regent Street, Main Street and down the parade
Rang the hooves of the Ridge and Coolcullen Brigade

Across the slopes of Slieve Bargy as evening had set
The horses they ploughed on all lather and sweat
While the wind and the frost played a cold serenade
In the ears of the Ridge and Coolcullen Brigade

It was late at night when most were in bed
The convoy reached Coolcullen with bacon and bread
There was no state reception nor loud cannonade
To welcome the Ridge and Coolcullen Brigade

And now across the hillside each gay cavalier
Is looked on as Gilpin in bold Paul Revere
The trip to the Antarctic's been put in the shade
By the trek of the Ridge and Coolcullen Brigade

There are no leather medals no civic address
No photos taken to put in the press
But manys the family their table had laid
By the deeds of the Ridge and Coolcullen Brigade

Singe hey for the Highlands sing low for the low
Three cheers for the lads of the Star Rodeo
Those great overlanders that grand cavalcade
Now known as the Ridge and Coolcullen Brigade

When Valerie and Andy and I moved to Coolcullen, Co. Carlow, in 1976, it was an old-world place where we encountered many's the kindness from the finest of neighbours. Our house was on the Protestant road at a thousand feet overlooking Coon Village, its valley and river.

I soon got to know all and to dig out any old songs or characters in the area. I played in Reddy's Coalmine Bar, Leo Conway's in Castlecomer, Larkin's of Kanesbridge, Sheeran's of The Ridge, The Arkle in Gowran and farther afield in Kilkenny, Carlow and Muckalee. Before long I had myself a grand little circuit of pub gigs and I lowered it up.

This is one of the songs I gleaned on the Castlecomer Plateau. I wrote a couple of other songs: 'Langstrom's Pony' and an adaptation of 'The Kilruddery Hunt', but they are lost. Before leaving I involved myself with a group of young people in Castlecomer and we ran a wonderful festival in 1978. I hoped it would continue but without the workaholic it fizzled out.

All of the men in 'The Ridge and Coolcullen Brigade' were known to me. The song was revived in 1977 when a fall of snow refreshed memories of 1943. During that period Andy spent time in hospital in Kilkenny, and Val and Mother were snowbound in Kilkenny for a week – I was off balladeering in West Germany.

Bridget O'Malley
Author unknown

Bridget O'Malley you have my heart shaken
With a hopeless desolation I'll have you to know
It's a wonder of admiration your quiet face has taken
Your beauty will haunt me wherever I go

The white moon above the pale sands, pale stars above the palm trees
Are gold beside my darling but no purer than she
Gazing upon cold land, stars drowning in the warm sea
The bright eyes of my darling are always on me

My Sunday is weary my Sunday is grey now
My heart is a cold thing my heart is a stone
All joy is dead in me, my life has gone away now
Another has taken my love for his own

The day is approaching when we were to be married
It's rather I'd die than live only to grieve
Oh meet me my darling when the sun sets o'er the Boreen
I'll meet you there on the road to Drumleigh

This song reads like a translation from Irish. The language is awkward, but suggests a beautiful song back down the line.

I was foostering around on the fringe of a wild bunch. I often ended up in a mad house in New Ross, Co. Wexford. The man of the house was on the fringes of madness and the craziness would begin after closing time when the social drinkers had gone home. There, in the midst of it one night, a man sang this song. On paper it is no great shakes, but the way I heard it that night shook me to the core. I was drunk and the song sobered me. I recognised the desolation, the awful, mind-numbing depression – it was a defining moment in my alcoholic life. Despite it, I drank on for a further ten years, but my drinking was ruined. I tried both to sing the song and to record it, neither to much avail.

There were two bottles of wine burning a hole in the boot of the car. By the time I'd driven the 160 miles I was reconciled to opening them without delay and once they were down it was an easy job deciding to go to the pub for ten pint bottles of stout. This meant that on Monday morning I was suffering a quiver that needed settling. I duly began settling it between 2.30 and 5pm when I drank six or seven pints in Kelly's pub in Ennis, Co. Clare. I then drove to Dublin, stopping at Matt the Thrashers, Portlaoise and Newbridge. I arrived in Rialto and did a quick wash and shave and out to meet a music associate for a 'business meeting'. I drank one bottle of stout, one dry sherry, a half-bottle of Riesling, two vintage ports and then we shared two bottles of Chateauneuf, numerous ports and more wine – how much I don't know. As this progressed I was also doing Valium and cocaine and, at the end, I remember some hashish in the equation.

The result of this was that for four days I was extremely ill; I had jitters, hot and cold flushes, my heart was paining, my liver was sore and my limbs all ached. Valerie was worried about me and fed up with me, the children were confused and I was feeling stupid, awkward and determined never to do it again. But, of course, I did.

Ten years later, I was trying so hard to give up booze that some days I'd try and write down previous days' madness in the hope that I might shock myself into sobriety. It never worked.

In This Heart
by Sinéad O'Connor

In this heart lies for you
A lark born only for you
Who sings only for you
My love my love my love

I am waiting for you
For only to adore you
My heart is for you
My love my love my love

This is my grief for you
For only the loss of you
The hurting of you
My love my love my love

There are waves on the weather
Soon these tears will have cried
All lonliness have died
My love my love my love

I will have you with me
In my arms only
For you are only
My love my love my love

When Gay Byrne honoured my songs with a dedicated *Late Late Show*, I leapt at the opportunity to try and sing with some different musicians and singers. I played once more with Moving Hearts; Planxty members were scattered around the globe. I did an old version of 'Spancilhill' with Shane McGowan and the Hothouse Flowers, I sang with Maire Ní Broanáin, Eleanor Shanley, Mandy Murphy, I duetted with Daniel O'Donnell, the music went on and on and I sang this song with Sinéad O'Connor who also wrote it. She had sung previously on the *Voyage* album, and we had periodically kept in touch.

For me it was an emotionally charged evening. I tend to get very emotional betimes, and on many occasions that night I welled up but kept the lid well tightened – some men cry while others have heart attacks! Check out Dan Penn's song 'Stand Up and Cry Like a Man' – maybe I'll be singing it in time for inclusion.

Insofar as I can recall I appeared on the *Late Late Show* twenty-two times between 1972 and 1999. I can recall Planxty and The Chieftains trying most unsuccessfully to duet together, singing 'Nancy Spain' for Eamonn Andrews' beautiful daughters, giving my chair to the Taoiseach Mr Haughey when he suddenly appeared on The Dubliners tribute show, forgetting my words while duetting with Paul Doran on 'Make it Work' (and not one person in the country noticed), the Paul McGrath tribute, singing with Daniel, on and on it went and each and every time Gay Byrne welcomed me warmly onto his stage. He always paved the way for me and made it easy to sing on his show. He also welcomed Mother into Studio One on a number of occasions and they hit it off – the pair of them.

Wickham and Connors
Author unknown

Come all you young fellows that's jolly and wholesome
I pray pay attention and listen to me
Concerning a battle of two bully champions
On the hill of Ballingeary 'twas plain for to see
The first was Jim Wickham who's mentioned in history
Of his famous deed and his courage so bold
The next was Pat Connors that fisherman of Britain
As I was a witness the truth I'll unfold

We were in Ned Blayney's that famous tavern
That is celebrated for selling sour beer
The drink went around we got intoxicated
When Connors for action he soon did declare
He said I'm Pat Connors that famous bold hero
I never was conquered in county or town
He threw off his coat and he roared holy murder
And rushed like a tiger to knock Wickham down

When Wickham saw Connors in such a great passion
Poor Wickham did seem for to crouch by the wall
And Connors he being overpowered by liquor
At half time he struck out at nothing at all
Wickham got up and his nose it was bleeding
'Tis only a cold that I caught the other day
He looked all around him in such a dazed fashion
Is there nobody here for to show me fair play

Oh there's nobody here but your own darling Leisha
Just you wait a minute 'til I go for Phil
Mrs Wickham turned round and she faced all the company
Saying my husband the best man that stands on this hill
The next round they parried and chuckled each other
And Wickham he cried out don't tear me auld clothes
Mrs Connors determined to end the battle
With the heel of her shoe she broke poor Wickham's nose

So we'll go back to Blayney's and drink there contented
Success to those heroes for their art and skill
Well if youse had a been there you'd have died of the laughter
To witness the battle that day on the hill

I was sixteen and over in London for my first summer of work in 1961. I met a townie in a pub in Southall and we struck up together for a night. Towards closing time my buddy was mad for a fight. Thanks be to God there were no takers for poor Joe Hughes could not fight his way out of a paper bag and this boy was not too far behind him. It was my first experience of fighting for the hell of it.

I was in a pub in Fulham in 1966. It was famous for its music and the playing was of a high degree. Come closing time and the select few would get the nod for the lock-in. There might be an occasional bit of quiet eccentric music but, after hours, this would have been the exception. Usually it was a card game, 110 with partners. Then, as the drink and the night wore on, there could be romance of a basic kind or, as on one famous occasion, arm-wrestling. The landlord was either a dry-drunk or a raving lunatic on the drink and he challenged the room to arm wrestle. Everyone chose to ignore him except a Bannerman who responded to the call. They put £20 a man on it which was a good week's wages. They commenced a best of three and the room fell into a pissed silence. They won one apiece and the stage was set for a great showdown. The Bannerman was weakening and almost bent down to the counter when he lifted up a heavy glass ashtray and broke it over the landlord's head. He swiped the £40 and out the door with him like a grey-hound from the traps.

Stupid, harmless violence but it was not always funny. Sometimes there is a terrible price to pay. I was invited once to share my experience, strength and hope as a recovering alcoholic with a group of long-term prisoners. There were six men in the room and three of them had done their crimes in blackouts. They were serving life sentences for crimes they could not remember.

I was in a nightclub in Oxford Street, Manchester in 1968. I was playing the hard man. I challenged a fellow over a woman and we went outside. He held a gun to my head. He was an armed detective. Then he took me back in and bought me a large Bacardi. It wasn't all folk clubs and song-searching.

Most of the violence I've witnessed in my life has been alcohol-related. Someone was watching over me. 'Wickham and Connors' reminds me of harmless fun; no innocent was injured.

Devious Twarth
by C. Moore

He called me
A devious twarth
Later that night
Embittered in bile
I lay listening
To their frantic guffaws
When silence came
My blood began to boil
As I lay there waiting
For the next round of cawphoos

We were on the Moving Hearts bus. We needed a band meeting. I was pushing and pushing to get the collective to do things my way. I was pulled up by a fellow Traveller and for years I've held on to these two words. He called me a devious twarth.

Of course, the fact that he uttered the words does not necessarily give them legitimacy, but today, at least I can look at them and acknowledge the possibility that he was absolutely right – maybe.

These accursed resentments: it is akin to carrying a burning coal in one's hand in the hope of meeting the subject of one's bitterness.

I acknowledge that I've not always been the type to follow. I was never asked to join any of the bands; I needed to make the running and form them myself. Today, nothing much has changed except I am more content doing what I'm able to do. I no longer feel inadequate, rather I'll try and do the best I can with the gifts I've got. One of the difficulties of making the running is that lingering resentments can sometimes be created.

Has there ever been a true collective? Someone must surely be the first to dream.

Innishvickallaune
by C. Moore

Stormy wild and free
Alone, deserted in the sea
All your children sailed ashore
The island people are no more

On Innishvickallaune

Ancient moods recoil
As beauty queens and ballad bands
Are flown out against the wind
To stand amongst the seagulls screaming

On Innishvickallaune

Wild birds fiercely turn
To fly in anger through the skies
Freaked by coarse intrusion
Of a nature long despised

On Innishvickallaune

Green Connemara marble
Blue Liscannor slate
Amazonian timbers
Gilted mirror, glass ornate

All flown out against the wind

To Innishvickallaune

I knew a man called Siney Crotty. We shared a few bottles of stout mainly in Slattery's of Capel Street of a Wednesday night. He was a lovely man to sing a quiet song – he'd sing it in your ear in the midst of mayhem and every note and nuance would be grand. He lived for the bit of music and told me many good yarns about his life, some of which was spent on Innishvikallaune, an island in the Blaskets off Co. Kerry, purchased by Charlie Haughey.

The Ciskei Miner
Patrick Burke and C. Moore

It's a long and dusty road from the ranch upon the Veldt
To the shanty town of mud, flies and squalor
The man from Soweto picks the ripened crop
In the orchard of the Afrikaaner
Beneath the scorching sun he sweats for a paltry sum
No rest 'til the bossman gives the order
Now he's old and lame and he remembers how he came
To end his days as a starving Kaffir

And the walls of the laager are crumbling
The day of the Kraal is returning
Your pass laws are being defied, repent or you'll be crucified
Soweto, Soweto is rising

It's a long hard road the Ciskei Miner goes
Five hundred miles from home he has to travel
To work twelve hours at a time deep down in the mine
Digging gold for an Afrikaaner
To Johannesburg the profits go, miners wages are kept low
If he strikes he knows he will be broken
With shotguns and CS gas upholding the ruling class
With jackboots the Springbok law is spoken

I received this song from a neighbour, Patrick Burke, in Monkstown in 1986. I worked it and demoed it and even sang it a few times but it never became a part of the repertoire, nor did I ever record it. When Wally Page gave me the song 'Biko Drum' I took to it quickly and I'm afraid that 'Ciskei Miner' had to give way.

I remember singing this to Kadar Asmal. Today, Kadar is a minister in Mandela's government but then he was a lecturer in Trinity College, Dublin. He invited me into the inner sanctum of Trinity one day for lunch and I sang this for dessert. It was a cold room which, to this visitor, appeared to have its own apartheid in operation. At that time Kadar and Louise Asmal were hard-working members of the Irish Anti-Apartheid Movement.

Writing this reminds me of another day, another lunch as guest of Tony Gregory in the Leinster House feeding trough. Tony and I sat alone in the midst of the pack of wolves. It was a most enjoyable experience and a few TDs came across to welcome this balladeer into their midst. But for every one who did, there were two whose demeanour suggested I was not welcome. That, of course, could be down to my paranoia, or a bad egg for breakfast.

Today, the Laager is still crumbling in Soweto and Portadown, but the Afrikaaner drums are still rattling down the Garvaghy Road.

All the Tides that Flow
by C. Moore

I opened up my heart to those whose anger made my blood run cold
And I bared my soul to those whose eyes were filled with hurt and pain
I sought love in the midst of sin and hatred
And every waking hour I was afraid

I sought light down in the darkest places
Sweet music where the loudest noise was made
Comfort in the dampest coldest corners
And I played where the dangerous games were played

But when I turned to you my love
All those lonely years came to an end
I learned that every twist and turn had been vital to my journey
And that there is more to life than simple fun and games

I learned that as I lay cold and frightened down those endless alleys
Leaves fell from the trees and new buds began to grow
As I tossed and turned within my nightmare dreaming
Raindrops fell gently from the foliage and streaming towards the ocean
Became a part forever more of all the tides that flow

Around the year of 1986 I wrote this lyric. It was a first-time write. Since then I've re-written and re-shaped it a hundred times or more but I always end up back at the beginning, so I'm leaving it simply as it is. It is difficult and seems wrong because it was difficult and always seemed wrong.

I can remember so many names but no poems. All the players from the Kildare team of 1956, but none of the poets. The Moorefield team of 1962, but not the poets. The Manchester United team of 1968, but not one poet.

I thank God for all the songs. I used never meet the poets, but I have been blessed with songs.

He Was a Quare One
Author unknown

My love is o'er the ocean my love is o'er the sea
My love is o'er the ocean and I'm in the family way

Oh! He was a quare one fol de dee get outa that
He was a quare one I'll tell you

And if you go to the Curragh Camp just call on number nine
You'll see three squaddies standing there and the best-looking one is mine

And if you go to Francis Street that's if you go at all
Take a look at the writing on the wall say a prayer for the way I walk

And if you go to fight the Boers that's if you go at all
Make sure you fight from a deep, deep trench or you won't come back at all

Me love lies o'er the ocean my love lies o'er the sea
Me loves lies o'er the ocean left me in the family way

So hand me down me petticoat and hand me down my shawl
So hand me down me petticoat for I'm off to the Linen Hall

21 January 2000

In September 1999 I released the album *Traveller* and it went to number one in the charts. The album was very well received despite being a radical departure from previous work. I started back gigging and opened at Vicar Street, Dublin where I planned to do twelve nights. Everything was progressing well until I suffered an angina attack. I was hospitalised and upon release thought to dip my toe back in the waters of performance, but it simply did not work out. It seems like my pump can no longer handle the adrenaline that gigging brings on.

That part of my life has ended. It is now 45 years since I first stood on a stage to sing, and this new life takes a lot of getting used to. I still sing everyday. I'm recording some songs and writing this book and slowly gaining acceptance of the new landscape.

Fol de dee get outa that.

The Siren's Voice
by C. Moore

She picked up a handful of earth
And kissing it she cried
The song of our village has come to an end

Then she heard the siren's voice
And the siren's voice was singing

Ireland of the welcomes, one hundred thousand welcomes
Christian holy island, one hundred thousand welcomes
Land of the Holy Father, one hundred thousand welcomes
Land of saints and scholars, one hundred thousand welcomes
Ancient city of the Black Lagoon, céad míle fáilte
Dublin of the rare auld times, céad míle fáilte
Heart of the rowl, céad míle fáilte
Where the green snot river flows, céad míle fáilte

Again she heard the siren's voice
And the siren's voice was singing

Black life white life pro life
Black life white life pro life
Black lies white lies no life

Then she heard the siren's voice
And the siren's voice was singing

No niggers or knackers or wogs, no refugees
No dia in muire sez she, no refugees
No divorce in heaven sez she, no refugees
Míle fáilte my arse sez she, míle fáilte my arse

Living off our land
Living off our hard-earned surplus
Causing housing shortage and unemployment
Living off our hard-earned surplus

They're coming here to save us
To save the white babies
They're coming here to save us
Saving white babies' souls
A penny for the white babies

Many years ago I predicted that a time would come when Mass in Ireland would be celebrated mainly by black priests, and that time is getting nearer with each passing year. Vocations in Ireland have all but dried up and is it any wonder? It will not be long before young priests and nuns from emerging countries will come to Ireland to 'save the white babies'. They will come to Bognia to give comfort and succour and spiritual sustenance in the wake of the Celtic Tiger.

As the tide of racism rose, fuelled by fanatics and cynical politicians, I wrote this song for the 1999 *Traveller* album. It has received no airplay to date, but I'm happy with the way it sits amongst the other tracks. Anyway, I did not write or record it for airplay but to express one of my own views of 'The Tiger's Island'.

Lovely Young One
by C. Moore and Wally Page

Oh my lovely young one
When you took your leave last night
You offered me no teardrops
No kisses no goodbyes
No simple explanation
You walked out the door
Leaving Tír na n Óg
For Tír na n Oíche

Oh my lovely young one
I'm left standing at your wake
My eyes are searching
But I can find no trace
Of your final footsteps
As you walked out the door
Leaving Tír na n Óg
For Tír na n Oíche

Oh my lovely young one
Oh my lovely young one
Gone from Tír na n Óg
To Tír na n Oíche

I had tried, unsuccessfully, for many years to write a lament for the families of young suicide victims. A number of friends had lost loved ones and I wanted to express my own hurt and pain when confronted with their terrible loss. Three years ago I received a letter from one such mother, a complete stranger to me, who asked me to write a song for her daughter. With no indication or forewarning, this young woman had taken her life.

'Lovely Young One' is the simple result. I struggled to write a third verse, to resolve the lyric. For months I tore up verse after verse until it dawned on me that there was no more to be said, it could neither be resolved nor explained.

I brought the lyric to Wally Page who wrote a beautiful melody and who also played on the recording. Sadly, the song has not been played on the airwaves. However, I did receive a lovely letter from the woman who asked me to write the song. She described it as a fitting memorial to her beautiful daughter – a memorial she can carry with her wherever she goes. The song, thank God, has served its purpose.

July 1999

My friend Donal McCann is laid to rest in Monaseed, neary Gorey, Co. Wexford. He was the most honest man I ever met. I said goodbye to him last week, the day before he entered the hospice. He shared so much with me and taught me about the love of God and the great gift of acceptance. He never once complained. Our paths had crossed occasionally over 25 years but in the last two years his illness brought us together and it became a friendship that I will always cherish. One of those friendships where two fellows can sit and say absolutely nothing and yet feel camaraderie.

God rest you my dear brother.

Urgency Culture
by C. Moore and Leo Pearson

Urgency culture
Information overload
Hot-bed of nothing
Holocaust of silence
Violence of apathy
Consumed by security
Intuition
Becoming obsolete

Disenchanted
Ruled by the rational
Fearing the spiritual
Living in the analysis
Intuition
Becoming obsolete

Let me hear the voice of an innocent child
Hear the source of mystery
Listen to the voice of an innocent child
Hear the source of mystery

These are the opening lines from my 1999 album *Traveller*: words I've heard on the radio, down the phone, on the street, words from Tom Berry, Pat Clarke, Joe Young, Noel Bradshaw, words that express my fears, my hope, my powerlessness, my utter dependence.

Me and Bibi
by C. Moore

I dreamt that I met Bibi Baskin and Bibi said to me
Tell me Christy, where did it all begin?
Well Bibi 'twas '43 or '44 in The Majestic Ballroom in Tramore
My father asked my mother out for a slow foxtrot
And some time later I was born into a very musical family
Daddy rose at five each morning and taking down his pipes
Began by gently fiddling with his chanter
Then Mother would rise and having stirred the gruel
She began to let the air into her weathered concertina
And there they'd sit the whole day long playing their slow airs and mazurkas

'Agus cupla focal anois mar geall ar do "earliest influences"
'Mar a diertear' sez Bibi
In the late Forties I was heavy into Percy French
Until one night I heard Count John sing Gounod
And I began to listen to Sonny Ghent, Woodner Quinn and John Hartfleet
Until one Tuesday night in 1956 me and Joe Coffey heard Bill Haley in The Palace
One, two, three o'clock four o'clock rock.
Goodnight Percy sez I and gave me soul to rock & roll
I resigned from The Altar Boys and climbed into my drainpipes
I pulled up my luminous socks and
'I'm just a lonely boy, lonely and blue, I'm all alone with nothing to do'
I was playing hard to get in my blue suede shoes

Plugging into 208 for Gene Vincent and Billy Eckstine
Yea Bibi I gave my soul to rock & roll
Until one Thursday night I was riding home from Devotions
And it dawned upon me
My entire repertoire in 1959 was outside the realm of my experience
Like there I was heading across the bog on my bike
Singing 'Riding along on my automobile'
It's all very well for Chuck Berry going down in the back of his pink Cadillac
But I was still trying to get Miss Kildare up on the bar of my bike
Would you like to come to dreamland, Pauline?
Albert has Dicky on tonight

It was time to seek out something more organic
Neither vegan nor macrobiotic but leaning a bit more to the Kildare side
I found it one night twiddling the knobs on the Panasonic
Half-way between Hilversum and Athlone — FINE GIRL YOU ARE
So I swapped my blue suede shoes for a pair of sandals
Pulled on my Báinín sweater and started training my ponytail
With three chords and Rosin the Bow I was away on a hack
Vamping the bull fiddle and sleeping under a bush
It was the life of Reilly, £3 a night and all I could drink
Then Bob Dylan came and ruined the bloody lot of it.
Everything went shaggin' progressive.
The winds of change came blowing in across The Curragh from Woodstock.
I pulled out of my sandals and climbed on to my platforms
Out of my Levis into my flares
Gave up the bottles and stopped the pints
I was dropping acid and rolling joints
I was seeking The Knowledge expounding on The Ramalama
Into the mystic in a Volkswagen Van
The karma was good and the Moroccan wasn't too bad either

Far out. Too much. All the way.
Jasus Bibi I was so far out I ended up in Gütersloh
Playing slow airs and singing songs for all the Vass in Doolins
Eintopf and Toten Hosen another bottle of Schnapps there Gunter
Me and Jimmy Faulkner living on Schmaltz in Bremen
We got so homesick in Hamburg that we couldn't go home at all
Back in Brest at feeding time the Bretons bombarded me
With Celtic ooze and bonhomie
And when I tumbled from the Planxty wagon in Lorient
I knew that something bad was wrong
For the van continued on its lonely way

Up, up and away again all on my lonesome
Bating it out in The Baggot
Getting lost in Bergen and down on my hands and knees in The Lowlands low
I wandered into Liechtenstein and met with Princess Nora on top of the gold-plated false tooth mountain
The trip got badder and badder
Albert Hall, Carnegie Hall and The Isaac Butt Memorial Hall
For the Pontiff in The Phoenix Park and Nancy in The Reagan Lounge
In the town of The Little Potato

I was climbing The Barricades to sing for Petra Kelly
I was dancing with The Blanket Men round and round the romper room
While Mairéad whispered me about The Armagh Women
Higher and higher up The Barricade like The Great Liberator
But sure I couldn't get away from myself
The hero balladeer stripped naked, space invaded
Probed and beaten – red diesel all the way
Stir them up – lock them up – blow them up
Until my heart stopped

Yeah, me docs were down at heel
And the Agit Prop doesn't fuel the pension fund
Like there's twenty-eight counties in Ireland
There they are Bibi
Longford, Westmeath and Roscommon
And there's no by-pass around Strokestown
We're gladhandling the Moola
Pocketing the Shamboola
Stroking the Payola

And that's the story Bibi (so far)

What's the Life of Man
Author unknown

As I was a-walking one morning at ease
A-viewing the leaves that had fell from the trees
All in full motion appearing to be
And those that had withered they fell from the tree

What's the life of a man any more than a leaf
A man has his seasons so why should we grieve
For although in this world we appear fine and gay
Like a leaf we must wither and soon fade away

If you'd seen the trees but a few days ago
How beautiful and green they all seemed to grow
A frost came upon them and withered them all
A storm came upon them and down they did fall

If you look in the churchyard there you will see
Many that have passed like a leaf from a tree
When age and affliction upon them did call
Like a leaf they did wither and down they did fall

And so I arrive at the final song in this collection. I rediscovered it among my papers written in a copy book from the Sixties. I have no recollection of where I heard it, but I do have a vague melody floating around in my distant memory. And so it goes, we write songs and sing them, we use the notes and the words that float on the air and, like leaves, like little seeds, they are carried on the wind where sometimes they will fall on fallow earth and gain root. Decades and generations later the verse will ring out on the air, the chorus will rise and shine for a moment and then fade away.

Discography

Details of all other compilations, collaborations, books, videos, etc. can be found on the websitehttp://www.christymoore.net

Albums

	1969	Paddy on the Road	1984	Ride On
	1970	Prosperous	1985	Ordinary Man
■	1971	Planxty	1986	Nice and Easy
■	1972	Well Below the Valley	■ 1986	Planxty Arís
■	1973	Cold Blow, Rainy Night	1986	The Spirit of Freedom
	1975	Whatever Tickles Your Fancy	1987	Unfinished Revolution
	1976	Christy Moore	1988	The Christy Moore Compilation
	1978	The Iron Behind the Velvet	1989	Voyage
	1978	Live in Dublin	1991	Collection '81–'91
	1978	H-Block	1991	Smoke & Strong Whiskey
■	1979	After the Break	1993	King Puck
■	1980	The Woman I Love	1994	Live at the Point
	1981	Christy Moore and Friends	1996	Graffiti Tongue
▲	1981	Moving Hearts	1997	The Collection Part II
▲	1982	The Dark End of the Street	1999	Traveller
■	1983	Words and Music	2001	This is the Day
	1983	The Time Has Come	2002	Live at Vicar Street

■ With Planxty;   ▲ With Moving Hearts.

Singles

■ 1972 Three Drunken Maidens

■ 1972 Cliffs of Dooneen

　 1975 Humours of Ballymagash

　 1976 Nancy Spain

　 1978 Ninety Miles to Dublin

　 1979 Anti-Nuclear 12"

　 1980 John O'Dreams

■ 1981 Timedance 12"

▲ 1981 Landlord

▲ 1982 All I Remember

▲ 1982 Hiroshima Nagasaki Russian
　　　　Roulette

　 1982 The Time Has Come

　 1983 Knock

　 1983 Don't Forget Your Shovel

　 1983 The Wicklow Boy

■ 1983 I Pity the Poor Immigrant

　 1984 Ride On

　 1984 Back Home in Derry

　 1984 Hey! Ronnie Reagan

　 1984 Lisdoonvarna

　 1985 They Never Came Home

　 1985 Delerium Tremens

　 1985 Ordinary Man

　 1985 Another Song is Born

　 1985 Sweet Music Roll On

　 1985 The Reel in the Flickering Light

　 1986 Make it Work

　 1987 Natives

　 1987 Biko Drum

　 1987 Messenger Boy

　 1987 Dying Soldier

　 1989 The Voyage

　 1989 Joxer Goes to Stuttgart

　 1989 Missing You

　 1991 Welcome to the Cabaret

　 1991 Fairytale of New York

　 1991 Smoke and Strong Whiskey

　 1991 If I Get an Encore

　 1994 Big Issue Single

　 1994 Away You Broken Heart You

　 1995 North and South

　 1996 God Woman

　 1996 Strangeways

　 1999 The Raggle Taggle Gypsy

　 2000 One Last Cold Kiss

Index of songs

Abbeville 514
After the Deluge 12
Aisling 125
All I Remember 250
All the Tides that Flow 533
Allende 70
Among the Wicklow Hills 375
Andytown Girl 470
Another Song is Born 170
Armagh Women, The 458
As I Roved Out 223
Avondale 401
Away You Broken Heart You 246

Back Home in Derry 56
Ballad of Eamon Byrne, The 353
Ballinamore 138
Ballindine Eviction 487
Banks of the Lee, The 207
Biko Drum 67
Billy Gray 140
Black Is the Colour
    (of my True Love's Hair) 24
Blackjack County Chains 297
Blackwater Side 347
Bleacher Lassie of Kelvinhall, The 265
Bless this Guitar 468
Bogie's Bonny Belle 46
Boning Hall 184
Bord Na Móna Man 512
Boy from Tamlaghduff, The 294
Boys of Mullaghbawn 494

Bridget O'Malley 522
Bright Blue Rose 117
Burning Times 40

Carrickfergus 405
Casey 151
Ciskei Miner, The 531
City of Chicago 35
Cliffs of Dooneen, The 209
Clyde's Bonnie Banks 268
Cold Blow, Rainy Night 366
Continental Céilí 100
Crack Was Ninety in the Isle of Man,
    The 142
Cricklewood 356
Croppy Boy 496
Crow on the Cradle, The 453
Curragh of Kildare, The 235

Dalesman's Litany, The 257
Dark End of the Street, The 211
Dark-Eyed Sailor 333
Delerium Tremens 105
Deportees Club 194
Derby Day 134
Devious Twarth 529
Don't Forget your Shovel 34
Don't Get Me Started 516
Dunlavin Green 396
Dunnes Stores 423
Dusty Diamondtina 281
Dying Soldier 182

Easter Snow 289
El Salvador 76
Encore 155

Fairytale of New York 22
Faithful Departed 82
Farewell to Pripyat 277
First Hunger Strike Song 483
First Time Ever I Saw your Face, The 144
Foggy Dew 327
Folk Tale 187
Follow Me Up to Carlow 237
Ford's Siamsa Cois Lee 498
Foxy Devil 411

Galtee Mountain Boy, The 114
Galway to Graceland 474
Gander, The 510
Giuseppe 123
Go, Move, Shift 146
God Woman 189
God's Truth 504
Good Ship Granma 518
Good Ship Kangaroo 306
Grannie's Dustbin Lid 449
Green Island 311
Gresford Disaster, The 462

Hackler from Grouse Hall, The 313
Hands Across the Lough 196
Hands Off the GLC 464
Hard Cases 243
He Was a Quare One 534
Hey! Paddy 466
Hey! Ronnie Reagan 304
Hey Sandy 364
Hiroshima Nagasaki Russian Roulette 132
Holy Ground, The 329
House in Carne 447

I Pity the Poor Immigrant 193

I Wish I Was in England 360
In this Heart 524
Innishvickallaune 530
Irish Ways and Irish Laws 109

James Connolly 233
James Larkin 358
January Man, The 112
Jesus Christ and Jessie James 451
Joe Doherty 471
Joe McCann 416
John O' Dreams 241
Johnny Connors 49
Johnny Jump Up 212
Joxer Goes to Stuttgart 61
Jug of Punch, The 351
Juice of the Barley for Me 508

Kerry Recruit, The 438
Kevin Barry 349
Kilkenny Doll 502
Knock 94

Lakes of Ponchartrain, The 263
Landlord 403
Lanigan's Ball 230
Lawless 121
Least We Can Do, The 373
Leaving of Liverpool 342
Liffeyside 338
Limerick Rake, The 220
Lisdoonvarna 148
Little Beggarman 441
Little Drummer 368
Little Mother 371
Little Musgrave 172
Lock Hospital 362
Looking for the Entrance Fee 185
Lord Baker 177
Lovely Young One 537
Ludlow Massacre, The 159

Luke Kelly 291

McIlhatton 88
Mad Lady and Me 384
Margaret Thatcher 485
Matty 103
Me and Bibi 540
Mea Maxima Culpa 51
Meeting of the Waters, The 457
Messenger Boy 420
Metropolitan Avenue 382
Middle of the Island, The 42
Minds Locked Shut 205
Missing You 98
Moorefield 472
Morrissey and the Russian Sailor 413
Mrs McGrath 455
Mullaghmore 175
Musha God Help Her 340
Mystic Lipstick 386

Nancy Spain 85
Natives 15
New Galway Races 299
Night Before Larry Was Stretched, The 399
1913 Massacre 162
Ninety Miles to Dublin Town 273
No Time for Love 107
North and South 196

Off to Sea Once More (Shangai Browne) 319
Old Man's Song, The 335
Old Triangle, The 287
On the Blanket 445
On the Bridge 136
On the Mainland 191
On the Run 380
Once I Had a Love 317
One Hundred Miles from Home 492
One Last Cold Kiss 111

Only Our Rivers Run Free 267
Ordinary Man 17
Other Side, The 77

Paddy on the Road 354
Pair of Brown Eyes, A 119
Panhandlers of Ireland 480
People's Own MP, The 283
Phone Tap Squad, The 489
Plane Crash at Los Gatos 279
Pretty Boy Floyd 394
Pride of Petravore, The 37

Quiet Desperation 58

Raggle Taggle Gypsy, The 129
Reel in the Flickering Light, The 64
Remember the Brave Ones 378
Ride On 80
Ridge and Coolcullen Brigade, The 520
Riding the High Stool 203
Rocks of Bawn 434
Rocky Road to Dublin 323
Rory Is Gone 201
Rose of Tralee, The (Me and the Rose) 252
Rosin the Bow 388

Sacco and Vanzetti 157
St Brendan's Voyage 74
St Patrick Was a Gentleman 315
St Patrick's Arrival 409
St Patrick's Dance in San Fernando 476
Sam Hall 427
Scallcrows 397
Scapegoats 218
Scariff Martyrs, The 285
Section 31 239
Singer, The 302
Singing Bird 28
Siren's Voice, The 535
Sliab Gallion Braes 392

Smoke and Strong Whiskey 153
Soldier Boys 275
Someone to Love Me 407
Song of Wandering Aongus, The 66
Sonny's Dream 96
Spancilhill 270
Spanish Lady 325
Stall the Digger Sham 478
Strange Ways 51
Streams of Bunclody 436
Streets of London 344
Suffocate 418
Sullivans John 321
Sun Is Burning in the Sky, The 216
Sweet Carnloch Bay 429
Sweet Music Roll On 248
Sweet Thames Flow Softly 226

Take It Down 425
Tell It to Me (What Put the Blood) 259
They Never Came Home 167
Three Drunken Maidens 443
Tiles and Slabs 199
Tim Evans 331
Time Has Come, The 60
Tippin' It Up to Nancy 214
Travelling People, The 293
Tribute to Woody 390

Trip to Jerusalem 90
Two Conneeleys, The 72
Two Devines and Breslin, The 500

Unfinished Revolution 165
Unquiet Grave 431
Urgency Culture 539

Van Dieman's Land 261
Veronica 490
Viva la Quinte Brigada 53
Voyage, The 44

Wave Up to the Shore 228
Weela Weela Waile 507
Welcome to the Cabaret 20
Well Below the Valley, The 127
Whacker Humphries 26
What Price Justice 505
What's the Life of Man 543
Whiskey in the Jar 308
Whiskey, You're the Devil 460
Wickham and Connors 526
Wicklow Boy, The 92
Wise and Holy Woman 86

Yellow Bittern, The 208
Yellow Triangle 180

Index

Ahakista (Co. Cork) 260
Aiken, Jim 45
Alphonsus, Br 83
America 9, 36, 65, 255, 304,
    376–7, 471, 476, 496
    anti-American songs 71
Anderson, Freddie 358
Andrews, Harvey 364
'Anti-Nuclear' (record) 217
anti-nuclear protest 108,
    133, 217, 277–8, 320,
    447–8, 453–4
Aran Islands 72–3
Armagh Women, The 136,
    459
Askeaton (Co. Limerick)
    221
Askew, Roger 255
Asmal, Kadar 531
asylum seekers 435
Australia 9, 34, 69, 87, 137,
    194, 297, 316, 361, 408,
    416–17, 479
Baggot Inn (Dublin) 13,
    109, 211
Bailey, Roy 40
Bain, Aly 47
Baker, Don 69
Ballyhaunis (Co. Mayo) 95,
    224, 374
Ballyvourney (Co. Cork)
    189, 255
Bantry (Co. Cork) 147
Barr na Cuíge (Co. Mayo)
    95
Barrett, Bertie and Olive 32,
    88
Barronstown (Co. Kildare)
    32, 37, 351, 386
Barry, Kevin 349, 350

Barry, Maggie 23, 357, 511
Baz and Suzie 81
Beggarmen, The 24
Behan, Brendan 287
Behan, Dominic 8, 354, 355,
    401
Berry, Tom 539
Big Issue 493
Biko, Steven 68
Birmingham Six 27, 219,
    467, 505
Black, Mary 96
Blake, Norman 140, 141
Blanket Men protest 89,
    274, 283, 296, 459 see
    also H-Blocks; Hunger
    Strikes
Bloom, Luka see Moore,
    Barry
Boardman, Harry 24, 280
'Bold Fenian Men' 325–6
Bono 196, 197, 272
Bothy Band, The 68, 213
Bourke, Ciarán 91
Bowe, Johnny 356
Bowen, Michael 495
Bowyer, Brendan 501
Boyle (Co. Roscommon)
    127, 128, 224
Bracken, Sam 345
Bradford 18, 25, 216, 258
Bradshaw (Halifax) 257–8
Bradshaw, Noel 539
Brady, Paul 264
Bragg, Billy 34
Brandon (Co. Kerry) 75
Brazen Head, The 89
Brazil, Noel 382, 418
Brennan, Leon 369
Brennan, Robbie 68

Breslin, Charlie 500–1
Briggs, Annie 411
Broderick, Mick 358
Browne, Jackson 12, 13
Browne, Ned 274
Bulfin, Ned 225
Burke, Joe 511
Burke, Kevin 68, 112, 113
Burke, Patrick 531
Burns, Robbie 235, 236
Burren Action Group 175
Butler, Jean 517
Byrne, Anne 437
Byrne, Catherine 411
Byrne, Conor 36
Byrne, Eamon 353
Byrne, Eilish 31, 36, 68, 141,
    251
Byrne, Gay see also Late Late
    Show 524–5
Byrne, Packie Manus 23,
    280
Byrnes, Mairtín 23, 356

Caddick, Bill 241
Cadle, Peter 165, 468
Caesar's Palace (Bunclody)
    9, 156
Cahill, Joe 58
Calnan, Brian 14, 109
Cameron, Alastair 258
Campbell, Ian 216–17, 335,
    336, 345
Cannon, Sean 370
Cape Clear Island 10, 491
Carnegie Hall (New York) 9,
    34
Carnsore Point 108, 133,
    149, 228, 447–8, 453
Carthy, John 353

Carthy, Martin 25, 411, 475
Casey, Bishop Eamon 152
Casey, Mick 264
Cashel (Co. Tipperary) 62, 134
Cassidy, Maurice 124
Castlebar (Co. Mayo) 13, 374
Castlecomer (Co. Carlow) 521
Catholic Church 40, 42, 52, 83–4, 152, 166, 189, 309, 327–8, 415, 435, 446, 452
Cawley, Anthony 288
Channel Islands 85
Chariot, The (Ranelagh) 163
Chernobyl 277–8
Chevron, Phil see Ryan, Philip
Chicago 36
Chieftains, The 149, 525
Christy (film) 211
Christy Moore Band, The 474
Christy Moore Collection, The 336
Claffey, Paul 374
Clancy, Liam 171, 388
Clancy, Willie 25, 510, 511
Clancy Brothers, The 8, 23, 91, 308, 329, 414–15, 437
Clannad 59, 68, 174, 213
Clare, County, music in 271–2
Claremorris (Co. Mayo) 21
Clarke, Mr 14, 109
Clarke, Mick 47
Clarke, Fr Pat 42, 539
Clay, Sara 143
Cleethorpes (Lincs) 17, 345
Clonmel (Co. Tipperary) 62, 114–15 347, 404, 487–8
Coakley, Pat 130
Coffey, Joe 152
Cold Blow, Rainy Night 367, 369
Collins, Clive 334

Collins, Patrick 99, 411
Comerford, Joe 50, 410
Comerford, Natie 213
Communist Party 217, 336, 519
Concerned Parents Against Drugs 27
Congleton (Cheshire) 207, 224, 441–2
Conlon, Festy 357, 511
Conlon, Gerry 467
Conlon, Giuseppe 123–4, 219
Conneff, Kevin see also Chieftains, The 334
Connolly, Billy 358
Connolly, Frank 108
Connolly, James 234
Coolcullen (Co. Carlow) 9, 45, 249, 371, 521
Cooney, Bob 263, 336, 519
Cooney, Steve 411
Cork 19, 141, 251, 405, 453, 492, 499
Corky (Christy's pal) 101
Corries, The 25, 48
Costello, Elvis 99, 194
Costello, Ger 182
Coughlan, Mary 99
Cowan, E. 218
Craigavon 137
Creagh, Seamus 213
Creighton, Andy 374
Cronin, Elizabeth 306, 307, 309
Crosbie, Harry 238
Crosby, Richie 204
Crotty, Siney 530
Crowley, Jimmy 212, 213
Curragh Military Camp 171, 364–5
Curry, Mick 121, 122
Cuypers, Josef 28, 171

Daly, Miriam 284
Danny and the Valtones 109
D'Arcy, Margaretta, 458, 459
De Danaan 68, 213
Dempsey, Damien 251
Dennehy, Tim 277

Denver, Nigel 25
Derry 18, 32, 57, 89, 108, 139, 239
    Civil Rights movement 163, 345
Devine, Micheal and David 16, 500–1
Dirty Nelly's (Co. Waterford) 78
Doherty, Joe 34, 471
Doherty, Kieran 13
Doherty, Martin and Lyn 87, 408
Doherty, Moya 124
Doherty, Paddy 149
Dolan, Joe 90, 91, 411
Donald, Keith 14, 211
Donohoe, Jim 16, 17, 18, 81, 118, 189, 255, 464, 465, 479
Donohoe, Peter 81
Donovan 405
Doolin (Co. Clare) 481
Doran, Felix 511
Doran, Paul 15, 16, 525
Dowling, Annie 147, 494–5
Dowling, Bridie 37–8, 147, 351–2, 494–5
Dowling, Frank 147, 494–5
Dowling, Pat 334
Downes, Tony 24, 280
Doyle, Bob 55
Doyle 'Ructions' 225
Dranouter 120
Drew, Ronnie 437, 507 see also Dubliners, The
Dublin Folk Festival 68
Dubliners, The 90, 91, 197, 291–2, 370, 525
Duhan, Johnny 18, 44, 76, 492, 493
Dunmanus Bay 188, 271, 386
Dunne, Pecker 321
Dwyer brothers 23
Dwyer, Finbar 357
Dwyer, Michael 356
Dylan, Bob 163, 193, 390

Eades, Peter 81
Early Grave Band, The 453

Edge, The 196, 197
Edinburgh 158, 234, 264
Egan, Martin 151, 152
Elliots of Birtly 262
emigration 99, 435 see also
    immigration; refugees
English, Des 24
Ennis, Séamus 128, 289–90,
    511
Enniskillen 135
environmentalism 115,
    175–6, 186, 277–8, 402,
    411–12, 425, 488, 497
Enya 59

Fairport Convention 474
'Fantastical Feats of Finn
    McCool' 264
Farrell, Liam 356
Farrell, Mairéad 23, 350,
    470
Farrow, Jessie 380
Faulkner, Jimmy 68, 112,
    113, 234, 244, 411
Finer, Jem 22
Finn, Mick 283
Finnegan, Kay 249
Fisher family 262
Fitzgerald, Paddy 347
Flanagan, Fr Henry 66, 171,
    241, 243, 411
Flatley, Michael 124, 517
Flint, Hughie 249
Floating Dublin Blues Band
    69
Flood, John 300
Flynn, Colm 112, 113
Flynn, Kevin 370
folk revival 216, 415, 456
Forum Theatre, The
    (Waterford) 118, 179
Fox, Mattie 9, 16, 136, 149,
    169, 170, 237–8
France 68, 166, 340, 370
Franks, Mark 81
Friel, Tom and Maisie 511
Furey, Finbar 47

Gallagher, Colm 64, 65, 476,
    477
Gallagher, Rory 201–2, 397

Galvin, Patrick 233, 234
Galway 57, 78, 90–1, 101,
    283, 300, 411
    Teac Furbo 291
Germany 9, 16, 68, 254, 370,
    478–9
Ghent, Sonn 171
Gibbs, John 109, 110
Glandsman, Martino 479
Glasgow 8, 201, 414
    Folk Centre 216, 345
    Scotia Bar 265–6, 358
    sectarianism in 358–9
Glastonbury 156
Glen O' The Downs 116
'Glennon, 'Scoop' 320
Gorman, Michael 357
Goulder, Dave 112
Graffiti Tongue 113, 180,
    397, 402
Greaves, Muriel 46
Gregory, Tony 532
Grehan Sisters, The 24, 25,
    91, 127, 128, 224, 317,
    324
Grehan, Tony 224, 317
Grehan's Bar (Boyle) 127,
    224
Grogan's Pub (Dublin) 383,
    401
Guerin, Veronica 491
Guildford Four 123, 219
Guthrie, Woody 57, 91,
    157–8, 159, 160, 162,
    163–4, 168, 279, 280,
    331, 394
Halifax 257–8, 266, 345,
    433
Halloran, Patsy 114, 115
Hames, Peter 17, 18
Hand, Owen 46, 158,
Hanly, Mick 13, 250, 251,
    445 see also Moving
    Hearts
Harding, Mike 24, 318, 366,
    367
Harding, Rosemary 24
Harney, Martin 114
Haughey, Charles 95, 350,
    515, 525, 530
Havens, Richie 66

Hayes, Joanna 78
H-Block (album) 9, 89, 274
H-Blocks (Long Kesh) 9, 13,
    57, 60, 88–9, 145, 239,
    274, 283–4, 296, 424,
    459, 471, 483–4
Heaney, Joe 91, 309, 407,
    408, 437, 511
Henderson, Hamish 47
Hennessy, Christie 34, 420
Higgins, Mick 364
Hill, Paul 467
Hogan, Sean 115
Horan, Fr James 95, 374
Hothouse Flowers 524
Huddersfield 266
Hudson, Clive 14, 170
Hughes, Mr and Mrs 60,
    295
Hughes, Francis 295–6
Hughes, Joe 527
Hull 216, 231–2, 262
Humphries, John 27
Hunger Strikes 13, 60, 88,
    145, 240, 283, 296,
    483–4 see also H-Blocks
Hurson, Martin 13, 446
Hutchinson, Pearse 267
Hynes, Ron 96, 97

'I'm a Bogman' 228, 513
Imlach, Hamish 8, 24, 25,
    85, 91, 96, 345, 358
immigrants 99, 193, 194–5,
    482 see also emigration,
    refugees
In the Name of the Father
    123
Irish Republican Army 57,
    206, 295, 500–1
    bombing campaign
    218–19, 497
'Irish Ways and Irish Laws'
    16, 58, 166
Iron Behind the Velvet, The
    217, 410
Irvine, Andy 21, 59, 158,
    334, 369, 370, 379, 411,
    443 see also Planxty
Isaacson, Ernie 45
Isaacson, Sheila 249

Isaacson, Sid (Cid) 14, 62, 68, 78, 109
'It Was Bigger Than Woodstock' 300
Italy, on tour in 369–70

Jahnke, Karsten 479
Johnston, Arthur 358
Johnston, The 147, 235, 293
Jones, Nick 475
Jordan, Peggy 347
Joyce's Collection (of songs) 236, 421
Jug of Punch Folk Club (Birmingham) 216

Keane, John B. 356
Kehoe, Annie 78, 115, 404
Kellighan, Matt 14, 109
Kelly, Luke 8, 91, 291–2
Kelly, Nicky 27, 93, 160
Kelly Live 124
Kilkenny 440, 502, 503, 521
Killarney 80
   Gleneagles Hotel 78, 95, 136
King, Geraldine 459
King, Norman 213
King, Philip 211
King Puck 145, 256, 336
Kyle, Danny 358

Lane, R. 297
Lange, Don 70
Late Late Show 320, 524–5
Leader, Bill 334
Ledwidge, Francis 120, 242
Leeds 25, 179, 216, 258, 267, 334
Levitas, Maurice 55
Liechtenstein 68
Limerick 78, 221
Lisdoonvarna (Co. Clare) 149, 150
Little, Marie 24
Live in Dublin 111, 269
Liverpool 244
Livingstone, Ken 464
Lloyd, Bert 130, 309
London 15–16, 81, 99, 158, 193, 237–8, 317, 334,

344, 355, 404, 410, 505–6, 511
Christy moves to 8, 23, 131, 324, 347, 356, 527
Finsbury Park 156, 163, 391
folk clubs 81, 216, 527
   Forum, The 15, 41
   Singers Club 8, 144–5, 216
Royal Albert Hall 9, 406
Tolpuddle Martyrs concert 464
Longstaffe, John and Pauline 54
Loughlin, Stevie 356
Lunny, Donal 48, 59, 92, 108, 200, 224, 242, 255, 411, 492
   collaboration on songs 60, 88, 137, 235, 236
   friendship with Christy 249, 421–2
   with Moving Hearts 9, 12, 14, 109, 379, 421
   with Planxty 21, 334, 367, 369, 370, 421
   at Portlaoise Prison 34, 93
   produces albums 421, 422
   Ride On 76, 80, 81, 96, 421
   see also Moving Hearts; Planxty
Lunny, Frank (Jnr) 431, 432
Lunny, Frank (Snr) 422
Lyle, Graham 248

McAliskey, Roisin 311
'McAlpine's Fusiliers' 102, 332, 481
Mac An Easpaig, Aiden 219
McBeath, Jimmy 46, 47
McCall, Davina 238
McCann, Donal 538
McCann, Eamon 240
McCann, Fra 274
McCann, Joe 417
MacCarthy, Jimmy 18, 80, 98, 99, 117–18, 134–5, 384, 386
McCarthy, Tom 75
McClelland, Martha 40
McColgan, John 124
McColl, Callum 145

McColl, Ewan 8, 18, 91, 144, 145, 146, 147, 226, 227, 282, 293, 311, 312, 331, 345, 518, 519
McColl, Neil 16, 145
McConnell, Cathal 267
McConnel, Michael 267
McCrea, Josh 158
McDaid's pub (Dublin) 44, 248–9
McDonald, Hugh 281
McDonald, Jake 163, 405
McEvoy, Eleanor 234
McEwan, Derek 227, 345
McFadden, John 369
McFarlane, Brendan 88, 274
McGann, Tommy 481, 482
McGettigan, Charlie 109
McGlinchey, Dominic 23, 288
McGlynn, Arty 59
McGowan, Pat Paul 238, 329
McGowan, Shane 18, 22, 23, 119, 125, 126, 524
McGowan, Turlough 329–30
McGrath, Paul 62, 525
McGuane, Mick 209, 437
McGuire, Sean 23
McIlkenny, Dick 505, 506
McKenna, Ted 437
McLoughlin, Tommy 225
McMahon, Robbie 270, 271
McNelis, Declan 68, 112, 113
McPeake family 262, 279, 280
McTell, Ralph 158, 344
Maguire, Brian 50, 99, 243, 322, 411
Maguire, John 304
Maguire, Sean 357, 511
Maguire family 123, 219
Maher, Titch 204
'Make It Work' 16, 525
Makem, Tommy 8, 65, 414, 415
Manchester 8, 24–5, 227, 258, 318, 367, 474, 527–8

Christy moves to 317, 357
MSG 25, 216, 318, 362
St Clare's Folk Club, 24,
    279–80
Manuel, Ian 232
Marsden Rattlers, The 47
Mayo, County 13, 95, 224,
    373–4
Mean Fiddler, The (Dublin)
    18, 19
Meehan, Paula 41, 187
Meeting Place, The
    (Dublin) 67, 68–9, 80,
    149, 152, 288
Melody Maker 433
Men of No Property, The
    108, 451
Milltown Malbay 277, 510
Minogue, John 271
Mohangi, Shan 430
Molloy, Matt 174, 369, 511
    see also Chieftains, The
Molloy, Tony 59
Moloney, Mick 235, 265
Moloney, Paddy 117 *see also*
    Chieftains, The
Momam, Chuck 211
Monolulu, Prince 381, 430
Moore, Andy (father) 8, 29,
    31, 36, 37–9, 141, 147,
    171, 298, 352, 364, 381,
    401–2, 427–8, 473 178,
    185,
Moore, Andy (brother) 31,
    36, 55, 141
Moore, Andy (son) 9, 16,
    45, 54, 72, 96, 242, 255,
    298, 321, 371, 481, 521
Moore, Anne *see* Rynne,
    Anne
Moore, Barry 31, 35–6, 141,
    228–9, 239, 298, 378,
    513
Moore, Caitlín 9, 45
Moore, Brian 451
Moore, Christopher
    (grandfather) 37, 352
Moore, Christy
    anti-nuclear protest 108,
    133, 217, 320, 447–8
    453–4

army days 276, 439–40
bank career 8, 114–15,
    130, 150, 199, 221–2,
    271, 347, 415, 487
and building workers 34,
    99, 332, 482
childhood 8, 28, 30, 31–2,
    38–9, 83, 152, 171, 251,
    325, 326, 327–8, 381,
    401–2, 457, 494–5
and the Church 40, 42, 52,
    83–4, 152, 166, 189, 309,
    327–8, 415, 435, 446,
    452
and drink 9, 25, 32, 115,
    174, 204, 208, 231, 232,
    314, 338–9, 377, 389,
    401, 460–1, 501, 522–3
and drugs 9, 25, 118, 208,
    362–3, 389, 523
    Concerned Parents
    Against Drugs 27
environmentalism 115,
    175–6, 186, 277–8, 402,
    411–12, 425, 488,
    497
family 8, 9, 28–33, 35–6,
    37–9, 45, 54, 55, 72, 141,
    298, 397, 419, 420–1
parents *see* Moore, Andy;
    Moore, Nancy
and H-Block campaign
    see H-Blocks
and Hunger Strike
    campaign *see* Hunger
    Strikes
illness 9, 175, 297–8, 523,
    534
learns to sing 171, 457
meets and marries Val 8,
    44, 249
music and painting 99,
    243–4
oil rig, works on 392–3
on picket lines 424
and politics 133, 163–4,
    217, 336, 345–6, 425,
    519
nationalism 126, 349–50,
    425
views formed 115, 217

see also Northern Ireland
prison experience 287–8
and racism 99, 160, 181,
    397, 464, 531–2, 536
and refugees 435
restlessness in Newbridge
    429
self-reflection 204, 207,
    214–15, 320, 338–9,
    340–1, 342–3, 360–1,
    386–7, 400, 401–2, 414,
    420, 421, 427–8, 496–7,
    501, 529, 534
and sexual equality 41,
    42–3, 136–7, 165–6, 189
spirituality 40, 83–4, 87,
    118, 189, 298, 342–3
and sport 62–3, 115, 258,
    321–2, 365, 381, 473
and suicide victims 537–8
and Travellers 48, 49–50,
    128, 147, 519
vegetarianism 186
views on
child abuse 52, 397, 507
corruption 76, 349–50,
    359, 425, 446, 485–6,
    497
meat industry 186, 271,
    397, 412
WORK
audiences 14, 15–16,
    18–19, 21, 42, 60, 65, 99,
    137, 155–6, 179, 244,
    245, 251, 254–5, 307,
    369, 370, 417, 432, 467,
    499
in prisons 27, 287–8
profiles of 41, 135, 137,
    144, 161, 234
benefit gigs 160
bootleg albums 171, 287,
    336–7
court action against 9, 27,
    136, 168–9, 170–1
Eurovision Song Contest
    517
fees from early gigs
    112–13, 130–1, 163,
    227, 318, 344, 347, 355
and films 211, 410

cancels tour 9, 175, 297, 298
music business 237–8, 309–10, 344–5, 359, 427, 432–3
Christy manages band 68, 112–13
co-operative bands 108, 529
demos sent to Christy 281–2
and media 330
recording studios 80–1, 334, 363, 432–3
musical influences 23, 24–5, 28, 31, 91, 127, 157–8, 171, 249
musicians admired 411
simplicity in music 379
performances 15–16, 17–19, 21, 41, 60, 73, 99, 101–2, 120, 194, 217, 244–5, 379, 405, 505–6
early gigs 24, 25, 47, 216, 241, 267, 344–5, 347, 356–7, 390–1, 441–2, 443
emotions during 14, 15–16, 111, 118, 135, 156, 179, 193, 233–4, 254–5, 340–1, 397, 420, 421, 432
first sessions 271, 300, 321, 349
in prisons 27, 34, 89, 93, 287–8
skirmishes at 143, 359, 527
records first album 355
repertoire 42, 153–4, 179, 234, 251
early 115, 145, 221, 235–6, 293, 442
encores 155–6, 345
opening numbers 13, 21
'secret drawer' 48
set lists 16, 113, 244
on radio 8, 47, 191
songs
banned 44, 57, 168–9, 170, 239–40

beauty of 16, 48, 128, 179, 207, 307, 324, 332, 340, 343, 347, 456, 511, 543
criticism of 34, 57, 71, 109–10, 143, 234, 367, 320, 359, 417, 451, 475, 499
emotion of 99, 111, 118, 128, 141, 260, 475, 509, 522
importance of 475, 494
joy of 347, 398, 468–9, 533
power of 164, 246–7, 394–5, 408, 432, 456, 463
writing 17, 23, 99, 106, 136–7, 168, 179, 186, 189, 197, 255, 513, 533, 537, 539
on television 8, 69, 123–4, 200, 238, 316, 320, 489
see also Late Late Show
on tour 13, 78–9, 95, 112–13, 174, 224–5, 369–70, 443, 478–9
road accident 113
see also Moving Hearts; Planxty
Moore, Eilish see Byrne, Eilish
Moore, Gavin 36
Moore, Juno 9, 16, 45, 52, 54, 72, 166, 251, 298
Moore, Nancy (née Power) 9, 28–33, 38, 141, 147, 171, 228, 352, 419, 422, 473, 521, 525
Moore, Pádraic 9, 16, 45, 54, 72, 298
Moore, Terry 31, 36, 54, 113, 141, 326, 473
Moore, Thomas 457
Moore, Val 8, 16, 44–5, 52, 54, 55, 72, 156, 160, 166, 249, 290, 298, 307, 342, 343, 371, 481, 491, 521
Moorefield GAA Club 228, 300, 473
Morley, Sheridan 191
Morrison, Van 81, 238

Morrissey, Eamon 374
Morrissey, Johnny 54, 425
Mother Redcap's (Dublin) 228, 251
Mountjoy Prison 287, 288, 349
Moving Hearts 12–14, 108, 109–10, 168, 182, 378–9, 380, 421, 474, 524, 529
repertoire 70, 83, 380
Moynihan, Johnny 367
Mulhearn, Joe 449
Mulhearn, Johnny 18, 100, 101, 103, 104, 243, 244
Mullaghmore (Co. Clare) 175–6, 397
Mulqueen, Ann 209
Mulready, Peter 437
Mulvanney, Maeve 437
Munnelly, Tom 127
Murphy, Mrs 285, 286
Murphy, Ber 204
Murphy, Charles 40
Murphy, Mandy 80, 524
Murphy, Mary and Kathy 75
Murphy, Noel 24–5, 355
Murray, Gerry 95, 373
Murray, Michael 115
Murray, Tony 314

Nelson, Rosemary 446
New Ross (Co. Wexford) 522
New Zealand 9, 297
Newbridge
childhood in 8, 31, 38, 134, 152, 171, 322, 352, 473
Curragh Military Camp 171, 364–5
first concerts in 171, 347, 349
restlessness in 23, 429
roots in 386–7
Ní Broanáin, Maire 524
Ní Dhonail, Triona 70
Niemoeller, Pastor 180
'Ninety Miles to Dublin Town' 57
Northern Ireland 57, 88,

123–4, 136, 139, 182, 239, 284, 417, 450, 500, 532
Bloody Sunday 206, 397, 466
British attitude towards 110, 206, 219, 311, 345
Christy's hopes for 274, 446, 497
IRA 57, 206, 218–19, 295–6, 497, 500–1
RUC, sectarianism of 446, 450, 501
see also Blanket Men protest; H-Blocks; Hunger Strikes
Norway 371–2
Nugent, Kieran 274
Nugent, Dr Patrick 298, 302, 303

O'Beirne, Aidan and Síle 112
O'Brien, Colm 264
O'Broin, Joe 78
O'Connor, Nuala 211
O'Connor, Peter and Biddy 54, 55, 78
O'Connor, Sinéad 43, 524
O'Doherty, Eamon 416, 417
O'Donnell, Austin 351
O'Donnell, Brendan 200
O'Donnell, Daniel 524, 525
O'Donohue's pub 209, 248, 408, 419, 436–7
O'Flynn, Liam 21, 59, 117, 267, 334, 370, 411, 443
see also Planxty
O'Hara, Patsy 240
O'Hara, Peggy 60, 240
O'Keeffe, Mick 291
O'Keeffe, Pádraic 411
O'Kelly, Donal 500, 501
Oldham Tinkers, The 24
O'Leary, Alan 17, 18
O'Leary, Dermot 232
O'Lochlainn, Colm (song collection) 222, 421
O'Maonlaói, Liam 264
O'Neill, Eoghan 14, 96, 379
O'Neill, Robbie 242

O'Neill, Terry 14, 109
Ordinary Man 59, 65, 168, 170, 269, 421
O'Riordan, Michael 54, 55
O'Sullivan, Thaddeus 410
Outfit, The 182
Owens, Jesse 91, 437

Paddy on the Road 8, 355, 432–3
Page, Jim 132, 133, 403
Page, Wally 18, 49, 67–8, 86, 152, 153, 154, 275, 276, 466, 531, 537–8
Palmer, Gary 417
Pappalardi, Felix 111
Parkinson, Billy 204, 381, 430
Parnell Folk, The 427
Pavarotti 376
Pearson, Leo 188, 402, 539
Pegg, Bob and Carol 334
Penn, Dan 211, 525
Pennine Folk, The 262
Peoples, Tommy 411
Planxty 21, 36, 59, 68, 72, 83, 90, 108, 163, 227, 248, 249, 263, 291, 336, 374, 525
Christy leaves 9, 68, 421
on Eurovision 517
formed 8, 21, 405, 421
re-formed 367, 421
repertoire 21, 85, 111, 128, 141
on tour 174, 369–70, 443, 478–9
police *see also* RUC 9, 14, 89, 99, 218, 219 284, 345–6, 353, 489
Portlaoise Prison 34, 58, 93, 287–8
Potts, Tommy 347
Power, Ellie (née Sheeran) 30, 32, 147, 217, 325, 326, 327
Power, Jack 30, 31, 325–6, 327–8
Power, Jimmy 30, 120, 193, 326
Power, Nancy *see* Moore, Nancy

Power, Paddy 365
Prendergast, Darky 430
Prior, Maddy 443
Prosperous 8, 80, 309, 334, 421

Quinn, Declan 211
Quinn, Woodner 365

Rafferty, Gerry 96
Rakes of Kildare 421
Randall, Colin 200
Raymond, Br 152
Reagan, Ronald 304
Regan, John 267
refugees 435
Reid, Jimmy 204
Reilly, John 91, 127–8, 129, 166, 177, 179, 214, 224, 259, 260, 309, 411
Revolutionary Struggle (organisation) 133
Ride On 9, 44, 76, 80–1, 96, 182, 421
Riney, Imelda 200
Riverdance 123, 124, 517
Robertson, Jeannie 47, 309
Roche, Adi 34
Rohr, Peggy 264
Rohr, Tony 16, 264
Roland, Raymond 23, 356–7
Rolfe, Nigel 42, 43, 199, 201, 202
Ronan, Martin 133, 447, 448
RUC, sectarianism of 225, 228, 254, 446, 450, 501
Rush, Barney 85, 122, 142
Russell, Micho 145
Ryan, Nicky 59, 170, 370
Ryan, Philip 82, 83
Ryan, Terry 242
Rynne, Andy 91, 207, 209, 224, 334, 399
Rynne, Anne 31, 36, 141
Rynne, Davoc 224, 432
Rynne, Donnaca 420–1

Sabey, Denis 258
Salford 291
Samuel, Walter 255

Sands, Bobby 56, 57, 88, 89, 240, 350, 424, 450
Scariff (Co. Clare) 112, 113, 199, 347
Scotland 25, 47–8, 158, 216, 264, 432 *see also* Glasgow
Scott, Bruce 283
Scottish Trades Union Council 234
Scullion, Colm 88
Seeger, Peggy 70, 145, 312
Seeger, Pete 282
Shanley, Eleanor 194, 524
Shannon, Dave 345
Shannon, Jim 149
Sheeran, Joe 119–20, 242
Sheeran, Kathleen 241–2
Sherkin Island Festival 73, 213
Sheridan, Jim 410
Sherlock, Roger 23, 356
Shine, Noel 141
Singing Jenny Folk Club (Huddersfield) 266
Sinnott, Declan 12, 14, 76, 80, 81, 96, 379, 380–1, 411 *see also* Moving Hearts
Slowey, Nancy and Marie 171
Small, Judy 137
Small, Tony 158
Smith, Sam 123, 124
Smoke and Strong Whiskey 126
Southend-on-Sea 233

Spain 54, 96–7
Spanish Civil War 54, 336, 519
Spillane, Davy 13, 14, 109
Spillane, Paddy 68
Spirit of Freedom, The 182–3
Stardust Club (Dublin) 168
Stewart, Belle 309
Stewart, Davey 46, 47
Stewart, Philip 246
Stewarts of Blair 262
Strong, Rob 69
Sweeney's Men 91
Switzerland 108, 174, 370

Taylor, Kevin 357
Taylor, Paddy 357
Thatcher, Maggie 465, 484, 485–6
Thomastown (Co. Kilkenny) 168
Thompson, Richard 474–5
Thurles (festival) 156
Time Has Come, The 93, 106, 421
Tomelty, Frances 411
Toronto 36, 169, 197, 264
Tozer, Brian and Sally 232
Tralee 255, 453
Traveller (album) 9, 40, 45, 111, 188, 207, 260, 422, 534, 536, 539
Travellers (community) 48, 49–50, 128, 147, 519
Trout, Tony 213
Tulla (Co. Clare) 199, 271, 286

Turley, John 284
Turner, Pierce 18, 340, 375, 376

Unfinished Revolution 119, 421
Union Folk, The 441–2

Vallely, Fintan 138, 139
Valley Folk, The 24, 318
Verso, Norman 14, 109, 174
Vicar Street Project, The 298
Voyage 43, 44, 144, 421, 524

Wales (RAF camp gig) 143
Walker, Johnny 467
Wallenstein, Abi 479
Walsh, Fr Joe 200
Warshaw, Jack 107, 108
Waterson, Mike 232, 261, 262, 263, 264, 411
Watersons, The 25, 91, 262, 309, 411
Weldon, Liam 25, 234
Westerman, Floyd 13, 58
Whatever Tickles Your Fancy 111, 112, 147, 260
Whelan, Bill 124, 379, 517
Whelan, Jim 447
White, Jimmy 321
Whitehead, Dikon 238
Williamson, Roy 48
Woods, John 68

Yeats, W.B. 66
Young, Fr Joe 42, 539

Picture credits

John Minihan Photography Foreword, 59, 205, 235; Unknown 13, 17, 64, 74, 77, 78, 90, 95, 99, 107, 118, 150, 186, 202, 213, 242, 269; Jill Furmanovsky Photography 14, 237, 272, 277; Family collection 20, 22, 25, 26, 40, 43, 47, 70, 72, 120, 123, 146, 152, 162, 166, 167, 192, 206, 207, 211, 216, 232, 239; Derek Spiers Photography 45, 55, 57, 67, 80, 85, 108, 113, 119, 128, 143, 151, 188, 225, 226, 245, 246, 250, 260, 266, 267, 271; Turlough Rynne 63, 87, 140, 184; Harry Gibney 29; Janet Rohr 31, 84; Dave Campbell 32; Willie Matthews 34; Fergus Bourke 35; Valerie Moore 50, 68, 227; Imlach family 53; George Doyle 111; John Taylor 129; Pádraic Moore 132; Ali Hewson 145; Nugent family 155; Jim Donohoe 156; Andy Moore III 158; Dona Lenihan 164; Frank McGowan 168; Pat Egan 174; MISE 180; Brendan Grace 183; Davoc Rynne 195, 212; *Sunday World* 197; *Melody Maker* 219; Barry Moores camera 233; An Phoblacht 249; Frank Fennell Photography 256

Lyric credits

'After the Deluge' written by Jackson Browne and reproduced by kind permission of Wixen-Polin Company, California; 'Natives' written by Paul Doran. Copyright Bal Music Ltd; 'Ordinary Man' written by Peter Hames and reproduced by kind permission of Folkus Music; 'Fairytale of New York' written by Shane McGowan and reproduced with his kind permission; 'Don't Forget Your Shovel' written by Christie Hennessy (with some new lyrics by Christy Moore) and reproduced with the kind permission of Christie Hennessy; 'City of Chicago' written by Barry Moore. Copyright Bal Music Ltd; 'Burning Times' written by Charles Murphy. Copyright Bal Music Ltd; 'Middle of the Island' written by Nigel Rolfe and Christy Moore. Copyright Bal Music Ltd; 'The Voyage' written by Johnny Duhan and reproduced with his kind permission; 'Johnny Connors' written by Christy Moore and Wally Page. Copyright Bal Music Ltd; 'Back Home in Derry' written by Bobby Sands. Copyright Bal

Music Ltd; 'Quiet Desperation' words and music by Floyd Westerman and Jimmy Curtiss © 1990 Clara Music Publishing Corp, USA. Reproduced by permission of EMI Songs Ltd, London, WC2H 0EA; 'The Reel in the Flickering Light' written by Colm Gallagher and reproduced by kind permission of Colm Music ASCAP; 'Biko Drum' written by Wally Page. Copyright Bal Music Ltd; 'Allende' written by Don Lange. Published by Barking Spider Music (admin. by Bug Music); 'The Two Conneeleys' written by Christy Moore and Wally Page. Copyright Bal Music Ltd; 'El Salvador' written by Johnny Duhan and lyrics reproduced with his kind permission; 'Ride On' written by Jimmy MacCarthy. Copyright Universal Music; 'Faithful Departed' written by Philip Chevron and reproduced by kind permission of Rockin Music, a division of Ace, UK; 'Nancy Spain' written by Barney Rush and reproduced with his kind permission; 'Wise and Holy Woman' written by Christy Moore and Wally Page. Copyright Bal Music Ltd; 'McIlhatton' written by Bobby Sands. Copyright Bal Music Ltd; 'Trip to Jerusalem' written by Joe Dolan and reproduced by his kind permission; 'The Wicklow Boy' written by Christy Moore and Donal Lunny. Copyright Bal Music Ltd; 'Sonny's Dream' written by Ron Hynes and reproduced by kind permission of Morning Music Ltd, Canada; 'Missing You' written by Jimmy MacCarthy. Copyright Universal Music; 'Continental Céilí' written by Johnny Mulhearn. Copyright Bal Music Ltd; 'Matty' written by Johnny Mulhearn. Copyright Bal Music Ltd; 'No Time for Love' music and lyrics by Jack Warshaw; 'Irish Ways and Irish Laws' written by John Gibbs; 'The January Man' words and music by Dave Goulder © 1969. Reproduced by kind permission of Robbins Music Corp Ltd, London WC2H 0EA; 'Bright Blue Rose' written by Jimmy MacCarthy. Copyright Universal Music; 'Lawless' written by Mick Curry. Copyright Bal Music Ltd; 'Aisling' written by Shane McGowan and lyrics reproduced with his kind permission; 'Hiroshima Nagasaki' written by Jim Page and lyrics reproduced with